On Foot Through Europe

A TRAIL GUIDE TO SCANDINAVIA

INCLUDES: *Denmark, Finland, Greenland, Iceland, Norway and Sweden*

Here's What Europe's Walking Organizations Say About this Book

"The most complete reference for the hiker in Germany." —LUDWIG LENZ, 3rd Direktor, Deutscher Alpenverein (German Alpine Club), Munich.

"Extraordinarily comprehensive." —JOHN NEWNHAM, assistant secretary, The Ramblers' Association, London.

"Excellent. Many more or less experienced alpinists could learn quite a lot on how to prepare a tour and on what to do in cases of emergency."— LUCETTE DUVOISIN, general secretary, Schweizerische Arbeitsgemeinschaft für Wanderwege (Swiss Footpath Protection Association), Basel.

"A very comprehensive and most valuable book." —DR. SONJA JORDAN, Österreichische Fremdenverkehrswerbung (Austrian National Tourist Office), Vienna.

"I was very impressed. This book will be of great value to all hikers who want to go to other countries." —FINN HAGEN, Den Norske Turistforening (Norwegian Mountain Touring Association), Oslo.

"You've done a helluva good job assembling and organizing a truly awesome amount of data. You seem to have thought of every contingency— and then some—so the prospective walker will be able to plan his vacation well in advance of departure. . . . This guide should become something of a classic in its field—a backpacker's Baedeker." —STEPHEN R. WHITNEY, former managing editor, Sierra Club Books, and author of *A Sierra Club Naturalist's Guide: The Sierra Nevada*.

"Your work is very complete and accurate (something we find seldom, even in our own country)." —FREDDY TUERLINCKX, general secretary, Grote Routepaden (Long-Distance Footpath Association), Antwerp.

"I am really impressed with the enormous work that you have been able to do in a short time—and by the amount of knowledge and experience that you show!" —INGEMUND HÄGG, Svenska turistföreningen (Swedish Touring Club), Stockholm.

"A Bible of European hiking opportunities." —EDWARD B. GARVEY, member of the Appalachian Trail Council Board of Managers and author of *Appalachian Hiker: Adventure of a Lifetime.*

On Foot Through Europe

A TRAIL GUIDE TO SCANDINAVIA

INCLUDES: *Denmark, Finland, Greenland, Iceland, Norway and Sweden*

by Craig Evans

Walking, Backpacking, Ski Touring, Climbing—Everything You Can Do On Foot

QUILL
New York 1982

Library of Congress Catalog Card Number: 82-601

ISBN: 0-688-01191-8 (pbk)

Printed in the United States of America

First Quill Edition

1 2 3 4 5 6 7 8 9 10

Behind the Scenes

MANY PEOPLE HAVE contributed to this book—people in tourist offices, weather bureaus, forestry services, sport shops and tour organizations. In addition, the members of Scandinavia's mountain touring and ski touring associations and walking organizations have been especially helpful. Without the assistance of these people—and the time and effort they devoted to answering questions, researching information and reviewing the final manuscript—this book would not have been possible.

To all who helped prepare the manuscript—typists, translators, proofreaders, friends—I also owe my sincere gratitude.

And to those who helped the most, a special thanks:

For reviewing the entire manuscript, helping offset my American bias and providing otherwise hard-to-get information:

Arthur Howcroft, president of the European Ramblers' Association's Walking Committee and a tour leader for England's Country-Wide Holidays Assocation.

Ingemund Hägg, secretary of the European Ramblers' Assocation's Walking Committee consultant to the Svenska turistföreningen (Swedish Touring Club) and author of *Walking in Europe,* a 40-page booklet on where to get information to go walking in 25 countries, published in English by the Swedish Touring Club, 1978 (a handy booklet, incidentally, that is well worth owning).

For providing information on walking and ski touring in their areas, and for reviewing for accuracy the chapters on their countries:

DENMARK

Palle Grønlund and *Mogens Persson* of the Dansk Vandrelaug, Copenhagen.
Jøren Hansen of the Århus Turistforening, Århus.

FINLAND

Martti Helenius, Suomen Matkailuliitto (Finnish Travel Association), Helsinki.

Matti Höök, marketing director, Finnish Tourist Board, Helsinka.
Marja-Sisko Pihl, Suomen Latu (Finnish Ski Track Association), Helsinki.
Teemu Salonen, chairman, Suomen Latu, Turku.

GREENLAND

Mogens Persson, Dansk Vandrelaug, Copenhagen.

ICELAND

Davíd Ólafsson, Ferdafélag Islands (Iceland Touring Club), Reykjavik.
Kjartan Lárusson, director, Ferdaskrifstola Ríkisins (Iceland Tourist Bureau), Reykjavik.
Ragna Samuélsson, manager, Fedamálarád Islands (Iceland Tourist Board), Reykjavik.
Njáll Símonarson, general manager, Úlfar Jacobsen, Reyljavik.

NORWAY

Alfred Andersen, director, technical section, Foreningen til Ski-idrettens Fremme, Oslo.
Finn Hagen, Den Norske Turistforening (Norwegian Mountain Touring Association), Oslo.
Elisabeth Hyerdahl-Jensen, Landslaget for Reiselivet i Norge (Norwegian National Tourist Office), Oslo.
Harald Julsrud, Den Norske Turistforening, Oslo.

SWEDEN

Gunnel Bäckström, Sveriges Turistråd (Swedish Tourist Board), Stockholm.
Hans Nelsäter, Fredrik Pripp, Kaj Lönnborg and *Olle Melander,* Svenska turistföreningen (Swedish Touring Club), Stockholm.
Staffan Thorssell, Sverek, Domänverket (Swedish Forest Service), Solna.

There was also the enormous dedication of the people who made the trail guide series come to physical reality. The basic team was: Ed Meehan who drew the maps, Brian Sheridan who did the illustrations, Vincent Torre who designed the cover and Elisabeth Kofler Shuman, my research and editorial assistant.

There was also Stephen R. Whitney, my editor, whose involvement in this book escalated beyond that of simply an editor, and whose commitment to its completion became much more than he—or his wife—ever bargained for. As deadlines approached and the size of each chapter swelled, he evolved from copy editor and devil's advocate to co-author, writing first short sections of unfinished chapters from my notes, then whole chapters. And I, in turn, became his rewriter and editor. Together, we were able to complete seven books, ensure their accuracy and oversee every detail of their production, a job I could never have accomplished alone and still have met the final deadline.

In this book, he co-authored the chapter on Iceland.

Finally, there was William Kemsley, Jr., president of Foot Trails Publications, Inc., whose own passion for detail sustained his unfaltering belief in this trail guide series through all of its growing pains, despite the advice of his accountants. Few publishers would have put up with so much when lesser books could have been produced much more economically. Yet he rarely asked that compromises be made. He only asked that it be done. And done well.

Thank you, each of you. You've been great friends.

Craig Evans
Washington, D.C., 1981

How to Use this Book

THIS BOOK IS PACKED with information. It describes every aspect of walking, backpacking, climbing and ski touring in Denmark, Finland, Greenland, Iceland, Norway and Sweden: all the places you can go, the maps and guidebooks you need, where you can get information on trail lodgings and camping, the weather conditions you can expect and the telephone numbers to call for weather forecasts. There's even a list of special fares on trains, buses, boats and airplanes that can save you money. And more: detailed descriptions of each mountain region, national park and wilderness; the clothing and equipment you will need; walking and skiing tours you might like to take advantage of; what you should know about wilderness travel and property rights; even some tidbits of history and folklore.

There are also hundreds of addresses—places you can write for maps and guidebooks, obtain train and bus schedule information and get specific answers on walking, ski touring and traveling in particular areas. And you get a lot more than just an address. Everything is spelled out: the information and services available, the languages in which inquires can be made and, if useful publications are available, what their titles are and what information they contain.

The result is a complete sourcebook to all the information available on walking, backpacking, ski touring and climbing in Scandinavia.

The area codes for all telephone numbers have been listed in parenthesis. For example, the number listed for the Svenska turistföreningen in Stockholm is (08) 22 72 00. (08) is the area code.

- To reach this number from within the same area—say, Stockholm itself—omit the area code and dial only the telephone number: 22 72 00.

- To reach this number from a different area within the same country—say, Storlien—dial the entire number as shown: (08) 22 72 00.

- To reach this number from a different country—say, Switzerland—first refer to the front pages of the telephone directory to find the appropriate country code for Sweden. From Switzerland this number is 00 46. Next, dial the area code *minus* the initial zero: (8). Then dial the telephone number 22 72 00. Hence: 00 46 (8) 22 72 00.

All the telephone numbers are listed in the *Address Directory* at the end of the chapters on each country.

This book has been designed to make finding the specific information you need as easy as possible. The table of contents lists the major divisions in each chapter, plus some minor divisions, so you can turn right to the page where, say, the services provided by the walking organizations or the emergency telephone numbers for search and rescue are given. The name of each organization has been set off from the rest of the text by means of a darker type face and additional spacing so it can be found easily—again and again. And all the addresses and telephone numbers are listed in an alphabetical *Address Directory* at the back of each chapter so you only have one place to look when you need to use one. There is even a section entitled *A Quick Reference* at the end of the chapters on each country, which gives you the page numbers where the most important information is located on walking in that country.

Another help: this book was bound so you can remove pages—and thus save lugging the entire book along—when you just want one chapter on the trail for easy reference. To remove pages: 1) open the book to the first page you wish to remove; 2) bend the book open as far as it will go; 3) turn to the end of the section you wish to remove; 4) again, bend the book open as far as it will go; 5) with one hand, hold down the pages on either side of the section you wish to remove; 6) with the thumb and index finger of the other hand, grasp the top part of the section at the point where it attaches to the spine, and 7) slowly pull the section away from the spine. The pages should come out in a complete section, with all the pages attached to one another.

When you wish to return a chapter you have removed to the book, simply slip it back into the space where it belongs. Then put a rubber band around the book so the loose sections don't fall out.

Finally, one last note: every attempt has been made to ensure the information in this book is both complete and accurate. Nonetheless, those who worked on the book—myself, the reviewers in each country, copy editors and typesetters—are not perfect. An occasional mistake might have slipped past. Two numerals in a telephone number might have been transposed and never caught. A name may have been misspelled or a valuable guidebook overlooked. If so, it was not intentional.

There are the inevitable changes to consider, too. All addresses, telephone numbers and prices were verified prior to publication. But people and organizations move, telephone numbers change and prices go up. Hence, I cannot accept responsibility or liability for any inaccuracies or omissions.

Prices, of course, change constantly. *Those quoted are meant only as guides.* For each year after 1981; expect a yearly increase of *at least 15 percent.* Maybe more.

This book describes the opportunities in the different regions of Scandinavia. Six other books cover the rest of Europe:

On Foot Through Europe: A Trail Guide to Austria, Switzerland & Liechtenstein

On Foot Through Europe: A Trail Guide to the British Isles

On Foot Through Europe: A Trail Guide to West Germany

On Foot Through Europe: A Trail Guide to Spain & Portugal

On Foot Through Europe: A Trail Guide to France & the Benelux Nations

Use this or any of the area guides in conjunction with *On Foot Through Europe: A Trail Guide to Europe's Long-Distance Footpaths,* which gives you an overview of walking in Europe and tips on how to plan your hikes. All the background information available—and the places where you can get it—is here. It includes how to get information by mail, how to get to and stay along the trails, how to follow the paths safely, what to do in an emergency, and what equipment to bring, and many other facts to get you started hiking through Europe.

I welcome your comments. If you find an address or telephone number has changed, or you think some additional information should have been included in the book and was not, please let me know. Write to me at: Foot Trails Publications, Inc., Bedford Road, Greenwich, Connecticut, 06830 U.S.A.

Contents

Where & How to Go Hiking in Scandinavia

Difficulty:
What the Footpath Gradings Mean

The footpaths described in this book have been graded according to their difficulty. These gradings are based upon the *Schwierigkeitsgrade*—or difficulty gradings—developed for walkers in Austria. They are:

Easy (Schwierigkeitsgrad A & B). A path across either level or gently undulating terrain. Differences in altitude are small—less than 250 meters. The path requires minimal effort. It can be walked in any weather. Suitable for families with young children.

Easy to Moderately Difficult (Schwierigkeitsgrad C). A path across hilly terrain or mountains of medium height (up to 1,800 meters in altitude). The path presents few complications: climbs and descents are rarely steep, altitude differences are less than 600 meters and route finding is generally not difficult. Except in extremely bad weather, the path can be walked without great effort.

Moderately Difficult (Schwierigkeitsgrad D). A path with regular climbs and descents. Sections of the path may cross steep, rocky or marshy terrain. Some sections may also be above treeline or partially obstructed with undergrowth. The path generally can be walked without difficulty in good weather—providing you are physically fit, have the proper equipment and know how to use a map and compass. In bad weather use caution. Check with local authorities before you set out to be sure you are aware of any peculiarities in the local weather and path conditions.

Difficult (Schwierigkeitsgrad E). A strenuous route across rough terrain. Climbs and descents are steep and difficult. Precipices, swiftly flowing streams, thick undergrowth or snowfields may be encountered. In some places use of a map and compass may be essential to follow the route. On particularly exposed or dangerous sections safety devices—such as fixed cables and ladders—may be installed along the path. No climbing skills nor climbing equipment are required. Sections of some routes, however, will require that you are sure footed and are not subject to acrophobia. Novices and families with young children should not attempt such a route. In bad weather, *all* walkers should avoid it.

For Experienced Mountain Walkers Only (Schwierigkeitsgrad F). An extremely difficult route—across glaciers, on routes with exposed or dangerous sections (and no fixed cables or other safety devices), or cross-country through rough terrain where accurate route-finding with a map and compass is essential. Climbs and descents are steep and treacherous and may require rock climbing (up to Class II). Stream crossings are tricky and may require use of a rope. Severe, quick-changing weather conditions also may be encountered. To follow this route mountaineering experience is imperative, as is specialized equipment—crampons, ice axe or rope—and knowledge of its use.

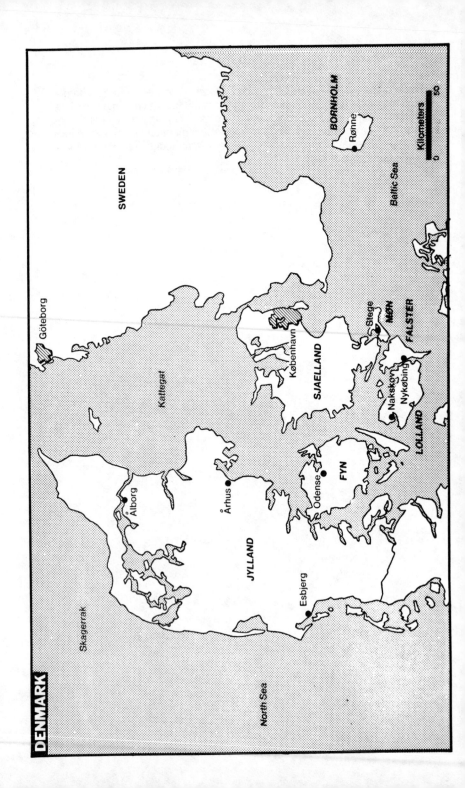

Denmark

DENMARK IS BEST KNOWN as a country for bicycling, canoeing, sailing, fishing, horseback riding and as a place to spend a leisurely holiday on a farm or at the seacoast. When it comes to walking, even many Danes ignore their own countryside. Nonetheless, Denmark is a pleasant country in which to walk.

But to do so requires persistence. Maps are difficult to find. Few guidebooks exist. And the Danish Tourist Board in Copenhagen is of little help. The only central source of information is the *Dansk Vandrelaug* (DVL), Denmark's main walking organization. But even the DVL is primarily concerned with walking in Sweden and Norway, and with organizing guided treks to Greenland.

The impression is misleading. There are 44 state forests and 12 private forests with footpaths. Coastal footpaths encircle the island of Bornholm. There is one long-distance footpath—the Danish section of European Long-Distance Foothpath E-6—that stretches from Kruså on the German border, across Funen and on to Roskilde, not far from Copenhagen. It is possible to walk along sections of the 1,000-year-old Hærvejen (The Ancient Army Road) that stretches up the center of Jutland from the German border to Viborg. In addition, many local tourist offices publish sketch maps and short route descriptions to footpaths in their areas.

In fact, with the appropriate Geodæstik Institut maps and information from local tourist offices, you can find numerous possibilities for both short and long walks. But to get the information to walk, you have to be sure you go to the right source.

It is worth the effort.

Although Denmark's highest point, Yding Skovhöj in Jutland, is only 173 meters (567 feet) high, the country is hardly flat. It has gently rolling hills and green pastures scattered with small lakes, woods and thatched-roof cottages. It also has more than 7,400 kilometers (4,600 miles) of coastline with vast dunes, cliffs, fjords and wide, sandy beaches.

Nearly three-quarters of Denmark's land area (total: 43,000 square kilometers) is occupied by the peninsula of Jutland (Jylland), which lies to the north of Germany. The remainder is made up of about 500 islands of which about 100 are inhabited. The most important of these are Zealand

(Sjælland), Funen (Fyn), Lolland, Falster and Bornholm, a granite island with many cliffs and ravines located in the Baltic Sea southeast of Sweden.

On the Jutland Peninsula, there are extensive tracks of moorland, marsh and heath in the west and low hills and valleys in the east. Zealand has a pastoral landscape with delightful beach woods, large lakes and moated castles. And Funen is a panorama of green pastures, flower gardens, old towns and magnificent castles and manors surrounded by moats.

Towns are rarely far apart, and few areas are uncultivated or truly deserted. Yet you often have the feeling of being far from civilization and, in some areas, you can walk for hours without meeting another person or seeing a house.

Most footpaths are located in isolated localities and coastal areas. For the most part, the paths are gentle and—with one or two exceptions—short.

Local tourist offices throughout Denmark are efficient and provide several services in addition to giving out maps and information. Some, for instance, rent bicycles. Several also operate a *Meet the Danes* program that allows you to spend an evening with a Danish family at no cost.

All personnel in the tourist offices are required to speak English, French and German. Because English classes are mandatory in school, most Danes speak at least some English. In addition, many Danes speak German and a few speak French.

Trail information is not so multilingual. With few exceptions, it is published only in Danish. But, even in the smallest town, you can usually find someone to help translate it.

Flora & Fauna

During the time of the Vikings, vast oak forests covered much of Denmark. Now, only about one-tenth of Denmark is forested, and beech is the dominant tree. There are also stands of Norway spruce and, on the moorland of west Jutland, several large coniferous forests have been planted. There are still oak trees to be found and an occasional elm. In addition, juniper flourishes on the chalky hillsides on the island of Møn, south of Zealand.

On Jutland there are extensive heather-clad hills and heaths. Much of northern Jutland is covered with sandhills, on which only mare's-tail grass and gorse are able to flourish.

Animals include the red and roe deer, hare and fox. There are also many storks, especially in the marshlands of west Jutland where cartwheel structures have been placed on the roofs of many houses to encourage the birds to nest there.

Danish Nature & the Law

Because Denmark's natural areas are limited, several strict laws have been enacted to preserve them. You should respect these laws.

On the beach, you are allowed to walk nearly everywhere. Motorized vehicles are forbidden. On private beaches, you are allowed to fish and bathe, providing your stay is short and you do not get any closer to a habitation than 50 meters.

In several public forests, you can travel only by foot. Bicycles, motorcycles and automobiles are banned. Foot travelers can also enter private forests. But here, you must stay either on the roads or the footpaths.

Most dune areas, heaths and marshes are open to walkers. Those off limits will be fenced.

Open fires are forbidden, as is digging wild plants and breaking branches from young trees.

Also, you can walk only between 7 a.m. and sunset.

Climate

Denmark has a maritime climate with mild winters and temperate summers. Daytime temperatures during the summer range between 18° and 25° C. (64-77° F.). The warmest months are July and August, when temperatures sometimes reach 30° C. (86° F.). Summer evenings are long, but often chilly. The weather is also changeable; sunny days can be interrupted by sudden showers.

The winter is rainy with isolated periods of frost. The coldest month is February with an average daytime temperature of 0° to 3° C. (32-37° F.). Between October and April many days are dull and gray.

Annual rainfall averages about 600 mm (24 inches) on Jutland and the principal islands, and about 450 mm (18 inches) on Bornholm. Most of the rainfall occurs during the late summer and autumn. Spring is the driest season.

Prevailing winds are westerly, and even inland, there is usually a breeze.

You can walk for most of the year in Denmark. The most desirable months to do so, however, are from May to September.

Weather Forecasts

Weather forecasts are broadcast every morning on Radio 3 in Copenhagen. The forecasts are given in German at 7:45 a.m., in Danish at 8 a.m. and in English at 8:15 a.m.

Where to Get Walking Information

The Dansk Vandrelaug can provide information on European Long-Distance Footpath E-6—known in Denmark as *Europæiske Fjernvandrevej Nr. 6*—as well as limited information on *Hærvejen*—the Ancient Army Road. In addition, the DVL gives away brochures on nature trails in the state forests, sells a handbook to Denmark's youth hostels—*Danmark Vandrerhjem*—issues guest cards to the hostels and camping passes to Denmark's campgrounds, organizes weekend hikes and bicycle tours in Denmark, and runs a series of walking tours to Norway, Sweden, Bornholm and Greenland.

Dansk Vandrelaug (for its address and telephone number, see the *Address Directory* at the back of this chapter). Staff speaks Danish, English and German.

You can also obtain walking information from the **Danish Tourist Board** (see *Address Directory*) and the **Københavns Kommunes Biblioteker,** the main public library in Copenhagen. The library has a set of the 1:25,000, 1:50,000 and 1:100,000 Geodæstik Institut maps, which you can look at to plan walks. The set of 1:25,000 and 1:50,000 maps, however, is not complete. The library also has two books on Hærvejen with English summaries: *Ad Hærvejens Spor* by Børge Mosumgaard and *Langs Hærvejen* by Hjalmar Ørnholt and Wermund Bendtsen. It is located across the square from the Dansk Vandrelaug office.

Beyond this, your best sources of information are the pamphlets and sketch maps available from local tourist offices.

Maps

Maps in a scale of 1:25,000, 1:50,000 and 1:100,000, plus a free index and price list, can be obtained from:

Geodæstik Institut (see *Address Directory*). Open weekdays from 10 a.m. to 3 p.m.

The Geodæstik Institut publishes its indexes, catalog and price lists in both Danish and English. The keys to symbols on many maps are also translated into English, and a few maps include a German translation of the symbols.

Because of Denmark's low-lying terrain, it is best to use the 1:25,000 maps, which provide more accurate topographical information.

You should also obtain your maps by mail in advance of your trip, or plan to visit the Geodæstik Institut in Copenhagen. If you visit the office in Copenhagen, be prepared to ask directions, for it is difficult to find. The office is a 10-minute walk from Rådhuspladsen (Town Hall Square):

Go across Rådhuspladsen to where Frederiksberggade (Copenhagen's main walking street) starts. Tivoli Gardens is at your back. Turn right on Vester Voldgade. Walk up Vester Voldgade for six blocks. The sixth street you come to is Ny Kongensgade. Turn left. You will cross a bridge, then pass through an archway and enter Rigsdagsgården, a large square. Walk along the right hand side of the square. Just before you exit the square you will come to two archways: one straight ahead, and one on your right. Go through the archway to your right. Walk straight ahead for about 75 meters (250 feet). You will pass a parking lot and see a small park to your right. The first doorway on your left is the entrance to the Geodæstik Institut.

For information on orienteering maps, see "Orienteering" under the section on *Other Activities* later in this chapter.

Guidebooks

Few guidebooks exist to the footpaths in Denmark. And those that do exist can hardly be considered trail guides in the normal sense.

DVL Publications

The Dansk Vandrelaug publishes three leaflets to European Long-Distance Footpath E-6:

- *Europæisk Fjernvandrevej Nr. 6—Fyenshav-Kruså.* Covers the section of trail across southern Jutland.
- *Europæisk Fjernvandrevej Nr. 6—Nybord-Bøjden.* Covers the section of trail on the island of Funen.
- *Europæisk Fjernvandrevej Nr. 6—Roskild-Korsør.* Covers the section of trail on Zealand.

Each of the leaflets includes a strip map in a scale of 1:100,000 on which the footpath has been marked in red. Red symbols also show where youth hostels, hotels and campsites are located along the path; where buses, trains and ferries can be found; and where tourist information offices are located. On the back, there is a sketchy description of the path and a list of suggested reading. All information on the leaflet is translated into English and German. The leaflets are free on request. When ordering please enclose an international postal reply coupon.

Another useful publication available from the DVL is its member magazine, *fritidsliv*. It describes the activities of the DVL and lists its weekend hikes in Denmark, as well as the tours it organizes for DVL members abroad.

Pamphlets on State and Private Forests

There is a series of pamphlets to the nature trails in Denmark's state forests—or, in Danish, the *Vandreture i Statsskovene*. There are 44 pamphlets in the series. They are published by:

Direktoratet for Statsskovbruget (see *Address Directory*).

A map showing the locations of the state forests is also available on request from the Statsskovbruget (State Forestry Office).

There are also 12 pamphlets to walks in Denmark's private forests. These are published by:

Dansk Skovforening (see *Address Directory*).

Each of the state and private forest pamphlets includes a short description of the forest and of the various routes within it, along with a sketch map on which the footpaths are color-coded according to length. With one or two exceptions, the pamphlets are published only in Danish. Nonetheless, the footpaths can be followed by simply referring to the sketch maps.

A complete set of the pamphlets can be obtained from the Danish Tourist Board in Copenhagen (see *Address Directory*). In addition, local tourist offices can give you the pamphlets to nearby forests. All the pamphlets are free.

Trailside Lodgings

For the walker, Denmark's youth hostels are convenient stopping places. Many are located near footpaths in the state forests. Five are within 10 kilometers of Hærvejen and six are located around the coast of Bornholm. Some are quite lovely, too. Several hostels are old manors and a few are thatched-roof cottages. Many also have rooms for families.

Information on the hostels can be obtained from tourist offices as well as from:

Herbergs-Ringen (see *Address Directory*). Open weekdays from 9 a.m. to 4 p.m. The head office of Denmark's youth hostel association. Gives away the brochures to the nature trails in the state forests. Also publishes a useful hostel list in Danish:

- *Danmark Vandrerhjem.* Includes maps to show where the hostels are located in each town, as well as a sketch of each hostel to show you what it looks like. (The handbook is also available from the Dansk Vandrelaug.)

Besides the hostels, there are many lodging possibilities in most towns. In some places, you can rent a cottage for a week or more. You can also stay in one of the graceful Danish inns. Lists of lodgings can be obtained from local tourist offices. They will also find rooms in private homes and make reservations in hotels and youth hostels.

Camping

Denmark has more than 500 authorized campsites. If you intend to camp, you must stay in one of these sites. Camping is not permitted in private fields. Open camping is also forbidden in state and private forests, on the beach and on the moors and heathland of Jutland.

Even to stay in the authorized sites, you must purchase a camping pass. The pass and a list of campsites can be obtained from the Dansk Vandrelaug or from:

Dansk Camping Union (see *Address Directory*).

The pass can also be obtained from the first campsite visited.

A free brochure, *Camping—Denmark,* gives the addresses and telephone numbers of campsites and youth hostels throughout Denmark. It is available from any branch office of the Danish Tourist Board.

Water

Tap water is safe throughout Denmark. You should, however, avoid drinking from natural water sources. Because settlements are close together, you should have no difficulty finding a place to fill your water bottle.

Equipment Notes

No specialized equipment is required for walking in Denmark—just stout shoes, rain and wind protection, and spare warm clothes.

Walking Tours

Weekend hikes are organized in various parts of Denmark by the Dansk Vandrelaug. The hikes are open only to members of the DVL. Guests, however, are welcome. Although foreigners can join the club, it is helpful if you speak a little Danish. Details are available from the DVL.

Day-long and weekend competitive walks are held throughout the year by Marchforeningen "Fodslaw." At the end of the walk, badges are awarded on the basis of your performance. Fodslaw also organizes the international *Hærvejsvandringen* each July. This march follows Denmark's historic Hærvejen. Participants must complete the 300-kilometer route in seven days. All lodgings, food and luggage transport arrangements are handled by Fodslaw. A calendar of events, plus brochures on the *Hærvejsvandringen*—in English and German—are available from:

Marchforeningen "Fodslaw" (see *Address Directory*). Open Mondays from 10 to 12 a.m. and Tuesdays through Friday from 2 to 5 p.m.

Weekend walks are also organized by the:

Dansk Gangforbund (see *Address Directory*). A calendar of walks is available on request.

Other Activities

Bicycling

Denmark is a cycle-minded country. For good reason, too. Its green, rolling countryside and numerous small back roads make it an ideal country for the cycler. Information on cycling in Denmark, and the places where bicycles can be rented, is available from any local tourist office or the Danish Tourist Board. Information can also be obtained from:

Dansk Cyklist-Forbund (see *Address Directory*).

Another possibility for cycling is the *Holiday on 2 Wheels*. This is a ready-made cycling holiday that includes your bicycle, maps, lodgings and food. Most of the tours are eight days long. You choose your own dates and the people you ride with, pay your money, and the tour organizer takes care of the other arrangements for you. Information is available from:

Fyntour (see *Address Directory*).

The Dansk Vandrelaug also organizes two week-long, all-inclusive tours that you follow on your own—one in North Zealand and one in South Zealand. Information sheets (in English) describing the tours are available on request from the DVL.

Orienteering

Competitive orienteering has become increasingly popular in Denmark. During almost any weekend of the year, people are out in the woods with their maps and compasses, running from one marker to another against time and dozens of other orienteers. You can also practice on your own. More than 125 orienteering maps in a scale of 1:15,000 and 1:20,000 are published by the Dansk Orienterings-Forbund.

A free index to the maps, entitled *Orienteringskort,* and a calendar of orienteering meets, the *Kursuskalender,* is available from:

Dansk Orienterings-Forbund (see *Address Directory*).

Special Train & Bus Fares

A dense network of rail lines covers Denmark, supplemented with buses on quieter stretches. Tickets are issued at all stations for trains and buses as well as for connecting ferry crossings. As a rule, bus tickets can also be bought on the buses.

Large fare reductions are available for families, groups and people over 65 years of age. Children under 4 years travel free; those between the ages of 4 and 12 at half price. There are also three money-saving tickets that are available from most rail stations:

Nordic Tourist Ticket. Good for unlimited rail travel throughout Denmark, Norway, Sweden and Finland. Both 21-day and one-month tickets are available.

One-month ticket. Good for unlimited travel between all stations in Denmark.

Take-five ticket. Good for 5 days of unlimited travel within a 17-day period.

Young people under the age of 26 can purchase a BIGE ticket from Dansk Vandrelaug. The ticket is valid for two months and provides a considerable savings on roundtrip rail travel to many destinations in Europe either starting or arriving in Denmark.

Useful Addresses & Telephone Numbers

General Tourist Information

In Denmark:
Danmarks Turistråd (see *Address Directory*).

Abroad:
Branch offices of the Danish Tourist Board are located in EUROPE: Amsterdam, Brussels, Hamburg, London, Munich, Oslo, Paris, Rome, Salzburg, Stockholm and Zurich; JAPAN: Tokyo; and the U.S.A.: Los Angeles and New York.

London: The Danish Tourist Board, 169-73 Regent Street, London W1R 8PY. Tel. (01) 734 2637 and 734 2638.

New York: Danish National Tourist Office, 75 Rockefeller Plaza, New York, New York 10019. Tel. (212) 687-5609.

Sport Shops

There is only one chain of shops in Denmark that specializes in hiking and climbing equipment.

Spejder Sport. Located in Copenhagen on the west side of Ørsteds Parken (a 15-minute walk from Rådhuspladsen). Smaller shops are located in Lyngby, Odense, Århus and Aalborg. (see *Address Directory* for their street addresses and telephone numbers). The shops stock maps to the mountain regions of Norway and Sweden. They also sell a guide—in Danish—to walking in Greenland. They do not, however, have any information on hiking in Denmark. The shops are not large, but they have a good stock of equipment.

Search & Rescue

In case of an accident on the trail, call:

Police emergency: Tel. 0. 0. 0.

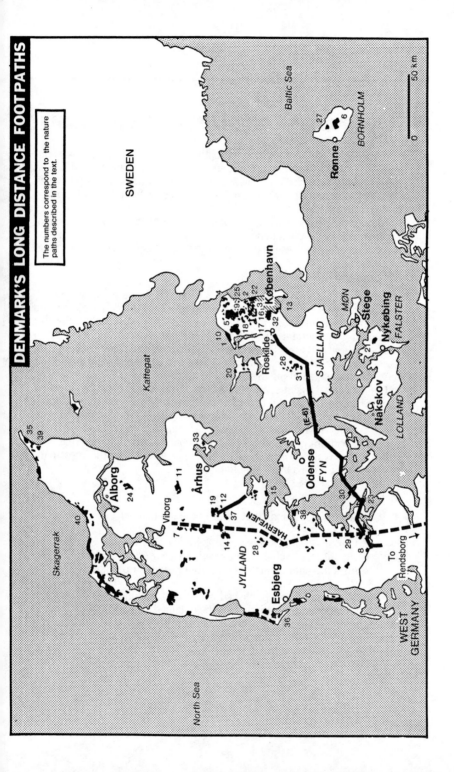

DENMARK'S LONG DISTANCE FOOT PATHS

The numbers correspond to the nature paths described in the text.

SWEDEN

Baltic Sea

BORNHOLM

Rønne

København

Roskilde

SJAELLAND

MØN

Stege

Nykøbing

FALSTER

Nakskov

LOLLAND

Odense

FYN

(E-6)

Kattegat

Ålborg

Viborg

Århus

HAERVEJEN

JYLLAND

Esbjerg

To Rendsborg

WEST GERMANY

Skagerrak

North Sea

50 km

0

Denmark's Long-Distance Footpaths

The only marked long-distance footpath in Denmark is *Europæisk Fjern-vandrevej Nr. 6.* The path currently stretches from Germany to Roskilde on the island of Zealand. Eventually it is to be continued to both Copenhagen and to Helsingør (Elsinore), where it will link up with the Swedish portion of E-6.

To walk the path's entire 256 kilometers requires about 10 days. Each of its three sections—on Jutland, on Funen and on Zealand—can also be walked separately. These take from three to four days to walk.

Lodgings and Bus Service

Lodgings and campsites are not always located near the path. As a result, you must sometimes take a bus at the end of your day's walk to find lodgings, and then return to the path by bus the next morning. For this reason, it is important to obtain the *Europæisk Fjernvandrevej Nr. 6* leaflets published by the Dansk Vandrelaug (see the section on *Guidebooks* earlier in this chapter). These show where lodgings and bus services are located along the path.

The walking is gentle and takes you through some of the loveliest countryside in Denmark. You can also travel light if you stay in youth hostels and other lodgings along the way. A tent and sleeping bag are necessary only if you intend to stay in campsites.

Several portions of the path follow small back roads. In these areas, you will have to walk on the shoulder of the roadway. For the most part, however, these roads have little traffic.

Maps and Guidebooks

As yet, the only guidebook that exists to the footpath is:

- *Kompass—Wanderführer: Europäischer Fernwanderweg E 6* (in German), Deutscher Wanderverlag (see *Address Directory*). Describes the entire length of E-6, from Roskilde to Yugoslavia.

In addition, the leaflets published by the DVL include a list of books in English, German and Danish that can be obtained from most bookstores in Denmark, or perused in Copenhagen's main library. These will give you additional information on the areas through which the footpath passes, but they make no reference to the footpath.

The maps necessary to walk the path are:

E-6, Section 1

Across Jutland from Kruså to Fynshav (ferry crossing to Funen). **Length:** ca. 60 kilometers. **Walking Time:** 3 days. **Path Markings:** White crosses.
Maps:
• Geodæstik Institut 1:25,000, sheets 1211-I-SV, NV, and NØ; 1211-II-SØ; and 1311-IV-NV.

E-6, Section 2

Across Funen from Bøjden to Nyborg (ferry crossing to Zealand). **Length:** 87 kilometers. **Walking Time:** 3 days. **Path Markings:** White crosses.
Maps:
• Geodæstik Institut 1:25,000, sheets 1312-I-SV, SØ and NØ; 1312-II-NV; and 1312-III-NV, SV, SØ and NØ.

E-6, Section 3

Across Zealand from Korsør to Roskilde. **Length:** 109 kilometers. **Walking Time:** 4 days. **Path Markings:** White crosses.
Maps:
• Geodæstik Institut 1:25,000, sheets 1412-I-NV and NØ; 1412-IV-NØ; 1413-II-SØ; and 1513-III-NV, NØ, SV and SØ.

One other long-distance walk in Denmark is along Hærvejen, the Ancient Army Road in Jutland. This road, or rather what is left of it, was already in existence when Nordic pilgrims used it in the year 1070 to flock into southern Europe. It has been traveled by merchants, soldiers, oxen drivers and highwaymen, and, hence, has played an important role in Danish history.

Today small, quiet roads follow much of its route from Viborg to the German border. Parts have been paved with asphalt. But other sections have been left as they were and are still scattered with runic stones and old bridges.

Towns are located close enough to the route so that it is possible to find food and lodging each night. There are also many nearby campsites.

Because Hærvejen is not a footpath in the typical sense, there are no path markings to aid you in following it. Its route, however, is marked on the Geodæstik Institut maps. Several tourist offices in nearby towns also publish brochures that include maps of its route.

Hærvejen

From Viborg to Flensburg, Germany. **Length:** ca. 300 kilometers. **Walking Time:** 10-12 days. **Path Markings:** None.
Maps:
• Geodæstik Institut 1:25,000, sheets 1211-IV-NØ and SØ; 1212-III-NØ and SØ; 1212-IV-SØ, NØ and NV; 1213-III-SV, SØ, NV and NØ; 1213-IV-SØ and NØ; 1214-I-NV and SV; 1214-II-NV; 1214-III-NØ and SØ; 1214-IV-NØ and SØ; 1215-III-NØ, SØ and SV; and 1215-IV-SØ.

Bornholm

Bornholm is an island of granite cliffs, beech woods, rocky ravines and round fortress churches. The white sand on its southern beaches is so fine that European kings and princes of the past used it for ink blotting. Inland, cultivated fields alternate with fir and pine woods, tracts of heather and broad-leafed forests of ash and oak, hornbeam, cherry trees, alder and hazel. Small, idyllic townships with half-timbered houses are scattered across the island. Runic stones and prehistoric remains abound. And for the gourmet there is the island delicacy—smoked Bornholm herring.

The island is truly a delight. You can walk practically anywhere. Motor traffic on its roads is limited. Youth hostels and campsites are everywhere to be found. And it has the best weather in Denmark.

The island is small—only 567.5 square kilometers (219 square miles). At its widest point it is only 40 kilometers (25 miles) across. It is also isolated. It can be reached by air (45 minutes from Copenhagen's Kastrup Airport) or by ship (seven hours from Copenhagen, two and a half hours from Ystad, Sweden, and two hours from Simrishamn, Sweden). But it is worth the trip.

Bornholm receives 25 percent less rainfall than the rest of Denmark. Temperatures are mild. It also has a long summer, with warm weather beginning in the spring and lasting into autumn. Because of this, it supports a rich variety of unusual and rare plants, a few of which are found nowhere else in Europe.

The best times to walk on Bornholm are May-June and September-October. During these months, the plant life is at its most beautiful, and the weather is stable. Also, some prices are reduced, and lodgings are easier to find.

Useful Addresses

See *Address Directory:*

Bornholms Turistbureau. Located in Bornholm's largest town; old townscape with half-timbered houses and merchant's buildings. Provides general tourist information for the entire island. Also can provide information on the island's footpaths. Useful publications available from the office include:

* *Vandreture i Statsskovene—Almindingen-Bornholm.* State Forestry Office pamphlet to nature trails in the Almindingen Forest in the heart of Bornholm. (Number 6 on the map showing *Denmark's Long-Distance Footpaths.*)

* *Vandreture i Statsskovene—Rø Plantage Bornholm.* Pamphlet to the footpaths in the state forest in North Bornholm. (Number 27 on the map, showing *Denmark's Long-Distance Footpaths.*)

* *Hotelliste.* Lists the addresses, telephone numbers, opening and closing dates and prices in Bornholm's 100-plus hotels and pensions. Also gives the addresses and telephone numbers of its youth hostels, campsites and local tourist offices.

Nordbornholms Turistbureau. Located near Hammeren, a hilly, heath-covered granite point on Bornholm's northernmost coast; said to be the finest cliff walk in Denmark. The office provides information on North Bornholm. It can also supply German translations of the State Forestry Office pamphlets to Almindingen and Rø Plantage.

In addition to these offices, there are six other tourist offices on Bornholm, located in **Gudhjem** (characteristic herring smoke houses; near a forest lake surrounded by monoliths and burial mounds), **Hasle** (seaport with a granite church and runic stones; cliff footpath), **Neksø** (near Paradisbakkerne—Paradise Hills—a splendid rocky area of forest and lakes, rift valleys and heathland; footpaths to Rokkestenen—rocking stone—a 25-ton rock; to Gamleborg, remains of Iron Age castle of refuge; and to Gryet, grove with 62 monoliths), **Svaneke** (market town with narrow, steep streets; near Randkløve Skår, an area of rugged cliffs and deep ravines with a lovely coastal footpath), **Tejn-Sandkås** (located on an exciting stretch of coast with rugged cliffs, clumps of woodland, caves and grottos) and **Aakirkeby** (old market town in Middle Ages).

Addresses and telephone numbers of these offices can be obtained from either the Bornholms Turistbureau or Nordbornholms Turistbureau.

Maps

Bornholm is covered by the 1:25,000 Geodæstik Institut maps, sheets 1812-III-NV, NØ and SØ and 1812-IV-NV, SV, and SØ. All footpaths on the island are indicated on the maps.

Suggested Walks

One of the most spectacular walks on Bornholm is along its 150 kilometers of coastline. The walk can be made in six days with overnight stops in each of Bornholm's youth hostels. Or you can camp along the way.

Part of the walk is on footpaths, part on roads. If you prefer not to walk the roads, even though they have little traffic, you can cut the walk down to four days and stick to the footpaths. Or, if you like company, you can join one of the walking tours that the Dansk Vandrelaug organizes each summer along this route.

Day 1. From Rønne to Hasle by woodland footpaths. Overnight at campsite or youth hostel in Hasle.

Day 2. From Hasle to Sandvig. Along a cliff path to Hammershus, ruins of a 13th century castle, thence around the Hammeren promontory through tracts of heather, birch and pine on Denmark's most spectacular cliff walk. Overnight at campsite or youth hostel in Sandvig.

Day 3. From Sandvig to Gudhjem. Along an exciting stretch of coast with rugged cliffs, partly on road. Overnight at youth hostel or one of the three campsites in Gudhjem.

Day 4. From Gudhjem to Svaneke. Along cliff and shore paths through Randkløve Skår. Overnight at youth hostel or one of the two campsites in Svaneke.

Day 5. From Svaneke to Dueodde, a magnificent National Trust dune area with unusually white, fine sand. Along coast roads, partly on short footpaths. Overnight at youth hostel or one of the two campsites at Dueodde.

Day 6. From Dueodde to Rønne. Through dunes, woodland and heather, mostly on roads.

In addition to the walk along the coast, there are waymarked footpaths in the Almindingen State Forest, the third largest in Denmark. These lead you through varied vegetation and past small ponds to Rytterknaegten, Bornholm's highest point (162 meters); to Ekkodalen, a rift valley; to

Bastemosen, a marsh with rare plants; and to Gamleborg, with mounds that are the remains of a Viking Age castle.

Other rewarding day hikes can be made in Paradisbakkerne (Paradise Hills) and in the Rø Plantage State Forest.

Footpaths in these areas range from 2 to 10 kilometers in length.

Fyn (Funen) & Its Islands

Funen has aptly been called Denmark's garden island. It has a pleasant, undulating countryside where green fields, fruit trees and farms alternate with wooded groves, storybook castles and numerous well-kept villages. Some of Denmark's best preserved manor houses are located on the island. Around Fåborg, a quaint town with numerous lanes and courtyards, is a hilly, forested landscape known as the Funen "Alps." Odense, now one of Denmark's main industrial towns, is where Hans Christian Andersen was born and reared. And off the south coast are two lovely islands, Ærø and Langeland, with manor houses, old churches and small towns that include many half-timbered houses from the 17th and 18th centuries.

Both islands can be reached from Svendborg, an old shipping town on Svendborg Sound, with a lovely beachside hostel and several short footpaths along the sound and in nearby forest areas.

To plan walks on Funen, it is best to refer to the Geodæstik Institut maps. The pamphlets available from the local tourist offices do not encompass all the walking possibilities on the island. One lovely area for short walks, for instance, is the Funen "Alps." Yet there is no pamphlet available to the footpaths in the area.

For the most part, footpaths are few and short. The only possibility for a long walk is on the section of European Long-Distance Footpath E-6. And even E-6 follows back roads most of the way across the island.

Because of the scarcity of long footpaths some walkers may be tempted to strike off cross-country through private forests and fields. Don't. The Danes are extremely protective of their privacy and property rights. As a result, trespassing laws are strict. Stick to the footpaths and small back roads.

Useful Addresses

See *Address Directory:*

Turistforeningen for Faaborg og Omegn. Provides general tourist information on the town of Fåborg and its surroundings. Gives away one pamphlet useful to walkers:

• *Ture i Danske Skove—Hvidkilde.* Shows the footpaths in the private forest around Hvidkilde, an old manor house with a good restaurant, between Fåborg and Svendborg.

Langeland-Rudkøbing Turistkontor. Provides general tourist information on the island of Langeland, accessible by bridge from Svendborg. The island has lovely, undulating scenery, sandy beaches, forests and small, idyllic villages. Footpaths are few, but it is possible to plan walks on the island with the Geodæstik Institut maps. One useful publication available from the office is:

• *Ture i Danske Skove—Tranekær.* Shows the locations of footpaths in the private forest surrounding the lovely Tranekær Castle near a charming village of the same name.

Turistforeningen for Middelfart. Bridgetown linking the island of Funen with the Jutland Peninsula. There are three short footpaths on the Hindsgavl Peninsula near the town. English and German translations of route descriptions to the paths are currently in preparation.

Nyborg Erhvers- & Turistkontor. Provides general tourist information. Also publishes a sketch map that shows the locations of five short walks (1.3 to 4.5 kilometers in length) near the town. To obtain the sketch map, ask for the *Nyborg Vandrerute Kort.*

Odense Turistkontor. Provides general tourist information. Also gives away one pamphlet useful to walkers:

• *Ture i Dankse Skove—Langesø.* Shows the locations of footpaths in the forest surrounding Langesø, a lovely manor house about 15 kilometers northwest of Odense.

Svendborg Turistkontor. Provides general tourist information. Gives away the pamphlet to *Hvidkilde* (a half hour walk from the town), as well as:

• *Svendborg er himmelsk!—også til fods.* Shows the locations of five short walks in and around Svendborg. Also includes sketch maps of each walk. Footpaths on the maps are color-coded according to length.

Turistkontoret Ærøskøbing. A small, isolated island with idyllic villages and old, half-timbered farmhouses; reached by ferry from Svendborg. There are no marked footpaths on the island, although you can walk on its winding roads. The office provides general tourist information and will find a room for you in a private home, farm or hotel.

Maps

The 1:25,000 Geodæstik Institut maps that cover the walking regions— South Funen, Langeland and Ærø—are:

South Funen: sheets 1211-O-NØ and SØ; 1311-I-NV; 1312-I-NV, SV, NØ and SØ; 1312-II-NV, SV, NØ and SØ (covers the area around Svenborg); 1312-III-NV, NØ and SØ (sheets 1312-III-NØ and 1312-II-NV cover the Funen "Alps"); and 1312-IV-NV, SV, NØ and SØ.

Aerø: sheets 1311-I-SV and 1311-IV-NØ and SØ.

Langeland: sheets 1311-I-NØ and SØ; 1311-II-NØ; 1412-III-NV and SV; and 1411-IV-NV.

Guidebooks

The pamphlets to footpaths in the private forests—Ture i Danske Skove— can be obtained free from any branch office of the Danish Tourist Board, as well as from the local tourist offices on Funen.

Suggested Walks

If you do not mind walking on back roads, the walk along European Long-Distance Footpath E-6 takes you through some of the loveliest areas on Funen. For details on the path, see the section on Denmark's Long-Distance Footpaths.

Jutland
(Jylland)

For the walker, Jutland is one of the best places to go in Denmark. It has more and longer footpaths than any other region in Denmark. Its terrain is varied. And though localities where you can find food and lodging are rarely more than 30 kilometers apart, it is possible to walk in solitude for kilometer after kilometer.

Nearly 45 towns have marked footpaths within walking distance of the town limits. The local tourist offices in about half these towns publish short route descriptions and sketch maps. In the remainder of the towns, the tourist offices will mark the route on a map and give you directions to the trail. There are also 20 state forests, with marked nature trails, on the peninsula.

One of the loveliest areas in Jutland is the Danish Lake District, near the town of Silkeborg. Here, where east Jutland's fertile, beech-clad countryside and the rolling hills of central Jutland meet, is a chain of lakes formed by Denmark's longest river, the Gudenå. Old tow paths still exist along much of the river. There are also numerous footpaths through heathland and woods on the hills above the lakes, as well as in the forests surrounding Silkeborg.

Along the west coast, solitary moors stretch out toward the shifting dunes and white sand of the beaches. Open meadows and marshes attract migratory birds for nesting in the spring. The land is low, scattered with fishing villages, farmsteads, white village churches, beech woods and spruce plantations.

At Limfjord, where the Vikings used to gather their ships for raids across the North Sea, there are ancient burial mounds and other relics from the Viking past. Many traces of prehistoric man have been found in Himmerland, a wooded region in North Jutland. There are also runic stones, stone burial chambers and excavations of Iron Age settlements along the east coast fjords, which cut deeply inland between green meadows and tree-clad slopes.

Paths in the state forests are usually marked with red, yellow or blue circles painted on trees. Where there are no trees, colored posts are driven into the ground alongside the path. Some paths in Jutland, however, are not marked. On these, it is advisable to supplement the published route description with the appropriate Geodæstik Institute maps.

Useful Addresses—Nordjylland (North Jutland)

See *Address Directory:*

Erhvervs- og Turistkontoret Fjerritslev. Located in Han Herred, to the north of Limfjord. Near the Svinkløv Klitplantage State Forest. The tourist office distributes three publications useful to walkers:

• *Vandreture i Statsskovene—Svinkløv Klitplantage Fjerritslev.* State Forestry Office pamphlet to nature trails in the Svinkløv Forest (number 40 on the map accompanying the section on *Denmark's Long-Distance Footpaths).*

• *NR. 9 Wanderblatt über Waldtouren in Svinkløv und Umgebung.* Describes 10 short walks in the Svinkløv State Forest. Written in German.

• *NR. 10 Wandertouren in Han Herred.* Describes nine short walks in the countryside surrounding Fjerritslev. Written in German.

Turistforeningen for Frederikshavn. Located on the northern tip of the Danish mainland. Ferry service from the town connects with Læsø, a small island of heather, woods, meadows and dunes. The office can provide information on three marked footpaths in the Bangsbo Forest, south of Frederikshavn. It also distributes a pamphlet and a sketch map to other local walks:

• *Ture i Danske Skove—Dronninglund.* Short route description in Danish and sketch map to nature trails in the Dronninglund Forest between Frederikshavn and Ålborg.

• *Åsted Ådal-Fredningen.* A sketch map to marked footpaths and a keep-fit trail in the Åsted Forest west of Frederikshavn. Information on the map is in Danish. The tourist office, however, will translate the information into English, German or French for you.

Turistforeningen for Hobro. Located in Himmerland. Near an excavated Viking encampment. Also near Rold Skov/Rebild Bakker, Denmark's largest woodland area. Publications available from the office include:

• *Rold Skov/Rebild Bakker Jutland.* Describes the Rold Forest and Rebild Hills (number 24 on the map showing *Denmark's Long-Distance Footpaths),* as well as the lakes, meadows and moorland in the area. Gives a brief description of walks.

• *Vandreture i Statsskovene—Rebild Bakker Himmerland.* State Forestry Office pamphlet to nature trails in the Rebild Hills. (Number 24 on the map showing *Denmark's Long-Distance Footpaths.)* Written in Danish. Also available in English.

- *Ture-Ide 2*. A pamphlet written in Danish, German and English. Includes a sketch map of three marked footpaths in the Bramslev Hills and Valsgaard Brook valley near Hobro.

Skagen Turistforening. An old fishing hamlet located in a scenic area of marsh, moorland and dunes. The northernmost town on Jutland. Near two state forests with footpaths. Pamphlets to the footpaths are available from the tourist office:

- *Vandreture i Statsskovene—Skagen Klitplantage*. Number 35 on the map, showing *Denmark's Long-Distance Footpaths*.
- *Vandreture i Statsskovene—Bunken Klitplantage Skagens Odde*. Number 39 on the map, showing *Denmark's Long-Distance Footpaths.*.

Turistforeningen for Thisted og Thy. Located on Limfjord. Near the Vandet Sø State Forest. Publications available from the office include:

- *Vandreture i Statsskovene—Klitplantagerne Ved Vandet Sø, Thy*. (Number 34 on the map, showing *Denmark's Long-Distance Footpaths*..) State Forestry Office pamphlet and sketch map to nature trails. A translation in German of the 18 walks in the forest is also available from the tourist office.
- *Velkommen til Frøstrup*. Describes four tours of up to 30 kilometers in the forest and moorlands northeast of Thisted. Includes a sketch map.
- *Vandreture i Statsskovene—Skov og Klitvæsenet Tved Plantage*. A sketch map to six short footpaths in a forest and marsh area nine kilometers north of Thisted. (Near number 34 on the map, showing *Denmark's Long-Distance Footpaths*.)

Useful Addresses—Midtjylland (Central Jutland)

See *Address Directory*:

Århus Turistforening. A very helpful tourist office, located in an old town with a beautifully preserved old quarter. The office can provide information on footpaths in the immediate vicinity as well as on footpaths in the Danish Lake District. Publications available from the office include:

- *Natursti Horsens-Silkeborg*. A sketch map and route description in Danish to a 61-kilometer footpath between Horsens and Silkeborg. Follows an abandoned railway line through a beautiful and varying landscape. Marked with green arrows. Several campsites and youth hostels are near the path.

• *Natursti Ebeltoft-Gravlev.* A sketch map and route description in Danish to an 8-kilometer walk between Ebeltoft and Gravlev on the peninsula northeast of Århus. Follows an abandoned railway line through a nature reserve around the Stubbe Lake. Marked with green arrows. There are campsites in Ebeltoft and a youth hostel in Gravlev.

• *Vandreture i Statsskovene—Mols Bjerge.* State Forest office pamphlet to two footpaths in the undulating Mols Bjerge country, located on a peninsula across the Kaløvig Bay from Århus. (Number 33 on the map showing *Denmark's Long-Distance Footpaths.*) Beautiful views across two bays.

• *Brabrand Sø.* Describes a 17-kilometer walk around the lake of Brabrand on the western outskirts of Århus. Includes a sketch map.

• *Natursti Århus.* Written in Danish, German and English. Describes a nature trail in the Marselisborg Forest south of Århus. Includes a sketch map.

• *3 kondi-stier i Riis skov—Idrætshøjskolen i Århus.* A sketch map to three keep-fit trails in the Riis Forest Park inside the town. The Århus youth hostel is located in the park.

• *Scanticondi stier.* A sketch map and short description in Danish to three short footpaths in Skaade Bakker, a wooded area south of Århus.

• *Cyklistkort for Arhus Kommune.* A sketch map with an explanation of symbols in Danish and English. Shows the locations of bicycle routes and footpaths in and around Århus.

• *Marselisborg Woods—From the city to Hørhaven* and *Marselisborg Woods—From Hørhaven to Moesgaard Beach.* Two pamphlets written in English. Describe a seven-kilometer footpath from Marselisborg Palace in Århus along the Århus Bay to Moesgaard Beach. Sketch maps are included.

Turistforeningen for Ebeltoft-Mols-Kaløvigegnen. Located in an idyllic township with many old half-timbered houses dating from the 17th century. Can provide help with planning walks on the peninsula east of Århus. Also distributes the pamphlets to the *Natursti Ebeltoft-Gravlev* and *Vandreture i Statsskovene—Mols Bjerge* (number 33 on the map showing *Denmark's Long-Distance Footpaths),* both of which are located nearby.

Grindstedegnens Turistforening. Located almost dead center in Jutland. Provides several useful publications to footpaths in the area. Also will tell you where other footpaths are located. Publications available from the office include:

• *Ballesbækgård Rørbæk Sø.* A short route description in Danish and sketch map to footpaths in a nature reserve on the Rørbæk Sø Lake.

The nature reserve is located about three kilometers from Hærvejen and five kilometers south of Nr. Snede.

- *Natursti Haraldskær-Bindeballe.* A route description in Danish and sketch map to a 12-kilometer footpath in a forest area south of Nørup, between Grinsted and Vejle.
- *Vandreture i Statsskovene—Engelsholm Skov Vejle.* State Forestry Office pamphlet to nature trails in the forest area south of the Engelsholm Sø Lake outside Nørup. (Number 28 on the map, showing Denmark's Long-Distance Footpaths.)
- *Something about Billund.* A tourist brochure written in English. Includes a paragraph of description on Grene Sande, a nature reserve between Billund and Hejnsvig to the east of Grindsted. There are two marked footpaths in the nature reserve. Information on walking the paths can be obtained from the Grindsted tourist office.

The tourist office also publishes 10 sketch maps and route descriptions in Danish to tours on back roads in the surrounding area. Although the tours are designed primarily for cyclists, they can also be followed by walkers. Lengths of the tours range from 14 to 45 kilometers. In addition, there is a 10-kilometer footpath and keep-fit trail between Grindsted and Sønder Omme. No route description exists to this path. The tourist office, however, will mark its route on a map and give you directions to the path.

Holstebro Turistkontor. Located south of Limfjord in a moorland district. Near a black grouse sanctuary. Useful publications available from the office include:

- *Vandreture i Klosterheden.* A pamphlet similar to those published by the State Forestry Office. Includes a sketch map and route description of 12 footpaths in the Klosterheden Forest northwest of Holstebro. (Located below number 34 on the map showing Denmark's Long-Distance Footpaths.) Written in Danish.
- *Gå tur i Holstebros plantager.* Includes sketch maps and short route descriptions to footpaths in four forests on the outskirts of Holstebro.
- *Venå Kort.* A sketch map to the roads, footpaths and forest areas on the island of Venå in Limfjord.
- *Naturen i Ringkjøbing Amt.* A pamphlet in Danish describing 33 nature areas surrounding Holstebro. Includes eight sketch maps on which footpaths are marked. The key to symbols used on the maps is translated into English and German.

Horsens Turistforening. A fjordside town on the east coast of Jutland with picturesque lanes, 18th century houses and court interiors. Beginning point for the 61-kilometer footpath through the Danish

Lake District to Silkeborg. There is also an 8-kilometer footpath along Horsens Fjord between Horsens and Haldrup, and several short footpaths in the Uldrup Bakker (Uldrup Hills) and Sondrup Plantage (Sondrup Plantation) on the northern edge of the fjord, about 10 kilometers east of Horsens. No route descriptions exist to these paths. Information on walking them, however, is available from the tourist office. The office can also supply the State Forestry Office pamphlet to footpaths in the Stagsrode Forest, 20 kilometers south of Horsens:

• *Vandreture i Statsskovene—Stagsrode Skov.* Number 15 on the map showing *Denmark's Long-Distance Footpaths.*

Turistforeningen for Odder. Located on the east coast of Jutland between Århus and Horsens. There are many footpaths in the area, although there are few maps or route descriptions available. Best to refer to the 1:25,000 Geodæstik Institut maps, sheets 1314-III-NØ, SØ, NV and SV. Two useful publications available from the office include:

• *Welcome to the Odder-Country.* A general tourist information brochure with a short description of a 7-kilometer walking tour and 30-kilometer bicycle tour. A series of pictures and short descriptions in English describe the routes for the two tours.

• *Tilmeldingskupon.* A sketch map to a 10-kilometer footpath in the forest area southwest of Odder. The walk begins and ends at the market square in the middle of Odder. It is marked with yellow stripes painted on buildings and trees.

Silkeborg Turistforening. Located in the Danish Lake District. Beautiful area with tree- and heather-covered hills, lakes, streams and numerous footpaths. Near Denmark's second highest "mountain," the 147-meter high Himmelbjerget. A very helpful tourist office. Publications available from the office include:

• *Vandreture i Statsskovene—Velling-Skovene Byrup.* State Forestry Office pamphlet to the footpaths in the Velling Forest, 10 kilometers south of Silkeborg. (Number 37 on the map showing *Denmark's Long-Distance Footpaths.*)

• **Vandreture i Statsskovene—Slåensø Silkeborg.** *State Forestry Office pamphlet to a 7-kilometer footpath around the lake of Slåen, six kilometers south of Silkeborg. (Number 12.)*

• **Vandreture i Statsskovene—Nordskoven Silkeborg.** *State Forestry Office pamphlet to the footpaths in the Nordskoven Forest, on the outskirts of Silkeborg. (Number 19.)*

• **Vandreture i Statsskovene—Harrild Hede.** *State Forestry Office pamphlet to the footpaths in the Harrild Heath, about 25 kilometers west of Silkeborg. (Number 14.)*

- **Natursti Horsens-Silkeborg.** *A sketch map and route description in Danish to the 61-kilometer footpath between Horsens and Silkeborg. Follows an abandoned railway line through hills and forests and past lakes. Several campsites and youth hostels are near the path.*
- **Hærvejen.** *A sketch map and short description in Danish to the Ancient Army Road that passes about 10 kilometers to the west of Silkeborg.*
- **Tur-2—Silkeborg-Ry.** *A sketch map and route description in Danish to a 40-kilometer walk around the Silkeborg lakes.*

Other footpaths around Silkeborg are indicated on the 1:25,000 Geodæstik Institut maps, sheets 1214-I-NV, SV, NØ and SØ, and 1214-IV-NØ and SØ.

Skjern Turistkontor. Located in a fertile river valley near Ringkøbing Fjord on the west coast of Jutland. Two publications available from the office are:

- *Ture i Danske Skove—Dejbjerg.* Sketch map and route description in Danish to footpaths in the Dejbjerg, a private heathland and forest area five kilometers north of Skjern.
- *Ture i Danske Skove—Birkebæk.* Sketch map and route description in Danish to footpaths in the Birkebæk Forest south of Herning, 25 kilometers east of Skjern.

Viborg Turistkontor. An ancient town on Hald Lake. Beginning point of the Hærvejen. Publications available from the office include:

- *Vandreture i Statsskovene—Hald-Turene.* State Forestry Office pamphlet to footpaths in the heathland and moors surrounding Hald Lake. (Number 7 on the map showing *Denmark's Long-Distance Footpaths.)*
- **Vandreture i Statsskovene—Fussingsø-Turen.** *State Forestry Office pamphlet to footpaths in the forest area on Fussingsø Lake, located 25 kilometers west of Viborg. (Number 11.)*
- **On Foot in the Viborg Area.** *A pamphlet in English with short descriptions of nearly 40 walks in the forest and heathland areas surrounding Viborg.*

Turistforeningen for Vinderup. A small town located between Skive and Struer on the south side of Limfjord. A useful publication available from the office is:

- *Trave en Tur i rakkernes fodspor.* A sketch map and description of seven short walks in the Hjerl Hede, a heathland and lake area about five kilometers east of Vinderup. The pamphlet includes summaries in English and German of the path descriptions.

Useful Addresses—Sønderjylland (South Jutland)

See *Address Directory:*

Turistforeningen for Åbenrå. An old seaport located on Åbenrå Fjord on Jutland's east coast. Useful publications available from the office include:

* *Vandreture i Statsskovene—Sønderskov og Hjælm, Åbenrå.* State Forestry Office pamphlet to footpaths in the Sønderskov and Hjælm forests outside Åbenrå. (Number 29 on the map showing *Denmark's Long-Distance Footpaths.)*
* **Vandreture i Statsskovene—Frøslev-Lyngpolde-Turen.** State Forestry Office pamphlet to footpaths in the Frøslev Forest area on the Danish-German border, 25 kilometers south of Åbenrå. *(Number 8 on the map showing* **Denmark's Long-Distance Footpaths.)**

Handerslev Turistforening. Old market town located on Handerslev Fjord. Publications available from the office include:

* *Handerslev Omegn.* A nicely done pamphlet with a map in a scale of 1:40,000. Shows the locations of forests, lakes, beaches and footpaths in the countryside surrounding Handerslev. Footpaths can be followed by using the fold-out map in the back of the pamphlet. A German translation of the route descriptions and other information in the pamphlet, entitled *Handerslev Umgebung,* is also available from the office.
* *Geheimratssteig.* A route description in German to a 15-kilometer path through woodlands that begins in Handerslev. No sketch map is included.
* *Christiansfeld, Handerslev, Vojens.* A general-information tourist brochure in English. The section on Christiansfeld includes a sketchy description of a walk through fields, past streams and over wooded hills in the countryside surrounding the town.

Kolding Turistbureau. An old frontier and fortress town located on Kolding Fjord. Publications available from the office include:

* *Ture i Kolding bys skove.* A sketch map and route description in Danish to two footpaths—5 and 10 kilometers in length—in a wooded area on the outskirts of the town.
* *Vandreture i Statsskovene—Stenderup Skovene Kolding.* State Forestry Office pamphlet to footpaths in the forest areas on the

Stenderup Peninsula east of Kolding. (Number 38 on the map showing *Denmark's Long-Distance Footpaths.*)

Turistforeningen for Sønderborg. Important town in Danish history. Located on Sønderborg Sound across from the German mainland. Publications available from the office include:

- *Vandreture i Statsskovene—Nørreskoven På Als.* State Forestry Office pamphlet to footpaths in the Nørreskov Forest on the northern coast of the Als Peninsula, 15 kilometers north of Sønderborg. (Number 30 on the map showing *Denmark's Long-Distance Footpaths.*)
- *Vandreture i Statsskovene—Sønderskoven På Als.* State Forestry Office pamphlet to footpaths in a forest area one kilometer east of Sønderborg. (Number 23 on the map showing *Denmark's Long-Distance Footpaths.*)

Varde Turistforening. An important commercial town for centuries. Located north of Esbjerg in western Jutland. The office distributes the State Forestry Office pamphlet to footpaths in a forest plantation on the Skallingen Peninsula, 25 kilometers to the west of the town:

- *Vandreture i Statsskovene-Ho Klitplantage Varde.* Number 36 on the map showing *Denmark's Long-Distance Footpaths.*

Vojens Turistforening. A small town located on Hærvejen, 15 kilometers west of Handerslev. The office publishes a pamphlet in English covering a series of footpaths that wander through the countryside south of the town:

- *Paths at Jels and Oksenvad.* Describes points of interest along the paths between Jels and Oksenvad. Includes a sketch map.

Guidebooks

The State Forestry Office pamphlets can be obtained from most tourist offices throughout Jutland. For the sake of simplicity, however, they have been listed only under the towns closest to the state forests.

Walking Tours

Several tourist offices in the towns surrounding Limfjord arrange one- and two-day walks in the Limfjord countryside. Information on the tours is available from the tourist offices in Farsø, Fjerritslev, Lemvig, Nykøbing Mors, Skive, Struer, Sydthy, Thisted, Viborg and Vinderup.

Suggested Walks

Two of the most pleasant walks on Jutland are the 61-kilometer *Natursti Horsens-Silkeborg* and the 40-kilometer *Tur 2—Silkeborg-Ry* in the Danish Lake District. Information on the paths and on lodgings along their routes can be obtained from the Silkeborg tourist office.

Lolland, Falster & Møn

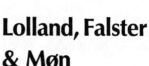

These three idyllic farming and fishing islands are strung in a semicircle below the southern tip of Zealand. The islands are scattered with manor houses, old churches and pretty villages. Møn is said to be the most attractive Danish island, perhaps because of Møns Klint, a magnificent stretch of chalk cliffs on the island's eastern coast. The beech-covered cliffs rise 128 meters (420 feet) above the sea and are carved into numerous fanciful shapes. Atop the cliffs is a state forest with footpaths and a campsite.

Lolland and Falster are primarily pastoral, their main attraction being their fine, sandy beaches. Both islands lie on the main rail line between Copenhagen and Germany. Møn is reached by bridge from Zealand.

The number of footpaths on the islands is limited, and none are more than eight kilometers in length. Nonetheless, there are enough trails on the islands for a series of pleasant day hikes.

Useful Addresses

See *Address Directory:*

> **Turistbureauet for Nakskov.** Largest town on the island of Lolland. The office distributes two publications that are of use to walkers:
>
> • *Ture i Danske Skove—Rudbjerggård Vindeholme Lolland.* Route description in Danish and sketch map to three short footpaths in a private forest on the southeast coast of Lolland.

- *12 Naturområder i Storstrøms Amt.* A pamphlet with sketch maps to 12 nature reserves on Lolland, Falster, Møn and southern Zealand. Several of the reserves have short footpaths.

Nykøbing Turistforening. Old-world townscape on the island of Falster. Publications available from the office include:

- *Ture i Danske Skove—Corselitze Falster.* Route description in Danish and sketch map to three short paths in a private forest on the east coast of Falster.
- *Vandreture i Statsskovene—Borremosen.* State Forestry Office pamphlet to footpaths in a forest and marsh area in the center of the island, seven kilometers northeast of Nykøbing. (Number 21 on the map showing *Denmark's Long-Distance Footpaths.*)

Møns Turistforening. A small market town with a well-preserved medieval town gate. The office distributes two pamphlets—one in Danish and one in German—to footpaths in the privately owned forest area above the Møns Klint cliffs:

- *Ture i Danske Skove—Klintholm Møn.* Written in Danish. Includes a sketch map.
- *Touren in Dänischen Wäldern-Klintholm Mön.* Written in German. Includes a sketch map.

Publications in English describing the archeology and geology of Møns Klint are also available from the office.

Maps

The three islands are covered by the following 1:25,000 Geodæstik Institut maps:

Lolland: sheets 1411-I-NV, SV and SØ; 1411-II-NV, SV, NØ and SØ; 1411-III-NV and NØ; 1411-IV-NØ, SØ and SV; 1511-III-NV and SV; and 1511-IV-SV.

Falster: sheets 1510-IV-NØ; 1511-III-NV, SV, NØ and SØ; and 1511-IV-NV, SV, NØ and SØ.
Møn: sheets 1511-I-NV and NØ; 1511-IV-NØ; and 1512-II-SV and SØ.

Suggested Walks

The most pleasant hikes on the three islands are in the wooded Klintholm Estate above the cliffs of Møns Klint. Of the three footpaths in the estate, two hug the cliffs, zigzagging up and down them to follow in some places the shore at their base, in others the beech-covered cliff tops. Several prehistoric remains and burial mounds are scattered throughout the estate. There is also a keep-fit trail, a camping site and a hotel on the estate grounds. Total length of the paths in the estate is 22 kilometers.

Sjælland (Zealand)

Zealand is an island of pastoral beauty with delightful beech woods, green rolling pastures and large lakes. Denmark's principal tourist attractions are located on the island—the cities of Copenhagen, Roskilde and Helsingør; the old manor houses and castles of North Zealand; and the pleasant lakeside and beach resorts of Hornbæk, Fakse Ladeplads and Jyderup.

Few footpaths on the island are long. But they are numerous, particularly in North Zealand, which has the highest concentration of state forests in the country. Zealand has 16 state forests in which you can walk—14 of which are located in North Zealand. In addition, the island contains five private forests with footpaths.

As in the rest of Denmark, walking is not regarded as a prime tourist attraction. The result is that information on footpaths outside the state forests is sketchy—and hard to come by. For this reason, it is advisable to obtain a full set of the State Forestry Office pamphlets to Zealand from the Danish Tourist Board in Copenhagen and to plan your walks from these. A trip to the Copenhagen library to look at the 1:25,000 Geodæstik Institut maps that cover North Zealand is also useful. This will help you locate footpaths and small backroads along which you can walk outside the state forests. Then you can buy the maps you need for your walk from the Geodæstik Institut in Copenhagen.

The State Forestry Office pamphlets are also available from tourist offices in the towns near the state forests. But few of the offices stock a full set of the pamphlets for Zealand. And only four publish sketch maps to local footpaths. These are listed below.

Useful Addresses

See Address Directory:

Turistforeningen for Hillerød. Site of Frederiksborg Castle. Located in the center of North Zealand between two forest areas—Gribskov, a 5,676-hectare (14,000 acre) woodland on the shores of Esrum Sø Lake, and Rågårds Mose. State Forestry Office pamphlets to the forest footpaths are available from the office. A 26-kilometer bicycle route also starts in the town and follows back roads through Gribskov to Gilleleje, a beachside resort on the north coast of Zealand. The bike route can be walked. A pamphlet is available from the tourist office:

• *Gang-og Cykelsti.* Describes the marked bicycle route in Danish. Includes three sketch maps of the route. A German translation of the pamphlet is also available from the office.

Turistforeningen for Køge. A charming old market town with many well-preserved buildings. Located on the east coast of Zealand, 38 kilometers south of Copenhagen. Several nearby woodlands have footpaths, for which the tourist office can provide pamphlets:

• *Vandreture Køge Ås Gammelkjøgegård.* A sketch map and short description of a meadow and woodland area surrounding a manor house west of Køge. The pamphlet is published by the tourist office. It is written in English, Danish and German.

• *Ture i Danske Skove—Vemmetofte.* A route description in Danish and sketch map to two footpaths and a keep-fit trail in a forest area near Fakse Ladeplads, 25 kilometers south of Køge.

• *Ture i Danske Skove—Vallø.* A route description in Danish and sketch map to three footpaths in a woodland surrounding Vallø, a Renaissance castle two kilometers south of Køge.

Næstved Turist- og Servicekontor. The largest town and center of southern Zealand, with a lovely countryside setting. Several footpaths have recently been marked in the woodlands surrounding the town. No documentation on the footpaths has yet been published. The tourist office, however, can tell you which woodlands have footpaths and give you directions to them.

Odsherreds Turistforening. Located on the northwestern tip of Zealand, a lovely area of bays and inlets with long stretches of sandy beaches, large moors, fir plantations and beech woods. A state forest area with short footpath, Sonnerup Skov, is seven kilometers west of Nykøbing on the coast. There is also a 12-kilometer long bicycle route and footpath along Isefjord, south of Nykøbing. A sketch map to the path is available from the tourist office:

• *Tingstien langs Isefjorden.*

Roskilde Turistforening. An historically important town with many beautiful old buildings. Located at the southern tip of Roskilde Fjord in North Zealand. The town is the current end-point of European Long-Distance Footpath E–6, which winds its way north from Yugoslavia to Denmark. A sketch map to the section of trail crossing Zealand is available from the tourist office. The office also distributes sketch maps and route descriptions in Danish to footpaths in three woodland areas near the town:

• *Ture Vest for Roskilde—Boserup Turen och Kattinge Turen.* A two-page description and map of two unmarked footpaths and bike routes—15 and 17 kilometers in length—west of Roskilde. The routes pass in front of the Roskilde youth hostel. The tourist office will give those who do not speak Danish a verbal "briefing" to help them follow the paths.

• *Vandreture i Københavns Kommunes Skove—Bidstrup Skovdistrikt.* A brief description and sketch map of a footpath in a woodland 15 kilometers southwest of Roskilde.

• *Ture i Danske Skove—Skjoldenæsholm og Bidstrup.* A brief description and sketch map of three footpaths in a private woodland adjoining the Bidstrup Skovdistrikt.

Slagelse Erhvers- & Turistkontor. An old, established town in which little of antiquity remains because of many fires. Located on the edge of a forest area in southwest Zealand. Few sketch maps exist of footpaths in the surrounding countryside, although the tourist office is good about providing suggestions for walks. It can also provide a pamphlet for footpaths in a nearby state forest, Stensbøg Skov, as well as a sketch map it publishes of footpaths in the woodlands on the outskirts of the town:

• *Trelleborg Marchen.*

Guidebooks

The State Forestry Office publishes 17 pamphlets describing the footpaths in Zealand's forest areas. The locations of the state forests and the local tourist offices from which the pamphlets can be obtained are:

• *Vandreture i Statsskovene—Sonnerup Skov.* Located near Nykøbing SJ on the Odsherreds Peninsula in northwest Zealand. (Number 20 on the map showing *Denmark's Long-Distance Footpaths.*) Pamphlet available from the Odsherreds Turistforening in Nykøbing.

• *Vandreture i Statsskovene—Tisvilde Hegn-Turen 1.* Located six kilometers north of Frederiskværk on the coast of North Zealand. (Number 1.) Pamphlet available from the tourist offices in Frederiskværk and Tisvilde.

- **Vandreture i Statsskovene—Tisvilde Hegn-Turen II.** *Located nine kilometers north of Frederiskværk. (Number 10.) Pamphlet available from the tourist office in Frederiksværk.*

- **Vandreture i Statsskovene—Teglstrup Hegn Helsingør.** *Located three kilometers north of Helsingør (Elsinore) in North Zealand. (Number 4.) Pamphlet available from the tourist office in Helsingør.*

- **Vandreture i Statsskovene—Gribskov-Turen.** *Located on the outskirts of Hillerød in North Zealand. (Number 5.) Pamphlet available from the Turistforeningen for Hillerød.*

- *Vandreture i Statsskovene—Rågårds Mose Hillerød.* Located three kilometers south of Hillerød. (Number 18.) Pamphlet available from the Turistforeningen for Hillerød.

- *Vandreture i Statsskovene—Tokkekøb Hegn-Turen.* Located six kilometers south of Hillerød. (Number 9.) Pamphlet available from the tourist office in Hillerød.

- *Vandreture i Statsskovene—Folehaven Hørsholm.* Located on the outskirts of Hørsholm on the rail line between Copenhagen and Helsingør in North Zealand, 15 kilometers east of Hillerød. (Number 25.) Pamphlet available from the tourist office in Hørsholm.

- *Vandreture i Statsskovene—Rudeskove-Turen.* Located between Hørsholm and Holte, 18 kilometers north of Copenhagen. (Number 2.) Pamphlet available from the tourist office in Hørsholm.

- *Nature Trails in the State Forests—Jægersborg Dyrehave.* A woodland of magnificent beech trees with a deer park near Klampenborg, 10 kilometers north of Copenhagen. (Number 22.) The pamphlet, written in English, is available from the Danish Tourist Board in Copenhagen.

- *Vandreture i Statsskovene—Skovene ved Buresø Slangerup.* Located three kilometers southeast of Slangerup, to the east of Frederikssund in North Zealand. (Number 17.) Pamphlet available from the tourist offices in Frederikssund and Hillerød.

- *Vandreture i Statsskovene—Nørreskove-Turen.* Located southeast of Farum on the shores of the lake of Fure Sø between Copenhagen and Hillerød. (Number 3.) Pamphlet available from the tourist offices in Hørsholm and Hillerød.

- *Vandreture i Statsskovene—Jonstrupvang Li. Hareskov.* Located two kilometers north of Ballerup below the lake of Fure Sø. (Number 16.) Pamphlet available from the tourist offices in Hørsholm and Hillerød.

- *Vandreture i Statsskovene—Kongelunden.* Located on Amager Island south of Copenhagen, not far from Copenhagen's Kastrup Airport. (Number 13.) Pamphlet available from the Danish Tourist Board in Copenhagen.

- *Vandreture i Statsskovene—Vestkoven København.* Located between Ballerup and Albertslund east of Copenhagen. (Number 32.) Pamphlet available from the Danish Tourist Board in Copenhagen.

- *Vandreture i Statsskovene—Store Bøgeskov Ringsted.* Located on the lake of Gyrstinge Sø, 10 kilometers northwest of Ringsted in central Zealand. (Number 26.) Pamphlet available from the tourist offices in Ringsted and Sorø.

- *Vandreture i Statsskovene—Stensbøg Skov og Akademihaven Sorø.* Located on the outskirts of Sorø on the lake of Sorø Sø in central Zealand. (Number 31.) Pamphlet available from the tourist offices in Sorø and Slagelse.

Suggested Walks

In addition to the nature trails in the state forests, there is one long-distance footpath on Zealand—the section of European Long-Distance Footpath E-6 stretching from Korsør to Roskilde through central Zealand. In many areas, the 80-kilometer footpath follows backroads. Nonetheless, it passes through pleasant countryside, and traffic on the roads is light—so you still can enjoy your hike. The purist may wish there were less macadam and more path. But it is the only opportunity for a walker to truly stretch his or her legs on Zealand. Details on the footpath are included under the section on *Denmark's Long-Distance Footpaths.*

For short day hikes, one of the best places to base yourself is in Hillerød, from which the footpaths in seven state forests are easily accessible.

Address Directory

A

- *Århus Turistforening,* Rådhuset, DK-8000 Århus C. Tel. (06) 12 16 00.

B

- *Bornholms Turistbureau,* Box 60, v/Havnen, DK-3700 Rønne. Tel. (03) 95 08 06 and 95 08 10.

D

- *DVL,* see *Dansk Vandrelaug.*

- *Danish National Tourist Office, New York,* 75 Rockefeller Plaza, New York, New York 10019. Tel. (212) 687-5609.
- *Danish Tourist Board, London,* 169-73 Regent Street, London W1R 8PY. Tel. (01) 734 2637 and 734 2638.
- *Danmarks Turistråd,* H.C. Andersens Blvd. 22, (vis-a-vis Radhuset) 1553 Copenhagen V. Tel. (01) 11 14 15.
- *Dansk Camping Union,* C. Kongevej 74, D-1850 Copenhagen V. Tel. (01) 21 06 00.
- *Dansk Cyklist-Forbund,* Kjeld Langesgade 14, DK
- *Dansk Gangforbund,* Idrættens Hus, Brønby Station 20, DK-2600 Glostrup. Tel. (02) 88 58 27.
- *Dansk Orienterings-Forbund,* Idrættens Hus, Brønby Station, DK-2600 Glostrup. Tel. (02) 45 77 30.
- *Dansk Skovforening,* Amalievej 20, DK-1875 Cph.V
- *Dansk Vandrelaug,* Kultorvet 7, DK-1175 Copenhagen K. Tel. (01) 12 11 65.
- *Deutscher Wanderverlag,* Haussmannstrasse 66, D-7000 Stuttgart 1, Germany.
- *Direktoratet for Statsskovbruget,* Strandvejen 863, DK-2930 Klampenborg. Tel. (01) 63 11 66.

E

- *Emergency:* Tel. 0.0.0.
- *Erhvervs- og Turistkontoret Fjerritslev,* Danmarksgade 1, DK-9690 Fjerritslev. Tel. (08) 21 15 71.

F

- *Fyntour,* Møllergade 20, DK-5700 Svendborg. Tel. (0045) 921 07 41.

G

- *Geodætisk Institut,* Rigsdagsgården 7, DK-1218 Copenhagen K. Tel. (01) 11 60 17.
- *Grindstedegnens Turistforening,* Østergade 25, DK-7200 Grindsted. Tel. (05) 32 21 12.

H

- Hadersle Turistforening, Apotekergade 1, DK-6100 Hadersle. Tel. (04) 52 55 50.
- Herbergs-Ringen, Vesterbrogade 35, DK-1620 Copenhagen V. Tel. (01) 31 36 12.
- Holstebro Turistkontor, Brostræde 1, DK-7500 Holstebro. Tel. (07) 42 57 00.
- Horsens Turistforening, Kongensgade 25, Postbox 184, DK-8700 Horsens. Tel. (05) 72 31 32.

K

- Københavns Kommunes Biblioteker, Kultorvet 2, DK-1175 Copenhagen.
- Kolding Turistbureau, Helligkorsgade 18, DK-6000 Kolding. Tel. (05) 53 21 00.

L

- Langeland-Rudkøbing Turistkontor, Gåsetorvet 1, DK-5900 Rudkøbing. Tel. (09) 51 14 44.

M

- Marchforeningen "Fodslaw," Reberbanen 12, DK-8800 Viborg. Tel. (06) 62 45 21.
- Møns Turistforening, Storegade 5, DK-4780 Stege. Tel. (03) 81 44 11.

N

- Næstved Turist- og Servicekontor, Banegårdspladsen, DK-4700 Næstved. Tel. (03) 72 11 22.
- Nordbornholms Turistbureau, Hammershusvej 2, Sandvig, DK-3770 Allinge. Tel. (03) 98 00 01.
- Nyborg Erhvers- & Turistkontor, Gl. Torv 4, DK-5800 Nyborg. Tel. (09) 31 02 80.
- Nykøbing Turistforening, Østergade 2, DK-4800 Nykøbing. Tel. (03) 85 13 03.

O

- Odense Turistkontor, Rådhuset, DK-5000 Odense. Tel. (09) 12 75 20.

- *Odsherreds Turistforening*, Algade 52, DK-4500 Nykøbing SJ. Tel. (03) 41 08 88.

R

- *Roskilde Turistforening*, Fondensbro v/Domkirken, DK-4000 Roskilde. Tel. (03) 35 27 00.

S

- *Silkeborg Turistforening*, Torvet 12, DK-8600 Silkeborg. Tel. (06) 82 19 11.
- *Skagen Turistforening*, Sct. Laurentiivej 18, DK-9990 Skagen. Tel. (08) 44 13 77.
- *Skjern Turistkontor*, Banegårdsplads, DK-6900 Skjern. Tel. (07) 35 18 18.
- *Slagelse Erhvers- & Turistkontoret*, Bredegade 8, DK-4200 Slagelse. Tel. (03) 52 22 06.
- *Spejder Sport, Aalborg*, Borgergade 5, DK-9000 Aalborg. Tel. (08) 13 87 33.
- *Spejder Sport, Århus*, Åboulevarden 54-58, DK-8000 Århus C. Tel. (06) 13 36 13.
- *Spejder Sport, Copenhagen*, Nøbre Farimagsgade 39, DK-1364 Copenhagen K. Tel. (01) 12 55 22.
- *Spejder Sport, Lyngby*, Lyngby Hovedgade 57, DK-2800 Lyngby. Tel. (02) 87 04 67.
- *Spejder Sport, Odense*, Kongensgade 55, DK-5000 Odense. Tel. (09) 11 24 18.
- *Svendborg Turistkontor*, Møllergade 20, DK-5700 Svendborg. Tel. (09) 21 09 80.

T

- *Turistbureauet for Nakskov*, Axeltorv, DK-4900 Naskov. Tel. (03) 92 21 72.
- *Turistforeningen for Åbenrå*, H.P. Hanssensgade 5, DK-6200 Åbenrå. Tel. (04) 62 35 00.
- *Turistforeningen for Ebeltoft-Mols-Kaløvigegnen*, Torvet 9, DK-8400 Ebeltoft. Tel. (06) 34 14 00.
- *Turistforeningen for Faaborg og Omegn*, Havnegade 2 DK-5600 Faaborg. Tel. (09) 61 07 07.
- *Turistforeningen for Frederikshavn*, Brotorvet 1, DK-9900 Frederikshavn. Tel. (08) 42 32 66.

- *Turistforeningen for Hillerød,* Torvet 1, DK-3400 Hillerød. Tel. (03) 26 28 52.
- *Turistforeningen for Hobro,* Vestergade, DK-9500 Hobro. Tel. (08) 55 22 88.
- *Turistforeningen for Køge,* Vestergade 1, DK-4600 Køge. Tel. (03) 65 58 00.
- *Turistforeningen for Middelfart,* Algade 62, DK-5500 Middelfart. Tel. (09) 41 17 88.
- *Turistforeningen for Odder,* Banegårdsplads 3, DK-8300 Odder. Tel. (06) 54 26 00.
- *Turistforeningen for Sønderborg,* Rådhustorvet 7, DK-6400 Sønderborg. Tel. (04) 42 35 55.
- *Turistforeningen for Thisted og Thy,* Store Torr 6, DK-7700 Thisted. Tel. (07) 92 19 00.
- *Turistforeningen for Vinderup,* Vinjes Torv, DK-7830 Vinderup. Tel. (07) 44 22 85.
- *Turistkontoret Ærøskøbing,* Torvet, DK-5970 Ærøskøbing. Tel. (09) 52 13 00.

V

- *Varde Turistforening,* Torvet 5, DK-6800 Varde. Tel. (05) 22 07 30.
- *Viborg Turistkontor,* Nytorv 5, DK-8800 Viborg. Tel. (06) 62 16 17.
- *Vojens Turistforening,* c/o Vojens Bibliotek Billundvej 5, DK-6500 Vojens. Tel. (04) 54 11 44.

A Quick Reference

In a hurry? Turn to the pages listed below. They will give you the most important information on walking in Denmark.

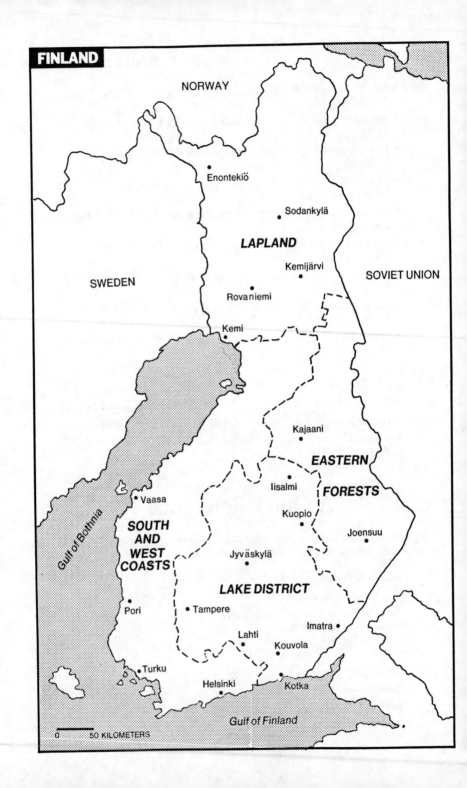

FINLAND

NORWAY

SWEDEN

SOVIET UNION

• Enontekiö

• Sodankylä

LAPLAND

• Kemijärvi

• Rovaniemi

• Kemi

• Kajaani

EASTERN

• Iisalmi

FORESTS

• Kuopio

• Joensuu

• Vaasa

SOUTH AND WEST COASTS

Gulf of Bothnia

• Jyväskylä

LAKE DISTRICT

• Pori

• Tampere

• Imatra

• Lahti

• Kouvola

• Turku

• Helsinki

• Kotka

Gulf of Finland

0   50 KILOMETERS

Finland

FINLAND—OR, AS it is known in Finnish, *Suomi*—is, after Iceland, the most northerly country in the world. Tucked between the Gulf of Bothnia and the Soviet Union with nearly one-third of its total length lying above the Arctic Circle, Finland is also the repository of some of the largest remaining wilds in Europe: a land undulating with forest and marsh and glistening with lakes.

Because of the Gulf Stream, its climate is not as severe as might be expected. Average temperatures in Finland are considerably higher during all seasons than in other countries at the same latitude. The population is small—only 4.7 million people—and the density of people per square kilometer is one of the lowest in Europe. As a result, it is easy to find large, uninhabited wilderness regions in which to roam. Even in southern Finland, where the majority of the population is concentrated, there are large tracts of wilderness. (The wilderness region of Nuuksio, for instance, is a mere 30 kilometers from Helsinki, Finland's capital and largest city.) It has more marshland than any other country in Europe. Almost a third of Finland's total area of 337,000 square kilometers (130,085 square miles) is covered by peatlands. Forests cover 68 percent of the country, making it the most heavily wooded country in Europe. It also has more than 60,000 lakes, the largest of which is Iso Saimaa in the southeast (4,400 square kilometers).

Though much of Finland is comparatively low, it is far from flat. Everywhere there are rocky outcrops, ridges, valleys and hollows, many of which contain lakes. In the Lake District of central Finland small settlements are scattered along back roads, and dairy farms and harbor towns nestle on the wooded shores of the hill-bound lakes. Just north of Rovaniemi, a few kilometers below the Arctic Circle, the rail line ends and Lapland begins. This gently rolling land has occasional lakes, crystal clear rapids and few towns. It also contains the highest peaks in Finland— 1,328-meter (4,380-foot) Haltitunturi, 1,316-meter (4,318-foot) Ridnitchohkka and 1,144-meter (3,753-foot) Kahperusvaara. This is the land of the Lapps, a handful of whom still herd their reindeer across the tundra during the long winter nights and summer days of the far north.

Marked footpaths are few—only about 1,000 kilometers altogether.

Instead, there is an unwritten law, an "everyman's right," that, save for a few reasonable restrictions, a person may walk where he or she wishes in the countryside. Orienteering with a map and compass has always been more popular in Finland than walking on a marked trail. But this takes experience. In Finland's rolling terrain there are few prominent landmarks, and it is quite easy to get lost in its forests and on the Lapland fells. In the northern hiking areas, where villages are few and widely scattered, it is necessary to carry a tent, sleeping bag and *all* of your food. Knee-high rubber boots should also be worn, especially in Lapland, where the ground is soggy and streams must be forded. Even well-waterproofed leather boots will soak through in a few hours—if water doesn't come over the tops first.

For less experienced hikers there are marked routes near many towns and villages, particularly in the Lake District. These usually range between two and 10 kilometers in length, although one route that is currently being marked in central Finland stretches for 297 kilometers (184 miles) between Viitasaari and Halli through Saarijärvi, Suolahti, Jyväskylä, and Jämsä. An additional 134 kilometers of spur trails lead from this path to Korpilahti, Multia and Keuruu. There are also several relatively long, marked trails in Finland's national parks, such as the 70-kilometer *Karhun Kierros*—Bear's Tour—which runs through the Oulanka National Park. But the marking of trails has only recently begun. And though Lapland has many forest tracks and hiking routes—some of which follow reindeer trails—the majority are unmarked.

Because of this, walkers who are not intimately familiar with wilderness travel—and the special conditions that prevail in Finland—should first take part in one of the guided hikes arranged by Soumen Matkailuliitto (Finnish Travel Association) or Suomen Latu (Finnish Ski Track Association), before striking off on their own. (Information on guided hikes, wilderness treks and winter ski tours is given in the section on *Walking & Skiing Tours* later in this chapter.)

In the winter there are countless opportunities for cross-country skiing. In fact, there is much more emphasis on cross-country skiing than on hiking in Finland. Like the sauna (which every house in the country seems to have), skiing is a Finnish institution. In some remote areas it is still a principal mode of transport. Each February, school children are given a week's skiing holiday. Even one of the principal sources of information on hiking in Finland—Suomen Latu—was originally a ski touring association.

Near villages and towns, the more popular ski routes are marked with red triangles or rings painted on trees or, often, with colored pennants and plastic streamers. There are also numerous unmarked skiing routes, many of which are indicated on Finnish maps.

Whether you cross-country ski or hike in Finland, certain precautions are essential: you should brush up on your map reading and orienteering skills, always be sure to carry a map and compass (even for short hikes on marked trails), bring the proper clothing and equipment, and buy a Finnish-English dictionary. Although the country is bilingual (Swedish is spoken by 7 percent of the population, located primarily on the southwest and west coasts), Finnish is the dominant language, and all of the few guidebooks that exist are written in Finnish. Many educated Finns speak Swedish and, in the cities, many speak English or German. But few Finns speak French. In the countryside you sometimes find that sign language is the only way to communicate.

Despite Finland's unwritten law of "everyman's right," walkers have a responsibility to respect property rights. To light a fire on private land requires the owner's permission. And if there is a gate, it should be closed and latched behind you.

Near the Russian border in eastern Finland, care must also be taken to not cross into—or over—the no-man's land that separates the two countries. On the Finnish side, the border zone is marked with yellow rings painted on trees. The Russian side is dotted with sentry posts and is heavily patroled. If you cross over, you are likely to be spotted. And saying that you misread your map is no excuse. You are still an intruder—and subject to all the consequences that may follow.

Everyman's Right

Since ancient times, there has been a traditional right in Finland to move freely on other people's land without permission. There is no specific legislation that guarantees this right, although a number of different laws have set forth guidelines to define it. The latest definition is included in the 1973 Committee Report on Recreation Areas. According to the report, Everyman's Right consists of:

1. The right to move freely in the countryside when hiking, bicycling or skiing except: a) in the immediate vicinity of another person's house (such as in the courtyard), b) in cultivated fields or gardens, c) in meadows and newly painted forest plantations and d) where it is specifically prohibited by official order, such as in strict nature reserves. Private notices (i.e. "No Trespassing" signs) without legal authority do not cancel this right.

2. The right to move freely on open lake and river systems, as well as on ice.

3. The right to swim, pitch a tent, picnic or otherwise stay temporarily in places where free movement is allowed. (You are, however, urged to stay away from houses, courtyards and other buildings, such as barns, saunas and tool sheds, so you do not pose a nuisance.)

4. The right to take water for drinking and household purposes from springs and other natural water sources that are not specifically for private use.

5. The right to pick berries, mushrooms and wildflowers (excepting protected species) in areas where free movement is allowed.

6. The right to fish and hunt on specified sea zones along the coasts during the appropriate seasons and to angle under some restrictions in the municipality of one's residence. An official fishing license (obtainable in post offices) and hunting license are required.

These rights apply principally to Finnish citizens, although foreign visitors also enjoy the same benefits. It is implicit, however, that the exercise of these rights must not cause any damage to the natural vegetation, the wildlife or private property and must not be a disturbance to other people.

Hence, it is imperative that you observe standard wilderness ethics and camping practices. Always act with common courtesy and respect. In fact, on private land the best policy is still: if you see the property owner, ask permission before you hike across his or her property or set up a tent. The reception will be a lot friendlier if you do.

Flora & Fauna

With the exception of a narrow region along the south coast where oak trees grow, Finland's forests are made up almost entirely of pine (44 percent), fir and spruce (37 percent) and birch (16 percent). At higher latitudes in Lapland, the first tree species to disappear is the spruce, followed by the pine until, at tree limit, only dwarf birches remain. Beyond the tree limit is a vast region of fragile tundra that is easily damaged. Here, a moment of carelessness or disregard—building a fire, digging a trench around a tent, even walking off the established track—can destroy vegetation that will take at least from 15 to 25 years to recover. Also, because the climate in Lapland is so cold, metal, glass and plastic waste remain unchanged in the environment for centuries. Even a discarded orange peel may last for as long as two years.

No matter where you hike, you should be conscious of your impact on the environment and take all litter (including cigarette butts if you smoke) home with you. In Lapland and in the outer Archipelago of southwest Finland, this is critical.

More than 100 species of plants are protected against picking. It is also forbidden to break off the branches of trees and bushes. Berries and mushrooms, on the other hand, may be picked. In some years the inhabitants of Lapland have the sole right to pick cloudberries, so before picking them you should ask one of the local tourist offices about the latest regulations.

Many wild animals, including several of Finland's 350 species of birds, are also protected. Finland's wildlife is still diverse and plentiful and includes wild reindeer, elk, bear, beaver, wolf, lynx, marten and fox. In fact, it was the wildlife that attracted the first Finnish-speaking settlers to this northern land of forests, peatlands and lakes nearly 2,000 years ago. Others, including the Lapps, were here before then. Until the last 150 years, Finland always had more animals than people. Since then, however, many species of wildlife have nearly disappeared or have been sharply reduced in number.

The last native beaver was shot in 1868. And by 1900 the wild reindeer had almost disappeared. Bear, wolf, wolverine, lynx and golden eagle were progressively pushed north and east into the last expanses of virgin forest, where the impact of humans was still negligible. By 1920, the osprey was nearly extinct and, 20 years later, the arctic fox disappeared because its fur was in demand.

Some improvement came with the Nature Conservation Act of 1923. Ospreys began to increase. Beavers were reintroduced from Norway and North America, as were the alien muskrat, white-tailed deer and pheasant. Mink have escaped from mink farms and adapted successfully to conditions in Finland. The wild forest reindeer also returned in 1950 after an absence of nearly 50 years. According to Russian experts, however, this animal requires unspoiled wilderness areas—both forests and bogs—to live and reproduce, and, even in Finland, such areas are rapidly disappearing under the pressures of forestry, the drainage of peatlands and the need for local employment. Finally, despite protection, only 15 to 20 pairs of whooper swans remained in their native marshes in 1950, the result of being illegally hunted for food.

The balance between humans and wildlife is still fragile. With protection, swans and lynxes are increasing and gradually expanding their ranges. White-tailed deer are fairly common, numbering more than 40,000. Arctic foxes are also regularly seen in northernmost Lapland, although their numbers are still very small. Measures have been taken to protect the golden eagle, and the peregrine falcon, practically extinct a few years ago, has made a slight recovery. There are also nearly 120,000 elk.

Bear, wolf and wolverine are seen in many of Finland's national parks as well as in areas where reindeer herding is still practiced. But because these animals interfere with the herds, they are only partially protected. Also, unlike in many of the national parks in the U.S.A., these animals have not become accustomed to the presence of people and have yet to learn that a walker's rucksack is an easy source of food. Hanging your food at night out of reach of animals is still advisable, but not a necessary prerequisite to ensure you will have breakfast the next morning.

The viper is the only poisonous snake in Finland and is most commonly found in the southern half of the country, within the fir zone. It usually does not present a problem to hikers, but a bite should receive immediate medical attention. Insects, however, are another matter entirely. The buzzing arctic summer, especially from mid-June to mid-August, brings clouds of arctic mosquitoes, gnats, no-see-ums and black flies. The mosquitoes are not malaria-bearing, but insect repellent and, in boggy areas, no-see-um-proof netting to protect your face are essential.

Climate

Despite its extreme northern location, Finland has a surprisingly moderate climate. It summers are as warm as those in Great Britain or the New England states of the U.S.A. Winters are cold, but no colder than those around North America's Great Lakes. In July, temperatures may climb as high as 32° C. (90° F.) on the warmest days, even in Lapland. Temperatures in February may plunge as low as *minus* 30° C. *(minus* 22° F.) in Helsinki, and as low as *minus* 40° C. *(minus* 40° F.) on extremely cold days in Lapland. Averages are more moderate: 13° to 20° C. (55° to 68° F.) in July, and *minus* 3° to *minus* 14° C. (26° to *minus* 7° F.) in February. Summer, when average daytime temperatures are above 10° C. (50° F.), usually lasts for 110 to 120 days in the south and from 50 to 85 days in the north.

In midsummer southern Finland has 19 hours of daylight. At the 70th parallel in northern Finland, there are 73 days of perpetual daylight in summer, and 51 days of unending night in winter. The Midnight Sun, which can be seen on the Arctic Circle starting about June 6, is continuously above the horizon from May 16 to June 27 on the 70th parallel.

Statistically, some precipitation falls every other day in Finland. But amounts are small. Southwest Finland receives an annual average of 700 mm (27 inches) of precipitation, while northwest Finland receives an average of only 400 mm (16 inches). The driest period of the year is spring; the wettest, autumn. Nearly 40 percent of the precipitation is in the form of snow. Southern Finland is usually snow-covered for about four months of the year, while much of Lapland is snow-covered for seven months.

Weather Forecasts

There is no telephone number in Finland that can be called to obtain recorded weather forecasts. Instead, general weather forecasts are reported in local newspapers and during news broadcasts on radio and television.

In Helsinki news broadcasts in English are given during July and August on radio 557 at 8:35 a.m., 10:30 p.m. and 11 p.m.

Elsewhere, you can contact the local tourist office and ask what the forecast is for the day. Or better yet, call the meteorological office at the nearest airport—their forecasts will be much more precise. Most tourist offices will make this call for you if you offer to pay any toll charges. You can also look up the number for the airport meteorological office in a local telephone directory. The number will generally be found in the front pages of the directory. And language should be no problem. All the airport meteo staffs speak English. Although weather forecasts are not provided, information on the current climatic trends in various regions of Finland can be obtained from:

Ilmatieteen laitos (Institute of Weather Science). For its address, see the *Address Directory* at the back of this chapter. Staff speaks Finnish, Swedish, English and German.

Where to Get Walking Information

There are two central organizations that provide information on walking in Finland:

Suomen Latu (Finnish Ski Track Association). For its address and telephone number, see the *Address Directory* at the back of this chapter. Staff speaks Finnish, Swedish, English, French and German. Can provide information on fell walking, hiking and cross-country skiing in Finland. Organizes numerous guided hikes, wilderness treks, ski tours, and ski weeks in various parts of Finland. Runs courses to teach ski techniques, first aid and orienteering. Also helps maintain the network of fell cabins at Saariselkä (see the section on *Trailside Lodgings*). Suomen Latu can help you plan walking and skiing itineraries and will provide assistance in making the necessary arrangements. The voluntary association also has more than 130 local clubs which can assist you in their areas. Finnish publications available from Suomen Latu include:

* *Keski-Suomi Retkeilijän Suomi.* A free leaflet with a sketch map published by Keski-Suomen Maakuntaliitto in Jyväskylä. Describes the 297-kilometer hiking route now being marked between Viitasaari and Halli in central Finland, as well as its 134 kilometers of spur trails. A German translation of the leaflet, *Mittelfinnland Wanderland,* is also available.

* *Virkisty Retkeillen Keski-Suomen Ulkoilureiteillä.* A map in a scale of 1:400,000. Also published by Keski-Suomen Maakuntaliitto. Shows the hiking route between Viitasaari and Halli, along with the locations of hotels, farm accommodation and camping sites. Includes a brief description—in Finnish—of each section of the route. Should be supplemented with larger-scale maps.

* *Kesälomalle* (On Your Summer Vacation). Issued annually. De-

scribes the one- and two-week guided hiking trips that are organized each summer by Suomen Latu throughout Finland. Gives full details, including prices.

- *Talvilomalle* (On Your Winter Vacation). Issued annually. Describes the numerous guided ski track hikes, ski weeks, wilderness treks and winter camping trips organized each winter by Suomen Latu, most of which are in Lapland. Gives full details, including prices.

- *Vesiretkeilyreitit.* A guidebook describing 51 canoeing and hiking routes on Finland's lake and river systems. Includes maps and all other necessary information.

- *Finnland—Heimat des Skilanglaufs* (Finland—Home of Cross-Country Skiing). Written in German. A guidebook to cross-country skiing in Finland with information on technique, equipment, international cross-country skiing events and Finland's principal ski touring centers.

- *Suomen Latu ry.* A small booklet with text in Finnish, Swedish, English and German. Describes the history, activities, and organization of Suomen Latu.

- *Suomen Latu: Osoitemuistio.* Issued annually. Lists the addresses, telephone numbers and officers of each of Suomen Latu's local member associations.

- *Latu ja Polku* (Ski Track and Path). Suomen Latu's member magazine, published eight times a year.

Suomen Matkailuliitto (Finnish Travel Association). See *Address Directory.* Established to promote tourism, wilderness excursions and camping in Finland. Runs numerous guided trips and outdoor activities, including wilderness hikes, ski trips, canoeing and bicycle tours, and winter hikes across the Arctic fells with overnight stays in snow caves. Publishes several guidebooks and hut lists (see the sections on *Guidebooks* and *Trailside Lodgings*), as well as several tourist guides and lodging lists. Also runs Matkailuliitton Matkatoimisto (the F.T.A. Travel Agency), a complete travel service that plans itineraries, arranges bookings and issues tickets on all means of transport. Very good about providing information. The staff will tell you how to get to the hiking routes throughout Finland and, if you make an appointment to drop into the office, they will help you with the translation of essential material in the guidebooks. Staff speaks Finnish, Swedish, English and German. In addition to the guidebooks and lodging lists, its Finnish-language publications include:

- *Kesälomaopas* (Summer Vacation Guide). Issued annually. Describes the various guided "fell weeks," wilderness hikes and other outdoor activities organized each summer by Suomen Matkailuliitto. Gives full details, including prices.

- *Talvilomaopas* (Winter Vacation Guide). Issued annually. Describes the guided ski trips, Arctic fell hikes and winter camping trips organized by Suomen Matkailuliitto. Gives full details, including prices.

- *Suomen matkailuopas* (Tourist Guide to Finland). Describes the principal sights in cities and rural communities throughout Finland. Lists lodging possibilities and gives the addresses of tourist offices. Includes maps.

- *Lapin matkailutieto* (Tourist Information on Lapland). An encyclopedia to the different communities, sights, hiking trails and lifestyles in Lapland. Includes a list of lodgings.

- *Pohjois-Norjan matkailu- ja retkeilyopas* (Tourist and Hiking Guide to North Norway). Describes roadside sights, communities, campsites, hiking trails, mountain huts and fishing facilities in Northern Norway.

- *Matkailumaailma* (Travel World). A travel magazine with articles on tourism in Finland and abroad. Published for members of the Finnish Travel Association.

- *Leirintä ja Retkeily* (Camping and Hiking). A member magazine with topical articles on camping, hiking and skiing in Finland and abroad. Also includes information on caravanning (travel with a car-trailer).

Finland's Walking & Skiing Associations

There are numerous associations devoted to walking and skiing in Finland. Some, such as Suomen Latu, are voluntary service associations, while others, such as Suomen Matkailuliitto, are tourist organizations. In addition, there are several municipal associations that organize outdoor activities, help create and mark hiking and skiing routes, and handle bookings in lodgings. The structure and aims of these organizations are sometimes vastly different. Nonetheless, each can provide you with valuable information on hiking and skiing. You can also become a member of Suomen Matkailuliitto and Suomen Latu, which will qualify you for discounts in many trail lodgings and save you money on their publications and organized activities.

Of the associations, the most important for the foreign hiker and skier are the following:

See *Address Directory:*

Keski-Suomen Maakuntaliitto. A regional working group created by several cooperating municipalities in central Finland. Oversees the establishment and marking of the 431-kilometer network of footpaths between Viitasaari and Halli, Finland's first system of marked long-distance footpaths. Can provide information on walking and cross-country skiing in Finland's lake district and eastern forests. Also publishes a leaflet and 1:400,000 map to the long-distance footpath network in central Finland. Staff speaks Finnish, Swedish, English and German.

Lapin Matkailu. A regional tourist association in northern Finland. Can provide information on walking and cross-country skiing in Lapland. Also handles bookings for lodgings in holiday cottages, holiday villages and farmhouses. Staff speaks Finnish, Swedish, English and German.

Pirkanmaan Taival. A community-based center that provides information on the Pirkanmaa district around Tampere. The group is composed of associations in rural districts and townships, each of which organizes outdoor activities and hiking trips. It works to improve the design of footpath maps and path markings, promotes trips to Pirkanmaa and publishes reports on new paths. A consultation group, composed of members from the 25 municipalities that border Pirkanmaa in the north, also participates in the association. Pirkanmaan Taival publishes a yearly bulletin that provides information on organized hikes, ski tours and competitive events. It also handles bookings for lodgings in holiday cottages, holiday villages and farmhouses. Staff speaks Finnish, Swedish, English and German.

Suomen Latu. This is the oldest of Finland's organizations for physical recreation activity. It is also the representative for Finland in the international European Ramblers' Association. Founded in 1938, Suomen Latu has 130 member clubs throughout Finland and in excess of 25,000 members. It is primarily a voluntary service organization which organizes and directs outdoor activities in which every Finnish citizen (and foreign visitor)—member or not—can take part. In 1946 it initiated cross-country ski events known as "People's Skiings" in which more than a million people now participate each winter. In 1955 it organized *Pirkan Hiihto*—Pirkka's Skiing—a day-long 90-kilometer ski-track hike from Niinisalo to Tampere, the first of more than 300 such events that are now held each winter. Together with the Board of Forestry, the organization helped build a network of fell cabins at Saariselkä. And to mark its 40th anniversary in the winter of 1978, Suomen Latu opened more than 4,700 kilometers of cross-country ski routes, the longest of which was an 1,800-kilometer ski route stretching the length of Finland, from Helsinki to Utsjoki. Although most of these were temporary routes, Suomen Latu hopes to eventually develop many of them into routes that can be followed both on foot in summer and on skis in winter.

The organization tests skiing and hiking equipment, acts as a consultant to local governments and private organizations on physical recreation and, through its member associations, clears paths, and annually prepares and marks thousands of kilometers of ski tracks. In addition, Suomen Latu arranges:

1. More than 65 holiday weeks during the year for hiking and skiing;
2. Ten- to 20-day wilderness hiking and skiing trips, mainly in Lapland;
3. More than 200 ski-track hikes of from 10 to 90 kilometers in length;
4. A series of instructor and leader training courses, including a five-month course run in cooperation with Ammattikurssikeskus for hiking and tour guides, ski-instructor courses and both summer and winter courses for the leaders of wilderness hiking trips; and
5. A series of physical training programs and hikers' holiday weeks at training centers in Äkäslompolo, Kiilopää, Luumäki and Vuokatti.

Members of Suomen Latu receive its publications and discounts on its holiday weeks, guided hikes and other activities.

Suomen Matkailuliitto. Suomen Matkailuliitto is an independent central tourist organization with 41 regional associations throughout Finland and more than 29,000 members. Also a member of the European Ramblers' Association, it promotes tourism in Finland, organizes guided ski touring weeks and hiking tours led by Finnish fell guides, publishes guidebooks, helps maintain fell huts and camping sites, maintains an information service and data bank, and provides a variety of member services including a reservation service for hotels, fell cabins, campsites and numerous tourist excursions. In addition, it manages several holiday centers, sells maps and guidebooks and provides help in planning hiking, fishing, canoeing, bicycling and ski touring trips in Finland.

When it was founded in 1887, the fundamental aim of the Finnish Travel Association was to arouse interest in travel in Finland, both among Finns and foreign visitors, and to develop tourist facilities in the country. It maintained this role until 1968, when the general duties of promoting tourism in Finland abroad were transferred to the state. Although the emphasis of the association has varied throughout its history, it has always placed a high priority on individual member services, which span all aspects of tourism and leisure activity.

Members of the association receive its two magazines and can purchase its publications at a discount. Members also receive discounts in hotels, at campsites and on lake excursions and chartered bus trips, as well as on its guided hikes and ski touring weeks. In addition, members benefit from the reciprocal membership agreements that Suomen Matkailuliitto maintains with Den Norsk Turistforening (Norwegian Mountain Touring Association) and Svenska turistföreningen (Swedish Touring Club), which allows them to stay in the mountain huts in those countries at reduced rates.

Maps

A wide range of maps is available that can be used for orienteering, hiking and ski touring. These include:

Peruskartta (Basic Map) 1:20,000. The 2,740 sheets in this series cover all of southern Finland and a part of northern Finland. Each sheet covers an area of 10 kilometers by 10 kilometers, is printed in five colors and has a contour interval of five meters. When necessary 2.5-meter auxiliary contours also are used. Property boundaries are shown on the maps. Specially printed editions also show hiking and skiing routes and fixed orientation posts. About 100 sheets in the series have not been updated for as much as 20 years, and there may be several discrepancies between what these sheets show and what is found on the ground—new roads, for instance. These sheets are currently being revised and are expected to be updated by 1984. The index color-codes each sheet according to the year when the map was last revised (older sheets are pale yellow)—something to remember when you buy the maps. The maps are suitable for orienteering, hiking and ski touring.

Topografinen kartta (Topographical Map) 1:20,000. This map series is similar to the Basic Map, except that property boundaries are not shown and the maps are printed in only three colors. The series, with 972 sheets, covers the whole of northern Finland. Suitable for orienteering, hiking and ski touring.

Peruskartan pienennös (Reduction of Basic Map) 1:50,000. The 182 sheets in this series are a photographic reduction of the Basic Map. They cover most of the central Lake District and parts of the south and west coasts. Details are the same as on the Basic Map, except that the sheets do not show property boundaries and have been reduced in scale so each sheet covers a larger area. Another 39 sheets are currently in preparation. Suitable for hiking and ski touring. Also can be used for orienteering.

Topografinen kartta (Topographical Map) 1:50,000. The 78 sheets in this series are a photographic reduction of the 1:20,000 Topographical Map. The series is printed in three colors and covers most of Lapland. Another 19 sheets are currently in preparation. Suitable for hiking or ski touring. Also can be used for orienteering.

Ympäristökartat (Environs Map) 1:25,000, 1:40,000 and 1:50,000. The sheets in this series cover Finland's major towns and cities and their immediate surroundings. The contour interval is five meters. Details shown on the maps include marked hiking and ski touring routes, unmarked hiking and ski touring routes, fixed orientation posts, camping sites, holiday camps, youth hostels, fell huts, campfire rings, tourist information centers and first aid stations. The key to symbols is translated into Swedish, English and German. The maps are printed in six, and sometimes, seven colors. Ten sheets in a scale of 1:25,000 cover Nuuksio, Helsinki, Joensuu, Lahti, Lappeenranta, Jyväskylä, Oulu, Rovaniemi, Turku and Kajaani. One 1:40,000 sheet covers Hämeenlinna, and one 1:50,000 sheet covers Lieksa. These are the best maps available for hiking and ski touring near these towns.

Ulkoilukartat (Outdoor Maps) 1:40,000, 1:50,000 and 1:100,000. The 12 sheets in this series cover several of the most popular hiking and ski touring areas in northern Finland. Details are the same as on the Environs Maps. The key to symbols is also translated into Swedish, English and German. One sheet in a scale of 1:40,000 covers Luosto-Pyhätunturi; ten sheets in a scale of 1:50,000 cover Rukatunturi-Oulanka, Salla-Suomu, Ylläs-Levi, Pallas-Keimiö, Hetta-Outtakka, Kaunispää-Kopsusjä rvi (Saariselkä), Sokosti-Suomujoki (Saariselkä), Halti-Kilpisjärvi, Inari-Menesjärvi and Lemmenjoki, and one sheet in a scale of 1:100,000 covers Inarijärvi. These are the best maps available for hiking and ski touring in these areas.

Matkailukartat (Touring Maps) 1:100,000. The five maps in this series are similar to the Outdoor Maps and Environs Maps, except that they are drawn in a smaller scale. They cover the areas surrounding Helsinki, Hämeenlinna, Tampere, Turku and the Åland Islands in southern Finland. Because of the information they provide on the locations of lodgings and marked and unmarked trails, they are useful for planning walks and ski touring trips. They can be used on marked paths, but on unmarked routes they should be supplemented with the 1:20,000 or 1:50,000 maps.

Suomen tiekartta GT (Road Map of Finland, GT-edition) 1:200,000. Normally a road map in a small scale is of little use or interest to hikers. But the 19 sheets in this series are an exception. The maps have contour lines at 20 meter intervals and show the locations of holiday cottages, guesthouses, youth hostels, fell huts, campsites, tourist information centers, telephones and first aid stations, as well as the most important hiking routes. These maps are invaluable aids to planning hiking and ski touring trips. Once you have decided where you wish to go, they should be supplemented with the appropriate larger-scale maps. But they are still useful to carry along for the information they provide. The series covers the whole of Finland and is updated every two to four years.

Which Map to Choose

For hiking and ski touring, you should use the Outdoor Maps and Environs Maps for the areas they cover. Next choice goes to the 1:50,000 reduction of the Basic Map for southern Finland and 1:50,000 Topographical Map for northern Finland, again for the areas they cover. They are a fairly recent edition and, by using these maps, you won't have to buy—or carry—so many sheets. In difficult terrain, however, the 1:20,000 Basic Maps should be used in southern Finland and, in northern Finland, the 1:20,000 Topographical Maps. Elsewhere in Finland, there is no choice: the only maps suitable for walking and ski touring are the 1:20,000 Basic Maps in southern Finland and the 1:20,000 Topographical Maps in northern Finland.

Because so much of Finland has a low, undulating terrain and is covered by forests, large-scale maps (1:50,000 or larger) should always be carried. To prevent yourself from becoming lost, it is important, even on marked routes, to always follow proper map-reading practices.

Where to Buy Maps

Maps can be purchased from bookstores in many large towns and cities. In some of the popular tourist areas—Rovaniemi, Jyväskylä, Joensuu and Tampere, for instance—the tourist information offices also sell maps. Usually, only the maps to the surrounding area are stocked. On occasion you may be able to buy Touring Maps, Outdoor Maps or Environs Maps, but not the 1:20,000 or 1:50,000 maps you need. Therefore, it is best to obtain several of the 1:200,000 GT Road Maps by mail for planning your trip and then, before taking off for the hinterlands, to buy the specific large-scale maps you need from the Map Service in Helsinki. Or if you do not expect to pass through Helsinki, buy them by mail beforehand. The maps, free indexes and a price list (in Finnish, Swedish, English and German) are available from:

Maanmittaushallituksen kartanmyynti (Map Service of the National Board of Survey). See *Address Directory*. The retail outlet is located at Eteläesplanadi 10 (five doors down toward the bay from the Silja Line office—one of the companies that operates ships between Stockholm and Helsinki). Open weekdays from 8:30 a.m. to 4:30 p.m. The staff speaks Finnish, Swedish, English, German and French. Letters will be answered in the language in which you write. Service by mail is prompt.

Guidebooks

The number of guidebooks to hiking in Finland is limited. There are only four, all of which are published in Finnish:

• *Pohjois-Suomen retkeilyopas* (Hiking Guide to Northern Finland).

Describes 59 hikes for both hikers and skiers in Lapland, Kuusamo wilderness and the Kainuu fell area. Most of the hikes are on unmarked routes. Includes information on fell cabins and tent sites.

- *Saariselkä.* Describes 61 cross-country hikes in Saariselkä, a wilderness region in northeastern Lapland. Includes a sketch map and information on fell cabins.

- *Kilpisjärvi.* A tourist and hiking guide to Kilpisjärvi, a highland fell region in northwestern Lapland. Describes wilderness hikes, fishing facilities and special features of the flora and fauna.

- *Kultamaiden retkeilyopas* (Hiking Guide to the Gold Country). Describes cross-country hikes and fell cabins in the gold-panning areas of Lapland. Covers the Tankavaara, Laanila, Sotajoki, Ivalojoki and Lemmenjoki gold regions. Includes information on history, as well as maps and illustrations.

All the above guidebooks are published by Suomen Matkailuliitto—the Finnish Travel Association. The following guidebook is published by Suomen Latu:

- *Vesiretkeilyreitit.* Describes 51 hiking and canoeing routes on Finland's lake and river systems. Includes numerous maps and photographs.

All the guidebooks include detailed route descriptions, sketch maps, lists of maps required for each route and information on available camping and lodging facilities, as well as where reservations can be made. Even without a knowledge of Finnish it is possible to understand some basic information in the guides just by glancing through them. To understand any details, however, requires a Finnish-English dictionary or help from a Finn who is willing to sit down and translate the essential information for you.

The guidebooks can be purchased from Suomen Matkailuliitto (see *Address Directory*) and Suomen Latu as well as from some bookstores.

Several local hiking clubs and tourist offices publish leaflets that describe hiking and skiing routes. Occasionally, these are available in English or German.

A list of these leaflets, along with the outlets where they can be obtained, are included in the descriptions of the various hiking regions in Finland later in this chapter.

Trailside Lodgings

For the most part, lodgings are limited along Finland's hiking routes. In both the Lake District and southern Finland there are many hotels, tourist inns and youth hostels in towns near hiking areas and, occasionally, on the marked paths. But on unmarked routes, the lodgings are not always close enough together for you to stay in one each night. Similar accommodation can be found in northern Finland, although the lodgings are fewer in number and are often located a considerable distance from the area in which you intend to hike. There are also many holiday cottages—usually a fishing hut, hunting lodge, bungalow or lakeside cottage located in a rural setting—plus several holiday villages, which provide good bases for excursions into the countryside. Most of these are located in the south, however, and few accept reservations for less than a week.

In addition, Finland has many fell cabins—the Finnish version of the unstaffed mountain hut—of which more than 250 are located in northern Finland. Four of Finland's national parks also have fell cabins within their boundaries. Most fell cabins can be reached only by hiking cross-country with a map and compass. Few are located on marked tracks. The fell cabins have beds and a fireplace, but no mattresses, blankets or stoves. To stay in them, you must bring a sleeping bag, your food and cooking equipment. In April and July, when the huts may be crowded, carry a tent just in case there is no room left inside when you arrive.

In fact, if you intend to hike any distance in Finland, you must be prepared to camp. Otherwise, you must plan your hiking routes around the available lodgings and make advance reservations to ensure yourself a place to sleep each night.

The locations of lodgings are indicated on most of the Finnish maps (with the exception of the older sheets of the 1:20,000 Basic Maps and Topographical Maps). There are also several accommodation lists that provide details on the various lodgings in Finland. These include:

- *Finland: Hotels, Motels and Hostels.* Lists addresses, telephone numbers, number of rooms, prices (not guaranteed), facilities in rooms and the facilities in the hotels and surrounding area. Also gives the addresses and telephone numbers of booking centers. Includes a sketch map to show the locations of the lodgings. Descriptive information and the key to symbols are translated into Swedish, English, German and French. Free on request from the Finnish Tourist Board and Suomen Matkailuliitto (see *Address Directory*).

- *Finland: Holiday Villages.* Gives full details. Also notes which of the holiday villages are located near hiking routes and marked ski tracks. Includes a sketch map to show locations, as well as the addresses and telephone numbers of booking centers. Descriptive information and the key to symbols is translated into Swedish, English, German and French. Free on request from the Finnish Tourist Board and Suomen Matkailuliitto.

- *Suomen hotelliopas* (Finland Hotel Guide). Published by Suomen Matkailuliitto. Gives detailed information on 379 hotels, 60 motels and 206 lodging houses in Finland. Directions for using the booklet are in Finnish, Swedish, English and German. Available for a nominal charge from Suomen Matkailuliitto.

- *Lomakylät ja täysihoitolat* (Holiday Villages and Boarding Houses). Also published by Suomen Matkailuliitto. Describes more than 200 holiday villages with separate rental cottages, 150 boarding houses and 17 health spas in Finland. Directions for use are in Finnish, Swedish, English and German. Available for a nominal charge.

Youth Hostels

Finland has a network of about 130 youth hostels, including 16 hostels located north of the Arctic Circle, all of which can be easily reached on public transport. Most of the hostels are open only during the summer, although about 30 of the best-equipped hostels remain open all year.

Hostel wardens often can provide information on local hiking routes. During the summer, many of the hostels rent bicycles and those that remain open during the winter often rent skis. Meals generally are not provided, although coffee and refreshments are available in most hostels, and some have places where you can cook. Advance bookings are essential—at least for groups and families—and should be made direct to the hostels. There are no age restrictions.

The hostels are classified into four categories, according to their standard:

One-Star Hostels: equipped with basic facilities.

Two-Star Hostels: have running hot water and small rooms to accommodate families or small groups.

Three-Star Hostels: have running hot water, showers and a self-service kitchen. Breakfast is also served in some of the three-star hostels.

Four-Star Hostels: have all the facilities listed above, plus a lounge and meeting facilities. Meals are served. In addition, linen is included in the overnight fee.

Details on the hostels are included in two publications:

- *Retkeilymajat Vandrarhem* (Youth Hostel Handbook). Issued annually in March. Gives full details on each hostel. Also includes sketch maps showing the location of each. Information in the booklet is written in Finnish, Swedish, English and German, as is the key to symbols used to describe the hostels. Available for a nominal charge from Suomen Retkeilymajajärjestö (address below).

- *Finland: Camping Sites and Youth Hostels.* Gives details on the youth hostels as well as on Finland's network of more than 300 official campsites. Includes a sketch map to show locations, as well as the addresses and telephone numbers of booking centers. Descriptive information and the key to symbols is translated into Swedish, English, German and French. Free on request from the Finnish Tourist Board and Suomen Matkailuliitto.

Further information on the hostels can be obtained from:

Suomen Retkeilymajajärjestö (Finnish Youth Hostel Association). See *Address Directory*. Staff speaks Finnish, Swedish, English, German and French.

Tourist Hotels & Hiking Centers

Both Suomen Latu and Suomen Matkailuliitto run several lodging facilities geared specifically for hikers and skiers and other outdoor enthusiasts. These include:

1. Four four-star hostels run by Suomen Latu—Kiilopään Koulutus Keskus (Kiilopää Training Center), located near the Lapland community of Inari, 260 kilometers north of Rovaniemi; Latukartano, located in Luumäen, about 30 kilometers west of Lappeenranta in southeastern Finland; Ylläskartano, located in Äkäslompolo, Lapland; and the Vuokatti Sport Institute in Sotkamo.

2. Twenty F.T.A. centers run by Suomen Matkailuliitto, 13 of which are in Lapland. These include the Kukasjärvi Hiking Center; Kilpisjärvi Camping Center; hotels at Kultakero (Pyhätunturi) and Laanihovi; tourist hotels at Hetta, Inari, Ivalo, Kilpisjärvi, Pallastunturi and Utsjoki; a fell cabin at Saarijärvi; and camping sites at Ivalo and Kilpisjärvi.

Full details on these facilities are available from Suomen Latu and Suomen Matkailuliitto.

Fell Cabins

Two regional hiking guides published by Suomen Matkailuliitto—*Saariselkä* and *Kultamaiden retkeilyopas* (see the section on *Guidebooks*)—include information on the fell cabins in northern Finland. In addition, Suomen Matkailuliitto publishes a complete fell cabin list:

• *Pohjois-Suomen Autiotuvat* (Fell Cabins in Northern Finland). Gives a brief description of the location of each of the 250 fell cabins in northern Finland, the sheet number of the map on which each is located, lists its facilities and gives the names and telephone numbers of the associations responsible for the cabins. Notations after the name of each cabin indicate which are: 1) always open and free to users (indicated by RT or, in some cases, no notation appears after the name of the cabin), 2) locked, with keys available only to hikers who reserve space for a nominal fee (indicated by VT), and 3) located in a wilderness or isolated area (indicated by AT). The booklet also includes sketch maps to show where the fell cabins—and emergency telephones—are located in each region. The booklet is designed to be used in conjunction with the guidebook to hiking in northern Finland: *Pohjois-Suomen Retkeilyopas* (see the section on *Guidebooks*).

The booklet is available only in Finnish. It may be obtained from Suomen Matkailuliitto and Suomen Latu, as well as from some bookstores. Cost of staying in the locked fell cabins is approximately twice as much for foreign hikers, unless you are a member of a Finnish group.

To make reservations in the fell cabins you can contact either Suomen Matkailuliitto or:

Kiilopään Koulutuskeskus (see *Address Directory*).

Camping

Despite Finland's large amount of wilderness, there is a trend in the country to limit camping only to designated sites. This is intended as a protective measure to prevent damage to fragile plant communities in the wilderness areas. Whenever possible, you should use these designated sites or—at the very least—a tent site that has been used in the past. If neither are available, ensure that you pitch your tent on firm ground where you will cause a minimum of damage to fragile plant communities. On private land, you should also try to find the property owner to ask his or her permission to camp—simply as a matter of courtesy.

In a list of guidelines to camping in Finland, Suomen Matkailuliitto stresses that you should *never:*

1. Camp in meadows, cultivated fields or newly planted forest plantations;
2. Pull up plants by the roots;
3. Break off the branches of living trees or bushes;
4. Dig a trench around a tent;
5. Disturb nesting birds, nests or fledgings;
6. Leave litter; or
7. Light a fire on private land without the owner's permission.

There are designated campsites along many of the hiking routes in

Finland. On some routes, there are also special places where an open fire can be lit. The locations of both the campsites and fire pits are indicated on most hiking maps.

For the locations of commercial campgrounds, you can refer to one of the following publications:

- *Suomen leirintäalueopas* (Campsite Guide to Finland). Gives a detailed description of each of Finland's more than 300 official campsites. Includes maps showing the location of each site. The text is in Finnish with a brief introduction in English, Swedish, German and French. The table of symbols used to describe the campground facilities is also translated. Available for a nominal charge from Suomen Matkailuliitto (see *Address Directory*).

- *Reisen & Camping in Finnlande* (Traveling & Camping in Finland). Written in German. Describes the various camping possibilities in Finland, lists the telephone numbers and closing dates of Finland's commercial campsites, and includes a map showing their locations. Also includes several topical articles on travel, as well as information on youth hostels, hiking and hiking tours. Available for a nominal charge from Suomen Matkailuliitto.

- *Finland: Camping Sites and Youth Hostels*. See description under "Youth Hostels" in the section on *Trailside Lodgings*.

Lighting Fires

On all hiking trips you should use a camp stove rather than build fires. But, if for some reason you do build a fire in Finland, you must use an old fire ring and, in national parks, only areas that have been designated as fire pits. In wild areas you can build fires only from down wood. To light a fire always requires the permission of the landowner. Also, you must never build a fire in a forest or near a wooded area, except in an emergency— and even then you are held responsible for the consequences. Fell cabins provide split firewood for use in the cabin's fireplace, but you are obliged to replace it.

You should never build a fire or smoke tobacco in the wilderness during times of drought. When there is a danger of forest fires, warnings are given in newspapers and on radio and television: *kulovaroitus* means there is a risk of forest fire. At this stage, no open fire should be lit—not a match, not a pipe, not even a camp stove.

Water

A person might expect to safely drink water anywhere in the land of 60,000 lakes. Unfortunately, this is not true. Some of the Finnish lakes have been polluted by mercury released by the pulp and paper industry. In Lake Saimaa, for example, the rare Saimaa seal has been found to have large amounts of mercury in its tissues. Most of the lakes are still crystal pure. The problem is, without carrying a portable laboratory, you won't be able to tell which are and which aren't. So, if you do not already avoid lakewater as a matter of course for drinking, do so in Finland. You also should use caution when drinking from streams in southern Finland. Again, many are crystal pure, but some are not. As a precaution, fill up your water bottle whenever you can—at hotels, restaurants or farm houses—and then, if you have to rely on a natural water source . . . pray.

In northern Finland, caution is necessary only near settlements (where you will be able to get tap water anyway). Elsewhere in the north, you will be able to find pure, cold water from practically every natural water source.

Equipment Notes

In addition to maps and a compass, you will need a lightweight tent, preferably one with a dark-colored fabric (to cut out the Midnight Sun) and no-see-um proof netting that can be tightly sealed on all vents and entrances. Since heavy winds and rain may lash the Lapland fells, tents should have a full-size flap-free rain fly that can stand up in a gale. In the forests wind stability is not so crucial, but the pestproofing and rain protection is.

You should also bring a sleeping bag, as well as a camp stove (preferably the alcohol-burning Trangia), spare fuel, lightweight pots and the rest of your cooking gear. Plan out your menus and buy all the food you are going to need before you go into the wilderness. If you want to take freeze-dried food to save weight, a small selection is available from Partio Aitta in Helsinki (see *Address Directory*).

You should have one complete change of clothing, plus a warm sweater, wind protection and raingear. You will also need a pair of knee-high rubber boots and a light pair of sneakers for use in camp and on dry heathlands.

Finally, take insect repellent and for summer walks on the Lapland fells a hat and mosquito (or better yet, no-see-um proof) netting to protect your face.

Winter trips will require more equipment: suitable clothing for sub-zero temperatures, a dependable high-efficiency stove for melting snow for your water and a thin pair of silk gloves worn inside your mittens so you can handle metal equipment without risk of frostbite. (For more details on the equipment for winter travel, see *The Equipment Rack* in Part I.)

Crowded Trails

Because so much of the hiking in Finland is either on unmarked trails or cross-country with a map and compass, it is possible to walk for days without seeing another person—except perhaps in the evening in the fell cabins. Some routes, of course, are popular and much more heavily used. During July and August and, in Lapland, at the beginning of September after the bugs have subsided, many people converge on the national parks. The trails near tourist centers also may have many people on them. But no hiking route in Finland is really overcrowded.

Lapland and Kuusamo are the most popular hiking areas in Finland. The most popular route is *Karhun Kierros*—the Bear's Tour—which passes through Oulanka National Park in the Kuusamo district. In Lapland most trails are either unmarked or, if marked, their red-painted triangles, squares and circles on rocks or trees may have become indistinct. Consequently, you can find vast stretches of tundra and bog where you can be alone, even in September.

If you hike in Lapland, remember that the tundra is extremely fragile and deserves both respect and protection. In order to localize your impact upon the environment, stick to routes described in *Pohjois-Suomen Retkeilyopas*, even if you are tempted to navigate one of your own. In addition, simply following the guidebook routes with a map and compass requires considerable skill. Even if you are an experienced map reader, until you have walked on the Lapland fells and have become familiar with their special conditions, you are advised to join a guided party for your first trip—or, at the least, to follow one of the guidebook routes with a *minimum* of two other experienced persons.

Neither should you spend all of your time in Lapland. There are many other areas in Finland worth exploring on foot—the Lake District, the eastern forests, the inland bogs and marshes, and the southwest Archipelago. There are also more lodgings outside of Lapland, even a few places where you can hike without the weight of a tent or a week's worth of food.

Keep This in Mind

The Five Rules for Fell Visitors (freely translated from Finnish):

1. Never take a fell tour alone;
2. Equip yourself for any worst emergency;
3. Never overrate your capabilities;
4. Get to know the natural surroundings; and
5. Respect the fells.

Walking & Skiing Tours

Hiking trips with a Finnish fell guide are arranged by both Suomen Latu and Suomen Matkailuliitto (see *Address Directory*). The tours take you through wilderness areas in both southern Finland and Lapland and last from 7 to 20 days, depending upon the tour you choose. Both associations also arrange holiday weeks at centers around Finland which include hiking in summer and skiing in winter.

During the winter, the two associations arrange guided camping trips, several-day-long ski-track hikes (10 to 90 kilometers) and day-long path hikes (5 to 35 kilometers).

Guided ski treks across the Lapland fells also are arranged by Suomen Latu and Suomen Matkailuliitto, as well as by several winter sport centers. These last several days, with meals prepared over a fire in the open and accommodation in the log fell cabins.

Among the sport centers in northern Finland where guided ski treks take place are the following:

For all addresses, see the *Address Directory* at the back of this chapter:

Hetta (Enontekiö): A ski center located in an old Lapp and Sami center, 320 kilometers north of Tornio. It is about 30 kilometers north of the northern growth limit of the spruce, and 30 to 40 kilometers south of the northern limit of the pine. Several fells are located south of the community. Lodging possibilities in hotels, farmhouses and a campsite. Information is available from Kunnantoimisto Matkailuasiamies. Also from Suomen Matkailuliitto and Suomen Latu.

Kilpisjärvi: Located in the highest mountain region in Finland near the point where the Finnish, Swedish and Norwegian borders meet. One of the best regions for hiking and ski touring in Finland. A guidebook published by Suomen Matkailuliitto, *Kilpisjärvi*, describes hiking possibilities in the area. Lodgings include the Kilpisjärvi Hiking

Center, a tourist hotel and Saananmaja (Saana Cottage). Information is available from Kilpisjärven Retkeilykeskus. Also from Suomen Latu and Suomen Matkailuliitto.

Levitunturi: Located in Kittilä, 180 kilometers north of Rovaniemi. Several lodging possibilities. Information is available from Kittilän Kunnantoimisto Matkailuasiamies. Also from Suomen Latu and Suomen Matkailuliitto.

Pyhätunturi: The southernmost fell region in Finland. Starting point of the marked Pyhätunturi-Luosto hike. Located in Pelkosenniemi, 50 kilometers north of Kemijärvi. Information is available from Kemijärven, Kaupungin Matkailutoimisto. Also from Suomen Latu and Suomen Matkailuliitto.

Saariselkä: Located in Saariselkä fell area, 40 kilometers south of Ivalo and 260 kilometers north of Rovaniemi. One of Finland's best regions for wilderness hikes and ski tours. A guidebook published by Suomen Matkailuliitto, *Saariselkä* describes hiking possibilities and fell cabins in the area. Information is available from Saariselän Retkeilykeskus (Saariselkä Hiking Center), Kiilopään Koulutuskeskus (Kiilopää Training Center) and Inarin Matkailuyhdistys. Also from Suomen Latu and Suomen Matkailuliitto.

Äkäslompolo-Ylläs: Located in Kolari, 180 kilometers north of Rovaniemi. Several lodging possibilities. Information is available from Äkäs Hotelli.

The staffs in all the information centers speak Finnish, Swedish, English and German.

Booklets (in Finnish) describing the summer and winter guided trips arranged by Suomen Latu and Suomen Matkailuliitto are available on request (see *Where to Get Walking Information*). Or if you write and tell them where you want to hike or ski, the staff will write back with a list of the tours and their dates in those areas.

Fell Guides

If you wish to hire a fell guide—for summer or winter—you should first decide which area you wish to explore. Then contact either Suomen Latu or Suomen Matkailuliitto. Both organizations have fell guides to lead hikes in both Lapland and southern Finland.

Suomen Latu will put you directly in touch with their guides. They may also arrange for a guide to be available when you arrive and negotiate the fee for you. On request, Suomen Matkailuliitto will take care of all the arrangements—even down to booking your lodgings and transport.

When writing, you should tell them:

1. The area in which you wish to hike or ski;
2. The experience of participants;
3. The dates for which a guide will be required;
4. The equipment you will be bringing with you;
5. Your home address and telephone number and the last date you can be reached at that address; and
6. The address and telephone number where you will be staying in Finland, and the dates you can be reached there.

Information on Finnish fell guides can also be obtained from:

Eräoppaitten Yhdistys (see *Address Directory*).

Cross-Country Skiing

Finland has a vast network of cross-country ski tracks, many of which are marked and illuminated. The member associations of Suomen Latu prepare and mark several thousand kilometers of ski tracks each winter. In addition, there are numerous marked tracks at Finland's winter sport centers and around many towns.

But this is only the beginning. Not all of Finland's ski routes follow prepared tracks. Nor are they all marked. On hiking maps, you often see a series of wavy red arrows. These indicate slopes with generally good snow suited for ski touring. You also see two kinds of red dashed lines—one set with long dashes and another with short dashes. The long dashed lines indicated marked ski routes, the short dashed lines, unmarked routes. In some areas almost all the red lines have short dashes.

Surprisingly, no guidebook yet exists to the ski tracks of Finland. The guidebook published in German by Suomen Latu, *Finnland—Heimat des Skilanglaufs* (Finland—Home of Cross-Country Skiing), lists Finland's principal ski touring centers and international cross-country skiing events (and is highly recommended for anyone who wants to cross-country ski in Finland). It does not, however, describe individual ski touring routes. But with the Finnish maps, a guidebook is hardly necessary. The maps are among the best available anywhere for ski touring.

As with hiking during the summer in Finland, skiing on the unmarked routes and for long distances requires the proper equipment, expertise in the use of map and compass, and knowledge of the special conditions that prevail in Finland during the winter. In fact, because of Finland's cold temperatures and the possibility of blizzards, such expertise and experience is much more critical in winter, when a small error that might only be frustrating in summer can be fatal.

For trips of more than a day you should join one of the guided ski treks (see the section on *Walking & Skiing Tours*). Otherwise, stick to the marked tracks and—always—ski with at least two other companions.

Several of the areas having marked ski tracks are listed later in this chapter in the descriptions of the various regions of Finland. In addition areas offering cross-country ski instruction and rental equipment have been noted.

Further information on cross-country skiing in Finland can be obtained from Suomen Latu, its local member associations and Suomen Matkailiitto (see *Address Directory*).

How to Get to the Trails

Unlike those of other countries, the hiking and skiing routes in Finland do not always start and end in—nor for that matter, even near—a town. Most don't even pass through towns. Instead, to reach the routes, you often must take an intercity bus to a suburb or a spot alongside the road between two towns—and pray you get off at the right place. This is complicated by the fact that the routes might not even start near a scheduled stop.

To ensure you get off at the right spot, it is advisable to mark the starting point of the route on your map and then show this to the bus driver. He or she will then tell you when you should get off.

It is also necessary to find out where and when buses stop on the road at the other end of the route before you set out. If the scheduled stop is a long distance from where the route ends, you can flag the bus down as it approaches. But you will have to determine the approximate time it will pass by—then subtract an hour for error and possible delays enroute. In some places, there may only be one or two buses a day, so it is much better to be an hour early than a few minutes late.

Bus schedules can be obtained from tourist offices and from the various motor coach companies. Several detailed timetables are available. These bear a close resemblance to phone books and include bus schedule information for most routes in Finland. Unfortunately, these timetables do not include *all* of the routes—and the small ones that are left out are often the ones that will be of most use to you. For this reason, it is best to check *bus schedules locally.* If it still appears that the route you want to hike is isolated in the hinterlands, with nothing but long walks along country roads between the nearest bus routes, contact the local tourist bureau. Its staff will find out if there is bus service to that area and tell you which bus to get on and what time it leaves. (You can, of course, obtain this information from the bus stations in all towns, but the chance of finding someone who speaks your language is much better at the tourist bureaus.) Help on working out transportation connections to and from hiking routes can also be obtained from Suomen Matkailuliitto (see *Address Directory*).

Wherever a road links settlements in Finland, no matter how small, there will usually be some sort of bus service. This may be one of the State Postal Office buses, which carry the mail in rural areas along with 20 to 30 passengers. These are comfortable, on time and charge low fares.

Special Train, Bus & Air Fares

There are several ways in which you can save money on travel within Finland:

Air

Finland has one of the densest and cheapest airline networks in Europe. Among the 20 cities to which Finnair flies within Finland is Ivalo, 40 kilometers north of the hiking routes in Saariselkä. The flight takes only an hour and a half from Helsinki. By comparison, it takes one full day (20 hours) to cover the same distance by train and bus and costs nearly as much, plus you have to pay for meals and sleeping accommodation. Finnair also offers several reduced fares, including:

Finnair Holiday Ticket. This entitles you to unlimited air travel within Finland for 15 days. The ticket is available to any permanent resident of countries outside Scandinavia.

Tourist Ticket. This entitles you to reduced fares on some short routes and includes any necessary travel by rail, bus or boat for you to reach your destination.

Discounts. A discount of 25 percent is granted to groups of 15 or more persons as well as to families when one member travels for full fare. People over the age of 65 and full-time students with valid student identity cards are also entitled to discounts of 25 percent.

Rail

Finland has 5,900 kilometers of rail lines (only slightly more than the total length of its marked cross-country ski tracks). In southern Finland the rail network links most major towns, but in the north as towns become smaller and fewer between, the number of rail lines diminishes until, above the Arctic Circle, they disappear entirely. Children under four years of age ride free and those between the ages of 4 and 11 ride for half fare. Other reduced fares include:

Tourist Ticket. This is good for one-way or round trip journeys and includes any necessary connections by bus, boat and air.

Finnrail Pass. This provides unlimited first- or second-class rail travel for a period of 8, 15 or 22 days or one month. It can be purchased in railway stations and at ports of arrival in Finland. A foreign passport is a prerequisite for purchase.

Discounts. Groups of 10 or more persons receive discounts of 10 percent. Families also receive a discount of 50 percent for children ages 12 to 20 and a discount of 75 percent for children between 4 and 11 when two members of the family buy full fare tickets.

Bus & Motor Coach

In Lapland and many rural areas in Finland, buses are the major means of surface travel. Generally, the service—and the buses—are first rate. From Helsinki there are more than 300 express services daily, with connections to the most remote and isolated parts of the country. Bus stations throughout Finland have restaurants, shops and newsstands. Baggage almost always arrives with you at your destination, even when bus changes and different bus companies are involved. Fares are reasonable. Also, for each adult, one child under four years of age is carried free and children between the ages of 4 and 12 ride half fare. These reduced-fare tickets can be obtained at the time you purchase your regular ticket.

You can also buy a *Matkailulippu* (Tourist Ticket) in most travel bureaus or at the bus stations in Helsinki, Joensuu, Kajaani, Kemi, Kemijärvi, Kuopio, Lahti, Lappeenranta, Mikkeli, Oulu, Rovaniemi, Tampere, Turku and Vaasa. The ticket is valid for one month. You can stop and stay at any place enroute which is mentioned in the ticket book. Information about timetables, excursion possibilities, sights and accommodation are included in a leaflet, which you are given when you buy the ticket.

For further information on special fares and travel in Finland contact the Finnish Tourist Board (see *Address Directory*).

How to Get There

Non-stop airline service to Helsinki is available from 29 cities in Europe, Canada, the U.S. and the Far East. In addition, there are twice-daily sailings between Stockholm and Helsinki on the Silja Line and Viking Line ships (sailing time: 15 hours), as well as between several other cities in Sweden and Finland. Details are given in a leaflet available from the Finnish Tourist Board:

- *Finland: Timetables and Fares*

Information can also be obtained from the airlines that fly to Finland (Finnair, SAS, British Airways, Air France, Austrian Airlines, CSA, Interflug, LOT, Lufthansa, Malev, Aeroflot and Swissair, to name a few), as well as from the sailing companies:

> See *Address Directory*:
> **Silja Line (Stockholm) Ab,** Stockholm.
> **Silja Line, Reservations,** Helsinki.
> **Silja Line, Sales and Ticket Office,** Helsinki.
> **Viking Line,** Stockholm.
> **Viking Line,** Helsinki.

Useful Addresses & Telephone Numbers

General Tourist Information

In Finland:

Finnish Tourist Board (see *Address Directory*).

Abroad:

Branch offices of the Finnish Tourist Board are located in EUROPE: Amsterdam, Hamburg, London, Munich, Paris, Stockholm and Zurich, and in the U.S.A.: Los Angeles and New York.

London: Finnish Tourist Board, UK Office, Finland House Annexe, 53-54 Haymarket, London SW1Y 4RP. Tel. (01) 839 4048.

New York: Finland National Tourist Office, 75 Rockefeller Plaza, New York, New York 10019. Tel. (212) 582-2802.

Sport Shops

There are few shops in Finland that specialize solely in hiking and ski touring equipment. Instead, most shops tend to stock all types of sport equipment. One exception to this is the scout shop in Helsinki:

> **Partio Aitta** (see *Address Directory*). The shop is small and the selection of equipment limited, but should you need a replacement part, a pair of rubber boots, freeze-dried food or a new stove, this is the place to find it.

Bookstores

There is one bookstore in Helsinki that stocks a wide range of books in Swedish, English, German and French, as well as the hiking guides to Finland and most of the Outdoor, Environs and Touring Maps. It also has many books on Finland's flora and fauna:

> **Akateeminen Kirjakauppa** (The Academic Bookstore). See *Address Directory*. Catalogs of the titles in English and German are available on request.

Emergency Telephones in the Wilderness

Emergency telephones have been installed in many fell cabins and at other strategic locations in Finland's wilderness. Information on where these telephones can be found is included in *Pohjois-Suomen Autiotuvat* (see the section on *Trailside Lodgings*), the Fell Hut Booklet published by Suomen Matkailuliitto. The locations of the telephones are also shown on the sketch maps in the booklet, as well as on many hiking maps. You should always know where these telephones are located and how you can get to them quickly.

In case of an emergency:

1. Locate the nearest telephone;
2. **On telephones with all the numerals (0 to 9) on the dialing disk:** Dial 0 for the operator;
3. **On telephones with only 0 and 9 on the dialing disk:** Dial 09 for the operator;
4. **On telephones with no dialing disk:** If there is a button on the telephone: a) lift the receiver, and b) press the button for the operator;
   If there is no button on the telephone: Lift the receiver for the operator;
5. Tell the operator to connect you to the police (in Finnish: *Poliisi* pronounced: *Poli:si*); and
6. Tell the police:
   a) What has happened;
   b) What assistance is required;
   c) Where you are located; and
   d) Where the injured person is located.

Outside of the wilderness areas the same directions for the use of telephones to summon help apply.

Search & Rescue

Search and rescue operations are overseen by the Finnish Red Cross and carried out by the police. There is no charge for this service, although if a helicopter is required, the injured person may, in some cases, have to pay the cost of the helicopter and its pilot.

If a person is known—or suspected—to be overdue from his or her return from a wilderness trip, the police should be contacted *immediately*. The police will mobilize rescue units and lead the search. Once the person is found, notice of the extent of his or her injuries or illness will be relayed to the nearest hospital. Emergency transportation by land or air (depending upon the extent and severity of the injuries or illness) will then be arranged by the police or attending doctor.

If emergency transportation is arranged by the police or a doctor, all costs of both the search and rescue are paid by the Finnish government. If an airport is notified directly, however, the arrangement is considered a charter transportation and must be paid in full by the person who orders it.

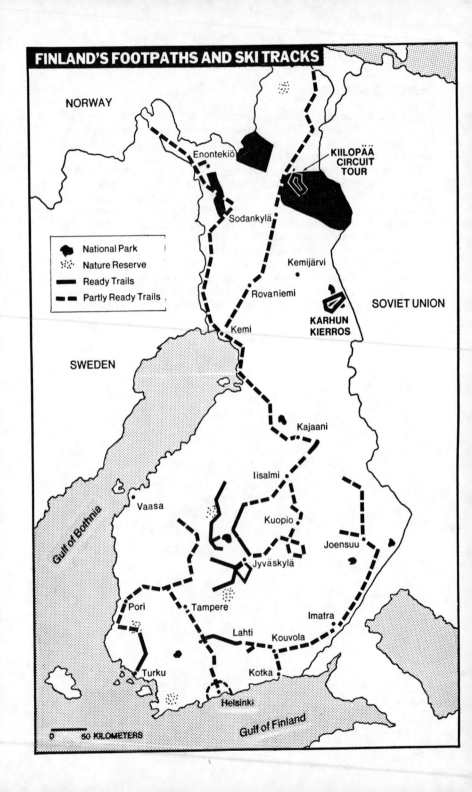

Finland's Long-Distance Footpaths

Finland has many long hiking routes—some of which are on unmarked tracks, others of which are cross-country treks that require orienteering with a map and compass. But there are only six long-distance footpaths. Of these, three are only partly marked, and the markings on a fourth are indistinct.

Hetta-Pallas Route

From the shores of the Ounasjärvi Lake, opposite the village of Enontekiö (Hetta), to the tourist hotel at Pallas (indicated on maps only as *Matkailukeskus*). Both have bus services. Passes through the Pallas-Ounastunturi National Park in northwestern Finland, an area of heath-covered fells up to 800 meters in height, with small lakes, spruce and birch, forest and bog. The route also can be extended an additional 70 kilometers on an unmarked route through a Special Conservation Forest—across the Äkäskero and Ylläs fells—to the small settlement of Ylläsjarvi. **Length:** 60 kilometers (37 miles). **Walking Time:** 4 days *minimum*; 9 days if the route is extended to Ylläs. **Path Markings:** Partially marked with white triangles. Signposted after the Rihmakuru fire pit.
Special Notes: A map and compass are essential to follow the route. All the comments under the section on *Equipment Notes* also apply. Emergency telephones are located in three of the fell cabins along the Hetta-Pallas Route. There are no telephones along the Pallas-Ylläs Route. Best time to walk the route is early September.
Lodgings: There are seven fell cabins on or near the Hetta-Pallas route with a total sleeping capacity of 76 persons. But there is a good chance the fell cabins will be crowded to overflowing. Bring a tent. There are also six campfire sites along the route and several designated tent sites. Along the Pallas-Ylläs Route there are no fell cabins and only three campfire sites.
Maps:
• Ulkoilukartta (Outdoor Map) 1:50,000, sheets *Hetta-Outtakka* and *Pallas-Keimiö*. If the route is extended to Ylläs, one additional sheet is also needed: *Ylläs-Levi*.
Guidebooks:
• *Pohjois-Suomen retkeilyopas* and *Pohjois-Suomen Autiotuvat* (see descriptions under the sections on *Guidebooks* and *Trailside Lodgings*).

Karhun Kierros (Bear's Tour)

From Rukatunturi to the Kuusamo-Salla road, one kilometer below the small settlement of Kuntakkivaara. Bus service at both points. Passes through the Oulanka National Park in northeastern Finland, an area of deep valleys, river canyons and rapids. **Length:** 70 kilometers (43 miles). **Walking Time:** 3 to 4 days. **Path Markings:** Signposted and marked throughout.
Special Notes: An easy route that many hikers take. Nonetheless, the *Equipment Notes* still apply. There is only one emergency telephone along the route—located in Virkkula, 11 kilometers from Rukatunturi.
Lodgings: There are six campfire and tent sites located along the route, as well as five fell cabins. A tent is advisable.
Maps:
• Ulkoilukartta (Outdoor Map) 1:50,000, sheet *Rukatunturi-Oulanka*.
Guidebooks:
• *Pohjois-Suomen Retkeilyopas* and *Pohjois-Suomen Autiotuvat*, both available from Suomen Matkailuliitto (see *Address Directory*).

Keski-Suomi ulkoilureitti

From Viitasaari to Halli in central Finland's lake district. Passes through the towns of Saarijärvi, Suolahti, Jyväskylä and Jämsä. **Length:** 299 kilometers, with an additional 134 kilometers of footpaths to Korpilahti, Keuruu and Multia. **Walking Time:** 15 days. **Path Markings:** Only a portion of the route has been marked. In these sections, it is marked variously with blue bars painted on trees and rocks, blue plastic streamers tied to the branches of trees and shrubs, and white signposts with a stylized symbol of a wood-grouse—the official Keski-Suomen symbol—and arrows, also in blue.
Special Notes: The route is generally easy walking through forests, past fields and lakes, and across meadows with purple heather, blueberries, raspberries and wild strawberries. It does, however, cross several dirt roads and logged areas. Because of the lack of markings, the route is difficult to follow in some places. A map and compass are essential.
Lodgings: There are hotels in most of the larger towns through which the route passes. But these lodgings are sometimes as much as 36 kilometers apart. A tent is necessary. There are 15 designated campsites along the route and three campsites along the spur trails. But even the distances between campsites and the last available lodgings are sometimes as much as 30 kilometers. Hence, you must plan on occasionally having to ask a landowner's permission to set up your tent for the night.
Maps:
• *Virkisty Retkeillen Keski-Suomen Ulkoilureiteillä* A special edition, 1:400,000 map on which the route has been marked, along with information on lodgings and campsites. Available from Suomen Latu or Keski-Suomen Maakuntaliitto (see *Address Directory*).

A list of the 1:20,000 and 1:50,000 maps that cover the route is also available on request from Keski-Suomen Maakuntaliitto.

Guidebooks:
- The only route description that currently exists is in Finnish and appears on the margin of the 1:400,000 map mentioned above.
- *Keski-Suomi retkeilijän Suomi* (leaflet). Gives an overview of the route, but includes little information of help in following the path on the ground. A German translation of the leaflet—*Mittelfinnland Wanderland* —is also available. Both may be obtained from Keski-Suomen Maakuntaliitto.

Further Information: Keski-Suomen Maakuntaliitto (see *Address Directory*).

Kevojoki Route

From the Inari-Utsjoki road (Route 970), half a kilometer above Kenestupa cottage on the southern shore of Kenesjärvi Lake to the Inari-Karigasniemi road (E-4), 15 kilometers east of the town of Karigasniemi on the Norwegian border. Follows a deep river canyon through Kevojoki National Park—Finland's northernmost park—an area of dwarf birches and fells. **Length:** 55 kilometers. **Walking Time:** 6 days *minimum*. **Path Markings:** Red-painted triangles on trees and rocks.
Special Notes: This is a walk for experienced hikers only. See the section on *Equipment Notes*. There are no emergency telephones along the route.
Lodgings: There is only one fell cabin in the park. A tent is essential.
Maps:
- Topografinen Kartta (Topographical Map) 1:20,000, sheets 3913/01, 3913/04, 3913/05, 3914/10 and 3932/01. Also:
- Topografinen Kartta (Topographical Map) 1:50,000, sheet 3913/2.

Guidebooks:
- *Pohjois-Suomen retkeilyopas* and *Pohjois-Suomen Autiotuvat*, both available from Suomen Matkailuliitto.

Sevetti-Nuorgam Tour

From Sevetti—a Lapp village and a vacation area of lakes, isthmuses, fast-flowing streams and many fells—to Nuorgam, the northernmost village in Finland. Bus service at both points. Near Sevetti at Ailejavri begins a thick pine woodland that continues to the lakes at Sundeejärvet. For the next 15 or 20 kilometers, the trail crosses a desolate wilderness, winding westward and north to a high point at Tshaaraoaivi (348 meters). The trail then moves through tundra landscape to the Norwegian border, where it reaches another high point at Kolmishoaivi (379 meters). Greener terrain occurs past Tshuomasvarri hill (438 meters), and marshy areas continue to Pajula, a cottage near Lake Polmak, and to Nuorgam. **Length:** About 100

kilometers. **Walking Time:** 5 to 7 days. **Path Markings:** Marked, but only intermittently.
Special Notes: For about 60 kilometers—between Polmakjärvi and Hahpagjavre (or Opukasjärvi)—the path passes through a completely desolate area. The only emergency telephone is at the head of the Pulmankijoki River. Northern Finland is particularly dangerous for inexperienced hikers (see the section on *Equipment Notes*).
Lodgings: Several fell cabins are located along the route, particularly at Leipäjoki, Tsuomasvaara, Tshaarajärvi, Iisakuijärvi, Opukasjärvi, Laavuvaara and Pajula. Most of these are maintained by the Department of Forestry: some are for rent and require reservations; others are free and unlocked. Inquire at Nuorgam or Sevetti.
Maps:
• Topografinen Kartta (Topographical Map) 1:50,000, sheets 3931/2, 3932/1, 3932/2, 3933/3, 3933/1 and 4911/2. Also:
• Topografinen Kartta (Topographical Map) 1:20,000, sheets 3934/01, 3934/02, 3934/04, 3941/01, 3941/04 and 3941/05.
Guidebooks
• *Pohjois-Suomen retkeilyopas* and
• *Pohjois-Suomen Autiotuvat.*

While not a long-distance footpath in the typical sense, one challenging hike you might want to take in the Saariselkä fells is:

Kiilopää-Circuit Tour

This is a demanding ski tour or hike across the tops of 10 fells in Saariselkä, all of which rise to more than 500 meters in elevation. The route can be followed either as a challenge performance or as a regular hike or ski tour. If you are able to complete the tour within 24 hours, you are entitled to a gold Kiilopää-Circuit medal. A silver medal is awarded for completing the tour within 48 hours, and a bronze medal for completing it within 72 hours. Beginning point for the hike is the Kiilopää Training Center (see *Address Directory*). Fell guides are available at the center during the season. **Length:** 70 to 90 kilometers, depending upon the choice of routes.
Path Markings: None.
Special Notes: See *Equipment Notes.* The route requires a high degree of proficiency in orienteering and top physical condition. It also must be followed at your own risk.
Lodgings: Three fell cabins.
Maps:
• Ulkoilukartat (Outdoor Maps) 1:50,000, sheets *Kaunispää-Koksusjärvi* and *Sokosti-Suomujoki.*
Guidebooks:
• None.
Further Information: Rules and information on the route are available from Suomen Latu (see *Address Directory*).

Finland's National Parks

Finland has 11 national parks in addition to several Strict Nature Reserves and Special Conservation Forests. The larger parks and conservation forests—most of which are located above the Arctic Circle—have fell cabins, tent and campfire sites and, occasionally, tourist hotels in the backwoods. Footpaths are often numerous, although few are marked. Because the parks are nature-protection areas, however, some special restrictions apply to hiking and skiing. To protect the flora and fauna some areas within the parks have been closed to entry. Such areas are marked on maps and signposted on location. Elsewhere in the parks you can move about freely. In the Strict Nature Reserves movement is restricted to established paths, and written permission is required from the National Board of Forestry to walk elsewhere.

The Parks

Kevojoki

Finland's northernmost park, located 25 kilometers south of Utsjoki. A region of rolling fells, small lakes and a broad river basin covered with dwarf birch. The park is cut by the Kevojoki River, which in some places narrows to white-water rapids between 100-meter cliffs.

Area: 343 square kilometers (131 square miles).

Access: There are no roads into the park. Access is by foot along the Kevojoki Route (see the section on *Finland's Long-Distance Footpaths*). There is bus service to both ends of the path.

Footpaths: Only one: the Kevojoki Route. The park originally was a Strict Nature Reserve in which movement within its boundaries was restricted to the footpath. Walkers are still encouraged not to diverge from the path.

Lodgings: One fell cabin is located at the southern boundary of the park. In addition, there are 10 designated tent sites within the park.

Maps:
- See the maps for the Kevojoki Route, in the section on *Finland's Long-Distance Footpaths*.

Further Information: Contact Suomen Matkailuliitto or Maa-jametsätalous ministeriön (the Bureau of Natural Resources). See *Address Directory*.

Lemmenjoki

Finland's largest park, located on the Norwegian border near the small settlement of Njurgulahti, 46 kilometers south of Inari (172 kilometers south of Utsjoki). A large roadless wilderness, the park is dominated in the east by fells that rise to heights of nearly 600 meters and in the northwest by the sharp, narrow range of the Skiehttšamtuddarak fells (555 meters). In the center is a broad plain with ridges of dwarf birch, scattered pine forest and long stretches of grassy fens. The northern limit of the pine and spruce bisects the park. Rivers are numerous. There are also many small streams with waterfalls that flow through deep gorges and canyons. The most important river is the Lemmenjoki, which flows between steep banks in places and forms several small lakes lined with gravel terraces and esker formations from the Ice Age. A stand of pines grows on the lower slopes of the Lemmenjoki Valley containing trees more than 600 years old. Higher up, the pines give way to the dwarf birches and finally, to heath and large boulder fields. The Lapps still herd reindeer in the park and, in some places, there are ancient hunting pits used by the Lapps' forebears several thousand years ago.

Area: 1,700 square kilometers (656 square miles).

Access: Route 955 between Kittila and Inari touches the southern border of the park (from which a short footpath leads into the southern fell region) but no road enters the park. Buses run from Inari to Njurgulahti, from which regular motorboat service to the park boundary is available in the summer. In addition, a footpath leads from Njurgulahti into the park.

Footpaths: There are two marked circular paths—2 kilometers and 23 kilometers in length—from the Ravadasjarvi fell cabin (drop-off point for the motorboat service).

Lodgings: Eight fell cabins are located within the park. Most of them can be reached only by traveling cross-country with map and compass. In addition, there are several designated campfire and tent sites. Njurjulahti offers a holiday village and family accommodation.

Maps:
• Ulkoilukartat (Outdoor Maps) 1:50,000, sheets *Lemmenjoki* and *Inari-Menesjärvi*.

Further Information: Contact the national park warden at Njurgulahti; the Forestry Administration, Inari District Office or Suomen Matkailuliitto (see *Address Directory*).

Liesjärvi

Located north of Helsinki in the sparsely populated "Tammela uplands" of southwest Finland. Encompasses spruce stands, lakes and an old farm.

Area: 1.5 square kilometers (.58 square miles).

Access: A two-kilometer road leads to the park from the Helsinki-Pori Highway. Bus service to the junction.

Footpaths: There are three marked paths—2.2, 4.6 and 5.4 kilometers in length.
Lodgings: Nearest camping area is 14 kilometers away in Tammela.
Map:
• Peruskartta (Basic Map) 1:20,000, sheet 2024/11.
Further Information: Contact the Forestry Administration, Hämeenlinna District Office (see *Address Directory*).

Linnansaari

This park comprises a group of rocky islands northwest of Savonlinna in Haukivesi Lake. Of the dozen or so islands scattered across 80 square kilometers, the largest is 4 kilometers in length. The islands have long bays, high rocky outcrops, narrow gorges and a variety of woodland types, some dominated by deciduous trees, others by spruce and pine. Animals include the rare Saimaa seal, a post-glacial relict of this freshwater area.
Area: 8 square kilometers (3 square miles).
Access: Only by water. There is no regular transportation service. A rowboat, however, can be hired from the Porosalmi holiday village on the shore of the lake.
Footpaths: None.
Lodgings: One tent site on the largest island.
Maps:
• Peruskartta (Basic Map) 1:20,000, sheets 3233/13, 3234/10, 4211/03 and 4212/01.
Further Information: Contact the Forestry Administration, Savonlinna District Office (see *Address Directory*).

Oulanka

Located near the Russian border just below the Arctic Circle, 46 kilometers north of Kuusamo. Contains several rivers, rapids and waterfalls; narrow, steep-walled canyons, flowering meadows and, in the north, large marshy peatlands that are difficult to cross. Most of the forest is pine.
Area: 107 square kilometers (41 square miles).
Access: There is a road through the park and bus service to Rukatunturi at the southern end of the Bear's Tour path.
Footpaths: Several marked trails, including Karhun Kierros—the Bear's Tour—and a 4.5-kilometer long nature trail.
Lodgings: There are several tent sites in the park, in addition to four fell cabins and a campsite.
Maps:
• Ulkoilukartta (Outdoor Map) 1:50,000, sheet *Rukatunturi-Oulanka*.
Further Information: Contact the Forestry Administration, Kuusamo Dis-

trict Office or Kuusamon Lomat Oy/Kuusamon Matkailutoimisto (see *Address Directory*).

Pallas-Ounastunturi

Located near the Swedish border in northwestern Finland, a few kilometers south of the town of Enontekiö. Encompasses a long range of rounded fells rising to 821 meters in height, plus many tarns and streams. Forest areas and bogs occur at the base of the fells and in the valleys. Old, moss-covered spruce stands in the southern part of the park give way to pine groves in the north. Above timberline, there is a wide range of heath vegetation, dominated by the dwarf shrub, which turns a brilliant red in autumn.

Area: 500 square kilometers (193 square miles).
Access: Several roads lead to the park from Kolari, Sirkka and Muonio. Suitable starting places for hikes into the park are the tourist hotels at Pallas and Hetta (Enontekiö), to which there are bus services.
Footpaths: The two main hiking routes are the Pallas-Hetta Route and Pallas-Ylläs Route (see the section on *Finland's Long-Distance Footpaths*). In addition, there are several unmarked trails in the Ylläs Special Conservation Forest to the south of the park.
Lodgings: There are three fell cabins inside the park, in addition to several tent sites and the tourist hotel at Pallas. Other lodgings are available at local farms and in hotels and hostels in the surrounding villages.
Maps:
• Ulkoilukartat (Outdoor Maps) 1:50,000, sheets *Pallas-Keimiö* and *Hetta-Outtakka*.
Further Information: Contact the national park wardens at the Pallasjärvi experimental area and at Enontekiö or the Forestry Research Institute, North Finland District (see *Address Directory*).

Petkeljärvi

A bleak pine heath with small bogs and marshy meadows. Includes part of a complex esker and lake sequence that starts at Lake Tolvajärvi, across the nearby border in Russia. Located 15 kilometers southeast of Ilomantsi (about 80 kilometers east of Joensuu) in southeast Finland.
Area: 6.3 square kilometers (2.4 square miles).
Access: A six-kilometer road leads to the park from the Möhkö Highway between Ilomantsi and the Russian border. Bus service is available.
Footpaths: There are two marked paths—3.5 and 5.5 kilometers in length—as well as the unmarked, 22-kilometer Taitajan Taival Route to Putkela village.
Lodgings: One campsite.

Maps:
• Peruskartta (Basic Map) 1:20,000, sheets 4243/06 and 4243/09.
Further Information: Contact the Forestry Administration, Ilomantsi District Office or Ilomantsin Kunta (see *Address Directory*).

Pyhä-Häkki

This is one of the largest remaining natural forest areas in southern Finland. About a third of the area is covered by dense spruce stands, above which tall primeval pines rise. Another third is an open, predominately pine forest, with many trees more than 450 years old. The park also contains both wooded and open bogs, as well as several small forest ponds. Located 85 kilometers north of Jyväskylä.
Area: 10 square kilometers (3.86 square miles).
Access: There is a road through the park between Saarijärvi and Viitasaari that is served by buses.
Footpaths: Two marked paths, 2.8 and 5.9 kilometers in length.
Lodgings: There is a campfire area within the park, a tent site 4.5 kilometers from the park boundary, and a camping area and hotel in Saarijärvi, 30 kilometers to the southwest.
Maps:
• Peruskartta (Basic Map) 1:20,000, sheets 2244/12, 2244/11 and 3222/03.
Further Information: Contact the Forestry Administration, Saarijärvi District Office (see *Address Directory*).

Pyhätunturi

This park gets its name from the large fell (540 meters in height) that dominates its low-lying forest and peatland. Once worshipped by the ancient Lapps, the fell has steep slopes, bare stony faces and deep valleys separating its five peaks. At the foot of the fell are pine and spruce forests and large aapa-fens. The park is connected to a large Special Conservation Forest area in the northwest, which encompasses the Luosto fell ridge and large peatlands. It is also the starting place for several hikes into this area.
Area: 31 square kilometers (12 square miles).
Access: A road runs along the eastern boundary of the park, with bus service from Kemijärvi to the Kultakero Hotel in Pyhätunturi.
Footpaths: A partially marked path, the 55-kilometer Pyhätunturi/Luosto Route, begins in the park. Several other hiking trails run through both the park and the Special Conservation Forest to the northwest.
Lodgings: Campfire areas and tent sites are located along the trails in the park. Near the park's eastern and northern boundaries are hotels, camping areas and guesthouses. Tent sites are available along the Pyhätunturi-

Luosto Route, and six fell cabins—three of which are also located on the route—are found in the region to the northwest of the park.
Maps:
• Ulkoilukartta (Outdoor Map) 1:40,000, sheet *Luosto-Pyhätunturi.*
Further Information: Contact the national park warden in Rovaniemi, or the Forestry Research Institute, North Finland Office (see *Address Directory*).

Rokua

This national park includes part of the ridge of Rokuanvaara, which rises from the peatland plains of northern Ostrobothnia above the central Lake District. Molded since the Ice Age by sea and wind, the region has dune formations, shore banks, flat sandy heaths and deep kettle holes with small tarns and bogs at the bottom. The forest floor is a barren pine heath, white with lichen.
Area: 4.2 square kilometers (1.6 square miles).
Access: The park is 14 kilometers from the Ahmas station on the rail line between Vaala and Oulu (take an express train from Helsinki to Oulu—7½ hours—then change to the Vaala local). There is also a road in poor condition that goes to the edge of the park, but the best way to visit the park is from the Utajärvi holiday center 2.5 kilometers north of the park.
Footpaths: Marked footpaths lead to the park from the holiday center.
Lodgings: There is a combined campfire and tent site in the park. Accommodation is also available at the holiday center (see *Address Directory*).
Map:
• Peruskartta (Basic Map) 1:20,000, sheet 3423/04.
Further Information: Contact the Forestry Administration, Vaala District Office (see *Address Directory*).

Strict Nature Reserves

Most of Finland's 15 strict nature reserves are left completely untouched for scientific reasons, and entry to them is forbidden without written permission from the National Board of Forestry. Six of the reserves, however, have trails open to the public along which you can walk to view the areas' flora and fauna. Anything that might disturb the natural state of the reserves—littering, picking berries and breaking branches from trees, building fires, and so on—is, of course, strictly forbidden. Also, you must keep to the paths.

Karkali. An oak forest located near Lohja between Helsinki and Salo. Has a 5-kilometer nature trail. Covers 1 square kilometer (.4 square mile).

Malla. A Scandic fell region located near Kilpisjärvi at the junction of the Norwegian, Swedish and Finnish borders. Persons who wish to hike the reserve's 11-kilometer trail must inform the warden at the Kilpisjärvi recreation center, or the tourist hotel in advance. Covers 30 square kilometers (11.6 square miles).

Salamanperä. A region of bleak peatlands and heathlands near Perho (between Suolahti and Kokkola) in central Finland. Has a 5.2-kilometer trail. Covers 12.7 square kilometers (4.9 square miles).

Sinivuori. A luxuriant forest with grass-herb ground cover south of Längelmäki (93 kilometers east of Tampere). Has two trails, .8 and .5 kilometers in length. Covers .6 square kilometers (.23 square miles).

Sompio. Encompasses the Nattastunturi fells and large aapa-fens. Located between Sodankylä and Ivalo in northern Finland, southwest of Saariselkä. A cartroad leads into the reserve from Vuotso (on the Sodankylä-Ivalo Highway). A 30-kilometer trail that starts near Kiilopää Koulutuskeskus (the Kiilopää Training Center, run by Suomen Latu) also leads into the reserve. Inside the reserve there are two trails, 1.5 and 12.7 kilometers in length, one of which leads to the top of the fell. Covers 181 square kilometers (70 square miles).

Vaskijärvi. A complex of raised peatlands in southwestern Finland. Located near Yläne, south of the Pyhäjärvi Lake between Turku and Pori. Has two trails, 2 and 2.5 kilometers in length. Covers 8 square kilometers (3.1 square miles).

Other Nature Protection Areas

In addition to the national parks and strict nature reserves, Finland has 173 nature protection areas (total area: 50 square kilometers) located on private land. These include bird sanctuaries, estate parks, 71 peatlands protected from drainage (843 square kilometers), and numerous:

Primeval Areas

Finland's 242 primeval areas (800 square kilometers) are kept completely untouched as examples of primeval nature. There are no footpaths or roads in the areas and entry to them is strictly forbidden.

Special Conservation Forests

Finland's 300 special conservation forests cover 1,501 square kilometers (405.7 square miles). They often are set aside specifically for hiking and recreation. Several of the forests contain primeval areas to which entry is forbidden, but otherwise you are free to roam at will. Many have trails, as well as tent sites and fell cabins.

On maps no differentiation is made between the symbols used for the boundaries of national parks, strict nature reserves, special conservation forests and primeval areas. All are indicated by a black dashed line that is shaded over with a solid red line. Small areas enclosed by these boundary lines are usually strict nature reserves or primeval areas, which you should avoid entering. If you see hiking and skiing routes indicated on the maps (red dashed lines), then you know you may walk in those areas.

Further information on the national parks, nature reserves and special conservation forests can be obtained from:

> **Maa-jametsätalousministeriön luunnonhoitotoimisto** (Bureau of Natural Resources, Ministry of Agriculture and Forestry). See *Address Directory.*

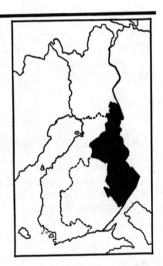

The Eastern Forests

Made up primarily of the provinces of North Karelia and Kainuu, this is a region of mountains and hills, vast forests, lakes and marshes, where rivers flow through deep canyons, plunge over waterfalls and cascade through rapids. Extensive tracts of wilderness cover Kainuu, south of the Arctic Circle. North Karelia has more and bigger towns, scattered fields, and tamer rivers, but its wilderness areas are just as unspoiled. They contain marshes with dead, but still-standing trees; tall pines; moss-covered bog patches on which cloudberries, blueberries and lingonberries grow; and low, pine-covered hills.

Along the Russian border to the east, much of the region is still uninhabited, crossed only by the Bard and Border Way, an ancient traveler's route connecting isolated villages which still have town histories, folk fiddlers and traditional craft workers. On the western shores of Lake Pielisjärvi in North Karelia, the Koli Fells rise to a height of 347 meters, the highest point in Karelia. A little further north in Kainuu are the seven hills of Vuokatti, situated beside the Sotkamo watercourse. These hills rise to 350 meters and are the site of a hiking center with keep-fit paths, exercise tracks, saunas and log cabin accommodation. Finally, just below Lapland and the Arctic Circle is the Kuusamo district, settled first by the Lapps and later by the Karelian peoples. Although Kuusamo does not belong to Lapland, its scenery and customs are so similar that it is often considered a part of the tourist district of Finnish Lapland. Here, fells rise up to 480 meters above deeply cut valleys and canyons, open rapids and the Oulanka National Park.

The opportunities for hiking and cross-country skiing—as well as for running rapids—are numerous. Marked footpaths, of course, are few, but there are several short marked routes in Karelia. In addition, the Kuusamo district includes the Bear's Tour (see the section on *Finland's Long-Distance Footpaths*). During winter, many cross-country ski tracks are marked, and a few are even illuminated, such as those near the winter sport centers at Kuusamo/Ruka, Koli and Vuokatti. In Kainuu, a guided hike during mid-September from Saukanmaja to Puolanka is arranged by the tourist office, Kainuun Matkailupalvelu.

When you aren't hiking or skiing, you can sample the region's culinary specialties: Karelian stew, brawn, salted whitefish, clabbered milk (a regional version of buttermilk) and rieska unleavened bread.

Useful Addresses

See *Address Directory:*

Lieksan Kaupungin Matkailutoimisto (Lieksa City Tourist Office). The town is located on the eastern shore of Lake Pielinen in North Karelia and is connected by boat to the Koli hills on the western shore, southern Finland's highest point. To the east extensive forests stretch to the Soviet border. The office provides general tourist information, information on guided day-long trips to shoot the rapids in the Ruunaa wilderness (25 kilometers to the east), and information on ski touring, hiking and accommodation in the Koli hills. Staff speaks Finnish, Swedish, English and German. Useful publications include:

- *Kolin Retkipolut/Hiking Trails in Koli*. A sketch map in a scale of

1:20,000 on which five trails have been marked. The trails, ranging from three to eight kilometers long, are color-coded according to their length. They can be linked up for longer hikes. The sketch map should be supplemented with the Peruskartta (Basic Map) 1:20,000, sheets 4313/07, 4313/08, 4313/10 and 4313/11.

Kuusamon Lomat Oy/Kuusamon Matkailutoimisto. Provides general tourist information on the Kuusamo district. Can help you with transportation connections to the starting point of Karhun Kierros—the Bear's Tour—the Oulanka National Park and to the cross-country ski tracks in the area. Also will mark the routes—and points of interest—on a map if you drop into the office. Staff speaks Finnish, Swedish, English and German. Useful publications include:

- *Karhunkierros.* A sketch map of the Bear's Tour that shows the locations of fell cabins, tent sites and camping areas along the route. Information is written in Finnish on one side of the sheet; in German on the other.

Kainuun Matkailupalvelu (Kainuu Tourist Service). Provides general tourist information on Kainuu. Also provides details on the marked hiking and cross-country ski trails in the area (see information below) and help in making transportation connections and booking lodgings. Staff speaks Finnish, Swedish, English and German.

Maps

For planning hikes and ski tours in the area, it is advisable to purchase the 1:200,000 *Suomen Tiekartta GT* (see the section on *Maps* earlier in this chapter). Hiking and cross-country ski routes and the locations of lodgings are indicated on the maps. Several sheets also have an index in their margins of the 1:20,000 maps, Outdoor Leisure Maps, Environs Maps and Touring Maps that cover the region. By referring to the index you can determine which sheets of the larger-scale maps will be required to follow each route. When you order the maps, however, you should request a set of indexes, since not all of the GT maps have indexes in their margins. The following GT maps cover the Eastern Forests:

Kainuu: Suomen Tiekartta GT 1:200,000, sheet 11.

Kuusamo: Suomen Tiekartta GT 1:200,000, sheets 13 and 15.

North Karelia: Suomen Tiekartta GT 1:200,000, sheets 6 and 9.

Guidebooks

- *Pohjois-Suomen retkeilyopas.* Covers the Kuusamo district.

• *Pohjois-Suomen Autiotuvat.* Gives information on fell cabins in the Kuusamo district.

Both guidebooks are available from Suomen Matkailuliitto (see *Address Directory*).

Suggested Walks

Among the marked trails in the region are:

Koli: Five trails, 3 to 8 kilometers in length. See the information on the sketch map, *Kolin Retkipolut,* above. Several lodging possibilities in campsites, youth hostels and hotels.

Kuhmo (Kainuu):

1. An 8-kilometer trail, "The Blue Trail," begins at the Moisiovaara Way, 21 kilometers from Kuhmo village. There are several campfire sites enroute as well as an outdoor shelter for overnight camping.
2. In the Iso-Palonen area there are two trails, 4 and 12 kilometers in length, campfire sites and outdoor shelters. The trails begin on the Maaselkä Way, 25 kilometers from Kuhmo village in the direction of Lentiira.
3. A network of orienteering check posts is located in the Multikangas area, 10 kilometers from Kuhmo toward Sotkamo. Information on these is available from the Kuhmo tourist information office in Kuhmo.
4. There is a network of several marked hiking trails, most of them short, at the Jauhovaara sporting area near Kuhmo village.

Kuusamo: Karhun Kierros, 80 kilometers (see the section on *Finland's Long-Distance Footpaths*).

Sotkamo (Kainuu):

1. In the Vuokatti area there are several marked trails that can be used for hiking in summer and cross-country skiing in winter. The lengths of these trails are 5, 8, 10 and 15 kilometers.
2. The partially marked, 28-kilometer "Vuokatti Hiking Trail" begins at Juurikkalahti, crosses 13 hills in Vuokatti and ends at the Vuokatti Sport Institute. Enroute, it is possible to stay overnight at Möykky cottage.
3. From Sotkamo, you can go by car or bus to a 4-kilometer trail leading to Hiidenportti (Devil's Gate), a park 42 kilometers from Sotkamo. Inside the park there is an outdoor shelter where you can camp overnight.

Suomussalmi (Kainuu): The Hossa wilderness area is located near the town. There are no marked hiking trails in the Hossa area, but guides are available on demand from the Kainuu Tourist Service (see *Address Directory*).

Further information on these hiking routes can be obtained from Suomen Matkailuliitto, as well as from the local tourist offices.

Cross-Country Skiing

Among the opportunities for cross-country skiing in the region are:

Kainuu: One of Finland's oldest winter sports centers is based at the Vuokatti Sports Institute near Sotkamo. It has 70 kilometers of marked tracks, 2.5 kilometers of illuminated tracks, ski instruction and rental facilities. Accommodation is also available. In addition, there are two cross-country ski tracks near the Hossa Holiday Village (Suomussalmi), 5 and 10 kilometers in length; three tracks (5, 10 and 15 kilometers in length) in Ämmänsaari village, some of which are illuminated during the winter, plus illuminated tracks at Kajaani, Kuhomo, Paltamo, Puolanka and Hyrynsalmi.

Kuusamo: There is a winter sports center 25 kilometers north of Kuusamo village, *Kuusamo/Ruka*, with four marked tracks—5, 10, 12 and 20 kilometers in length—ski instruction and organized ski weeks. Accommodation is also available at the center. In addition, there are marked ski tracks at Kuusamo (5 and 7 kilometers in length) and Kitka (2 and 3 kilometers in length).

North Karelia: The winter sports center at Koli has marked ski tracks and equipment rental and is the site of the *Ahman Hiihto*, a 30-kilometer ski trek across the hills of Koli held each March.

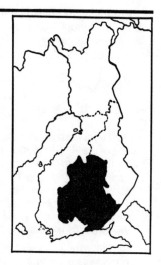

The Lake District

This region encompasses five provinces—Keski-Suomen (central Finland), Savo, Järvi-Savo (Lake Savo), South Karelia and North Pirkanmaa. Nowhere are you ever far from water. There are rapids and narrow waterways, such as those near Mäntyharju in South Savo; rivers such as the Vuoksi, which bisects Imatra and through which more water flows than in any other river in Finland; remote marshes; and, of course, the lakes. In fact, there is more water than land. Most of Finland's 60,000 lakes—including its largest lake, Saimaa—are here. But the country is also good for hiking and cross-country skiing. There are sparsely populated forest regions, ridges from which you can look out over unending lakeland panoramas, heather-clad meadows and lake shores with sandy beaches and rockbound inlets. There are also more kilometers of marked footpaths than anywhere else in Finland.

Small villages, farms and holiday cabins dot the wooded shores of many of the lakes. There are also several large towns and some large-scale industry, including pulp and steel mills, breweries and cement plants. But most of the region is still rural and the countryside is always easily accessible. Even near the large towns, there are forests, meadows and stretches of lakeshore where you can find solitude.

History lurks among the lakes as well. At the Astuvansalmi Straits near Ristiina in South Savo there are 4,000-year-old rock paintings. In east Savo, the shores of the lakes were once populated by Stone Age wanderers of the Cambric culture. Evidence of the Lapps, many of whom did not move north until the 16th century, can still be found. A few towns were built up around fortified walls and castles. And in the forests are many old wooden churches built by loggers and farmers in the early 18th century.

The region is more heavily settled than some of the other parts of Finland. You must occasionally walk along—or cross—back roads.

Property rights must also be respected. But, on the whole, people in the region are friendly, accommodation is plentiful and villages and towns are close enough together so that you can walk for several days without being weighted down with more than two or three days of food at a time.

Useful Addresses—Central Finland

See *Address Directory*:

Keski-Suomen Maakuntaliitto. Oversees the establishment and marking of the 431-kilometer network of footpaths between Viitasaari and Halli in central Finland. Can also provide information on walking and cross-country skiing elsewhere in central Finland and the eastern forests. Staff speaks Finnish, Swedish, English and German. **Useful Publications:** See the list of maps and guidebooks for the long-distance footpath Keski-Suomen ulkoilureitti in the section on *Finland's Long-Distance Footpaths*.

Keski-Suomi/Loma-Suomi. A very active tourist organization. Can provide general tourist information on all of central Finland, as well as on canoeing, running rapids, cross-country skiing and hiking. Staff speaks Finnish, Swedish, English, German and French. Useful publications include:

- *Keski-Suomi retkeilijän Suomi* (in Finnish) and *Mittelfinnland Wanderland* (in German). A brochure and sketch map giving a brief description of the Keski-Suomen ulkoilureitti long-distance footpath.
- *Virkisty Retkeillen Keski-Suomen Ulkoilureiteillä.* A map in a scale of 1:400,000 showing the route and locations of lodgings along the Keski-Suomen ulkoilureitti long-distance footpath.
- *Saarijärven ulkoilureitit* (in Finnish). A small booklet with sketch maps and route descriptions of three hiking routes near Saarijärvi, 59 kilometers north of Jyväskylä, one of which is in the Pyhän-Häkin National Park. The footpaths are 14, 17 and 20 kilometers in length. The booklet is useful simply for its sketch maps.
- *Saarijärven Seutu retkeilijän paratiisi* (in Finnish). A brochure describing the possibilities for canoeing and running rapids near Saarijärvi.
- *Laajavuoren Latukartta 1:25,000.* A two-color topographical map on which the routes of three cross-country ski and hiking tracks have been indicated and color-coded (in red, green and blue) according to their length. The tracks are 5, 10 and 15 kilometers in length and are marked during the winter. The map also includes an elevation chart to show the profiles of the ascents and descents of each route.

• *Laajavuori* (in English). A mimeographed sheet describing the facilities at the winter sports and outdoor leisure center in Laajavuori, 4 kilometers from Jyväskylä.

• *Keski-Suomen Läpihiihto* (in Finnish) and *Skiwanderung durch Mittel-Finnland* (in German). A mimeographed sheet describing the annual three-day ski-track hike from Ruuponsaari (near Viitasaari) to Summassaari (near Saarijärvi). Total length of the hike is 80 kilometers. It is held twice each year, once in mid-February and once in mid-March.

Useful Addresses—Pirkanmaa

See *Address Directory*:

Lahden Matkailutoimisto (Lahti City Tourist Office). Provides general tourist information on Lahti and its immediate surroundings. Staff speaks Finnish, Swedish, English and German. Useful publications include:

• *Hiihdon Maailmanmestaurruskipailut Lahti/Ski-Weltmeisterschaften Lahti Finnland/The World Ski Championships Lahti Finland*. A four-color topographical map showing the locations of the championship ski tracks, marked ski tracks and footpaths in Lahti.

Pirkanmaan Taival. Can provide information on walking and cross-country skiing in the Tampere region of the Lake District. Also arranges guided ski tours and competitions, running competitions and guided hiking tours. Staff speaks Finnish, Swedish, English and German. Useful publications include:

• *Pirkanmaan taival* (in Finnish). A brochure describing its various competitions and guided tours—more than 50 in total.

Tamperen Kaupungin Matkailutoimisto (Tampere City Tourist and Congress Service). A very helpful tourist office. Can provide general information on Tampere and North Pirkanmaa, as well as information on hiking, cross-country skiing and orienteering. Staff speaks Finnish, Swedish, English, German and French. Useful publications include:

• *Kaupin Ulkoilu- ja Urheilaulue.* A three-color topographical map in a scale of 1:20,000 showing the marked cross-country ski tracks, illuminated ski tracks and footpaths on the outskirts of Tampere. The paths are color-coded according to their length and use.

• *Pirkanmaan Ulkoilureitit* (Trails in the Surroundings of Tampere). A topographical map in a scale of 1:100,000 on which numerous footpaths are shown in the region north of Kuru, a small settlement

53 kilometers north of Tampere. Symbols on the map indicate: 1) hiking routes along a road, 2) hiking routes along a cart path, 3) hiking routes along a path, and 4) cross-country hiking routes across the terrain (unmarked), as well as the locations of open and locked fell cabins, tent sites, campfire sites, viewpoints, water wells, stores and camping areas. The paths are, so far, only partly marked with red or blue painted triangles on rocks and trees. Key to the symbols on the map is in Finnish, but the tourist office will translate them on request.

- *Kitusen Karhupolku* (The Kitunen Bear Path). A topographical map in a scale of 1:100,000 showing the 50-kilometer path beginning in Virrat, 120 kilometers north of Tampere. Symbols on the map indicate which parts of the route are along roads (about 15 kilometers) and which follow paths. The route is partially marked with red-painted triangles on trees and rocks.

- *Pirkanmaan taival* (in Finnish). A brochure describing the guided hikes and ski tours, as well as the skiing and running competitions arranged by the Pirkanmaan Taival (see the section on *Finland's Walking & Skiing Associations*).

- *Pirkan Hölkkä* (in Finnish). A brochure and sketch map describing the annual ski trek from Niinisalo to Tampere. Length of the trek is 90 kilometers. It is held every year on the first Sunday in March.

- Orienteering maps. Six maps in a scale of 1:15,000 showing the locations of fixed orienteering posts in the region surrounding Tampere. The six maps are: *Kauppi, Mustavuori, Lahdesjärvi, Vuorentausta, Pyynikki* and *Kintulampi*. Information on where these maps may be obtained is available from the tourist office.

- *Pohjois-Pirkanmaa*. A topographical map on which all the hiking routes in North Pirkanmaa have been indicated. Recently published by the Surveyor-General's office. Price of the map is 15 Fmk.

Urheilukeskus. Provides information on the Finlandia Ski Race, the largest ski track race in Finland. Held annually on the last Sunday in February. In 1979, the 75-kilometer race attracted about 7,000 participants. Staff speaks Finnish, Swedish, English and German.

Valkeakosken Kaupungin Matkailutoimisto (Valkeakoski City Tourist Office). Provides general tourist information on the town of Valkeakoski (44 kilometers south of Tampere) and its immediate surroundings. Staff speaks Finnish, Swedish, English and German. Useful publications include:

- *Retkeilyreitit Valkeakoski*. A sketch map showing the 34-kilometer footpath—marked with blue plastic ribbons—from Valkeakelta to Tampere. The sketch map should be supplemented with the 1:100,000 Matkailukartat (Touring Map), *Tampere* or, better yet, the 1:20,000 Peruskartta (Basic Maps).

- *Korkeakangas Valkeakoski.* A sketch map showing the routes of three marked cross-country ski tracks—5, 10 and 23 kilometers in length—south of Valkeakoski.
- *Eerolan Alue Valkeakoski.* A sketch map showing the routes of three cross-country ski tracks—8, 11 and 22 kilometers in length—north of Valkeakoski. The map also shows the routes of two lighted keep-fit trails, 2.9 and 2.3 kilometers in length.
- *Keskustan Ulkoilureitit Valkeakoski.* A sketch map showing the routes of two keep-fit trails—1 and 3.3 kilometers in length—the longest of which is lighted, in the center of Valkeakoski.

Useful Addresses—Savo

See *Address Directory*:

Kaupungin Matkailutoimisto Savonlinna (Savonlinna City Tourist Office). Provides general tourist information on Savonlinna and the surrounding area. There are several trails for hiking and cross-country skiing in the Pihlajaniemi area, 10 kilometers from Savonlinna, and in the Punkaharju area, 28 kilometers from Savonlinna. Information is available from the tourist office staff. Staff speaks Finnish, Swedish, English and German. Useful publications include:

- *Savonlinnan Luontopolut* (in Finnish). Describes the routes of the Pihlajaniemi path, 16 kilometers in length, and the Sunrijärvi path, 12 kilometers in length, in the Pihlajaniemi area. Includes a sketch map. The tourist office staff will help you translate the essential information.
- *Punkaharju* (in Finnish, English and German). Describes the lodging possibilities in the Punkaharju area.

Kuopion Kaupungin Matkailutoimisto (Kuopio City Tourist Office). Provides general tourist information on the area surrounding Kuopio. Staff speaks Finnish, Swedish, English and German. Useful publications include:

- *Kuopion Kaupungin Ulkoilukohteet ja -reitit.* A sketch map that shows the locations of bicycle paths and keep-fit trails.
- *Kuopion Kaupungin Ylläpitämät Kuntoladut.* A sketch map showing the locations of marked, unmarked and illuminated cross-country ski tracks in and around Kuopio.
- Orienteering Maps: *Jynkän Kiintorastikartta* 1:20,000, *Kuopion Suunnistajat Suunnistuskartta: Neulaniemi* 1:15,000 and *Kuopion Suunnistajat Suunnistuskartta: Puijo* 1:15,000. Five-color topographical maps showing the locations of fixed orienteering posts in the areas surrounding Kuopio.

Useful Addresses—South Karelia

See *Address Directory*:

Imatran Kaupungin Matkailutoimisto (Imatra City Tourist Office). Provides general tourist information on Imatra and South Karelia. The town has several marked keep-fit trails, two orienteering courses with fixed orienteering posts and numerous marked ski tracks. Information is available from the tourist office staff. Staff speaks Finnish, Swedish, English and German. Useful publications include:

- *Imatra: Opaskartta 1:75,000 Kansanhiihtoladut.* A single-color sketch map that shows the routes of marked cross-country ski trails and illuminated tracks in and around Imatra, with a total length of 82 kilometers.

Kaupungin Matkailutoimisto Lappeenranta (Lappeenranta Town Tourist Office). Provides general tourist information on Lappeenranta and its immediate surroundings (located near the beginning of the Bard and Border Way in the southern part of the Lake District near the Soviet border). A network of marked hiking trails is currently being created near the town. In addition, the town has 105 kilometers of marked cross-country ski tracks and three orienteering courses with more than 30 checking points on each course. A map showing the locations of the footpaths, ski tracks and orienteering courses is in preparation and should be available by spring, 1980. Staff speaks Finnish, Swedish, English and German.

Maps

For planning hikes and ski tours in the area, it is advisable to purchase the 1:200,000 *Suomen Tiekartta GT* (see the section on *Maps* earlier in this chapter). Hiking and cross-country ski routes as well as the locations of lodgings are indicated on the maps. Several sheets also have an index in their margins of the 1:20,000 maps, Environs Maps and Touring Maps covering the region. By referring to the index, you can determine which sheets of the larger-scale maps will be required to follow each route. When you order the maps, however, you should request a set of indexes, since not all of the GT maps have indexes in their margins. The following GT maps cover the Lake District:

- *Suomen Tiekartta GT 1:200,000*, sheets 3, 4, 5, 6, 8 and part of sheet 9.

Guidebooks

- *Saarijärven ulkoilureitit.* Describes three hiking routes near Saarijärvi, north of Jyväskylä. Available from Keski-Suomi (see *Address Directory*). Published only in Finnish.

• *Savonlinnan Luontopolut*. Describes the routes of two paths near Savonlinna. Available from Kaupungin Matkailutoimisto Savonlinna—the Savonlinna City Tourist Office. Published only in Finnish.

Suggested Walks

The possibilities are numerous. The two longest paths are the Keski-Suomen ulkoilureitti and Kitusen Karhupolku—the Kitunen Bear Path— 120 kilometers north of Tampere (see the information on the sketch map for this path under *Useful Addresses—Pirkanmaa*, above). There is a large network of footpaths and cross-country hiking routes north of Kuru, 53 kilometers from Tampere (again, see the information under *Useful Addresses—Pirkanmaa*), as well as several footpaths near Saarijärvi and Savonlinna. In addition, many towns around Lake Saimaa in South Karelia have marked paths—most of which are from two to five kilometers in length—near the town limits. For further information, refer to the sketch maps listed above, which are available from the local tourist offices.

Cross-Country Skiing

There are seven winter sport centers with marked cross-country ski tracks in the Lake District:

Ähtäri. Located 85 kilometers west of Jyväskylä. Has marked and illuminated ski tracks and facilities for equipment rental and accommodation. Offers ski week package arrangements. Also offers the opportunity to ski tour in a nearby nature park for wild animals.

Joutsa/Joutsenlampi. Located 70 kilometers south of Jyväskylä. Has 20 kilometers of well-illuminated ski tracks and facilities for accommodation.

Jyväskylä/Laajavuori. Located four kilometers from the center of Jyväskylä. Has 35 kilometers of prepared tracks, a 4.2-kilometer illuminated track, ski instruction, facilities for equipment rental, accommodation and a winter camping area.

Kuopio/Puijo. Located just outside Kuopio. Has 15 kilometers of marked ski tracks, a 5-kilometer illuminated track and facilities for equipment rental.

Lahti/Messilä and Tiirismaa. Site of the World Ski Championships in 1978. Has 150 kilometers of marked ski tracks, 15 kilometers of illuminated tracks, ski instruction and accommodation. The Tiirismaa Sports Center,

12 kilometers west of Lahti, also has marked ski tracks, ski instruction and facilities for equipment rental.

Nilsiä/Tahkovuori. Located 65 kilometers north of Kuopio. Has the steepest ski slopes in North Savo, as well as 25 kilometers of marked tracks, ski instruction, facilities for equipment rental and accommodation.

Viitasaari-Ruuponsaari. Located 100 kilometers north of Jyväskylä on Lake Keitele. Has 30 kilometers of marked tracks, a one-kilometer illuminated track, ski instruction and, in Viitassari, 15 kilometers away, facilities for equipment rental and accommodation.

This is by no means a complete listing of all the marked and illuminated cross-country ski tracks in the Lake District. But it should give you an idea of the opportunities that exist. Further information on cross-country skiing in the Lake District can be obtained from the local tourist offices.

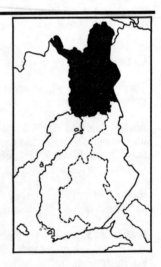

Lapland

Finnish Lapland is as large as Portugal, extending from the Arctic Circle near Rovaniemi almost to the Arctic Ocean in the north. Within this region is the largest area of untouched wilds in Europe—extensive highland areas, brooks and rivers, rapids and a world of rare plants and animals. Although many of Lapland's once-farflung inhabitants have moved together to form closer communities, it still has an ancient nomadic culture living side by side with modern industry. Lapland now has a population of 200,000 people (and just about as many reindeer) but it is sparsely populated. There are only four sizeable towns, one township and a dozen centers along the main roads. Lapland's capital, Rovaniemi (population: 30,000), is one of the largest municipalities in Finland, and its numerous power stations have made it an important center in Finland's energy industry. Even so, the overall population density of Lapland is less than two people per square kilometer.

The Lapps, who were the first people to live in Lapland, are today a small minority, numbering only about 3,500. But their culture still permeates the region. Each year at Easter the Sami Lapps hold a large church festival in Hetta (Enontekiö); reindeer racing championships are held in early spring at Inari. Reindeer herding is also still an important source of livelihood, especially since cultivated crops do not do well because of the harsh climate. At the annual reindeer roundups, there may be as many as 10,000 reindeer herded together on the snow-covered flanks of a single fell.

Lapland's culinary specialties also reflect the influence of the Lapps: reindeer stew, smoked reindeer, boiled reindeer, reindeer tongue, reindeer calf cutlets and reindeer steak. People, of course, do not eat only reindeer meat. They also enjoy fish (salmon soup, poached salmon, smoked salmon, whitefish, smoked whitefish, whitefish baked in the embers, and the like), dishes made from game such as ptarmigan, grouse and capercaillie, and liqueurs distilled from Arctic cloudberries, Arctic bramble and cranberries.

Because of Lapland's enormous size and sparse settlement, the opportunities for hiking and cross-country skiing are practically unlimited. Its skiing season is nearly seven months long, usually beginning in October and, in some parts of Lapland, lasting into May. There are marked and illuminated ski tracks near 13 winter sport centers. In addition, the frozen lakes and slopes and gullies of the Arctic fells can be skiied. The hours of daylight during the winter are, of course, limited (and nonexistent for part of the year), although the sun becomes visible above the horizon at the Arctic Circle as early as the end of January. But there is compensation. For part of the summer, the sun never sets. And then you can hike for hours in just about any direction.

Lapland has diverse scenery: from the farmlands in the south, vegetation alternates among forest, marsh and heath many times before the Arctic fells, with their dwarf birch, are reached. One of the best known and most popular hiking areas is the Saariselkä fell district in northeastern Lapland, site of the Saariselkä Excursion Center, which conducts guided hikes and ski treks and offers accommodation that includes Lapp delicacies and saunas.

The importance in Lapland of hiking and skiing with a guide or in a group is demonstrated each year by the many search parties organized for people who, despite warnings, thought they were experienced hikers and skiers. A few of these people have never been found.

Another important rule for winter, spring and summer travel is to wear brightly colored clothing so that if you become lost you can be easily spotted. In autumn, when frost turns the heath a deep, fiery red and trees display a spectrum of golden yellow, oranges and russets, bright apparel is useless and white clothing should be worn instead.

Useful Addresses

See *Address Directory:*

Lapin Matkailu. Can provide detailed information on hiking and cross-country skiing in Lapland—but only if you specify the area in which you intend to visit. Staff speaks Finnish, Swedish, English and German.

Inarin Matkailuyhdistys. Provides general tourist information on the region surrounding the towns of Inari and Ivalo in northeastern Lapland, including the Saariselkä fell region and the Kevojoki and Lemmenjoki national parks. Also can give you information on the possibilities for hiking and cross-country skiing, suggest good starting points and tell you what transportation connections are available to and from the routes you choose. Staff speaks Finnish, Swedish, English and German.

Rovaniemen Kaupunki Matkailutoimisto (Rovaniemi City Tourist Office). Provides general tourist information on Rovaniemi and Lapland. Also can provide limited information on hiking and cross-country skiing. Staff speaks Finnish, Swedish, English and German. Useful publications include:

- *Pohjois-Suomen retkeilyreitit* (a leaflet in Finnish). Gives the length, sheet numbers of maps and a brief description of 12 hiking routes in Lapland. Includes a sketch map.

- *Wanderrouten im Finnish-Lappland.* A mimeographed information sheet in German. Gives the length, location and sheet numbers of maps for seven hiking routes in Lapland.

- *Karhunkierros.* A sketch map and short route description of the Bear's Tour in the Kuusamo district. One side of the sketch map is written in Finnish; the other side in German.

Maps

For planning hikes and ski tours in Lapland, it is advisable to purchase the 1:200,000 *Suomen Tiekartta GT.* From these, you can decide which routes you might want to walk and determine which of the larger-scale maps you will have to buy. The following GT maps cover Lapland:

Southern Lapland and the Kuusamo District: Suomen Tiekartta GT 1:200,000, sheets 14 and 15.

Northwestern Lapland and the Pallas-Ounastunturi and Lemmenjoki national parks: Suomen Tiekartta GT 1:200,000, sheets 16 and 18. **Northeastern Lapland and the Saariselkä fells:** Suomen Tiekartta GT 1:200,000, sheet 17. **Northernmost Lapland and the Kevojoki National Park:** Suomen Tiekartta GT 1:200,000, sheet 19.

Guidebooks

* *Kilpisjärven retkeilyopas* (Hiking Trails in the Kilpijärvi Area).
* *Kultamaiden retkeilyopas* (Hiking Trails in the Gold Country).
* *Pohjois-Suomen retkeilyopas* (Hiking Trails in Northern Finland).
* *Saariselkä*.
* *Pohjois-Suomen Autiotuvat*. Lists the fell cabins in Lapland.

All the guidebooks are published in Finnish by Suomen Matkailuliitto. For more details, see the sections on *Guidebooks* and *Trailside Lodgings* earlier in this chapter.

Suggested Walks

Tirro-Karigasniemi Tour. From Tirro, situated on the Vasko River to Karigasniemi. Take a taxi or a bus from Inari to Kettukoski (literally fox waterfall). From Kettukoski walk two kilometers on a road to Tirro. The path is wider than average until Ritamaa, the first fell cabin enroute, and passes through dry wooded areas characteristic of Lapland. From Ritamaa to Mukkalompolo, the trail enters a wet, marshy, moss-covered lowland with colorful Lapland lichen, the indigenous reindeer food. From Mukkalompolo, another fell cabin location, the Muotka fell begins, including the Koarvikodsi fell, which is 395 meters high and has a steep southern side. The view from the top is spectacular. The Muotka fell continues until Kiella where a lowland area begins, which continues until the trail meets a road 2 or 3 kilometers before Karigasniemi. **Length:** About 60 kilometers. **Walking Time:** About 3 days. **Path Markings:** Path is marked, but not regularly.
Special Notes: The only telephone is at Karigasniemi. Path width changes at Ritamaa; marsh area noted above can be wet; see warning notes on northern Finland.
Lodgings: Free, unlocked cabins are located at Ritamaa, Mukkalompolo, and Stuorra-Avdshi (reached by following a narrow stream that flows into a pond). Other cabins can be reserved.
Maps:
* Ulkoilukartta (Outdoor Map) 1:50,000, sheet *Inari-Menesjärvi*.

Guidebooks:
• *Pohjois-Suomen retkeilyopas*, available from Suomen Maitkailuliitto.
• *Pohjois-Suomen Autiotuvat*, also available from Suomen Maitkailuliitto.

Kilpisjärvi-Halti Tour. Starting near the Norwegian border by the shores of Kilpisjärvi Lake, this tour heads northeast along the Finnish/Norwegian border to Saarijärvi near Halti. From Sanna Fell the trail passes Saanajärvi Lake on the north then crosses the southern slopes of Muurivaara and Salmivaara fells to the western shore of Saarijärvi Lake, where a cabin maintained by Suomen Matkailuliitto is located. The path continues north along a grass valley to Kuonjarvankka, then northeast along the river to the southeastern slopes of Kahperus. At the willow-rimmed Meekonjärvi Lake there is another cabin. The path crosses a rocky area and leads to the Vuomakasjoki River with its abundant fish. The trail then winds across the Pihtsusjoki River, which can be crossed most safely at its widest section. Here, a 17-meter high waterfall at Pihtsoskönkä can be seen. The last stop is Pihtsusjärvi, with campsites and cabins, a short distance from Halti. A demanding tour.
Length: About 100 to 110 kilometers (50 kilometers one-way). **Walking Time:** 5 to 6 days. **Path Markings:** None.
Special Notes: Telephones at Kilpisijärvi, Meekonjärvi (cabin location, reservations required), Pihtsusjärvi and Saarijärvi (Tsohepejärvi). Be careful about crossing the border into Norway.
Lodgings: Fell cabins are located at Saarijärvi, Meekonjärvi and Pitsusjärvi. Open cabins are at Meekonjärvi (free), Kuonjarjohka (free) and Pihtsusjärvi.
Maps:
• Ulkoilukartta (Outdoor Map) 1:50,000, sheet *Halti-Kilpisjärvi*.
Guidebooks:
• *Kilpisjärven retkeilyopas* and *Pohjois-Suomen retkeilyopas*, both available from Suomen Matkailuliitto.

Inari-Pielppajärvi Tour. A relatively short, non-wilderness tour from Inari, the center of Lapp civilization in Finland, to Pielppajärvi, the location of an old church (Pielppajärven Puukirkko). Begins at Juutuanjoki in Inari behind the Saame Museum. The trip back from Pielppajärvi can be made along Lake Inari, where boats can be hired. Stone structures along the route are the special interest on this tour. **Length:** 7 to 8 kilometers (oneway). **Walking Time:** 1 day (round trip). **Path Markings:** Paint markings on trees.
Special Notes: An easy route that affords plenty of time to enjoy Lake Inari and the other sights.
Lodgings: Many rooms can be rented in Inari.
Maps:
• Ulkoilukartta (Outdoor Map) 1:50,000, sheet *Inari-Menesjärvi*.
Guidebooks:
• *Pohjois-Suomen retkeilyopas*, available from Suomen Matkailuliitto.

Tulppio-Saariselkä Tour. Starting in Tulppio (about 160 kilometers north-east of Sodankylä, by way of Martti on Route 967) the trail runs along the Nuortti River, a favorite stream for fishermen. A fell cabin is located about 1.5 kilometers downstream from where the Kärekeoja River intersects the Nuortti. Further down the Nuortti, there is another cabin for hikers. To the north of this cabin is a long reindeer fence that the trail follows until Naltiotunturi. There, the trail crosses the Naltiojoki River (5 to 10 meters wide and 1 meter deep) and leads to another cabin for hikers. The trail continues across the Vierihaara River to Juusimantoselkä and Mantoselkä, an area of dried marsh and swamp. The reindeer fence then leads to the Manto-oja cabin, and across the Keski Haara swamp to the top of the Keski Haara reindeer separation and branding station, where another cabin, located 100 meters north of the reindeer fence, is located. Five kilometers farther along the reindeer fence are the Kokkopäät Fells and the Jaurijoki River cabin (called "Peuraselän Kämppä"). A number of different Saariselkä paths are possible from this cabin: one favorite is through the valley of Jauru, which is reached by going first to the Tahvontupa cabin, then to the "fairy tale" house at Siulanruoktu and finally to either Raja Jooseppi or Kaunispää. **Walking Time:** About 10 days. **Path Markings:** Unmarked.
Lodgings: As indicated above. The houses may be crowded during the reindeer season.
Maps:
* Ulkoilukartta (Outdoor Map) 1:50,000, sheets *Kaunispää-Kopsusjärvi* and *Sokosti-Suomujoki*.
Guidebook:
* *Pohjois-Suomen retkeilyopas*, available from Suomen Matkailuliitto.

Suomu-Jumisko Tour. This Arctic Circle trip begins in the village of Tonkopuri, a short walk from the No. 5 highway and winds past Suomutunturi Fell (409 meters), an area known primarily as a ski resort. By continuing across a number of narrow rivers, Matkajärvi Lake can be reached, followed by Matkaseläanlampi (a cabin location) and the Jumiskojoki River. Continuing south, you come to the resort village of Jumisko where there are a number of trail options to extend the walk.
Length: About 22 kilometers. **Walking Time:** 1 to 2 days. **Path Markings:** Unmarked.
Special Notes: Ask at Suomu where the best place to cross the Jumiskojoki River is at the time you will be there. From Jumisko there is a 10-kilometer marked path to Peniötunturi fell (409 meters).
Lodgings: Matkaselänlampi cabin.
Maps:
* Topografinen kartta (Topographical Map) 1:50,000, sheets 3631/2, 3532/2 and 3633/1 + 2.
Guidebook:
* *Pohjois-Suomen retkeilyopas*, available from Suomen Matkailuliitto.

For other hiking routes in Lapland, see the section on *Finland's Long-Distance Footpaths*.

Cross-Country Skiing

The main winter sport centers in Lapland include:

Hetta (Enontekiö). Located on the northern edge of the Pallas-Ounastunturi National Park. Has marked ski tracks, ski instruction, facilities for equipment rental and accommodation. Also organizes guided ski weeks into the Arctic fells.

Kilpisjärvi. Located near the point where the Finnish, Swedish and Norwegian borders meet in Finland's highest mountain region. Has marked ski tracks, ski instruction, facilities for equipment rental and accommodation. Organizes guided ski weeks and daily ski trips to Salmivaara, the Saarijärvi wilderness hut and the Kitsiputous fells.

Levitunturi. Located in Kittilä, 180 kilometers north of Rovaniemi. Has facilities for equipment rental and accommodation. Organizes guided ski weeks.

Luostotunturi. Located in Sodankylä, 130 kilometers north of Rovaniemi. Has two marked ski tracks, 3 and 10 kilometers in length, a 3-kilometer illuminated track, facilities for equipment rental and accommodation.

Olostunturi. A slalom center in Muonio, located on the Swedish border southwest of the Pallas-Ounastunturi National Park. Has 200 kilometers of marked ski tracks and accommodation facilities.

Pallastunturi. Located in the center of a group of 14 fells, 250 kilometers north of Rovaniemi. Has ski instruction, facilities for equipment rental and accommodation.

Rovaniemi/Ounasvaara and Pohtimolampi. Ounasvaara, near Rovaniemi, has 40 kilometers of marked ski tracks, 10 kilometers of illuminated tracks and facilities for equipment rental. Lodgings are available at the center, as well as in Rovaniemi.

Pyhätuntur. Located at Pelkosenniemi, 50 kilometers north of Kemijärvi. Has 50 kilometers of marked ski tracks, ski instruction, facilities for equipment rental and accommodation. Also organizes ski weeks.

Saariselkä. This is one of the best-known long-distance hiking and skiing regions in northern Finland and is the largest complete fell area in the country. It is located 250 kilometers north of Rovaniemi and 40 kilometers south of Ivalo. Numerous ski touring routes are possible. Facilities exist for ski instruction, equipment rental, accommodation and guided, week-long ski trips.

Sallantunturi. Located 150 kilometers east of Rovaniemi. Has marked ski tracks, facilities for equipment rental and accommodation. Also organizes guided ski trips, some to watch reindeer roundups.

Suomuntunturi. Located on the Arctic Circle in the Kemijärvi rural district, 130 kilometers east of Rovaniemi. Has two marked tracks, 3 and 18 kilometers in length, facilities for equipment rental and accommodation. Also organizes guided ski trips.

Yllästunturi. Located in the village of Äkäslompolo, in the Ylläs fell district, south of the Pallas-Ounastunturi National Park. Has marked tracks, ski instruction, facilities for equipment rental and accommodation. Organizes guided ski trips. During the holiday seasons it is also possible to take part in the Five Fells skiing expedition covering the Kesänki, Lainio, Pyhä, Kukas and Kuer fells.

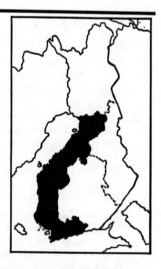

South & West Coasts

The south and west coasts of Finland are studded with rocky inlets, sandy bays, dunes and harbors cluttered with the masts of fishing boats and pleasure craft bobbing side by side on the tide. There are many small villages with wooden houses and narrow alleys, seaports, and cities with textile mills, leather-goods factories, glass works and large industrial plants. There are also many historical sites. The first Swedish adventurers visited this region as early as the 12th century, and today many towns in the region have a high percentage of Swedish-speaking people. Inland, there are wooded glens, hills, rock masses and broad gravel ridges left over from the Ice Age. In the north, broad fertile fields stretch across Ostrobothnia between low-lying peatlands and forests. And on the southwest tip of Finland, the string of islands that make up the Archipelago stretches across the sea between Finland and Sweden. Narrow sea inlets, some resembling the fjords of Norway, penetrate deeply inland on many of the islands. Much of the eastern part of the Archipelago has remained virtually untouched until recent times—a region of wilderness and wildlife that is sparsely populated throughout most of the year. Lodgings are limited and supplies are provided by mobile boat shops that visit the islands during the summer. But you can rent a cottage and use it as a base for wilderness trips in both summer and winter. You will, however, need a boat.

Footpaths on the south and west coasts are scattered. Most routes are short and are found only near towns, although there are several possibilities for longer cross-country hikes. There also are marked and illuminated cross-country ski tracks near many towns, though fewer tracks are found here than in other regions of Finland.

Useful Addresses

See *Address Directory*:

Ålands Turistförening. Provides general tourist information on the Archipelago. Can provide help in reaching the two footpaths on the islands—the 20-kilometer *Kejsarleden*, from the remains of the fortress of Bomarsund in Sund, through Viken in Saltvik (overnight lodgings) to Soltuna, a tourist center in Geta; and a five-kilometer path from Soltuna down to the seashore. Both paths are marked by cairns; neither has tent sites. Since camping is not allowed outside designated campgrounds, you must stay in lodgings at Sund, Viken and Soltuna. Further information is available from the tourist office staff. The staff speaks Swedish, Finnish, English and German.

Haminan Kaupungin Matkailutoimisto (Hamina City Tourist Office). Provides general tourist information on the city of Hamina, located on the southern coast of Finland near the Soviet border (see warning about crossing border at the end of the introduction to this chapter). There are five footpaths near the town, ranging from 2 to 5 kilometers in length (three of which are covered with sawdust), and 10 cross-country ski tracks, ranging from 2.5 to 10 kilometers in length (total length: 54 kilometers). All are marked. Further information is available from the tourist office staff. The staff speaks Finnish, Swedish, English, German and Russian.

Hangö Stads Turistbyrå. Provides general tourist information on the port of Hangö, located on the southernmost tip of Finland, east of Helsinki. There are two marked footpaths on the outskirts of the town, both of which are five kilometers in length, and can be combined for a 10-kilometer hike. The tourist office staff will mark the route on a map if you drop into the office. The staff speaks Swedish, Finnish, English and German.

Helsinki City Tourist Office. Provides general tourist information on Helsinki. Also publishes a series of city walking guides and can provide a map of bicycle routes in the city. Staff speaks Finnish, Swedish, English, German and French. Useful publications include:

• *Pyöräilyreitti/Cykelrutt.* A six-color map drawn in a scale of 1:30,000 on which bicycle routes throughout Helsinki have been drawn in red. Information on the map is in Finnish and Swedish.

• *Kävelykierros Helsingissä/På rundvandrig i Helsingfors/A walking tour in Helsinki/Auf Rundwanderung in Helsinki.* A series of route descriptions and maps to four different walking tours through the streets of Helsinki. The walks take you through areas of scenic and historic interest. Two of the walks are 3.5 kilometers in length; the others are 5 and 5.5 kilometers in length. The series is available in four languages: Finnish, Swedish, English and German.

Hyvinkään Kaupunki (Hyvinkää Municipal Recreation Office). Provides general tourist information on the town of Hyvinkää, located 56 kilometers north of Helsinki. The staff speaks Finnish, Swedish, English and German. Useful publications available from the office include:

• *Hyvinkään Kaupunki vapaa-aikatoimisto kartta: Sveitsin Kuntorata ja ulkoilureitit.* A sketch map in a scale of 1:10,000 on which a keep-fit track, divided into 1-, 3-, 5- and 7-kilometer loops, and a footpath and cross-country ski track, marked with orange streamers and paint, have been indicated. The footpaths and tracks are located in a forest-and-hill region to the west of the town. Information on the map is written in Finnish.

• *Hyvinkään Kaupunki Kiintorastikartta.* A four-color orienteering map in a scale of 1:25,000. Shows the locations of fixed orienteering posts in the forest-and-hill regions surrounding the town. Also shows several footpaths, most of which are unmarked. Information on the map is written in Finnish.

• *Hyvinkään Latuverkosto.* A sketch map in a scale of 1:100,000. Shows the locations of the cross-country ski tracks and outdoor cottages around Hyvinkää. The ski tracks are marked with orange plastic streamers. Their total length is 69.1 kilometers.

Keski-Pohjanmaan Matkailutoimisto (Central Ostrobothnia Tourist Office). Provides general tourist information on the city of Kokkola, located slightly more than midway up the west coast of Finland. Also can provide information on hiking in the province of Central Ostrobothnia, the eastern part of which contains the largest wilderness area in southern Finland. The staff speaks Finnish, Swedish, English and German. Among the hiking routes the office can provide information on are:

—Laajalahti. A recreational area seven kilometers south of Kokkola, with sand dunes and several short forest paths. There are also fixed orienteering posts. Orienteering maps are available from the tourist office. The office will also arrange contacts with orienteering organizations.

—Seljesåsen Holiday Village. Located 34 kilometers southeast of Kokkola in a region with lakes, forests and ridges. There are several short paths around the holiday village.

—Maasydämmenjärvi Holiday Village. A campsite with cottages located between Kikkola and Haapajärvi in eastern Ostrobothnia, about 30 kilometers north of the town of Reisjärvi. Several short footpaths wind through the forests around the campsite.

—Susisaari Holiday Village. Located on an island in a lake near the town of Reisjärvi. There are several trails in the wilderness region surrounding the lake. A long-distance hiking route, starting near the holiday village and extending nearly 80 kilometers to the south, is currently being cleared and marked.

—Valkeisenjärvi Holiday Village. Located 17 kilometers north of the town of Kinnula. There are several paths around the holiday village, in addition to the 80-kilometer route between Susisaari and Humalajoki.

—Iso-Koirajärvi. A large sport fishing area with several footpaths. Located in the eastern part of the province between Kinnula and Kvyjärvi. Accessible only on unpaved back roads.

—Humalajoki. A small country village with several hiking paths. Located near Perho, about 110 kilometers southeast of Kokkola. End point of the 80-kilometer hiking route between Humalajoki and Susisaari.

Full details on how to reach these areas are available from the tourist office. The office staff can also make reservations in the lodgings for you, make arrangements for guides and tell you which maps you will need to hike in the wilderness regions surrounding the various holiday villages.

Naantalin Kaupungin Matkailutoimisto (Naantali City Tourist Office). Provides general tourist information on the town of Naantali, located on the southwestern tip of Finland. The staff speaks Finnish, Swedish, English and German. A useful publication includes:

• *Hiihtoreitit.* A mimeographed sketch map on which the routes of cross-country ski tracks and footpaths surrounding the town are marked. In total, 34 kilometers of footpaths are indicated on the map. It also shows several ski tracks that each winter are marked across the ice in the town's harbor. All the routes are marked with colored plastic streamers. Several campsites located on the paths are indicated on the sketch map.

Turku City Tourist Office. Provides general tourist information on the city of Turku, located on the southwestern tip of Finland, and on the Archipelago. There is a 10-kilometer marked footpath on the island of Ruissalo near the town. The island also has a campsite and hotel. In the city there are 11 keep-fit trails, ranging from one to six kilometers in length, which are used as cross-country ski routes during the winter. An additional 100 kilometers of marked cross-country ski tracks, some of which are illuminated, surround the town. Full details are available from the tourist office. The staff speaks Finnish, Swedish, English and German.

Vaasan Kaupunki Matkailutoimisto (Vaasa City Tourist Office). Provides general tourist information on the city of Vaasa, located midway up the west coast of Finland. Also can provide information on a 15-kilometer footpath located on an island northwest of the city. Staff speaks Swedish, Finnish, English and German.

Varsinais-Suomen Matkailu-Yhdistys. Provides information on the regions around Turku, the oldest city in Finland, as well as on southwestern Finland's Archipelago. Brochures are available in Finnish, Swedish, English and German.

Maps

For planning hikes and ski tours it is advisable to purchase the 1:200,000 *Suomen Tiekartta GT.* These will help you locate hiking and cross-country skiing routes, show you where lodgings are located along the routes and aid you in determining which of the larger-scale maps you will need to follow the routes. The following GT maps cover the south and west coasts:

The South Coast (including the areas surrounding Hamina, Hangö, Helsinki and Hyvinkää): Suomen Tiekartta GT 1:200,000, sheets 2 and 3.

Southwestern Finland and the Archipelago: Suomen Tiekartta GT 1:200,000, sheet 1, or *Matkailukartat* (Touring Maps) 1:100,000, two sheets: *Åland Ahvenanmaa* and *Turku.*

The West Coast: Suomen Tiekartta GT 1:200,000, sheets 4 and 7.

Central Ostrobothnia: Suomen Tiekartta GT 1:200,000, sheet 10.

Guidebooks

At the moment, none. You can, however, check with Suomen Matkailuliitto to see if its guidebook *Etelä-Suomen Retkeilyopas* (Hiking Trails in Southern Finland) has been reissued.

Suggested Walks

See the information listed under *Useful Addresses* above.

Cross-Country Skiing

One winter sports center is located near Hyvinkää, 56 kilometers north of Helsinki, with marked cross-country ski tracks, ski instruction, facilities for equipment rental and accommodation. Another center is located at Vammala/Ellivuori, 50 kilometers west of Tampere.

Several other towns also have marked cross-country ski tracks near the town limits. Information on some of these is listed under *Useful Addresses* above. For further information, contact Suomen Latu or the local tourist office in the area in which you wish to ski.

Address Directory

A

- *Äkäs Hoielli*, SF-95970 Äkäslompolo. Tel. (995) 72/9171.
- *Akateeminen Kirjakauppa* (The Academic Bookstore), Keskuskatu 1, St-00100 Helsinki 10. Tel. (90) 65 11 22.
- *Alands Turistförening*, Norra Esplanadgatan 1, SF-22100 Marie hamm. Tel. (928) 12 140.

E

- *Emergency:*
  —On telephones with all the numerals (0 to 9) on the dialing disk: Dial 0 for the operator.
  —On telephones with only 0 and 9 on the dialing disk: Dial 09 for the operator.
  —On telephones with no dialing disk: If there is a button on the telephone: a) lift the receiver, and b) press the button for the operator.
  —If there is no button on the telephone: Lift the receiver for the

operator; tell the operator to connect you to the police (in Finnish: Poliisi pronounced: Poli:si.

- *Enontekiö Park Warden* Tel. (996) 51 261.
- *Eräoppaitten Yhdistys*, Chairman: Teuvo Katajamaa, SF-99835 Laanila. Tel. (997) 81 816.

F

- *Finland National Tourist Office*, 75 Rockefeller Plaza, New York, New York 10019. Tel. (212) 582-2802.
- *Finnish Tourist Board*, Helsinki, Kluuvikatu 8, SF-00100 Helsinki 10. Tel. (90) 650 155.
- *Finnish Tourist Board*, London UK Office. Finland House Annexe, 53-54 Haymarket, London SW1Y 4RP. Tel. (01) 839 4048.
- *Forestry Administration, Hämeenlinna District Office.* Tel. (917) 25 663.
- *Forestry Administration, Homantsi District Office.* Tel. (974) 1158.
- *Forestry Administration, Inari District Office.* Tel. (997) 11 951.
- *Forestry Administration, Kuusamo District Office.* Tel. (989) 2421.
- *Forestry Administration, Saarijärvi District Office.* Tel. (944) 21 662.
- *Forestry Administration, Savonlinna District Office.* Tel. (957) 21 051.
- *Forestry Administration, Vaala District Office.* Tel. (981) 65 131.
- *Forestry Research Institute, North Finland District,* Rovaniemi. Tel. (991) 15 721.

H

- *Haminan Kaupungin Matkailutoimisto* (Hamina City Tourist Office), Pikkuympyrankatu 5, SF-49400 Hamina. Tel. (952) 41 770.
- *Hangö Stads Turistbyrä.* Boulevarden 5, PB 14, SF-10901 Hangö. Tel. (911) 82 239 and 81 800.
- *Helsinki City Tourist Office,* Pohjoisesplanadi 19, SF-00100 Helsinki 10. Tel. (90) 1623 217 and 1693 757.
- *Hyvinkään Kaupunki* (Hyvinkää Municipal Recreation Office), Hyvinkäänkatu 1, SF-05800 Hyvinkää. Tel. (914) 11 920.

I

- *Ilmatieteen laitos* (Institute of Weather Science), Vuorikatu 24, SF-00100 Helsinki 10. Tel. (90) 17 19 22.
- *Ilomantsin Kunta.* Tel. (974) 1114.

114 FINLAND

- *Imatran Kaupungin Matkailutoimisto* (Imatra City Tourist Office), Keskusliikenreasema PL 22, SF-55121 Imatra 12. Tel. (954) 23 333 and 23 444.
- *Inarin Matkailuyhdistys,* P.O.B. 26, SF-99801, Ivalo. Tel. (997) 67 537.

K

- *Kainuu Tourist Service,* PL 79, SF-89601. Ämmänsaari. Tel. (987) 81 565.
- *Kainuun Matkailupalvelu* (Kainuu Tourist Service), Pohjolankatu 21 B, SF-87100 Kajaani 10. Tel. (986) 25 079.
- *Kaupungin Matkailutoimisto Lappeenranta* (Lappeenranta Town Tourist Office), Valtakatu 23, P.O.B. 113, SF-53101 Lappeenranta 10. Tel. (953) 13 120.
- *Kaupungin Matkailutoimisto Savonlinna* (Savonlinna City Tourist Office), Olavinkatu 35, SF-57130 Savonlinna/Nyslott 13. Tel. (957) 23 492.
- *Kemijärven Kaupungin Matkailutoimisto,* Hallituskatu 7, SF-98100 Kemijärvi. Tel. (992) 11 926 or 11 956.
- *Keski-Pohjanmaan Matkailutoimisto* (Central Ostrobothnia Tourist Office), Pitkansillankatu 39, SF-67100 Kokkola 10. Tel. (968) 11 902.
- *Keski-Suomen Maakuntaliitto,* Kauppakatu 22 A, SF-40100 Jyväskylä 10. Tel. (941) 14 720.
- *Keski-Suomi/Loma-Suomi,* Vapaudenkatu 38, SF-40100 Jyväskylä 10. Tel. (941) 17 150 and 10 866.
- *Kiilopään Koulutuskeskus* (Kiilopää Training Center), SF-99800, Ivalo. Tel. (997) 87 101.
- *Kiilopään Koulutuskeskos,* SF-9980 Ivalo. Tel. (997) 87 101.
- *Kilpisiärven Retkeilykeskus,* SF-99490 Kilpisjärvi. Tel. (996) 710.
- *Kittilän Kunnantoimisto Matkailuasiamies,* SF-99100 Kittilä. Tel. (994) 64/Kunta or 64/Kittilä 217.
- *Kunnantoimisto Matkailuasiamies,* SF-99400 Enontekio. Tel. (996) 51 261.
- *Kuopion Kaupungin Matkailutoimisto* (Kuopio City Tourist Office), Haapaniemenkatu 17, SF-70100 Kuopio 10. Tel. (971) 81 411 and 81 442.
- *Kuusamon Lomat Oy/Kuusamon Matkailutoimisto,* Kitkantie 20, SF-93600 Kuusamo. Tel. (989) 2412 and 2662.

L

- *Lahden Matkailutoimisto* (Lahti City Tourist Office), Hollolankatu 1, SF-15110 Lahti 11. Tel. (918) 40 141.
- *Lapin Matkailu,* Pekankatu 3 A, SF-96200 Rovaniemi 20. Tel. (991) 16 550.
- *Lieksan Kaupungin Matkailutoimisto* (Lieksa City Tourist Office), Pielisentie 3, SF-81700 Lieksa. Tel. (985) 21 400.

M

- *Maa-jametsätalousministeriön luunnonhoitotoimisto* (Bureau of Natural Resources, Ministry of Agriculture and Forestry), Hallituskatu 3 A, SF-00170 Helsinki 17. Tel. (90) 1601.
- *Maanmittaushallituksen Kartanmyynti* (Map Service of the National Board of Survey), PL 209, SF-00131 Helsinki 13. Tel. direct: (90) 660 554. Tel. operator: (90) 175 811.

N

- *Naantalin Kaupungin Matkailutoimisto* (Naatali City Tourist Office), Tullikatu 11, SF-21100 Naantali. Tel. (921) 751 090.

P

- *Pallasjärvi Park Warden,* Tel. (996) 8327.
- *Partio Aitta,* Yrjönkatu 34, SF-00100 Helsinki 10. Tel. (90) 643 622.
- *Pirkanmaan Taival,* Aleksis Kiven katu 14 B, SF-33210 Tampere 21. Tel. (931) 26 775.

R

- *Rokua Park holiday center.* Tel. (981) 427 613.
- *Rovaniemen Kaupunki Matkailutoimisto* (Rovaniemi City Tourist Office), Aallonkatu 2, SF-96200 Rovaniemi 20. Tel. (991) 16 270.
- *Rovaniemi Park Warden.* Tel. (991) 19 027.

S

- *Saariselän Retkeilykeskus* (Saariselkä Hiking Center), SF-99830 Saariselkä. Tel. (997) 81 826.
- *Silja Line (Stockholm) Ab,* P.O.B. 7070, S-103 82 Stockholm 7. Tel. (08) 226 660.

- *Silja Line, Reservations:* E. Makasiinikatu 4, P.O.B. 138, SF-00130 Helsinki 13. Tel. (90) 10 833.
- *Silja Line, Sales and Ticket Office:* Etelä esplanadi 14, SF-00130 Helsinki 13. Tel. (90) 13 133.
- *Suomen Latu* (Finnish Ski Track Association), Fabianink 7, SF-00130 Helsinki 3. Tel. (90) 17 01 01.
- *Suomen Matkailuliitto* (Finnish Travel Association), Mikonkatu 25, SF-00100 Helsinki 10. Tel. (90) 17 08 68.
- *Suomen Retkeilymajajärjestö* (Finnish Youth Hostel Association), Yriö nkatu 38 B, SF-00100 Helsinki 10. Tel. (90) 602 377.

T

- *Tamperen Kaupungin Matkailutoimisto* (Tampere City Tourist and Congress Service), Aleksis Kiven katu 14 B, SF-33210 Tampere 21. Tel. (931) 26 652 and 26 775.
- *Turku City Tourist Office,* Käsityöläiskatu 4, SF-20100 Turku 10. Tel. (921) 335 366.

U

- *Urheilukeskus,* SF-15110 Lahti. Tel. (918) 49 811.

V

- *Vaasan Kauounki Matkailutoimisto* (Vaasa City Tourist Office), Kaupungintalo, SF-65100 Vaasa 10. Tel. (961) 13 853.
- *Valkeakosken Kaupungin Matkailutoimisto* (Valkeakoski City Tourist Office), Sääksmäentie 2, SF-37600 Valkeakoski. Tel. (937) 41 800.
- *Varsinais-Suomen Matkailu-Yhdistys,* L-Rantakatu 13, SF-20100 Turku. Tel. (921) 11 333.
- *Viking Line, Helsinki,* Mannerheimintie 14, SF-00100 Helsinki 10. Tel. (90) 607 088.
- *Viking Line, Stockholm,* Stureplan 8, S-114 35 Stockholm. Tel. (08) 222 480.

A Quick Reference

In a hurry? Turn to the pages listed below. They will give you the most important information on walking in Finland.

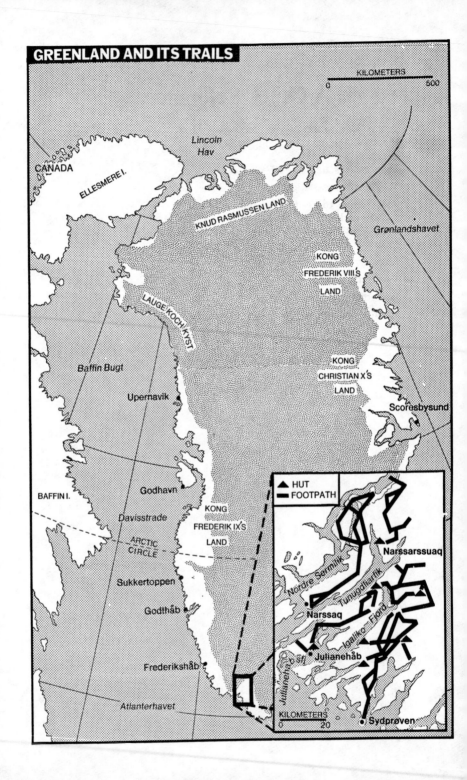

GREENLAND AND ITS TRAILS

KILOMETERS
0   500

Lincoln
Hav

CANADA

ELLESMERE I.

KNUD RASMUSSEN LAND

Grønlandshavet

KONG
FREDERIK VIII'S
LAND

LAUGE KOCH KYST

Baffin Bugt

KONG
CHRISTIAN X'S
LAND

Scoresbysund

Upernavik

Godhavn

BAFFIN I.

Davisstrade

ARCTIC
CIRCLE

KONG
FREDERIK IX'S
LAND

Sukkertoppen

Godthåb

Frederikshåb

Atlanterhavet

▲ HUT
■ FOOTPATH

Nordre Sermlik

Tunugdliarfik

Narssarssuaq

Narssaq

Igaliko Fjord

Julianehåb

Julianehåb

Sydprøven

KILOMETERS
0   20

Greenland

GREENLAND IS GEOGRAPHICALLY more a part of North America than of Europe. It is, however, a principality of Denmark and virtually all arrangements for hiking on the island are handled by Dansk Vandrelaug in Copenhagen.

With an area of 2,175,600 square kilometers (839,781 square miles), Greenland is the world's largest island—nearly 52 times the size of Denmark. Of its land area, 86 percent, or 1,833,900 square kilometers, is covered by ice. In some places, the massive ice cap is more than 2,700 meters (8,800 feet) thick. Along the coasts, granite peaks rise to an altitude of 3,733 meters (12,247 feet), towering above translucent blue icebergs that float in the sea. Deep fjords up to 300 kilometers in length indent the coastline, which is nearly 39,500 kilometers long—equivalent to the circumference of the entire earth at the equator.

Over much of the island, the glacial ice cap stretches its mighty paws into every valley, pushing crags and mountains into the sea with artillery-like crashes. But Greenland is not all glacier or polar ice. An area as big as Norway, or about 341,700 square kilometers, is free of ice. In the extreme south, flocks of sheep graze unattended for the greater part of the year. At Søndre Strømfjord, where plans are underway to create a system of hikers' huts similar to those in Sweden and Norway, fallow deer and musk oxen graze on mountainsides covered with a vividly colored Arctic vegetation. Along the west coast, the wooden houses of isolated fishing villages perch on the edges of the fjords. And along the north and east coasts, polar bear roam.

The island is the homeland of the largest Eskimo population in the world, the early ancestors of whom crossed Smith Sound from Canada with their dogs nearly 4,000 years ago. These were the Sarqaq, a Stone Age people who lived largely by reindeer hunting until about 500 B.C., when Greenland's mild climate grew cold again. For the next 500 years, Greenland was uninhabited. Then, about the time of Christ's birth, the Dorset race arrived from the West, a nomadic people who left images of themselves carved in wood and are considered to be the world's first igloo builders.

In the Viking Age, Greenland became the first place to be colonized in the Western Hemisphere when Norwegian and Icelandic settlers arrived in South Greenland around the year 986. The Viking settlements existed for five centuries and at one time included 300 farms and 16 churches as well as their own episcopal seat and two monasteries. Then in the 1500s, the colonies disappeared into the mists of legend and hearsay, leaving a few remains—and the Eskimos, who had created a highly developed hunting skill and, with the Greenland whale and seal as their source of food, warmth and clothing, spread their settlements in an almost continuous circle around the island.

In the 1700s, Greenland was rediscovered by Europeans and again colonized in 1721 by the dual kingdoms of Denmark and Norway. During the next two centuries, English, Scottish, Dutch and Basque whalers visited the island, as did explorers in search of the fabled Northwest Passage. Slowly, the Eskimos intermarried with Danes and Norwegians, and the concept of the Greenlander—or *Kalatdlit*—came into being.

Today, the island has a population of 49,500 inhabitants who live in scattered settlements, which range from small communities with a self-help hunter culture to modern towns with 3,000 to 4,000 inhabitants.

The human settlements, however, almost shrink into insignificance when compared with the rest of the island. Most of Greenland is still a vast, untouched wilderness of magnificent Arctic scenery, where the Midnight Sun sparkles over endless ice fields during the long summer months, and the Northern Lights sweep in violet curtains across the darkened winter skies.

Tourism is relatively new to the island (the first party of tourists arrived from Iceland on August 5, 1960)—and vastly different from anywhere else. The town-to-town distances are enormous, and transportation between them is by either helicopter or coastal steamer. Sometimes there can be up to three days—or even weeks in the more isolated spots—before the next plane or ship departs. The bigger towns have modern facilities and shops which can supply most of your needs. But the villages in the more isolated "outer" districts are not as well equipped, and you must sometimes bring your own sleeping bag and supplies of food if you expect to visit them. Telephone connections between Greenlandic towns are also rare and, where they exist, very expensive. As a result, it is difficult to travel on an individual basis in Greenland. You cannot casually go to the first town of your choosing and decide to move on when you feel like it. All travel arrangements must be carefully planned and you must make your hotel reservations prior to arrival in Greenland. In addition, ice, fog and storms can sometimes keep you weather-bound for days, or even weeks, and turn your travel plans (and budget) inside out.

In the principal hiking regions—around Narssarssuaq, Narssaq and Julianehåb in the south and along Søndre Strømfjord on the west coast— the terrain is rugged, the Arctic climate susceptible to sudden and unpredictable weather changes and the facilities for shelter limited. There are no trails or marked hiking routes. Instead, you must navigate by map and compass through regions with steep escarpments, deep rivers and scrub-covered slopes. The Dansk Vandrelaug in Copenhagen has, in cooperation with local sheep farmers and municipalities, opened seven mountain huts in South Greenland.

The huts provide a good base for tours of one to several days' duration. But none of the huts accommodate more than 20 people and to stay in them you must purchase a special permit from Dansk Vandrelaug in Copenhagen. Also, because the number of huts is limited, a tent and sleeping bag are virtual necessities for most hikes.

This combination of physically demanding terrain, extreme weather conditions and the difficulties of navigation across the island's untracked wilds makes Greenland a supreme challenge for the highly experienced wilderness hiker: a virgin land of glaciers, waterfalls, soaring mountains, iceberg-speckled lakes and torrential rivers where you must be totally self-reliant. It is no place for the casual or even moderately experienced hiker. There are some hiking routes with gradual ascents and easily followed landmarks, but a change in weather can make even these difficult or impossible to follow. Also, the facilities for a mountain rescue are still in their infancy, and rescue operations are greatly handicapped by the sheer size of the island and its fickle weather conditions. The only way a rescue party can know you are in trouble is if you are overdue or if a companion hikes out and tells them. Consequently, if one of the members of your party is injured, several days may pass before help arrives.

For these reasons, even experienced mountain walkers are advised to take part in one of the guided hiking tours arranged by the Dansk Vandrelaug or jointly by the Deutscher Alpenverein (German Alpine Club) and Österreichischer Alpenverein (Austrian Alpine Club).

These tours span varying grades of difficulty and are available for a duration of a few days up to several weeks. Special interest hikes are also available for those interested in botany, ornithology, zoology, geology, archeology and fishing.

The tours are by far the best way to introduce yourself to Greenland—if only because all the arrangements for food, transportation and lodgings are taken care of for you, while the problems of route finding are the responsibility of an experienced guide.

Should you prefer to hike on your own, you should nonetheless contact Dansk Vandrelaug well in advance of your arrival for specific information on the routes you intend to follow. Three 1:100,000 mountain maps and a Danish-language guidebook to hiking in South Greenland, prepared for the Udvalget for Vandreturisme I Grønland, can also be purchased from the Dansk Vandrelaug.

Flora & Fauna

Greenland's sparse vegetation is typical of Arctic tundra everywhere, consisting of shrubby heaths, sedges and turflike grasses sprinkled with a colorful diversity of hardy flowering plants. Around the fjords in the south there are two- to three-meter high willow-scrubs and, in some places, scattered birches.

The most important land animals are the reindeer, musk ox, polar bear, Arctic fox, lemming and Arctic hare. Coastal seas support whales, walrus and seals, all of which are hunted by the Greenlanders, particularly in the northern and eastern parts of the island. Land birds include the rock ptarmigan, eagle, falcon, snowy owl, grouse and snow bunting. Eider-ducks, auks, guillemots and many types of gulls breed along the coast.

During the summer, mosquitoes, midges and black flies can become a problem, and you will need a good supply of insect repellent to keep them away. All tents should have tightly meshed, gap-free insect netting. Insect netting to protect your face is also advisable.

Snakes are a different matter; none exist in Greenland. Polar bears do not roam in the principal walking areas so they rarely pose a danger.

Climate

Although Greenland stretches as far south as Oslo, its climate is much cooler. The polar current carries vast masses of ice from the Arctic Ocean down the island's east coast and around Cape Farewell, cooling the coastal areas. This produces a typical Arctic climate characterized by extreme weather conditions such as snow and ice storms, fog and, at higher altitudes, icing conditions. Weather changes along the coast are often sudden and may be accompanied by a severe temperature drop. The difference between daytime and nighttime temperatures can also be great.

Average daytime temperatures during the summer range from about 20°C. (68°F.) in the south to 5°C. (37°F.) in the north. Winter temperatures in the south rarely drop below *minus* 20°C. *(minus* 4°F.), but in the north they can plunge down to *minus* 40°C. *(minus* 40°F.).

Summer—from the beginning of June until the end of September—is the best time to hike. In the south, precipitation during this period is usually (but not always) in the form of rain. Normally, the greatest amount of precipitation falls during the month of July. Once or twice during the summer, a *fön* storm usually occurs in South Greenland. The *fön* is like a hurricane, starting with a perceptible rise in temperature, with heavy gusts of wind which grow stronger until, in the course of a few hours, they have reached hurricane force. Weather of this kind rarely lasts more than three days, often less. But it is not something to be caught unprepared in.

As the Julianehåb Turistforening advises: "The climate changes from region to region and from year to year, as do the drifting ice-conditions. The only thing you can predict is that it is absolutely unpredictable."

In other words, the best thing you can do is to be prepared for everything, including unforeseen difficulties and delays due to bad weather.

Weather Forecasts

Weather forecasts—as far as they can be trusted—are broadcast by radio from Godthåb and Julianehåb. No recorded telephone weather forecasts are available. The times of the forecasts are:

Godthåb radio, .700 megacycles: 7:30 a.m., 12:30 p.m. and 6:10 p.m. In Danish.

Julianehåb radio, 2129 kilocycles and WHF channel 24-25-26: 4:35 a.m., 10:35 a.m., 4:35 p.m. and 10:35 p.m. In Danish and English.

Where to Get Walking Information

For all information on hiking, climbing, glacier treks, the locations and availability of space in mountain huts, the hire of mountain guides and details on hiking tours, you should contact:

Dansk Vandrelaug (for its address and telephone number, see the *Address Directory* at the back of this chapter). Open weekdays from 9:30 a.m. to 5 p.m. and Saturdays from 9:30 a.m. to 12:30 p.m. Staff speaks Danish, English and German.

The DVL sells the only hiking maps and guidebook that have been published on Greenland to date. In addition, it can provide a brochure, entitled *Greenland Tours,* that contains full details on its guided hiking trips to Greenland. The brochure is available in both Danish and English.

Once you are in Greenland, questions about last minute details can be answered by the local tourist offices.

Letters to the local tourist offices are not always answered. Also, arrangements for overnight stays in the mountain huts and bookings for hiking tours are handled only by the Dansk Vandrelaug. Hence, if you plan to hike in Greenland it is essential that you contact the DVL before you arrive to ensure you obtain the proper information and do not overlook any necessary details.

Walking Clubs in Greenland

Walking clubs and alpine societies do not exist in Greenland. Instead, a private committee, known as the *Udvalget for Vandreturisme I Grønland*, is working in cooperation with local authorities to develop hiking in Greenland by publishing maps and route descriptions and establishing mountain huts. The committee is made up of the Dansk Vandrelaug as well as several Danish climbing clubs, including the Dansk Bjergklub, Spejdernes Fjeldgruppe, Dansk Fjeldvandrerklub, Katangut-gruppen and Grønlænderforeningen. The headquarters for the committee is in the Dansk Vandrelaug office in Copenhagen.

Maps

The best maps for hiking in Greenland are published by the Udvalget for Vandreturisme I Grønland:

* *Fjeldkort 1:100,000 over Narssarssuaq, Narssaq og Julianehåb*, one sheet.
* *Fjeldkort 1:100,000 over Søndre Strømfjord*, one sheet.
* *Fjeldkort 1:100,000 over Holsteinsborg*, one sheet.

The maps are overprinted with magnetic meridians to facilitate compass adjustments and are the most detailed topographical maps available to these areas. They can be purchased by mail from the Dansk Vandrelaug or in Greenland from the Julianehåb Turistforening (see *Address Directory*). When purchasing the maps you should specify whether you want the regular editions or the plastic-coated weatherproof editions. Advance payment is required for mail orders.

The rest of Greenland is covered by six series of maps published by the Geodætisk Institut in Copenhagen. Among these maps are:

Grønland 1:1,000,000. This is a series of topographical maps that will eventually cover all of Greenland. The maps are compiled in accordance with the specifications of the International Civil Aviation Organization, but without aeronautical information. Of the 14 maps planned, 8 have been published. They cover the majority of the island below a latitude of 76° North. While not suitable for hiking, these are the most detailed maps available to the ice cap in central Greenland.

Grønland 1:250,000. This is a series of 78 topographical maps which cover the west, south and east coasts of Greenland. Each sheet covers 1° of latitude. Outside of the areas covered by the 1:50,000 maps, these are the best maps available for hiking on the west coast of Greenland. Of the 78 maps, 6 remain to be published.

Grønland 1:50,000. This map series includes 160 sheets covering parts of the west coast and 67 sheets covering a portion of the east coast. The areas covered by the maps on the west coast include:

1. The region between Umanak and Sarqaq above Disko Bay;
2. The region between Christianshåb and Holsteinsborg south of Disko Bay;
3. The western half of Søndre Strømfjord; and
4. The westernmost coastal regions between Sukkertoppen and Godthåb.

The maps, plus free indexes and a price list, can be obtained from:

Geodætisk Institut (see *Address Directory*).

Many of the existing maps use the former spellings of Greenland place names, but a gradual introduction of a new orthography is taking place. As a result, the spellings of place names in route descriptions and tourist publications may not always agree with the way they are spelled on the maps.

Guidebooks

The only guidebook currently available to hiking in Greenland is:

* *Vandreruter i Sydgrønland* by Kirsten Kempel (in Danish), Udvalget for Vandreturisme I Grønland, 1976. Describes seven three- to eight-day hikes in South Greenland, as well as numerous day hikes from the mountain huts in the area. Includes maps. Available by mail from Dansk Vandrelaug (see *Address Directory*).

Trailside Lodgings

The only possibilities for trailside lodgings are in the 15 mountain huts established in South Greenland by the Udvalget for Vandreturisme I Grønland. On some of the hiking tours, you also can stay as the guest of Greenland's sheep breeders. But private accommodation is not arranged by any of the tourist offices when you are on your own, and you cannot depend upon unforeseen hospitality. In the bigger towns, lodgings are available in a variety of hotels. With these, you must make reservations through one of the Greenland tourist offices or a travel agent before you arrive on the island. Elsewhere, you must be prepared to camp.

The mountain huts in South Greenland are located within about a nine-hour walk of each other (in ideal conditions). Hence, a strong walker with a steady pace can walk from hut to hut. The huts are private property and are equipped rather simply (some still do not have mattresses). Most are owned by local sheep breeders, which gives you a chance to meet them. The huts typically accommodate from 12 to 15 people and are open from mid-June until the end of September.

To stay in the huts, you must purchase a special permit, or hut card, from the Dansk Vandrelaug. Without this, you will not be admitted to the huts. In addition, you must pay a nominal nightly fee at each hut. Because space is limited (the largest hut sleeps only 20 people), those who are hiking on their own should notify the DVL of their expected date of arrival. You should also have a sleeping bag and, since food is not available in the huts, all of your provisions.

Camping

Everyone who hikes on their own in Greenland must be prepared to camp—and to do so in severe conditions. Even many of the hiking tours depend upon tents. And on a hut-to-hut hike, if you are unable to reach one of the huts due to bad weather, a tent, sleeping bag and cooking equipment can mean survival.

Tents should be of a dark color to shut out glare from the Midnight Sun. They should also be able to stand up to gale-force winds, keep you dry in chilling rains and be pestproof enough to keep the pesky arctic insects where they belong: outside. Since you may be confined to your tent by the weather (or the bugs) a tent that gives you room to stretch out and store your gear out of the elements will also be appreciated.

In addition, you should have a waterproof ground covering, a sleeping pad to insulate you from cold ground and enough spare food and fuel to see you through a prolonged spell of bad weather.

You are free to camp practically anywhere you wish in Greenland. In the wilds, the only request is that you keep your impact to a minimum by observing basic camping practices. Several camping areas have been established near the bigger towns and you are urged to use these when you are in the vicinity (providing you prefer your tent and sleeping bag to a chance for a soft bed, clean sheets and a hot shower in one of the hotels). Elsewhere, if you are near a settlement, it is only common courtesy to ask permission to camp.

Equipment Notes

In addition to dependable camping equipment and a high-efficiency stove, you should have a wool cap, scarf and mittens; a windproof jacket; full-length raingear that will keep you dry in driving rain; a pair of short gaiters to keep water out of your boot tops; sufficient clothing to keep you warm in freezing—or, in case they occur, sub-freezing—temperatures; a full change of warm, dry clothes in the event the clothing you are wearing becomes wet; sunglasses, sun oil and a sun hat; insect repellent; insect netting for your face; a well-stocked first-aid kit for your entire party; a 50-meter length of 9 mm climbing rope per party to facilitate stream crossings; a map and compass; emergency rations; stout leather hiking boots; and a pair of knee-high rubber boots for soggy terrain.

When you sign up for one of the hiking tours, a detailed equipment list is sent to you. The tour organizers provide the tents, food, first aid supplies, cooking equipment, stoves and other necessary group equipment, such as wading ropes, although tour participants must sometimes help carry it.

Water

Drinking water may be safely taken from any natural source in Greenland. Water taken from lakes, streams and rivers is often cold, and should be allowed to warm up—either by setting your cup in the sun for a few minutes or by holding the water in your mouth before you swallow—to avoid stomach cramps. Water sources are numerous. Nonetheless, it is advisable to carry a water bottle so you can have water at hand if you are pinned down by bad weather in your tent. Carrying water in a water bottle also gives it a chance to warm up to air temperature.

Hiking Tours

The Dansk Vandrelaug organizes a series of 12-, 15- and 21-day hiking tours in Greenland. These range from tours where you are based in a single mountain hut, from which you take day hikes, to glacier treks. All the tours are led by experienced guides and include your roundtrip flight between Copenhagen and Narssarssuaq, local boat transportation, accommodation, meals and third-party liability insurance. The tours, of which there are nearly 10 from which to choose, with up to 40 possible starting dates, run from the end of June until the beginning of September. Full details on each tour, the dates they are available and their prices are included in a free brochure, entitled *Greenland Tours*, available in Danish and English from the Dansk Vandrelaug (see *Address Directory*).

The Österreichischer Alpenverein (Austrian Alpine Club) and Deutscher Alpenverein (German Alpine Club) also jointly organize three tours for 15, 19 and 21 days. Details on these tours are included in the alpine clubs' bi-annual catalogs of climbing courses and mountain tours—*DAV Berg- und Skischule* and *OEAV Bergsteigerschule*—which are available on request from:

> **Berg- und Skischule des Deutschen Alpenvereins** and:
>
> **Bergsteigerschule des Österreichischen Alpenvereins** (see *Address Directory*).

For safety, tour leaders maintain daily radio contact with each other. Also, most of the routes are along the fjords, which can easily be reached by boat in case of an emergency.

Before taking part in one of the tours, it is important to ensure you are physically fit—either by adopting a daily program of physical training, or by taking several extended mountain hikes before departure. Tour leaders are entitled to ask participants they consider unable to complete the walk to discontinue the tour and return by airplane or boat (at their own expense) to the tour base.

The DVL also stresses that "participants will be confronted with primitive conditions and have to adapt themselves to the fact that unforeseen events may happen on the way. The participants and the leader share all the practical duties (cooking, cleaning, setup camp, etc.). The group and the leader, in common, are responsible for the programme. If you can accept these conditions and not expect service at hotel level, an unforgettable adventure will be waiting for you. If not, these tours will be nothing for you."

The tour groups range in size up to a maximum of 15 people.

Expeditions

Greenland still has numerous mountains that have never been scaled and some that are still unnamed. For the experienced climber there are many possibilities for mountaineering, glacier scaling and treks across the ice cap.

Persons traveling to Greenland for these purposes, or to pursue similar sports, must report prior to departure to:

> **Ministry for Greenland** in Copenhagen (see *Address Directory*).

Applications must, among other items, contain information about the purpose of the expedition, destination, number of participants with names and qualifications and estimated duration of stay. Should the Ministry deem the expedition unjustifiable, the undertaking may be prohibited. The

Ministry may also decide that each expedition, prior to departure, must provide a financial guarantee to cover the costs of any possible rescue or search operation.

Useful Addresses & Telephone Numbers

General Tourist Information

For all of Greenland:

Danmarks Turistråd (The Danish Tourist Board). See *Address Directory*. Useful publications include:

- *Greenland: Land of Excitement* (in English). Gives a general description of Greenland, transportation information and several suggestions for sightseeing excursions on the island.
- *Facts about tours to and in Greenland* (in English). Gives good, succinct advice on the practical details of travel to Greenland. Includes descriptions of Greenland's towns and the addresses of tour operators.
- *Greenland: The Disko Bay* (in English). Describes areas of interest around Disko Bay on the west coast of Greenland. Includes information on the possibilities for dog sledding.
- *Greenland: South Greenland* (in English). Gives the most comprehensive information about hiking in Greenland. Also includes suggestions for four 4- to 7-day hiking trips, with brief details on each.

In local areas:

See *Address Directory*:

Godthab Turistkontor, Godthab.

Jakobshavn Turistkontor, Jakobshavn.

Julianehåb Turistkontor, Julianehåb.

Nanortalik Turistkontor, Nanortalik.

Narssaq Turistkontor, Narssaq.

Abroad:

Information on Greenland can be obtained from the branch offices of the Danish Tourist Board in EUROPE: Amsterdam, Brussels, Hamburg, London, Munich, Oslo, Paris, Rome, Salzburg, Stockholm, Zurich; AUSTRALIA: Sydney; JAPAN: Tokyo; and in the U.S.A.: Los Angeles and New York.

In New York: Danish National Tourist Office, 505 Fifth Avenue, New York, New York 10017. Tel. (212) 687-5609.

In London: The Danish Tourist Board, Sceptre House, 169/173 Regent Street, London W1R 8PY. Tel. (01) 734 2637.

Search & Rescue

A mountain rescue service, as exists in most European countries, has not yet been developed in Greenland. Rescue operations depend for the most part on volunteers and existing transportation facilities. Since there are few telephones or radios in the wilds that you can reach to call for help, it is essential that you notify local authorities prior to your departure to give them full details on the route you intend to follow, the number of people in your party and your expected date of return. Then, if you are overdue, the authorities will send out a search party.

In case of an emergency, you should be prepared to send two members of your party back to the nearest settlement for help. One member of your party should also be able to administer qualified first aid since, in certain areas, several days may pass before help arrives.

This situation makes it imperative that you have the proper medical supplies, emergency provisions and equipment to cope with an emergency. Needless to say, you should *never hike alone* in Greenland.

Information on the authorities in each area with whom you should leave a copy of your hiking itinerary is available from the local tourist offices.

How to Get There

The only practical way to reach Greenland is by air. Commercial flights are available from Copenhagen on SAS and from Reykjavik on Icelandic Airlines. The SAS flights serve Søndre Strømfjord four to five times a week during the summer and three times a week in the off-season. SAS also flies to Narssarssuaq twice a week during the summer. Icelandair flies to Narssarssuaq and Kulusuk and takes tourists on conducted tours in Greenland.

Information on the flight schedules and fares is available from the two airlines, as well as from the branch offices of the Danish Tourist Board (see *Address Directory*).

Transportation in Greenland

Helicopters provide most of the internal connections for passengers and mail in Greenland. From Søndre Strømfjord, the *Grønlandsfly* helicopters fly to all towns on the west coast from Frederikshåb in the south to Upernavik in the north. In addition, there are DC-6 aircraft connections to Kulusuk in East Greenland and Narssarssuaq in South Greenland. Coastal steamers operate on the west coast between Upernavik and Julianehåb from April to November, while local boats maintain scheduled service between the coastal towns and smaller communities. There are several conditions that apply to booking helicopter seats, since Greenlandair has to remain flexible in order to answer emergency calls for ambulance and rescue flights and to make connections between coastal steamers and mail drops (which take priority in front of passengers). Also, the schedules for coastal steamers are affected by drifting-ice conditions. For current information on schedules, fares and conditions for booking, you should contact the tourist offices prior to your arrival.

Address Directory

B

• *Berg- und Skishule des Deutschen Alpenvereins,* Fürstenfelderstrasse 7, D-8000 Munich 2, Germany. Tel. (089) 26 90 11.

D

• *Danish National Tourist Office, New York,* 505 Fifth Avenue, New York, New York 10017, U.S.A. Tel. (212) 687-5609.

• *Danish Tourist Board, London,* Sceptre House, 169/173 Regent Street, London W1R 8PY, England. Tel. (01) 734 2637.

• *Danmarks Turistråd* (The Danish Tourist Board), Banegårdspladsen 2, DK-1570 Copenhagen V, Denmark. Tel. (01) 11 14 15.

• *Dansk Vandrelaug,* Kultorvet 7, DK-1175 Copenhagen K, Denmark. Tel. (01) 12 11 65.

G

• *Geodætisk Institut,* Ringsdagsgarden 7, DK-1218 Copenhagen K, Denmark. Tel. (01) 11 60 17, ext. 2653 and 2654.

• *Godthab Turistkontor,* Box 605, DK-3900 Godthab.

J

• *Jakobshavn Turistkontor,* Box 99, DK-3952 Jakobshavn.

• *Julianehåb Turistkontor,* Box 128, DK-3920 Julianehåb. Tel. 38 4 44.

M

• *Ministry for Greenland,* Hausergade 3, DK-1128 Copenhagen K, Denmark.

N

• *Nanortalik Turistkontor,* DK-3922 Nanortalik.

• *Narsaq Turistkontor,* DK-3921 Narsaq.

A Quick Reference

In a hurry? Turn to the pages listed below. They will give you the most important information on walking in Greenland.

Search & Rescue, page 130.

Weather Forecasts, page 123.

Associations to Contact for Information:
   On Walking, page 123.
   On Hiking Tours, page 127.
   On Expeditions, page 128.
   General Tourist Information, page 129.

Maps, page 124.

Guidebooks, page 125.

Equipment, page 127.

Address Directory, page 131.

Iceland

ALTHOUGH ICELAND LIES in the middle of the North Atlantic Ocean, it is considered part of Europe, largely for reasons of history and culture. Today's Icelander is a descendant of Scandinavians from Norway and Celts from Scotland and Ireland, who settled the island in the 9th and 10th centuries A.D. The Scandinavians, however, made up the ruling class, and their language and institutions have dominated Icelandic culture from the beginning.

Europe's oldest parliament, the Althing, was founded in 930 A.D. at Thingvellir, northeast of Reykjavik. This beautiful area of lakes and lava cliffs is now set aside as a national park. Icelanders colonized Greenland—about 290 kilometers to the northwest—around the year 1000. Shortly thereafter, Icelanders led by Leif Eiriksson became the first Europeans to set foot in North America.

Iceland is easily the least densely populated of all European countries, with a quarter-million people inhabiting an island 103,000 square kilometers (39,756 square miles) in size. A third of the population lives in Reykjavik. The remainder is scattered in small coastal towns and villages and on isolated farms located in fertile lowland plains and valleys. The greater part of Iceland is mountainous and uninhabited.

Iceland is a rugged country born of volcanic fires and sculpted by glacial ice. It forms the northern outpost of the Mid-Atlantic Ridge, the great, largely submarine mountain chain that runs down the center of the Atlantic Ocean. The ridge marks the boundary between the great continental plates of Europe and Africa to the east and of the Americas to the west. Volcanic activity is frequent along the ridge, as molten rock from the earth's core pours upward through great rifts and out onto the sea floor. The continental plates move away from the ridge on either side, carrying the lava with them and opening new rifts from which more lava erupts.

Iceland is one of the most active volcanic regions in the world. It contains more than 200 post-Ice Age volcanoes, of which about 30 have erupted since the first settlers arrived. The most recent spectacular eruption occurred in 1973 on the island of Heimaey, off Iceland's southern coast, when 150 million cubic meters of lava poured into the

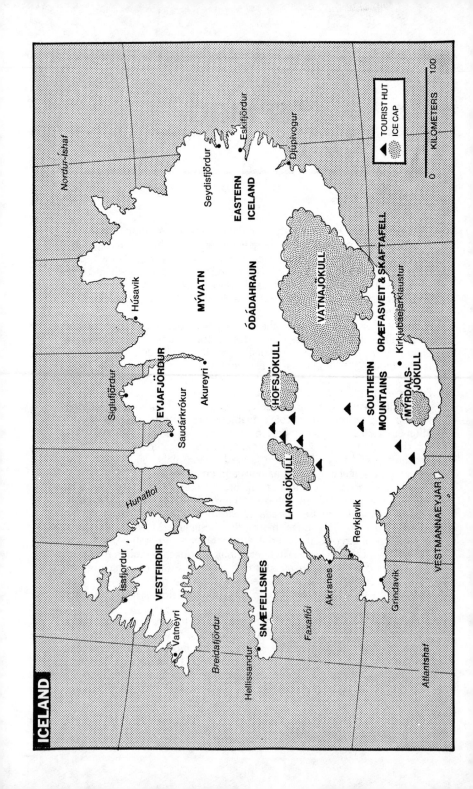

ocean and added 1.7 square kilometers of new land to the island. One-third of the local town was buried in lava, and fire bombs hurled from the volcano burned many buildings. Between 1963 and 1967, three islands rose from the sea in the same region as a result of volcanic eruptions. Of these, only Surtsey—with an area of 2.8 square kilometers—remains.

Iceland is composed entirely of volcanic rocks, mostly basalt. Its numerous mountains consist either of volcanoes or of older lava flows that have been deeply eroded by rivers and glacial ice. Lava fields cover huge areas on the island, especially in the Central Highlands. Other evidences of volcanic activity include geysers, mudpots, sulfur deposits, fumaroles, craters and hot springs.

Volcanic activity, however, has not been the only force shaping the Icelandic landscape. For millions of years, enormous glaciers have been sculpting craggy mountain peaks and gouging out steep-walled glacial valleys. On the north and east coasts in particular, valley glaciers once extended for miles toward the sea. When sea level rose in the warming period following the Ice Age, the waters flooded the lower portions of these valleys, creating the spectacular fjords found along these coasts.

Even during today's relatively warm climatic era, icecaps and glaciers cover 11,800 square kilometers—12 percent of the island. There are four very large icecaps and numerous smaller ones, most located in the southern half of the island, where moisture-bearing southerly winds first strike land and pass over the mountains. Vatnajökull, the largest icecap outside Greenland and Antarctica, sprawls over 8,400 square kilometers in southeastern Iceland. Beneath it and the other large icecaps lie buried volcanoes, which erupt from time to time and thereby produce torrential glacial floods.

Most of Iceland consists of a plateau between 600 and 800 meters in elevation. Here and there, volcanoes rise from the plateau to elevations of 1,000 meters and more. The volcano Hvannadalshnúkur, which is buried beneath Oræfajökull, a subsidiary icecap of Vatnajökull, rises 2,119 meters and is the highest point in Iceland.

Walking opportunities abound in Iceland. You can climb volcanoes, wander up glacial valleys green with meadow and marsh, cross high mountain passes white with perennial snow, follow rocky river gorges, explore the margins of icecaps, ramble across gentle uplands dotted with lakes and streams, scramble along rocky seacliffs where seabirds nest by the thousands or wander through remote valleys among abandoned farms.

Except in the immediate vicinity of settled areas, however, walking in Iceland is a serious business that should not be undertaken without adequate preparation. Most of the principal walking areas are rugged and remote. The weather can change abruptly—and usually does. Snows, freezes and gale-force winds can occur anytime during the summer. Marked footpaths are mostly lacking, although mountain tracks used by motor vehicles often provide walking routes. In many areas, however, cross-country travel is essential. The relatively few trailside huts that exist are small and usually located far more than a day's walk apart. Many areas have no huts whatsoever.

Because of such conditions, only highly experienced and well-equipped wilderness travelers should attempt to walk on their own in Iceland's rugged hinterland. And even they should walk only in the company of at least one, but preferably more, equally experienced companions. Walking in Iceland is a much wilder activity than even in the less populated mountainous regions of Europe. In this it is more akin to hiking in the wilder parts of North America.

Just because you lack experience in wilderness travel, however, does not mean you should not walk in Iceland. A variety of excellent tours and expeditions designed especially for walkers are available to all the principal walking regions on the island (see the section on *Walking Tours* later in this chapter). In many cases you can lay over at one of the Touring Club huts for a few days—time to explore the area on your own—and return on another tour. Some tour agents will also set up special trips for interested groups.

Jeep tracks crisscross the Central Highlands and extend into most other walking areas as well. These provide wilderness thoroughfares not only for the tour vehicles, but for those who plan to walk on their own. Unless you join a tour, access to walking areas is usually available only by four-wheeled vehicles, which can be rented in Reykjavik. It is also possible to walk across Iceland on the jeep tracks, a trip that would take at least two weeks—more if you include layover days.

Icelanders are a friendly people, but unless you speak Icelandic—a distinct Germanic language—communication may be difficult in some of the remoter districts. In Reykjavik and other large towns, many people also speak English or Danish. You will find the people who staff the offices of walking and tourist organizations to be very helpful in planning your walking trip in Iceland.

Flora & Fauna

Only one-quarter of Iceland supports continuous plant cover. Several factors have contributed to the sparsity of vegetation—glaciation past and present, volcanic activity, unfavorable climate and overgrazing. Ancient glaciers stripped the soil mantle from much of the island so that continuous vegetation today is confined largely to areas such as river valleys where soil has been able to accumulate. The Central Highlands are largely devoid of vegetation, for few plants can withstand the combination of cold, brief growing seasons and thin, rocky soils. The few species that do grow in the region are hearty arctic-alpine plants, and even they are sparsely distributed. Recent lava flows also support few or no plants, although several older flows at lower elevations support a distinctive cover of mosses and herbs not found in other areas.

When the first European settlers arrived in Iceland in the 9th century, woods covered the coastal lowlands between the sea and the mountains.

These woods consisted mostly of two species of birch, with a scattering of rowan, aspen and tea-leaved willow. Most of the original woodland was felled for fuel, and subsequent overgrazing, by exposing the soil cover to the wind, prevented the re-establishment of trees. Many formerly wooded areas are now largely or entirely devoid of vegetation. Others, however, support grasses and sedges. The finest remaining stands of birch occur in sheltered lowlands, notably at Hallormsstadarskógur in the east and at Fnjóskadalur and Vaglaskógur in the north. The Icelandic government is currently engaged in a reforestation program and to this end has forbidden grazing in a number of areas. Where this is the case, birch and introduced conifers have thrived.

Trees rarely occur above 400 meters, but meadows and shrubs occupy valley floors and adjacent slopes between 500 and 700 meters. Grasses and sedges are the most common vascular plants on the island. Among them grow a number of showy subarctic herbs and dwarf shrubs such as crowberry, bog whortleberry, bearberry, willow and dwarf birch. Large areas are also given over to combinations of moor, heath and bog.

Iceland's flora is small, consisting of only some 440 species of vascular plants. Most are European in origin, although a large number are circumpolar in distribution. A third of the species are hardy arctic-alpine types well adapted to cold climates, short growing seasons and thin, rocky soils. Iceland also supports some 450 species of lichen and 500 species of moss and allied plants. Lichens and mosses are the first plants to invade bare, rocky areas and in such places often form a distinctive plant cover.

Only one percent of Iceland is cultivated. The primary crop is grass, which is used to feed sheep and other livestock, the country's most important agricultural product. Turnips and potatoes are also grown, and tomatoes and flowers are important greenhouse crops. Another 20 percent of the island is used for grazing.

Only one land mammal—the arctic fox—is native to Iceland, and foxes are still common throughout the island. Reindeer were imported from Norway in the late 18th century, and a large herd still survives in the eastern highlands. Other imported mammals other than livestock include the mink, brown rat, black rat, house mouse and field mouse. Polar bears have occasionally traveled to Iceland on drift ice, but none have survived.

Offshore waters support 17 species of whales in addition to the common seal and gray seal. Fishing is Iceland's main industry, accounting for more than 80 percent of its exports. Cod, haddock, capelin and herring, which are abundant in the rich banks off the island, are the most important commercial species. Iceland's rivers and streams support Atlantic salmon, trout, char, common eel and stickleback.

Although nearly 250 species of birds have been recorded in Iceland, only 72 nest there regularly. Six species are common migratory visitors, and 30 more either winter on the island or visit it each year. Iceland is famous among birdwatchers for the huge nesting colonies on its coastal cliffs, where thousands of guillemots, razorbills, puffins, kitiwakes, fulmars and gannets can be observed. In addition, at least 15 species of waterfowl breed in great profusion at Lake Mývatn in northeastern Iceland.

Notable predators include the Iceland gyrfalcon and rare white-tailed eagle, both of which are protected by law.

There are no reptiles and amphibians in Iceland. The island is also free of biting insects such as black flies and mosquitoes. During July and August, clouds of midges, especially near lakes and wetlands, can be annoying because of their sheer numbers, but they do not bite.

Climate

Straddling the temperate and arctic zones, brushed by both the warm Gulf Stream and cold polar current, Iceland's climate is alternately influenced by northern and southern air masses. Weather can change rapidly—and usually does. Gales can arise out of nowhere at any time of the year. Clear days can suddenly turn gray and cold. Storms buffet the island all months of the year. As Icelanders are fond of saying, "If you don't like the weather, wait a few minutes." But the opposite is also true: you can begin a hike on a warm clear morning and find yourself struggling against wind, cold and snow by midafternoon. The need to be well equipped for almost any climatic contingency cannot be overemphasized. Failure to treat Iceland's changeable climate with due respect can become a matter not of mere discomfort, but of survival.

Winter temperatures are surprisingly mild for a land so far north. For example, in January, the coldest month of the year, the mean daily temperature is *minus* 1° C. (30° F.). The average daytime high and nighttime low for January hover just above and below freezing. And on Reykjavik's warmest day of the month, the temperature may soar to 8° C. (46.5° F.) or more. January temperatures in Reykjavik are thus comparable to those in Copenhagen and range somewhat higher than those in New York and Vienna.

Although winter temperatures are somewhat lower along the north and east coasts, they are still rather mild. And both districts experience higher January maximums resulting from the warm, dry Föhn winds that blow off the mountains. For the most part, however, temperature differences among the various regions of Iceland are slight, although the coldest days occur in the interior. Regardless of the region, however, temperatures drop as altitude increases.

Iceland's rather mild climate is produced by the warming effect of the Gulf Stream current, and by the prevailing southwesterly winds, which carry warmer southern air to the island. These same winds, however, often reach gale force along the southwestern coast, especially during the winter. Winds are less fierce along the protected northern and eastern coasts and calmest of all in the interior.

Summers are rather cool, with afternoon temperatures in the lowlands averaging only 12° to 15° C. (54° to 59° F.). The average temperature during July, the warmest month, is only 10° C. (50° F.). Frosts can occur any month of the year, especially in the interior, where nighttime temperatures in July can drop to *minus 7° C. (20° F.).* On the hottest day of the month, however, temperatures typically range from 17° to 22° C. (63° to 72° F.). The highest summer temperatures occur along the north coast and in the interior, where there is generally less cloud cover and winds than along the western and southern coasts.

The same southwesterly winds that moderate Iceland's climate also bring heavy precipitation to the island. Precipitation is greatest from October through January, but significant amounts fall throughout the year. May and June are the driest months, but even then, 40 mm (1.5 inches) or more per month is typical for most of the island. During October, the wettest month, precipitation in Reykjavik approaches an average of 100 mm (4 inches).

Precipitation is greatest along the south and southeastern coasts and on the southern slopes of the glaciers. Kvisker, the wettest point on the coast, receives about 3,000 mm (120 inches) per year. Amounts are even greater over the glaciers, where 5,000 to 6,000 mm (200 to 250 inches) per year is normal. This increase occurs because as moist air passes over the ice fields, it is cooled to such an extent that it is virtually wrung dry. As a result, the driest areas in Iceland occur on the leeward or northeastern side of the glaciers, where precipitation may drop to about 400 mm (16 inches) per year.

Snowfall is greatest in the mountainous areas. In the south it is usually necessary to climb above 600 meters to find reliable skiing conditions. Even so, Reykjavik, on the relatively warm southwest coast, is snow free only for an average of eight days in January. Snow cover is more reliable in northern Iceland, where even lowland areas usually have enough to support skiing. In the north, snow usually covers the ground from the last week in September to the third week in May; in the south, from the last week in October to the second week in April. Snow can fall in the mountainous areas any month of the year.

Weather Forecasts

Recorded weather forecasts in Icelandic can be obtained by telephone in Reykjavik:

Recorded Weather Forecasts: Tel. 17000.

If you don't speak Icelandic, your best bet is to telephone the weather bureau in Reykjavik. They will give you forecasts in English for any part of Iceland:

Vedurstofan (weather bureau): Tel. 86000.

In addition, the NATO base radio on MW band broadcasts weather forecasts in English each hour.

Where to Get Walking Information

Unless you plan to hire a guide or join an organized walking tour, thorough advanced planning is essential for a successful walking excursion in Iceland. You must know ahead of time what equipment and food to take, what lodgings are available near your route, and what arrangements you must make to get yourself to the start of your path. Iceland's climate and terrain can be unforgiving of shoddy preparation or lack of experience. Planning is best done before you reach Iceland, for the country does not have many of the walking facilities found elsewhere. Consequently, you may have to bring certain items of food and gear along with you.

Although information on specific footpaths remains scanty, you can obtain general information on walking from:

> **Ferdafélag Íslands** (for its address and telephone number, see the *Address Directory* at the end of this chapter). Staff speaks Icelandic, English and Danish.

The FI, or Iceland Touring Club, is the main walking organization in Iceland. It conducts walking and glacier trips, operates 26 mountain huts and conducts outings abroad for its members. It also publishes, in conjunction with the Iceland Geodetic Survey, a 1:750,000 topographical map of Iceland on which tourist huts and shelters and principal mountain tracks are shown. In addition, the Touring Club publishes a series of regional guidebooks. Written in Icelandic, these do not describe footpaths, but they can help you plan where to walk. The Touring Club can also suggest places to walk, trace routes on your maps, suggest food and equipment to take and help you with other arrangements for your trip.

Membership in the Iceland Touring Club is open to everyone and carries several benefits. First, members can stay at the club's mountain huts for reduced rates and have priority over non-members. Second, members receive reduced rates on club-sponsored tours both in Iceland and abroad. Third, they enjoy reciprocal privileges with members of the Norwegian Mountain Touring Association and the Swedish Touring Club. Finally, they receive an annual booklet in Icelandic describing available tours and various regions of the country.

Other Sources of Information

You can obtain a fact sheet on hiking and climbing from the Icelandic National Tourist Office (see *Address Directory*). The fact sheet is entitled:

- *Mountain Climbing and Hiking* (in English). In addition to general comments, the sheet also lists six hiking areas, although specific route descriptions are not included.

Iceland's international airline, Icelandair also publishes a pamphlet entitled:

- *Climbing and Ski-ing in Iceland* (in English). Gives information on terrain, glaciers, climbing and skiing centers, clothing and equipment.

The pamphlet is available from:

Flugleidir (Icelandair). See *Address Directory*.

Maps

If you plan to hire a guide or participate in an organized walking tour, you will not need topographical maps. But if you plan to walk on your own, especially cross-country, they are essential. So is a first-rate orienteering compass. Even people familiar with Iceland's uninhabited central highlands have occasionally lost their way.

Even equipped with the appropriate maps, you may encounter difficulties. Iceland's landscape is continually subject to alteration by volcanic activity. Whole landforms may disappear beneath lava, or new ones may appear overnight. Rivers also may alter course from year to year. As a result, maps drawn before 1957 may contain serious errors.

First-time visitors should be aware that many place names shown on the maps refer only to farms and rural churches rather than towns or villages. In addition, the "bridle paths" and "indistinct paths" shown on older maps may no longer be evident in the landscape.

Map difficulties of this kind are but one reason why unescorted walking expeditions into Iceland's rugged hinterlands should be left to highly experienced wilderness travelers well equipped for rugged terrain and inclement weather.

Landmælingar Íslands (the Icelandic Geodetic Survey) publishes two series of topographical maps suitable for walkers:

Atlasblöd (Atlas Map). This series is comprised of 87 sheets in a scale of 1:100,000 which together cover the entire country. Each sheet covers 1,760 square kilometers and shows principal footpaths, bridle paths and mountain tracks, sometimes in red. Contours are drawn in at vertical intervals of 20 meters. Shading and symbols indicate various types of vegetation and rocky terrain, as well as man-made features in the landscape. The key to symbols is printed on the bottom of each sheet in Icelandic, with translations in English and Danish.

Fjórdungsblöd (Quarter Sheet). The 117 sheets in this series are drawn in a scale of 1:50,000. Each sheet covers 440 square kilometers and shows the same features as the Atlas Maps except in greater detail. Contours are drawn in at 20-meter intervals. Quarter Sheets are currently available only for western Iceland and the south coast. Elsewhere, you must use the Atlas Maps.

Both map series are suitable for walking, although some sheets are outdated and, given the penchant of the Icelandic landscape for change, should be used with care—and sometimes downright skepticism.

Landmælingar Íslands, in conjunction with the Iceland Touring Club, also publishes a 1:750,000 Tourist Map of the entire island. This map is actually two maps in one: a topographical, shaded-relief map on one side and a road map on the other. Though unsuitable for use on the trail, the map is an excellent aid for planning where you want to walk. It shows the locations of towns, villages and hamlets; of churches, farms and abandoned farms; of principal roads, country roads and mountain tracks; and of mountain huts. Pasture and meadowlands are indicated in green, and topography is indicated by both contour lines and shaded relief. When ordering, ask for the Iceland Touring Club's *Tourist Map of Iceland*.

All the above maps, as well as a map index and price list, can be obtained by mail or in person from:

Landmælingar Íslands (see *Address Directory*). Staff speaks Icelandic, English and Danish.

The maps may also be purchased in most bookstores, including:

See *Address Directory*:
Bókaverzlun Sigfusar Eymundssonar, in Reykjavik.
Bókaverzlun Snæbjarnar, also in Reykjavik.
Bókaverzlun Larusar Blöndal, in Vesturer.

The Tourist Map of Iceland can also be purchased from the Iceland Touring Club.

You should buy all the maps you will need for your stay in Iceland before leaving Reykjavik. You cannot be certain of finding them in other towns.

Guidebooks

There are currently no guidebooks that describe the footpaths of Iceland. You can get a fairly good idea of what to expect on a given path, however, by consulting topographical maps—which indicate both landforms and vegetation—in conjunction with appropriate pamphlets describing the regions in which you wish to walk.

A useful set of regional guidebooks published by Ferdafélag Islands (see *Address Directory*). Includes some 50 titles, each devoted to a particular region. These booklets can be purchased at the FI office in Reykjavik.

In addition, Iceland's international airline publishes a series of pamphlets in English, French, German and Danish describing several of the more scenic regions. The following pamphlets are currently available:

- *Öræfasveit and Skaftafell—the National Park*
- *The Eastern Fiords of Iceland*
- *The Mývatn District—North Iceland*
- *Eyjafjördur District—North Iceland*
- *Hornafjördur and Southeast Iceland*
- *The Western Fiords of Iceland*
- *The Snaefellsnes Peninsula with Part of Dalasýsla District*

Each pamphlet describes the climate, geography, settlements and features of particular interest in each district. The pamphlets are written in English. They may be obtained free from Icelandair and the Iceland Tourist Bureau (see *Address Directory*).

Other useful guidebooks that may assist you in planning your walks include the following (for the addresses of their publishers, see the *Address Directory*):

- *Á Hringveg—Around Iceland* (in Icelandic and English). Published by Minjagripathjónustan. Describes points of interest in eight regions of Iceland, excluding only the uninhabited Central Highlands. Free upon request from the Iceland Tourist Bureau.
- *Handy Facts on Iceland* (in English). Published by *Atlantica* and *Iceland Review*. An excellent pocket-sized guide to the history, culture and natural features of Iceland. Available in most bookstores. Recommended.
- *Iceland in a Nutshell* (in English or German). Published by Örn og Örlygur (Iceland Travel Books). A complete reference guide to Iceland. Available in most bookstores. Recommended.
- *Iceland Road Guide* (in English). Published by Örn og Örlygur—Iceland Travel Books. Covers the entire road network in Iceland. Describes points of interest enroute. Available in most bookstores. Recommended.

Trailside Lodgings

Because Iceland's footpaths are mostly located in wild, unpopulated regions, trailside accommodation is sparse. The Iceland Touring Club maintains 26 mountain huts, but these are usually situated much more than a day's walk apart, and are often full, since they are used by a number of tour groups. As a result, you must be prepared to camp if you plan walks lasting two or more days.

There are six youth hostels in Iceland, most located in towns with access to local footpaths. In addition, travelers with sleeping bags—which should include most walkers—can find inexpensive lodging in what Icelanders call *Svefnpokapláss*—boarding schools and hotels that offer dormitory facilities without linen or blankets during the summer for reduced rates. Accommodation is also available in private homes in Reykjavik and Akureyri, and in certain farmhouses in the districts of Biskupstungur, Hreppar and Kjos in southern Iceland and in the district of Hunavatnssysla in the north.

Mountain Huts

The 26 mountain huts operated by the Iceland Touring Club are scattered throughout the Central Highlands, with a few in other districts. They have mattresses and coal stoves but little else. Some have dishes, but you shouldn't count on it; you should bring your own bedding, food and utensils.

Walkers using the huts are expected to clean up after themselves and carry their trash out with them. Groups and tours receive first priority, but if space is available individual hikers are welcome. Camping is also permitted near the huts. You don't have to be a club member to use the huts, but members receive discount rates.

You can reserve space at the huts through the Iceland Touring Club (see *Address Directory*). The club can also tell you whether a particular hut is likely to be available when you need it. You might thus be able to obtain lodging at a hut simply by revising your itinerary.

The locations of the huts are shown on the Touring Club's 1:750,000 Tourist Map (see the section on *Maps*). Even if you are unable or do not plan to stay in the huts, they provide good base camps for exploration. In addition, you may need to find one in case of emergency. A few are equipped with two-way radios, which are the only means of communicating with the outside world. Many huts, however, are not thus equipped.

The Iceland Touring Club is now building a system of huts located closer together, as well as a network of trails linking them. Work on this project was to be completed in the mountains of southern Iceland by the end of 1979. Full details on the new huts and trails can be obtained from the Touring Club.

There are also a number of primitive shelters scattered about Iceland that are not operated by the Touring Club. Abandoned farm buildings may also be used for shelter. The locations of many of these shelters are shown on the Touring Club's 1:750,000 Tourist Map.

Youth Hostels

The Icelandic Youth Hostels Association maintains youth hostels in Reykjavik, Akureyri, Seydisfjördur, Berunes and Vestmannæyjar. Dick Phillips (see *Address Directory*), a tour guide, operates a youth hostel at Fljótshlíd under the auspices of the Youth Hostels Association. The hostels at Reykjavik and Akureyri are open 12 months of the year. The others open in May, June or July and close in September or October. The number of beds ranges from 15 at Fljótshlíd to 60 at Reykjavik. The others have between 30 and 40 beds. In most of the hostels, individual rooms contain between two and six beds. Each of the hostels has a kitchen for preparing your meals; however, you must bring your own utensils. No food is served.

Advance reservations for the hostel at Fljótshlíd should be addressed to Dick Phillips. Reservations for all the other hostels should be addressed to:

Banalag Íslenzkra Farfugla (Icelandic Youth Hostels Association). See *Address Directory*. Publishes a brochure giving details on and a photograph of each hostel. A map shows the locations not only of youth hostels, but some of Iceland's mountain huts, svefnpokapláss and campgrounds. Written in Icelandic with English translations of essential information.

Svefnpokapláss

During the summer, some boarding schools and hotels provide inexpensive dormitory facilities for travelers with sleeping bags. No kitchen facilities are available, however. For instance, the Hotel Edda chain, which is operated by the Iceland Tourist Bureau, offers dormitory accommodation in eight of its hotels. The youth hostel brochure (described above) lists these svefnpokapláss along with 10 others. The address, telephone number and other details are given for each, and their locations are shown on the map printed in the brochure.

Hotels and Guesthouses

A list of hotels and guesthouses is available from Ferdamalarad Íslands—the Iceland Tourist Board (see *Address Directory*). The list does not include private homes and farmhouses that take in lodgers. For information on these, consult either your travel agent or the Iceland Tourist Board.

Camping

When walking in Iceland, you must be prepared to camp out. Huts are widely scattered and may be filled to capacity when you arrive. Fortunately, camping is permitted almost everywhere outside towns. Exceptions include fenced-in areas, cultivated ground, and a few spots within the national parks. Where camping is specifically prohibited, you will find a sign reading *Tjaldstædi bönnud*. Places specially set aside for camping will often be posted *Tjaldstædi*. When camping in the vicinity of a farm, obtain the permission of the farmer. In most cases it will be readily granted.

There are about 20 campgrounds scattered throughout Iceland near roads. All have sanitary facilities of one kind or another, and some have hot water and electrical outlets. The campgrounds at Húsavík and Laugarvatn have a swimming pool nearby. You can obtain information on camping, including a list of campgrounds, from both the Icelandic Tourist Bureau and the Iceland Tourist Board (see *Address Directory*).

When camping in Iceland, you should take special care not to damage the existing vegetation, which has at best a tenuous foothold in this land of thin soils and short growing seasons. When possible—and it almost always is—camp on barren ground. Once an area has been disturbed, it may take decades or longer for plants to re-establish themselves.

Finally, since no firewood is available in Iceland, campers must bring their own cookstoves. It is illegal to cut wood or pull up plants for fuel.

Water

Water from almost all lakes and streams in Iceland is safe to drink. Caution should be exercised only where contamination from livestock is a possibility. You should also avoid drinking the water from hot springs, which may be scalding. If used for cooking, however, this same water will save fuel. In some cases the water may have a rusty color from minerals. Such water is safe to drink, but may have an unpleasant taste.

Equipment Notes

When hiking throughout much of Iceland, you must be entirely self-sufficient. This means a heavy pack, but such is the price for the pleasure of walking through truly wild and rugged terrain. Essential gear includes a warm sleeping bag and ground pad, a lightweight tent able to withstand gale-force winds (the tent fabric should be dark enough to shut out the Midnight Sun), a portable campstove and fuel, cooking and eating utensils and all the food necessary for your trip. A rope is also essential for river crossings.

In addition, you should carry a good orienteering compass and topographical maps. Familiarize yourself with their use *before* setting out on your walk. Most walking routes in Iceland are poorly marked at best. Many require cross-country navigation.

Since summers are cool and the weather highly changeable, garments to protect you from wind, rain and even snow are essential. Wool clothing, including cap and mittens, offer the best protection. Blue jeans are not recommended and climbing breeches—or, as they are known to Americans, knickers—are the choice of experienced hikers.

A pair of sturdy hiking boots is recommended for Iceland's predominantly rocky terrain. But you should also take a light pair of knee-high rubber boots for crossing bogs and marshy areas. Insect repellent and netting to protect your face are essential to protect you from the clouds of midges that frequent both wetlands and the shores of streams and lakes in midsummer. Your tent should also have no-see-um proof netting that can be tightly sealed on all vents and entrances.

You can rent tents, sleeping bags, air mattresses, packs and campstoves from:

Tjaldaleigan (see *Address Directory*).

You should purchase all the food you need before setting off on your walk, for towns are few and far between in the main hiking districts. It is advisable, however, to bring as much food as you can with you into Iceland. At present, lightweight freeze-dried foods are not available in the country, and other foods are very expensive.

In selecting equipment, remember that most of Iceland is wild, rugged country subject to sudden changes in weather that even in midsummer can bring gales, snow, driving rain and sub-freezing temperatures. Equipment that can stand up to such conditions is a must. So too are emergency provisions. Even greater care, of course, is necessary if you plan to walk during the winter.

Crowded Trails

Crowded trails are not a problem in Iceland, where solitude is far easier to find than companionship.

Walking Tours

For the experienced, self-reliant wilderness traveler accustomed to foul weather and wild, rugged terrain, Iceland is a paradise. The scenery is everywhere magnificent and the opportunities for cross-country adventure virtually limitless. Even experienced mountaineers, however, should not travel in the interior by themselves. For most visitors the best way to explore Iceland on foot is to join one of the many available walking tours.

The tours are so numerous and varied that regardless of your experience, physical conditioning, special interests or available time you will be able to find one perfectly suited for you. There are literally hundreds to choose from, ranging from day-trips in popular hiking spots to two- and three-week-long expeditions to some of the remotest places in Iceland. Some tours utilize mountain huts; others require camping throughout; still others combine tents and huts. Most of the longer trips operate from one or more remote base camps from which walks of a few hours, a week or more may be taken. Several of the tours specialize in particular interests such as bird watching, geology or plant life. A few tours are available for walkers interested in climbing or glacier crossings. Most of the tours require that you provide your own food and gear. A few provide meals, although participants are expected to help with the cooking and clean-up. Insurance covers participants only while traveling in motor vehicles.

The following organizations offer walking tours in Iceland:

See *Address Directory*:

Ferdafélag Íslands (Iceland Touring Club). Offers the largest number of walking tours, ranging from one day to two weeks in length. Overnight accommodation is in the club's huts where possible; otherwise in tents. You must provide your own food and equipment. Transportation from the tour destination is provided from Reykjavik. In some cases, it is possible to book out on one tour, lay over between tours at one of the club's mountain huts, and then return to Reykjavik with the next tour. This arrangement provides you with a reliable base camp from which to take day-hikes on your own. You need not be a member of the Iceland Touring Club to participate in its tours. You can obtain a booklet (in Icelandic and English) listing the current year's tours by writing to the Touring Club Office in Reykjavik. The booklet is entitled *Ferdaáætlun/Iceland Tours*. Advanced booking for these tours can be arranged through your travel agent, Icelandair, the Iceland National Tourist Office or the Iceland Touring Club.

Útivist (Outdoor Life Club). Offers several 5- to 8-day tenting tours and well over 100 day tours. You must provide your own food and equipment. Transportation to and from the tour destination is provided from Reykjavik. You need not be a member of the Outdoor Life Club to participate. An annual brochure describing the tours and current prices is available upon request. The brochure is entitled *Útivistarferdir/Outdoor Life Tours.* Advanced booking can be arranged through your travel agent, Icelandair, the Iceland National Tourist Office or Útivist.

Dick Phillips. Offers numerous two- to three-week walking tours to remote districts. Huts are used when available, but most nights are spent camping. Hikes from one day to a week or more are conducted from base camps. Food is provided, but participants are expected to help cook, clean and carry their share of provisions. Walking gear is not provided. Motor tours are also offered for walkers and naturalists. Transportation is provided to and from Reykjavik. The cost of air travel from London or Glasgow to Iceland can be included in the tour price if desired. A booklet describing the tours is available upon request. The booklet, entitled *On Foot in Iceland,* describes the Icelandic countryside and tells walkers what to expect on the tours. It also includes information on special tours, car hire, transportation, camping, hostels, huts, maps, guidebooks and other useful matters. Advance booking for these tours is through Dick Phillips only. He can be reached from May through October at Fljótsdal, Fljótshlíd, Rang, Iceland (telephone via Hvolsvollur).

Bandalag Íslenskra Farfugla (Icelandic Youth Hostels Association). Conducts two- to three-day walking tours. You must bring your own food and gear. For information, write the association's office in Reykjavik.

In addition to the pre-packaged tours, groups wishing to arrange their own special tours may do so either through Dick Phillips or through:

Úlfar Jacobsen (see *Address Directory*). Offers 13-day Iceland Safaris that feature overnight camping. Guides will arrange walks for interested tour members. Jacobsen will also set up special walking tours for independent groups. You can avoid carrying food and cooking equipment on these tours by taking advantage of Úlfar Jacobsen's kitchen bus. Small parties can also make arrangements to meet the mobile kitchen at predetermined places along its scheduled route.

Dick Phillips will arrange special tours for periods up to two weeks for groups well-equipped and experienced in wilderness travel. He has provided such a service for the Ramblers' Association of Great Britain, the Caravanes de Jeunesse Belge, and the Sierra Club of the United States.

Hikers who wish to walk on their own may still find that the best way to get to the remoter walking districts is to go there with a tour. For this purpose a motor tour is just as useful as a walking tour. In many cases, you can arrange to be left behind by the tour at a certain spot and then rejoin the same tour, or another one, a few days later. In the interim, you are on your own, with all the pleasures and possible problems that implies. If this more adventurous approach appeals to you, make the appropriate arrangements ahead of time in Reykjavik.

Climbing & Climbing Courses

The Icelandic Alpine Club (ISALP), founded in 1977, organizes climbing tours. A few small local groups also conduct private climbing excursions, but for the most part these are open only to members and their guests. In addition, some of the walking tours feature climbing as an optional activity in certain areas. Climbing guides for individuals, however, are not available.

Even though Iceland has a large number of attractive peaks, it offers poor conditions for technical rock climbing. The volcanic rock composing the island is for the most part soft and crumbly, posing an extreme danger to climbers on steep pitches. For those who nonetheless remain interested in climbing in Iceland, information can be obtained from:

Icelandic Alpine Club (ISALP). See *Address Directory.*

A pamphlet entitled *Climbing and Skiing in Iceland* is also available upon request from Icelandair.

Cross-Country Skiing

Despite its northerly situation, Iceland offers surprisingly few opportunities for skiing of any kind. Temperatures in the lowland areas are for the most part too mild during the winter to sustain reliable snow. And there are relatively few ski facilities in the higher, snowier mountainous regions. The Icelandic government, however, plans additional facilities for the future. Currently, there are no cross-country ski tracks. Cross-country skiing is nevertheless possible in certain areas during the spring—and even the summer—when access by road becomes possible. Among the areas worth investigating are the Mountains near Akureyri in Northern Iceland (the Hlidarfjall Ski-Hotel is a 10-minute drive or one-hour walk from town); the mountains near Isafjördur (ski-hotel in the Seljalandsdalur Valley); the Kerlingarfjöll Mountains 200 kilometers north of Reykjavik (summer ski school); and the Tindafjallajökull Mountains 120 kilometers southeast of Reykjavik. Additional information on skiing in Iceland is contained in the pamphlet *Climbing and Skiing in Iceland,* available upon request from Icelandair (see *Address Directory*). The Iceland Touring Club can also suggest places to go.

Transportation to Hiking Areas

One of the main problems facing walkers in Iceland is arranging transportation to and from hiking districts. There are no railroads, so domestic transportation is by road or air. Buses serve most of the coastal districts accessible by road. Several walking areas are located near the scheduled bus routes. For example, if you want to walk in the mountains south of Akureyri, in Northern Iceland, you can take a bus from Reykjavik and upon arriving in Akureyri set off into the hinterlands on foot.

The greater part of the Central Highlands, however, as well as other remote districts, are not served by public transportation. The best way to reach these areas is to join a walking tour. But if you prefer to venture out on your own, you can rent a four-wheel drive vehicle in Reykjavik and some other towns. The cautions that apply to walkers venturing alone into Iceland's interior also apply to drivers. Most of the region is crossed only by unpaved mountain tracks. Some tracks are passable in summer by most motor vehicles; others are deeply rutted, indistinct or follow stream beds for short distances. These tracks are passable only by vehicles with four-wheel drive. The Iceland Touring Club's Tourist Map (see the section on *Maps*) shows the location of both types of mountain tracks and should be carried by anyone venturing off the main roads.

Rates for renting motor vehicles are based on a per-day and per-mile charge. Gasoline is not included. Renters must be at least 20 years old and have an international driver's license. Insurance is included in the cost of rental. A vehicle must be returned to its point of origin. Advance reservations will be necessary during the summer months.

Useful Addresses & Telephone Numbers

General Tourist Information

In Iceland:

See *Address Directory:*
Ferdaskrifstofa Ríkisins (Iceland Tourist Bureau). Staff speaks Icelandic, English and Danish. Useful publications include:

- *Iceland, A World of Difference* (in English). Gives general information on the history, culf17and scenic attractions of Iceland.
- *By the Roadside* (in English). Provides detailed descriptions of points of interest along the road from Reykjavik to Akureyri.

Ferdamálarád Íslands (Iceland Tourist Board). Staff speaks Icelandic, English and Danish. Useful publications include:

- *Iceland—Practical Information for Tourists* (in English). A brochure with information on air service, currency, climate and clothing, business hours, cultural facilities, restaurants, maps, tours, public transportation, hotels, camping and other matters of interest to visitors.

Ferdafélag Íslands (Iceland Touring Club). For details on the club and its publications, see the section on *Where to Get Walking Information*

Abroad:

Branch offices of the Icelandic National Tourist Office are located in the U.S.A.: Los Angeles and New York.

New York: Scandinavian National Tourist Offices, 75 Rockefeller Plaza, New York, New York 10019. Tel. (212) 582-2802.

Sport Shops

It is advisable to bring all of your hiking gear with you to Iceland. There are four sport shops in Reykjavik which have a selection of walking and mountaineering equipment, but the choice is limited and prices are high. If you have to make a last minute purchase, however, do so in Reykjavik. The selection of hiking gear in other towns is extremely restricted—and in many cases nonexistent. The four shops in Reykjavik are:

See *Address Directory*:

> **Geysir.**
> **Sportval.**
> **Skatabudin.**
> **Útilif.**

Search & Rescue

The Icelanders take search and rescue operations seriously. Nothing is spared to locate lost or injured parties. If necessary four or five planes may be sent up, along with a helicopter equipped with nurses and doctors. Obviously, an operation this thorough is expensive, and unless you have insurance covering such costs, your out-of-pocket expense can be sizeable.

In case of an emergency: 1) proceed to the nearest mountain hut for assistance; if you are lucky, it will have a two-way radio (most tour buses also have two-way radios), or 2) find the nearest telephone and call:

Slysavarnafélag Íslands (Lifesaving Organization of Iceland). Tel. 27111. 24-hour service.

Or call:

Hjálparsveit Skáta (Boy Scout Life Saving Association). Tel. 26430.

Walkers venturing into the remoter parts of the Central Highlands should bear in mind that should an emergency occur, it may take days to obtain assistance. This is but one more reason why only experienced wilderness travelers equipped for almost any contingency should attempt such trips. You should also be sure at least one member of your party is qualified to administer first aid. And *always:* be sure to notify local authorities prior to your departure to give them full details on the route you intend to follow, the number of people in your party and your expected date of return.

Iceland's Principal Walking Areas

Virtually all of Iceland outside the relatively few settled areas along the coast is open to walkers. Your choice of walks is limited only by your time, budget and abilities. To describe all the areas suitable for walking is impossible in a book this size. The following areas were chosen because they contain mountain tracks or other paths suitable for walking (which are shown on the recommended maps) in addition to one or more mountain huts maintained by the Iceland Touring Club. Cross-country possibilities, of course, are virtually limitless.

Further details on each area, plus information on other areas in which you can walk in Iceland, can be obtained from the Iceland Touring Club (see *Address Directory*).

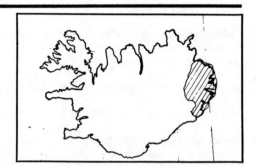

Eastern Iceland

The rugged east coast of Iceland consists of a succession of narrow fjords bounded on either side by steep mountain ridges that plunge into the sea. Small towns huddle at the head of several fjords, protected by the surrounding mountains from the fury of wind and sea. Inland, the terrain becomes gentler, the mountains giving way to a broad plateau dissected by glacial streams flowing northeast from Vatnajökull. Roads lead up both sides of the lush Fljotsdalur Valley, with its birch woods at Hallormsstadarskógur, extensive grasslands and meadows, and long glacial lake. At the head of the valley the snowcapped peak of Snæfell rises to 1,833 meters. Vatnajökull lies close at hand to the south. The rocks in this region are among the oldest in Iceland, consisting mostly of dark gray basalt accented with outcrops of lighter liparite. There is little sign of volcanic activity in the region, which is one of the few places in Iceland where you won't find lava fields or hot springs.

Trail Lodgings

The Iceland Touring Club operates a hut on the west side of Snæfell Peak and at Lambafell off the northeast side of Vatnajökull. Youth hostels are located at *Berunes* and *Seydisfjördur*.

Maps

- Landmælingar Íslands 1:100,000 Atlasblöd (Atlas Map), sheets 94, 95, 96, 103, 104, 105, 106, 113, 114 and 115. Also: Landmælingar Íslands 1:50,000 Fjórdungsblöd (Quarter Sheet), sheets 96-SA and 106-SV.

Suggested Walks

From Hrafnkelsdalur Valley road end to Snæfell. Up a narrow river valley with a flat meadow floor and steep rock walls. Leads to a long, narrow lake at the northwestern base of 1,833-meter Snæfell, Iceland's highest peak outside the Vatnajökullmassif. Excellent cross-country wandering and climbing opportunities. **Walking Time:** 3 days. **Difficulty:** Easy.
Maps:
• Ladmælingar Íslands 1:100,000 Atlas Maps 94 and 95.

From Stafafell to Vídidalur. Up a broad glacial valley, then over mountains to another valley at the eastern foot of Vatnajökull. Spectacular mountain scenery throughout. Numerous lakes and streams. Woodlands in upper Jokulsá í Loní Valley. **Walking Time:** 3 days. **Difficulty:** Moderately difficult to difficult.
Maps:
• Landmælingar Íslands 1:100,000 Atlas Maps 105 and 106.

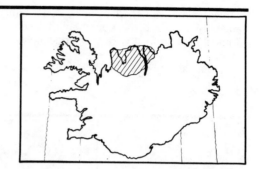

Eyjafjördur District

Akureyri, Iceland's second largest town, sits at the head of Eyjafjördur, a 60-kilometer-long fjord cut into the mountains of Iceland's north-central coast. To the west rise the Tröllaskagi Mountains, which are deeply indented by fertile, glacier-carved valleys. The peaks range between 1,200 and 1,400 meters in height. Several are covered by icecaps. Northeast of Akureyri, across the fjord, a second mountain mass rises steeply from the sea, occupying the entire peninsula dividing Eyjafjördur and Skjálfandi Bay to the east. A third mountain district extends south from Akureyri and includes 1,538-meter Kerling, the highest peak in North Iceland. These mountains are the main skiing area in the region, and the Hlídarfjall Ski Hotel is situated nearby.

Trail Lodgings

The Iceland Touring Club operates a mountain hut in the *Glerárdalur Valley* near Mt. Kerling. Lodging is available year-round in the nearby *Hlídarfjall Ski Hotel*. A youth hostel is located at *Akureyri*.

Maps

• Landmælingar Íslands 1:100,000 Atlasblöd (Atlas Map), sheets 52, 53, 61, 62, 63, 71, 72 and 73.

Suggested Walks

From Secondary Road 835 to Brettingsstadir. North along a mountain track through a glacial valley to the sea. Walking and climbing opportunities in the mountains on either side. Spectacular seacoast. **Walking Time:** 2 days. **Difficulty:** Easy.
Maps:
• Landmælingar Íslands 1:100,000 Atlas Maps 71 and 72.

From Akureyri to the headwaters of the Glerá River. Up a fertile glacier-carved valley with spectacular peaks on either side. Excellent climbing and cross-country hiking opportunities. Winter and spring skiing. **Walking Time:** 1 day. **Difficulty:** Easy to moderately difficult.

Map:
• Landmælingar Íslands 1:100:000 Atlas Map 63.

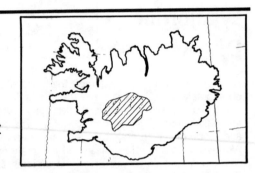

Langjökull & Hofsjökull

These two icecaps, the second and third largest in Iceland, dominate the western half of the Central Highlands. The terrain is mostly mountainous, but gentle glacial-outwash plains and river valleys lie between volcanic peaks and ridges. Vegetation consists largely of patches of meadow and marsh near lakes and streams. Elsewhere, gravel flats, boulder fields and lava fields are the rule. Glacial lakes and streams are numerous. Gullfoss, one of the largest and most beautiful of Iceland's many waterfalls, is located in the southern part of the region. Active thermal areas are found at Geysir, Haukadalur, Hveravellir and Kerlingarfjöll. The Thjórsá River, Iceland's longest, flows from the southern and eastern sides of Hofsjökull, the summit of which—at 1,765 meters—is the highest point in the region.

Trail Lodgings

Huts operated by the Iceland Touring Club are located at *Hagavatan, Herdulereidarlindir, Hlödufell, Hvannalindir, Hveravellir, Hvítárnes, Kerlingarfjöll, Kverkfjöll, Landmannalaugar, Snæfell, Sprengisandur, Thjófadalir, Thórsmörk* and *Tungafellsjökull*. In addition, numerous primitive shelters are scattered throughout the region. For hut locations, see the Iceland Touring Club's 1:750,000 Tourist Map.

Maps

• Landmælingar Íslands 1:100,000 Atlasblöd (Atlas Map), sheets 45, 46, 55, 56, 64, 65 and 66. Also:

• Landmælingar Íslands 1:50,000 Fjórdungsblöd (Quarter Sheet), sheets 46-SA and 46-SV.

Suggested Walks

From Gullfos Waterfall to Hveravellir. Possible sidetrips to Hagavatn, Kerlingarjöll and Thjófadalir. Across outwash plains, marsh and meadow, heath and lava fields; through river valleys; and past three large glacial lakes and numerous streams. Excellent views of Langjökull and Hofsjökull. Thermal areas at Hveravellir and Kerlingarfjöll. Summer ski school at Kerlingarfjöll. **Walking Time:** 6 days. **Difficulty:** Easy to moderately difficult.
Maps:
• Landmælingar Íslands 1:100,000 Atlas Maps 46, 55 and 56; and 1:50,000 Quarter Sheet 46-SA.

From Hjalparfoss Waterfall to Tungafellsjökull. Up the valley of the Thjórsá River to the marshes at the foot of the Hofsjökull, then on to the Touring Club hut at the foot of Tungafellsjökull. Views of Mt. Hekla and Hofsjökull. Marsh and meadow fairly common in the Thjórsá Valley, extensive near Hofsjökull. Follows the Gjáin Gorge on Thjórsá River. Numerous lakes and streams. **Walking Time:** 8 days. **Difficulty:** Easy to moderately difficult.
Maps:
• Landmælingar Íslands 1:100,000 Atlas Maps 56, 57, 65, 66 and 75.

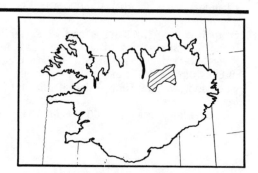

Mývatn District

Mývatn is a large, shallow lake situated on the western fringe of northeastern Iceland's vast lava fields, which extend 50 kilometers north of the lake and 110 kilometers southward. Evidence of volcanic activity abounds in the immediate area around the lake, including craters, table mountains, hot-water caves, the thermal area at Námaskard and such spectacular lava formations as the Dimmuborgir (the black castles). The lake itself is notable for its large populations of nesting waterfowl, which in summer number between 100,000 and 150,000. Fifteen species of ducks nest on the lake, including two North American species—Barrow's goldeneye and the harlequin duck—both of which are absent east of this region. Mývatn means "the lake of midges," and on hot, still summer days, clouds of these tiny insects hang over the lake. A few kilometers northeast of Mývatn, the Jökulsá á Fjöllum plunges abruptly over a lava wall to form the mighty Dettifoss waterfall, Europe's largest. To the west of Mývatn, in the Bárdadalur Valley, is Godafoss, the "Waterfall of the Gods."

Trail Lodgings

There are only a few primitive shelters in this district. For their locations, see the Iceland Touring Club's 1:750,000 Tourist Map.

Maps

• Landmælingar Íslands 1:100,000 Atlasblöd (Atlas Map), sheets 72, 73, 82 and 83.

Suggested Walks

From Mývatn to Grenjadarstadur. Follow a track northward from the lake up the Laxá River valley, noted for its spectacular lava formations and for Iceland's best salmon fishing. **Walking Time: 2 days. Difficulty: Easy.**
Maps:
• Landmælingar Íslands 1:100,000 Atlas Maps 72, 73 and 83.

From Highway 1, 18 miles east of Reyjahlid, to Ásbyrgi. Follows a mountain track northward along the east side of the Jökulsá á Fjöllum River. Short side trips possible to Dettifoss Waterfall and the grassy shores of Eilífsvötn Lake. Through meadow, heath, lava and, at Ásbyrgi, birch woodland. **Walking Time: 3 days. Difficulty: Easy.**
Maps:
• Landmælingar Íslands 1:100,000 Atlas Maps 82 and 83.

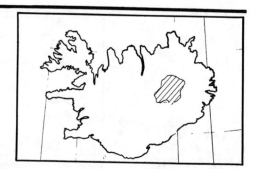

Ódádahraun

This vast volcanic tableland makes up the eastern half of Iceland's Central Highlands. It is a high, cold desert virtually devoid of vegetation. Rain-bearing winds from the southwest lose most of their moisture in passing over Vatnajokull, so that Ódádahraun, situated in the rain shadow of the icecap, receives less precipitation than anywhere else in the country. Most of the 9,000-square-kilometer region is covered with lava. (The region's lunar landscape was chosen by NASA as a training ground for U.S. astronauts.) In the center rises the volcano Askja (1,200 meters), which last erupted in 1961. Through the eastern part of this upland, the Jökulsá á Fjöllum River has cut a spectacular rocky gorge.

Trail Lodgings

The Iceland Touring Club operates huts at *Askja, Herdubreid* and *Kverkfjöll*. A few primitive shelters exist in the extreme western part of the region and along the Jökulsá á Fjöllum River. For hut locations, see the Iceland Touring Club's 1:750,000 Tourist Map.

Maps

- Landmælingar Íslands 1:100,000 Atlasblöd (Atlas Map), sheets 74, 75, 83, 84, 85 and 94.

Suggested Walk

From Highway 1 west of Grimsstadir to Askja. Follows a mountain track southward along the picturesque rocky gorge of the Jökulsá á Fjöllum River. Small lakes and ponds; extensive lava fields; Askja volcano, with its 45-square-kilometer caldera; 1,053-meter-high Oskjuvatn Lake near Askja. **Walking Time:** 8 days. **Difficulty:** Easy to moderately difficult.
Maps:
- Landmælingar Íslands 1:100,000 Atlas Maps 83, 84, 93 and 94.

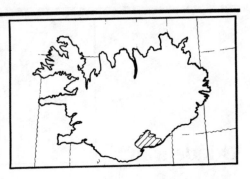

Öræfasveit & Skaftafell

Along Iceland's southeastern coast is the sprawling Vatnajökull, the largest icecap outside Greenland and Antarctica. Mountains buried beneath the icecap plunge steeply to a narrow coastal plain built out from the mountain wall by successive layers of black sand deposited by the glacier's numerous outwash streams. Oræfajökull, a smaller icecap that is part of Vatnajökull, is the highest point in Iceland (2,119 meters). Beneath it is buried the cone volcano Hvannadalshnúkur. Its great eruption in 1362 triggered an enormous glacial flood, which created the sandy wastes of Skeidarársandur and Breidamerkursandur. These sands are today crossed by numerous outwash streams, the courses of which shift from season to season. At the foot of Vatnajökull sits Skaftafell Farm, now a national park, which many people consider the single most beautiful place in Iceland. Skaftafell is situated on a fertile, rolling upland at the base of steep ice-capped peaks. To the south, the black sands of Skeidarársandur stretch to the Atlantic. Lush vegetation, including numerous plants found nowhere else in Iceland, cover the slopes.

Trail Lodgings

Campground at *Skaftafell*. Primitive shelter in the valley of the Núpsá River west of Skeidarársandur.

Maps

- Landmælingar Íslands 1:100,000 Atlasblöd (Atlas Map), sheets 77, 78, 87 and 88. Also:
- Landmælingar Íslands 1:50,000 Fjórdungsblöd (Quarter Sheet), sheets 77-SA; 78-NA, NV and SV; 87-NA, NV, SA and SV; and 88-NA and NV.

Suggested Walks

From Skaftafell to Grænalón Lake. Cross-country ramble up the Skaftafell uplands to the base of the Kristínartindar peaks. Continue down into the

Morsádalur Valley with its small woodland of rowan, willow and beech, then pass around the foot of Skeidararjökull and head up the Núpsá River valley to Grænalón Lake. Spectacular views of mountains, icecap and ocean. **Walking Time:** 3 days. **Difficulty:** Easy to moderately difficult.
Maps:
• Landmælingar Íslands 1:100,000 Atlas Maps 77 and 87; and 1:50,000 Quarter Sheets 77-SA and 87-SV. The rivers on Skeidarársandur have now been bridged and a road built across the sand. These features may not be shown on the maps.

From Fagurhólsmýri to Ingólfshöfdi. Across marsh, mudflat and sandpit to the summit of a grassy headland plunging 76 meters (250 feet) into the Atlantic. Superb views on a clear day of Myrdalsjökull to the west, of Vesturhorn Peak to the northeast, and of Vatnajökull to the north. Breeding grounds for puffin, fulmar, arctic tern, razorbill and oyster-catcher. **Walking Time:** 1 day. **Difficulty:** Easy.
Maps:
• Landmælingar Íslands 1:100,000 Atlas Map 88 and 1:50,000 Quarter Sheet 88-NA.

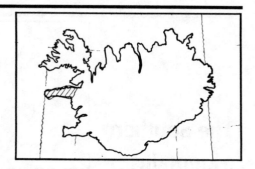

Snæfellsnes Peninsula

The Snæfellsnes Peninsula forms the northern coast of Faxaflói Bay. Across the water, 90 kilometers to the southeast, sits Reykjavik. From there, on a clear day, you can see the cone of Snæfellsjökull, which reaches a height of 1,446 meters and sits at the extreme western end of the Snæfellsnes Peninsula. This small icecap is the westernmost in Iceland. A range of mountains extends eastward from the icecap, forming the peninsula's backbone. The peaks drop abruptly to the north coast, but more gently to the south, where a broad fertile plain stretches from their bases to the sea. The northern shore is indented with fjords. Extensive lava fields surround Snæfellsjökull, tumbling down to the coast, where the sea has carved spectacular cliffs, seastacks and caves. Another lava field is located at Bjarnarhöfn on the north coast. The central mountains consist mostly of basalt, with lesser amounts of rhyolite, tuff and breccia.

Trail Lodgings

Two primitive shelters are located in the central mountains, each near one of the two roads that cross the range.

Maps

• Landmælingar Íslands 1:100,000 Atlasblöd (Atlas Map), sheets 5, 14 and 15. Also:
• Landmælingar Íslands 1:50,000 Fjórdungsblöd (Quarter Sheet), sheets 5-NA; 14-SA and SV; and 15-NA and NV.

Suggested Walk

From Arnarstapi to Snæfellsjökull. Climb through lava fields up the southeast slope of the volcano. **Walking Time:** 1 day. **Difficulty:** Moderately difficult.
Maps:
• Landmælingar Íslands 1:100,000 Atlas Map 5; or 1:50,000 Quarter Sheet 5-SA.

The Southern Mountains

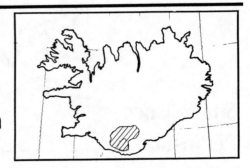

This rugged mountain region offers some of the most varied and spectacular scenery in Iceland. Sprawling Mýrdalsjökull, Iceland's fourth largest icecap, covers 1,450-meter Katla, a cone volcano, in the south. The snow-covered Hekla massif, Iceland's most famous volcano, rises in the west. Iceland's largest thermal area is located near Torfajökull, a small icecap north of Mýrdalsjökull. Another large thermal area is located at Landmannalaugar. The region's ice-sculpted lava peaks offer some of the finest mountain walking in Iceland. Many are covered with snow through late summer. In the southern part of the region lies the beautiful Thórsmörk Valley, a gentle green oasis surrounded by towering peaks and snowfields. At the head of the valley is the spectacular gorge of the Markarfljót River.

The valley is hemmed in by the Eyjafjallajökull icecap on the south, the enormous Mýrdalsjökull on the east and the spectacular Tindfjallajökull Mountains on the north. Across the mountains east of Landmannalaugar is the 32-kilometer-long volcanic fissure Eldgjá, Iceland's longest. It is 366 meters (1,200 feet) deep and 610 meters (2,000 feet) across. Here, too, is Ófærufoss, a spectacular double fall, the lower of which flows under a natural lava bridge.

Trail Lodgings

Huts operated by the Iceland Touring Club are located at Landmannalaugar, Markarfljót Gorge, Thórsmörk and Veidivötn.

A hut operated by Dick Phillips (see Address Directory) is located at Laugarháls, southeast of Torfajökull, and a youth hostel operated by Dick Phillips is at Fljótshlíd.

In addition, several primitive shelters are scattered through the region. For hut locations, see the Iceland Touring Club's 1:750,000 Tourist Map.

Maps

• Landmælingar Íslands 1:100,000 Atlasblöd (Atlas Map), sheets 57, 58, 67 and 68. Also:

• Landmælingar Íslands 1:50,000 Fjórdungsblöd (Quarter Sheet), sheets 57-SV, 58-NV and SV, and 68-SA.

Suggested Walks

From Thórsmörk to Veidivötn. Up the Markarfljót Valley to Hvanngil, across the mountains to Hvafntinnusker (hut), then north to Landmannalaugar and, finally, to the gentle grassy shores of Veidivötn Lake. Spectacular mountain scenery—river gorge, high peaks, perennial snow, numerous lakes and streams. Thermal area at Landmannalaugar has hot springs suitable for bathing. Gentler terrain in the lake-strewn Viedivötn region. A sidetrip from Landmannalaugar to Eldgja volcanic fissure—about 25 kilometers east—and the nearby Ófærufoss Waterfall is highly recommended. **Walking Time:** 10 days. **Difficulty:** Moderately to extremely difficult. Many steep ascents and snow crossings; extensive cross-country section.

Maps:

• Landmælingar Íslands 1:100,000 Atlas Maps 57, 58 and 67.

Up northeast slope from Skjólkviar to summit of Mt. Hekla. A long, but not overly difficult ascent of Iceland's most famous volcano. Extensive lava fields and numerous steaming vents. Perennial snow on summit, where the view is spectacular in all directions. **Walking Time:** 3 to 4 hours. **Difficulty:** Moderately difficult; easiest ascent route.

Maps:
• Landmælingar Íslands 1:100,000 Atlas Map 57; and 1:50,000 Quarter Sheet 57-SV.

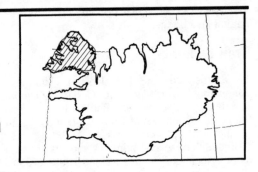

The Western Fjords

The large claw-shaped peninsula that makes up extreme northwest Iceland is known as Vestfirdir (the Western Fjords). It is attached to the rest of the island by a neck of land only about 16 kilometers across. It is a sparsely populated, largely mountainous region from which snowy tablelands plunge steeply to the shore. The coast is indented by numerous large fjords, the largest of which is Ísafjardardjúp on the north coast. The town of Isafjördur, which sits on the west side of the fjord, is the largest settlement in Vestfirdir. Three kilometers from town, in the Seljalandsdalur Valley, is a ski lodge which operates year round and serves as a convenient base camp during the summer for walks into the nearby mountains. The ridges dividing the fjords are made of ancient basaltic rock, and volcanic activity in the region has been slight in geologically recent times. The ridges are usually flat-topped and rise to heights of between 300 and 400 meters. The peninsula's highest peak, Kaldbakur, is just under 1,000 meters. On the east side of Ísafjardardjúp, the small icecap Drangajökull rises to 925 meters. The region north of the icecap is uninhabited except for a single lighthouse keeper at Látravík, on the extreme northeast coast. Vegetation in the region is scanty and usually confined to the shores of the fjords.

Trail Lodgings

A few primitive shelters are found in Vestfirdir. A youth hostel is located at Isafjördur. For hut locations, see the Iceland Touring Club's 1:750,000 Tourist Map.

Maps

• Landmælingar Íslands 1:100,000 Atlasblöd (Atlas Map), sheets 2, 3, 10, 11, 12, 13, 20, 21, 22, 23, 31, 32 and 33. Or:

• Landmælingar Íslands 1:50,000 Fjórdungsblöd (Quarter Sheet), sheets 2-SA; 3-NA, NV and SA; 10-SA; 11-NA, SA and SV; 12-NA, NV, SA and SV; 13-NA, NV, SA and SV; 20-SA and SV; 21-NA, NV, SA and SV; 22-NA, NV, SA and SV; 23-NA, NV, SA and SV; 31-SV; 32-NA, NV, SA and SV; and 33-NA, NV, SA and SV.

Suggested Walks

From Bæir to Hesteyri. A long, rugged trip on the lonely peninsula east of Ísafjardarjúp. Passes mountains, spectacular seacliffs, coastal marshes, abandoned farmsteads, nesting sites for abundant seabirds and numerous waterfalls. Provides close-up views of Drangajökull and the possibility to visit the peninsula's only inhabitant, the hospitable lighthouse keeper at Látravík. **Walking Time:** 8 days. **Difficulty:** Easy to very difficult; some cross-country travel is necessary.
Maps:
• Landmælingar Íslands 1:100,000 Atlas Maps 20 and 21; or 1:50,000 Quarter Sheets 20-SA and SV; 21-NA, NV and SV; and (optional) 21-SA.

Address Directory

B

• *Banalag Íslenzkra Farfugla* (Icelandic Youth Hostel Association), P.O. Box 1045, Reykjavik. Tel. 2 49 50.

• *Bókaverzlun Larusar Blöndal,* Skólavördustig 2, Vesturver. Tel. 15650.

• *Bókaverzlun Sigfusar Eymundssonar,* Austurstræti 18, Reykjavik. Tel. 18880.

• *Bókaverzlun Snæbiarnar* (English Bookstore), Hafnarstræt 4 og 9, Reykjavik. Tel. 14281.

D

• *Dick Phillips, see Phillips, Dick.*

E

• *Emergency: Slysavarnafélag Íslands* (Lifesaving Organization of Iceland), Grandagardi 14, Reykjavik. Tel. 27111. 24-hour service. Or call: *Hjálparsveit Skáta* (Boy Scout Life Saving Association), Hverfisgata 49, Reykjavik. Tel. 26430.

F

- *Ferdafélag Íslands* (Iceland Traveling Club), Öldugata 3, Reykjavik. Tel. 19533.
- *Ferdamálarád Íslands* (Iceland Tourist Board), P.O. Box 1184, Reykjavik. Tel. 15677 and 27488.
- *Ferdaskrifstofa Ríkisins* (Iceland Tourist Bureau), Reykjanesbraut 6, Reykjavik. Tel. 25855.
- *Flugleidir (Icelandair)*, Reykjavik Airport. Tel. 27800.

G

- *Geysir*, Vesturgotu 1, Reykjavik. Tel. 11350.

H

- *Hjálparsveit Skáta* (Boy Scout Life Saving Association), Hverfisgata 49, Reykjavik. Tel. 26430.

I

- *Iceland Touring Club*, see *Ferdafélag Íslands*.
- *Iceland Tourist Board*, see *Ferdamálarád Íslands*.
- *Iceland Tourist Bureau*, see *Ferdaskrifstofa Ríkisins*.
- *Icelandair*, see *Flugleidir*.
- *Icelandic Alpine Club (ISALP)*, Reykjavik. Tel. 36059.
- *Icelandic National Tourist Office*, see *Scandinavian National Tourist Offices*, or in Iceland, *Ferdaskrifstofa Ríkisins*.

L

- *Landmælingar Íslands*, Laugavegi 178, Reykjavik. Tel. 38245.

M

- *Minjagripathjónustan*, P.O. Box 4105, Reykjavik. Tel. 82574.

O

- *Örn og Örlygur* (Iceland Travel Books), Sidumuli 11, Reykjavik. Tel. 25722.

P

- *Phillips, Dick*, Whitehall House, Nenthead, Alston, Cumbria, CA9 3PS, England. Tel. Alston 440.

S

- *Scandinavian National Tourist Offices, New York,* 75 Rockefeller Plaza, New York, New York 10019, U.S.A. Tel. (212) 582-2802.
- *Skatabudin,* Snorrabraut 58, Reykjavik. Tel. 12045.
- *Slysavarnafélag Íslands* (Lifesaving Organization of Iceland), Grandagardi 14, Reykjavik. Tel. 27111. 24-hour service.
- *Sportval,* Laugaveg 116, Reykjavik. Tel. 14390.

T

- *Tjaldaleigan,* Umferdarmidstödin (Bus Terminal), Reykjavik. Tel. 13072.

U

- *Úlfar Jacobsen,* Tourist Bureau Ltd., P.O. Box 886, Austurstræti 9, Reykjavik. Tel. 13499.
- *Útilif,* Alfheimar 74, Reykjavik.
- *ÚTIVIST* (Outdoor Life Club), Lækjargötu 6, Reykjavik. Tel. 14606.

W

- *Weather:*
- *Recorded Weather Forecasts* (in Icelandic): Tel. 17000.
- *Verdurstofan* (weather bureau) for forecasts in English: Tel. 86000.

A Quick Reference

In a hurry? Turn to the pages listed below. They will give you the most important information on walking in Iceland.

Search & Rescue, page 152.

Weather Forecasts, page 139.

Associations to Contact for Information:
On Walking, page 140.
On Iceland's Principal Walking Regions, page 155.
Tourist Information, page 151.

Maps, page 141.

Guidebooks, page 142.

Equipment, page 146.

Address Directory, page 167.

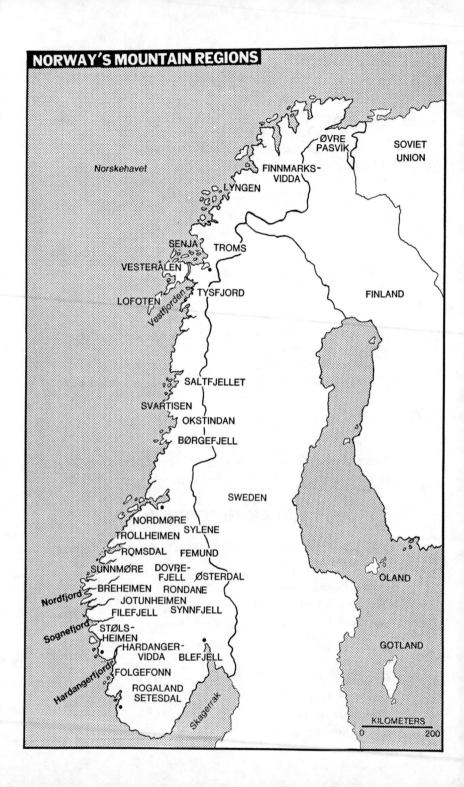

NORWAY'S MOUNTAIN REGIONS

Norskehavet

ØVRE PASVIK

SOVIET UNION

FINNMARKS-VIDDA

LYNGEN

SENJA

TROMS

VESTERÅLEN

FINLAND

LOFOTEN

TYSFJORD

Vestfjorden

SALTFJELLET

SVARTISEN

OKSTINDAN

BØRGEFJELL

SWEDEN

NORDMØRE

SYLENE

TROLLHEIMEN

ROMSDAL

FEMUND

SUNNMØRE

DOVRE-FJELL

ØSTERDAL

OLAND

Nordfjord

BREHEIMEN

RONDANE

JOTUNHEIMEN

FILEFJELL

SYNNFJELL

Sognefjord

STØLS-HEIMEN

GOTLAND

HARDANGER-VIDDA

BLEFJELL

Hardangerfjord

FOLGEFONN

ROGALAND

SETESDAL

Skagerrak

KILOMETERS

0   200

Norway

NORWAY IS A superb country for mountain touring—both on foot in summer and on skis in winter. Mountains cover 72 percent of the country, rising up to 2,469 meters (8,100 feet) above remote valleys, vast glaciers and rolling moors clad with wildflowers. From the coast, fjords thrust their way inland, winding between steep mountain walls, from which a myriad of waterfalls tumble earthward in white-foam plumes. Everywhere you go there is a majestic, awe-inspiring juxtaposition of water and mountain, glacier and forest, and rock and tundra.

Along the verdant shores of the fjords, small villages cluster around white clapboard churches against a backdrop of mountains. From such bays the slender, high-prowed Viking longboats sailed to England in the 9th century, leaving the Norwegian word *ransack* as a permanent momento. Higher up, rugged mountain plateaus stretch as far as the eye can see and the wild array of snow-capped peaks are reflected in thousands of mountain lakes, along the shores of which are scattered *seters* (summer farms) and the ancient remains of old reindeer hunting pits.

Nearly 7,000 kilometers of cairned paths wind through the mountainous terrain, passing lakes, glaciers and Stone Age hunting grounds; climbing peaks; and winding down to the shores of the fjords. Along the paths is a network of more than 200 mountain huts operated by Norway's local mountain touring associations in cooperation with *Den Norsk Turistforening* (the Norwegian Mountain Touring Association).

In the winter, marked and prepared ski tracks fanning out from more than 130 ski centers lead through forests, across moors and to the summits of mountain peaks. In Oslomarka alone—the hilly, wooded country surrounding Oslo—there are more than 2,200 kilometers of marked and prepared ski tracks, plus facilities for equipment rental, cross-country ski instruction and 54 lighted ski trails—a large number of which are accessible in less than half an hour from the National Theatre underground station in the heart of Oslo.

Much of Norway's high country is open and rugged, and in many places along the fjords, every meter of elevation has to be climbed from sea level. But there are also gentler, wooded walks. Forests cover 24 percent of the country and, in some of the national parks, include stands of 500-year-old spruce trees. There are also pine forests and, near the tree-limit, stands of gnarled birch.

With slightly more than 4 million people, Norway's population density is, next to Iceland, the lowest in Europe. The bulk of the population lives in small towns and settlements scattered in the valleys, near the fjords and on the flat coastal fringes of its islands. In the far north, there are some 20,000 people of Samic (Lappish) origin, 3,000 of whom are mountain Lapps who still live by raising reindeer. Residents of remote villages are usually friendly and receptive to travelers, and during the short days and long nights of the northern winter, candles burn in their windows, glowing with a cheerful welcome.

Near the populated settlements, there are farmlands, orchards and green, rolling dairy country. But less than 4 percent of Norway's land area is cultivated. The other 96 percent—the mountains and forests—is the realm of the hiker, mountaineer and ski tourer. An Act of Parliament (the Open Air Act of 1957) guarantees, with some reasonable restrictions, every Norwegian's right of access to this countryside, a right that foreigners also enjoy.

Because of Norway's extreme length, nearly half of which lies above the Arctic Circle, the scenery and weather conditions vary enormously from south to north. (If Norway were pivoted southward from the city of Kristiansand, it would reach to Rome, Italy, a distance of 1,752 kilometers—Europe's longest country). It also has 150,000 islands and an astounding 21,112 kilometers of coastline. As a result, the scope of opportunities for hiking and ski touring is enough to more than occupy one lifetime.

North-south distances are long, and the traveler who wants to go to Finnmark (Lappland) must invest substantial time and money. But east-west distances are short (ranging from a maximum width of 430 kilometers in the south, to a mere 6.3 kilometers near Narvik), and the majority of the mountain and forest country is easily accessible by train and bus.

Norway has two official languages—*Bokmål,* a Norwegianised Danish, and *Nynorsk,* built upon the village dialects, that developed as a medium for depicting country life. Though closely related, the two languages differ in pronunciation, grammar and vocabulary. In addition, many Norwegians, including a fair number in remote areas, speak English. A few also speak German or, occasionally, French. Tourist information is often translated into English and German, and the planning maps to South Norway's mountain regions, published by *Den Norsk Turistforening,* have keys in English. Moreover, one of the principal guidebooks to hiking in Norway is available in English *(Mountain Touring Holidays in Norway)* and German *(Bergwandern in Norwegen).*

Flora & Fauna

Norway's flora follows a succession typical of plant communities in the far north. At low altitudes in the south of the country, the forests are composed primarily of spruce and fir, with a few species of deciduous trees. As altitude and latitude increase, the deciduous trees gradually disappear and spruce is replaced by pine. At the forest limit, however, the pine is replaced by the deciduous birch as the dominant tree, which then gives way to thickets of willow and dwarf birch and, finally, to open moors in which nearly 200 species of mountain plants flourish.

Luxuriant plant communities of ferns, several species of grass and numerous flowering plants are occasionally found in moist, sunny openings within the birch forests. On the other hand, where the soil is dry and poor, the birch woods are sparse and the ground between the trees is mostly occupied by lichens, the most common of which is the whitish-yellow reindeer moss.

A comparable contrast in vegetation is found within the treeless zones. On steep, comparatively warm south-facing slopes, rocks, clefts and shelves provide shelter for a rich variety of plants. On the opposite side of the same ridge, scree and frost-broken rocks often dominate the landscape, and plant species are sparse.

As the makeup of the soil and its moisture content varies, the walker moves through a high-alpine world of lush meadows, vivid heath communities, patches of mountain berries and across bogs and fens with their variety of grasses, sedges and mosses. On the moist ground of snow-bed communities, you can sometimes stand in one place and count 40 different species of plants—each of which competes for your attention with a bright display of color. As you climb higher, the bilberry and willow thickets disappear and, finally, the heath and grass communities give way to the snow, ice, rock and scree of the upper alpine belt where the few remaining plants are small and well-hidden from the eye, but include some of Norway's rarest species, such as Arctic poppy, Norwegian sandwort, smoothing braya and ascending saxifrage.

On some mountain trails you can even pass through all of these communities in a single day's walk. And lest you pass unnoticing by the fragile blossom of a rare mountain plant, there is a handy, pocket-size booklet to help you identify the flora:

- *Mountain Flowers of Scandinavia* (available in English, Norwegian, Swedish and Finnish) by Olav Gjærevoll and Reidar Jørgensen, edited by Trondhjems Turistforening, F. Bruns Bokhandels Forlag, Trondheim. Available for a nominal charge from Den Norsk Turistforening (for its address and telephone number, see the *Address Directory* at the back of this chapter).

Norway's wildlife includes animals such as the hare, fox, wolverine, lemming and reindeer, which are found in the north and above the conifer limit in the mountains of South Norway. There are elk and roe deer in the forests of East Norway, red deer on the west coast, and a scattering of beaver, mink, marten and musk ox. The bear and lynx, once numerous, are now rare.

Many birds native to Norway also nest in Britain, and many that breed in Norway visit Britain as winter migrants. On the moors, ptarmigan and capercaillie are found, and on the coasts, numerous ducks and gulls.

The only dangerous snake is the viper, which is found only in the southern forests, and there rarely. A bite, however, should receive immediate medical attention. Mosquitoes, gnats and no-see-ums are seldom a major nuisance in western and central Norway, but they can drive you to distraction in Arctic Norway. For hikes during midsummer in the far north, insect repellent and tightly knit insect netting to protect your face are musts.

Climate

Because of the Gulf Stream and the general west-east circulation of the atmosphere, Norway has a fairly temperate climate—much warmer than one would expect from its extreme northerly location. During the winter, even harbors as far north as Hammerfest remain ice-free.

Summer normally extends from May until late September in the coastal regions and lowland valleys of western and central Norway. Average midday temperatures during this period range from about 13.3° C. (56° F.) to 20° C. (68° F.), with temperatures of 25° C. (77° F.)—or more—occasionally occurring in July.

In the mountains summer is shorter, lasting only from the end of June until the beginning of September, with the peak season from July 15 to August 15. As the altitude increases, air temperatures become cooler. Midday temperatures during July may reach 22° C. (71.6° F.) on some of the mountain plateaus in central and western Norway, but freezing temperatures (and sudden storms) are also possible.

In contrast, average temperatures in Oslo during January and February hover around *minus* 5° C. (23° F.). In Røros, located in central Norway 400 kilometers to the north, temperatures for the same period average about *minus* 10.5° C. (13° F.). And in some of the inland mountain ranges temperatures can sometimes dip as low as *minus* 40° C. (*minus* 40° F.).

Norway's northerly location has a significant effect on its hours of daylight. In North Norway, there is never any real darkness from the end of April until the middle of August and the sun remains continuously above the horizon from May 14 to July 30 at North Cape; from May 26 to July 19 in Narvick; and from June 5 to July 9 in Bodø. Conversely, there is almost continuous darkness in the far north during the winter months.

The moist, prevailing southwest winds that blow across Norway bring large amounts of precipitation. Bergen, sometimes called the wettest city in Europe, annually receives an average of 1,884 mm (74 inches) of precipitation. On the other hand, Oslo annually receives only 768 mm (30 inches) of precipitation, while Trondheim annually receives about 823 mm (32.5 inches). August is the wettest month throughout much of Norway, although Bergen receives the greatest amount of precipitation during the autumn and winter.

Snow may fall in Norway as early as October and often lasts into April. Many higher mountain regions, however, might not be fully snow-free until July. The towns of Oslo, Lillehammer and Geilo each receive an annual average of about 3.5 meters (11.5 feet) of snow. High mountain regions receive much more. As a rule, stable snow conditions—and therefore the ski season—last from the beginning of January through March.

As with any mountainous region, weather conditions can change swiftly, and walkers should be prepared for severe storms and low temperatures at any time of the year.

Weather Forecasts

Recorded weather forecasts in Norwegian can be obtained by telephone in Oslo and several large towns in Norway:

Recorded Weather Forecasts: Tel. 016.

Elsewhere, you can call the weather service directly. Its telephone number is:

Weather Service: Tel. 018.

Additional information also can be obtained by telephoning the Meteorological Institute in Oslo:

Meterologisk Institutt (see *Address Directory*). Tel. (02) 50 50 90.

Most operators at the weather services and the Meteorological Institute speak both Norwegian and English. If you call either of these numbers, however, you should specify:

1. That you wish to obtain a weather forecast;
2. The locality for which you wish a forecast;
3. The purpose for which the forecast is required; and
4. The weather features that are of interest to you (wind, rain and temperature, for instance).

Where to Get Walking Information

You can obtain information on practically every aspect of mountain travel in Norway by writing:

Den Norsk Turistforening (see *Address Directory*). Staff speaks English and German. Letters may also be written in French, although the response may be in English.

The DNT is an extremely active mountain touring association with nearly 90,000 members, of whom 8,000 are foreign members. Founded in 1868, the DNT operates mountain huts, marks summer and winter routes, and arranges numerous guided mountain hikes and mountaineering courses.

It also publishes a series of free planning maps to the most popular mountain regions in South Norway. In addition to showing the topographical maps covering each area and the locations of lodgings and shelters, each map indicates: 1) cairned routes, with the average walking times between mountain huts, 2) unmarked routes, and 3) routes across glaciers for which a guide is necessary.

The DNT also sells a 96-page booklet in English—*Mountain Touring Holidays in Norway*—and German—*Bergwandern in Norwegen*—which is one of the most complete resources available for planning hikes in any single country in Europe. Among the information included in the booklet is an overview of the opportunities for various mountain activities in Norway—hiking, climbing, spelunking, angling, horseback riding, and so on—a description of each of Norway's principal mountain regions, detailed information on trail lodgings, plus route descriptions for several suggested 5- to 10-day mountain hikes in each region.

Between the planning maps and *Mountain Touring Holidays in Norway* it is unlikely you will have many questions left, but if you do the DNT can provide the answers. It also can provide information on guided mountain hikes, climbing and climbing courses, and the hire of guides for glacier treks. In some cases, it will even make the necessary arrangements for guided hikes and climbs for you.

Finally, once your planning is done and you have decided where you want to go, the DNT can sell you the necessary topographical maps as well as Norwegian-language guides to hikes in each mountain region. If you are a DNT member and drop into its Oslo office, it can also supply keys to mountain huts which are kept locked.

The only thing the DNT cannot provide, in fact, is detailed information on cross-country skiing. But the Norway Travel Association publishes an annual brochure that fills this gap (for details, see the section on *Cross-Country Skiing* later in this chapter).

Norway's Mountain Touring Associations

The DNT cooperates with about 30 local mountain touring associations throughout the country. These associations mark paths, build and operate mountain huts, and arrange guided mountain hikes in their areas. Membership privileges between the DNT and the local mountain touring associations are reciprocal: a member of any of the associations is entitled to discounts in DNT's huts and on all of its arrangements and vice versa.

Foreign hikers who wish to join a mountain touring association in Norway should join the DNT. This will entitle you to:

1. Generous discounts and precedence over non-members for accommodation at the DNT and local tourist association huts;
2. Discounts on overnight stays at a number of private tourist huts;
3. Use of keys to locked mountain huts;
4. Complimentary copies of the DNT's yearbook and quarterly magazine (both in Norwegian; sometimes with summaries in English);
5. Advice and guidance for planning trips;
6. Participation in the DNT's conducted tours, meetings and courses; and
7. Discounts on fees for guides for crossing glaciers.

Full details on membership in the DNT, along with a membership application, will be sent on request.

Maps

For planning hikes in the mountain ranges of South Norway, you should first obtain the DNT's free planning maps to the regions you wish to explore. The planning maps are not suitable for use on the trail, but they will give you all the information you need to plot out hiking routes, decide where you are going to stay, and choose the points where you can replenish your provisions. The planning maps also show the names and sheet numbers of the 1:50,000 and 1:100,000 topographical maps that cover each region, so you can order the appropriate maps once your itinerary is finalized.

Planning maps are not yet available to all the mountain regions in North Norway, but routes can be planned by using the Cappelens Maps available from the DNT (listed below). You can also determine which topographical maps are required for hikes anywhere in Norway by referring to the *Kart Katalog* available from Norway's Geographical Survey office:

Norges Geografiske Oppmåling (see *Address Directory*). Staff understands English and German.

The map catalog, which includes an index and price list, is free on request. The survey office, however, does not sell maps. Instead, you must purchase topographical maps from the DNT or from international map outlets such as:

Edward Stanford Ltd. or:

GEO CENTER (see *Address Directory*).

Topographical Maps

Most of Norway is covered by 1:50,000 and 1:100,000 topographical maps (known respectively as the *Serie M711* and *Gradteigskart*). Neither series covers the entire country and in some mountain areas you may have to use 1:50,000 sheets to follow part of your route and 1:100,000 sheets for the remainder. Nonetheless, both series are suitable for mountain hiking.

In addition, there are special maps—known as *Turistkart*—which cover some of the most popular hiking areas in South Norway, plus several large-scale maps to popular winter sport centers on which ski tracks are marked *(Skikart)*.

The *Turistkart* range in scale from 1:100,000 to 1:250,000 and cover Hardangervidda, Jotunheimen and Rodane. They may be purchased from the DNT.

The *Skikart* are available in a scale of 1:50,000 and cover Gol, Oslo nordmark and Ringebu. These maps may be purchased from the DNT, as well as from bookstores in Oslo and from bookstores and local tourist offices in the ski areas.

Cappelens Maps

These are a series of small-scale tourist maps on which roads and principal mountain tracks are shown. Their scale makes them unsuitable for use in the mountains, but they are good for general planning. Their legends are also translated into English, German and French. The series includes:

Blad 1-2, 1:325,000. Covers the southern part of Norway as far north as Bergen.

Blad 3-4, 1:325,000. Covers the central part of southern Norway, from Oslo in the south to Ålesund and Røros in the north.

Blad 5-6, 1:325,000. Covers the region between Ålesund–Røros and Namsos–Grong. Includes Trondheim.
Blad 7-8, 1:400,000. Covers the region from Grong north. Includes the Lofoten Islands, Harstad and Narvik.
Blad 9-10, 1:400,000. Covers the rest of Norway, including Troms and Finnmark.
Blad 13, 1:1,000,000. Covers all of Norway.

All the sheets can be obtained from the DNT. A price list and details on the cost of postage and payment procedures is available on request.

DNT Planning Maps

The following planning maps may be obtained from the DNT:

Dovrefjell—Trollheimen—Møre—Romsdal
Fjellrute i Finnmark
Finse—Bygdin
Gausdal Vestfjell
Hardangervidda
Hardangervidda—Blefjell
Harstad
Indre—Troms
Jotunheimen—Breheimen
Koiestrøket
Narvikfjella
Østerdal—Femund
Rana
Rondane
Rondane—Lillehammer
Saltfjellet—Sulitjelma
Setesdal—Ryfylke—Heiane
Stølsheimen—Bergsdalen—Kvamskogen—Folgefonni
Sylene

Guidebooks

The DNT publishes several Norwegian-language guidebooks to the most popular mountain regions in Norway. These include:

• *Til Fots i Femundsmarka og Sylane*
• *Til Fots på Hardangervidda*
• *Til Fots i Jotunheimen*

- *Til Fots i Oslomarka*
- *Til Fots i Rondane—Dovrefjell—Trollheimen*
- *Til Fots i Setesdal- og Rogalandsheiene*
- *Fiske og Ferie Nordpå*
- *Sunnmøre*

Guidebooks with international symbols and abbreviations have also been published to the most prominent rock climbing areas in Norway: Hurrungane and Nordmøre (Innerdalen). A list of these guidebooks and their prices is available from the DNT (see *Address Directory*).

There is also an English-language guide to Romsdal:

- *Walks and Climbs in Romsdal, Norway* by Tony Howard, Cicerone Press. Available from the DNT, as well as from the publisher (see *Address Directory*) and selected booksellers in Britain.

In addition, a German-language guidebook is in the planning:

- *Kompass-Wanderführer: Norwegen*. Due sometime in 1981. Available from Deutscher Wanderverlag (see *Address Directory*).

For their overall coverage, however, the English-language and German-language editions of *Mountain Touring Holidays in Norway* (see the section on *Where to Get Walking Information*) are still unbeatable. In fact, between this one booklet and the appropriate topographical maps, it is unlikely you will need any other guidebook.

Trailside Lodgings

The DNT and Norway's local mountain touring associations operate more than 200 mountain huts and chalets along the cairned paths in Norway. Most of these huts, which range from large staffed chalets with more than 100 beds to small unstaffed huts with only four beds, are located in the mountain regions of South Norway. In North Norway the huts are few and, with only one or two exceptions, unstaffed.

There are also nearly 120 youth hostels, many of which are located near cairned paths, and hotels and guesthouses in towns near the mountain regions.

Mountain Huts

There are three kinds of mountain huts in Norway:

1) *Staffed chalets*. These are designed to enable hikers to spend their

nights in comfort and, in each, substantial meals are served. Some rooms have only two beds; others, four to six beds. Prices are less if you bring your own sheet sleeping bag, but if you wish, you can get crisp clean sheets for an additional charge during the summer. (During Easter sheet sleeping bags are required.) Full board is available and includes breakfast, a sack lunch with a thermos and dinner. Children under the age of 12 who are accompanied by their parents pay half price for regular meals and lodging; those aged 12 to 16 pay half price for lodgings when accompanied by their parents.

Opening and closing dates in the staffed chalets vary, but most are open from at least the end of June until the beginning of September. During the winter, the DNT huts are open from the Saturday before Palm Sunday through the Monday after Easter, except for huts around the Bergen Railway, which open two weeks before Easter. (Skiing from hut to hut at this time is exceedingly popular.) Several of the staffed huts also have self-service facilities for use outside the regular season. Reservations can be made only during the summer and only for stays of more than three nights. Hikers walking from hut to hut cannot reserve space in advance. The staffed chalets, however, cannot turn guests away even if all beds are taken. Hence, you can always be assured of getting accommodation—at least a mattress, blankets and floor space.

2) *Self-service huts.* These are fully stocked with bed linen and kitchen equipment, and have provisions for sale. Most are locked, although some self-service huts are open during the summer season. A key which fits all DNT huts is loaned to members, either at a neighboring hut or DNT's Oslo office. Sheet sleeping bags are required for overnight stays. Also, the huts are open only to members of the DNT and cooperating associations, and to hikers accompanied by members. There is a nominal charge for day use of the huts.

3) *Unstaffed huts.* These do not have provisions for sale, but are otherwise fully equipped. Most unstaffed huts are also kept locked, are open only to members and require a sheet sleeping bag for overnight stays.

Membership cards can be obtained in the DNT huts. Sheet sleeping bags are also for sale in the huts.

Further details on the mountain huts, including a list of the opening and closing dates for the individual staffed chalets and private staffed huts, can be obtained on request from the DNT (see *Address Directory*).

Youth Hostels

Norway's network of youth hostels is spread over the entire country from Kristiansand in the south to Honningsvåg in the north. Many of the hostels are large and modern, specially built for the purpose, while others are small and homey and located on farms or in private houses. During the summer season, several boarding schools are also used as hostels. Most of the hostels have four- to six-bed rooms, hot and cold water, showers and self-cooking facilities. Most also serve meals. A sheet sleeping bag is required. Several hostels have family rooms for young couples with children. In other hostels, families with children may request to be put in the same room.

Most hostels are open from May or June to mid-September, and a few are open all year. Advance bookings are essential for groups and are recommended for others in the larger towns and popular tourist resorts. Reservations should be made directly to the hostels. Several hostels that provide good bases for mountain hikes are listed in *Mountain Touring Holidays in Norway* (see the section on *Where to Get Walking Information*). Additional information on the hostels can be obtained from:

Landslaget for Norske Ungdomsherberger (see *Address Directory*). Publishes a list with full details on the hostels and a sketch map showing their locations. Information is written in Norwegian, English and German. The list, *Ungdomsherberger i Norge,* is free on request.

Hotels, Pensions & Guesthouses

Information on hotels and pensions throughout Norway is listed in a pamphlet available from the Norway Travel Association (see *Address Directory*):

- *Hvor Skal jeg bo Norge/Where to Stay: Norway.* Information is written in Norwegian, English, German and French. Gives full details on hotels, pensions and hostels, including prices and opening and closing dates. Free on request.

Small guesthouses, mountain lodges, boarding houses, chalets, farm guesthouses and mountain pasture farms—or *seters*—(including many that are convenient for hikers) are not always listed in the pamphlet. Local tourist offices, however, can provide information on these lodgings and, for a nominal charge, will help you find accommodation.

Camping

There are few restrictions on camping in Norway's uninhabited country. You may camp nearly anywhere you wish, so long as you adhere to two strict rules: 1) leave the place tidier than you found it, and 2) in wooded country, *never* build an open fire during the summer months (May to September). If a mountain hut has reached its overflow capacity and you wish to camp nearby, it is customary to first ask permission from the hut manager, who may have a preference where you set up your tent. Near farms or other habitations, you should always ask the owner's permission to camp.

Norway's Open Air Act of 1957—also known as the Great Open Air Charter—gives you the right to wander to your heart's content (and to camp) over 96 percent of Norway's land surface. But the 4 percent comprising Norway's farmland is out-of-bounds, and you are obliged to respect property rights.

Above tree limit, the vegetation is often easily damaged. Here, you should always be sure to camp on firm ground and to adhere to standard camping practices. Be careful since even one careless camper can destroy fragile ground cover that may take *20 years or more* to recover. For this reason, lush, wildflower-speckled meadows that look like such tempting campsites should be avoided.

Along the roads, there are nearly 1,200 commercial campsites in Norway, many of which are located in mountain areas. Some of the campsites also have inexpensive chalets or camping huts in which you can stay, although you will have to bring your own sleeping bag. Blankets and linen usually are not provided in the camping huts. A list of these campsites with an introduction and key to symbols in Norwegian, English and German may be obtained on request from the Norway Travel Association (see *Address Directory*):

- *Norge Campingplasser Ungdomsherberger.* Gives details on locations and facilities for each of Norway's campsites and youth hostels. Includes telephone numbers.

Opening dates at the campsites vary, but all are open from June 15 to August 25.

Water

You may safely drink the water from rivers and streams throughout Norway's mountain areas. Streams directly downstream from a large hotel should be avoided for drinking, as should rivers and streams in large cities. But streams and lakes near mountain huts are usually safe; to prevent fouling them, all wastes are regularly flown out from the mountain huts.

Equipment Notes

Because most mountain huts are located within a day's walk of each other, a walker can travel with a relatively light pack in Norway. Shorts and skirts are standard wear—and greatly appreciated on warm summer afternoons—but warm clothes and full length trousers should also be packed. Garments to protect you from wind and rain are essential, as is a wool cap and mittens.

Increasingly, many hikers are turning to blue jeans for their choice of longer pants, especially younger people. Blue jeans, however, are not recommended for trail wear and climbing breeches—or, as they are known to Americans, knickers—are still the choice of experienced hikers.

On dry ground, a pair of sturdy hiking boots should be worn. A light pair of knee-high rubber boots is also necessary, especially for crossing marshy areas. In the Arctic regions, insect repellent and netting to protect your face are essential. A pair of sunglasses is also recommended, particularly in areas where you may cross snowfields or glaciers.

For staying in mountain huts, you will need a sheet sleeping bag and towel (and, to save money and be able to use the self-service and unstaffed huts, a DNT membership card). If you intend to camp, you should bring a lightweight tent with a dark-colored fabric to cut out the Midnight Sun. The tent should be sturdy enough to stand up to gale-force winds since many of the places in which you may camp will be above the tree limit and open to the full force of storms. It also should have no-see-um proof netting that can be tightly sealed on all vents and entrances.

Provisions for camping can be bought in any town or village in Norway. Many of the Norwegian canned foods are delicious, including the bread known as *knekkebrød,* which will keep for weeks. But if you take canned foods into the mountains, be sure to bring the empty cans back out again. Even if you don't intend to camp, it is advisable to pack some *knekkebrød* and spreads to make your own lunch. It will be much cheaper than buying a sandwich at one of the huts.

Winter trips will require more equipment: suitable clothing for sub-zero temperatures, a thin pair of silk gloves worn inside your mittens so you can handle metal equipment without risk of frostbite and a warm sleeping bag.

Crowded Trails

Because a hiker can roam over so much of Norway's terrain, it is easy to find places where you can have a vast panorama of peaks, moors and forests entirely to yourself. In the more popular hiking regions in South Norway, mountain huts sometimes become crowded, but few cairned paths ever have a steady stream of hikers passing hither and fro. The sole exception to this is the Jotunheimen, where cairned paths, and especially the mountain huts, do become crowded between mid-July and mid-August. Mountain huts that are opened during Easter also become packed. Three other areas that receive a disproportionate share of use during mid-summer and Easter are Hardangervidda, Rondane and Trollheimen. But it is easy to avoid the crowds by either hiking elsewhere, or by hiking in the more popular areas after August 15.

Walking & Skiing Tours

The DNT organizes more than 170 guided tours through various mountain regions in Norway, both in summer and winter. These include mountain hikes, glacier tours, ski treks, dog sled tours and horseback trips. The tours span varying degrees of difficulty and are intended for hikers in average physical form. Normally, they last from one to two weeks. On the glacier tours, dog sled tours and horseback trips, no previous experience is necessary. The DNT also assists in planning trips and courses for groups with special interests. Details on the various arrangements can be obtained on request from the DNT (see *Address Directory*).

Climbing & Climbing Courses

All of Norway's peaks have been climbed, although the records of many of these ascents have been published only in Norwegian. Nonetheless, many new routes remain to be pioneered and the scope for new climbs of varying degrees of difficulty—particularly in Arctic Norway—is still considerable.

Guidebooks to climbs in Hurrungane, Romsdalen and Nordmøre (Innerdalen) can be obtained from the DNT.

For the less adventurous—or experienced—there are several climbing courses and tours in which you can participate. The DNT conducts climbing courses at Innerdalen each summer, in which participants learn the basic principles of rock climbing. The DNT also arranges glacier-walking courses to provide elementary, practical and theoretical knowledge about glaciers and glacier crossings. These courses are held at Finse, Krossbu, Flatbrehytta (Jostedal Glacier) and on the Svartisen Glacier. Prior experience is not necessary for any of these courses. Further information is available on request from the DNT.

Norsk Alpincenter

The Norsk Alpincenter, founded in 1967, is the only permanent school of its kind in Norway. Based in Hemsedal, it conducts beginning and advanced courses throughout Norway in rock and ice climbing, glacier touring, ski mountaineering, alpine ski touring, Nordic ski touring and white-water kayaking. Its staff consists of two permanent and more than 20 part-time instructors. It also offers courses and seminars for teachers and mountain rescue personnel, and qualification courses for instructors and guides. In addition, it provides information and advice on techniques, equipment, theory and instruction. A nonprofit organization, it publishes a thrice-yearly periodical *Mestre Fjellet* (Master the Mountains) and works to promote an understanding of nature and each person's responsibility for the environment. Further information is available from:

Norsk Alpincenter (see *Address Directory*).

Mountain Guides

Guides are available for glacier crossings in the most popular mountain ranges. They are usually based at—or at least can be contacted through—the local tourist lodges and staffed mountain chalets. Information can be obtained from the DNT (see *Address Directory*).

Guides for rock and ice climbs are not available in Norway.

Cross-Country Skiing

Norway is the home of cross-country—or, more aptly, *Nordic*— skiing. In fact, people have been skiing in Norway for more than 4,000 years. In some remote areas it is still a principal mode of transport. But above all, skiing is the country's national sport—and pasttime—in the winter. On Sundays, Norwegian families take *en masse* to prepared tracks in the woods and mountains. Events like the annual Birkebeiner Ski Race, held at Lillehammer each March, attract thousands of participants from all over the world and have been used as models for similar events in practically every country in the Western Hemisphere.

The first regular ski trails in the country were developed in the 1880s by the *Foreingen til Ski-Idrettens Fremme* (Society for the Promotion of Skiing). Since then, the number of prepared tracks—and the worldwide popularity of Nordic skiing—has mushroomed. Around Oslo alone there are now more than 2,200 kilometers (1,366 miles) of marked and prepared ski tracks. And this is just the beginning.

The *Statens Ungdoms- og Idrettskontor* (State Office for Youth and Sports)—or S.T.U.I.—provides funding for the development, marking and preparation of nearly 1,000 ski tracks throughout the country. Ski tracks are also prepared and marked by the DNT, local mountain touring associations and personnel at Norway's winter sport resorts and ski centers.

A comprehensive list of the places where you can ski tour in Norway is published each year by the Norway Travel Association (see *Address Directory*):

- *Norway: Snow-Sun-Fun* (in English, also available in German). Gives the names, locations, and transportation connections to ski centers throughout Norway. Includes information on the type of terrain, facilities for ski rental and instruction, lengths of ski touring trails, places where ski touring maps can be obtained, and a brief description of popular ski touring destinations for each center. Maps showing the locations of the ski centers are included.

This is the best list of its kind available in Norway. There are, however, several other sources of information available. The DNT, for instance, publishes a sketch map of its marked ski tracks in the Jotunheimen, Hardangervidda, Dovrefjell and Rondane:

- *Hytter og Kvistruter Vinteren* (Winter Huts and Ski routes). Free on request. Ski routes are marked with birch branches and only during Easter.

A sketch map of ski routes in the Trollheimen and Sylene mountains is available from:

Trondhjems Turistforening (see *Address Directory*).

Many ski centers also have maps of the tracks in their areas. Some of these maps are free; others must be purchased. In addition, a guidebook is published to Oslomarka, Norway's capital of ski touring:

- *På ski i Oslomarka* (in Norwegian) by Knut A. Nilsen Jr., published by Gyldendal Norsk Forlag in cooperation with Foreningen til Ski-Idrettens Fremme. Available from the Foreningen til Ski-Idrettens Fremme.

Further information on ski touring in Norway can be obtained directly from the various ski centers (their addresses are listed in *Norway: Snow-Sun-Fun)* or from:

See *Address Directory*:

Foreningen til Ski-Idrettens Fremme. Organizes the annual Holmenkollen Ski Festival in Oslo each year. Can provide information on Oslomarka. Staff speaks Norwegian, English and German.

Statens Ungdoms- og Idrettskontor (S.T.U.I.). Staff speaks Norwegian, English and German. Useful publications include:

- *Oversikt over Lysløyper i Norge* (Ski Trails in Norway). A mimeographed list with the locations and lengths of the ski trails for which the S.T.U.I. provides financial support, broken down by county. Does not provide the in-depth information contained in *Norway: Snow-Sun-Fun,* nor does it attempt to list all the ski trails in Norway. Only 100 kilometers of ski tracks in Oslomarka are included.

- *Nature Trails/Trim Trails* (in English). A booklet designed to set forth guidelines for the development, clearing, construction, marking and maintenance of nature trails, keep-fit trails and ski tracks in Norway. A handy booklet for anyone interested in trail construction and maintenance. Gives a good insight into the thought, planning and work that go into trail design, construction and maintenance, and hence, is recommended reading for any hiker or cross-country skier.

Special Train & Bus Fares

There is little money-saving news to report here. Long trips cost less per kilometer than short trips. Beyond that, there are no special fares that give you a price-break for travel on Norway's network of trains, buses and ferries. The only way to beat transportation costs is to be of a nationality so you can purchase a Eurail Pass before you arrive in Norway, or young enough so you can purchase an Inter-Rail Pass.

Useful Addresses & Telephone Numbers

General Tourist Information

In Norway:

Landslaget for Reiselivet i Norge (Norway Travel Association). See *Address Directory*. Staff speaks Norwegian, English, German and French. Useful publications include:

- *Norway—Land of Adventure* (in English). Provides general information on the attractions and sights throughout Norway. Includes the addresses and telephone numbers of local tourist offices. In German, the brochure is entitled: *Norwegen Urlaub für Entdecker,* and in French, it is entitled: *La Norwege Merveilleuse.*
- *Norway: Snow-Sun-Fun* (in English). Provides information on the places and facilities for cross-country skiing in Norway (see the section on *Cross-Country Skiing*). A German-language edition, *Norwegen: Shenee-Sonne,* is also available.
- *Mountain Touring Holidays in Norway* (in English). Described in the section on *Where to Get Walking Information.* Gives the best overall view of the opportunities for mountain hikes in Norway. Also provides information on other mountain activities, such as

orienteering and rock cave exploring. A German-language edition, *Bergwandern in Norwegen,* is also available.

- *Angling in Norway* (in English). Indispensable for the angler. Covers salmon fishing, trout fishing and seawater fishing in the same detail that *Mountain Touring Holidays* covers hiking.

Several other publications are also available, both from the Norway Travel Association and its branch offices:

Abroad:

Branch offices of the Norway Travel Association are located in EUROPE: Amsterdam, Brussels, Copenhagen, Hamburg, London, Paris and Stockholm; and in the U.S.A.: Los Angeles and New York.

London: Norwegian National Tourist Office, 20 Pall Mall, London SW1Y 5 NE. Tel. (01) 839 6255.

New York: Scandinavian National Tourist Offices, 75 Rockefeller Plaza, New York, New York 10019. Tel. (212) 582-2802.

Sport Shops

There are several sport shops in Norway where you can purchase equipment for hiking, cross-country skiing and climbing. One of the best, however, is located in Oslo:

Sport Co A/S (see *Address Directory*). Located less than 100 meters from the DNT's Oslo office. Very well stocked. Has climbing hardware, ropes, snow shovels, a full line of tents, sleeping bags, and boots—even double winter boots. A free catalog *Fjellsport* is available on request.

Search & Rescue

The local police are responsible for all search and rescue operations in Norway. Normally, there is no charge for this service. But a person may be charged in case of exceedingly stupid mistakes. Hence, if you get into trouble because you are ill-equipped or try to cross terrain where your ability (and common sense) dictate that you have no right to be, and you have to be rescued, it could cost you—a lot.

There is no central emergency telephone number for search and rescue.

In case of an emergency: 1) proceed to the nearest mountain hut for assistance, or 2) find the nearest telephone and call the local police.

The emergency telephone number for the police will be listed on the first page of telephone directories. The number you should call will be listed under: *Alarmtelefon Politi.*

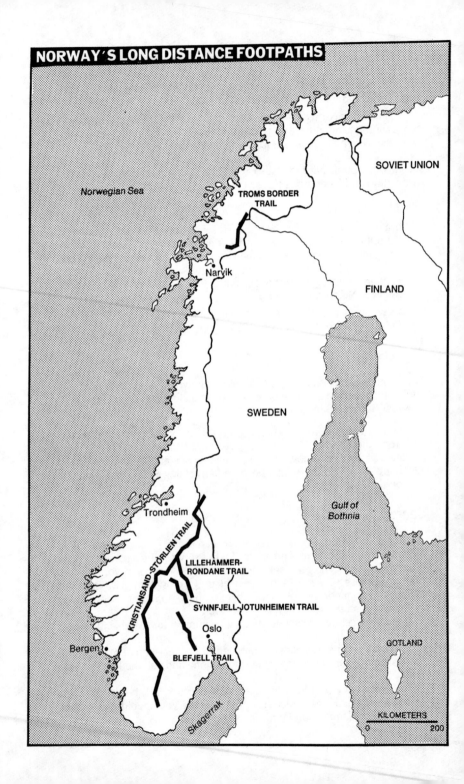

Norway's Long-Distance Footpaths

Technically, Norway has only four cairned routes that qualify as "long-distance footpaths"—routes that stand alone and span a long distance: the Blefjell Trail, the Lillehammer-Rondane Trail, the Synnfjell-Jotunheimen Trail and the Troms Border Trail. The possibilities for long-distance hikes in Norway, however, are practically unlimited. Simply by looking at one of the DNT's planning maps (see the section on *Maps*), you can easily plan several hikes of a week's duration. Virtually every one of the hikes suggested later in this chapter is for five days or longer. And if you follow some of the unmarked routes or strike off cross-country, the possibilities are even greater. Trail systems in the various mountain regions also can be linked together for long-distance hikes. For instance, cairned routes link Kristiansand, on the southern tip of Norway, and Storlien, east of Trondheim on the Swedish border, allowing you to walk nearly one-third the length of Norway. Such a hike would take about seven weeks (and, for those who are interested, is described below).

Route markings vary in their consistency throughout Norway. Hence, it is necessary to always carry the appropriate topographical maps and a compass—and be sure you know how to use them. Markings consist of cairns—piles of stones—on which a red T has often been painted. Signposts have also been placed at most bridges, fords and junctions. Unmarked routes indicated on the DNT's planning maps and on topographical maps often follow a mountain track, but lack cairns and signposts. Such tracks, however, can disappear without warning on rocky or marshy ground.

Before beginning a hike, you should always plot out your route on a DNT planning map (at least in those areas for which they exist), so you can decide where you are going to restock your provisions, pinpoint the locations of overnight lodgings and estimate the walking times between them. Walking times indicated on the DNT planning maps, however, should not be taken as gospel. Remember, they are *average* walking times, without allowances for rest stops, lunch breaks or time for photographs, and can increase significantly in bad weather.

From Kristiansand to Storlien, Sweden

Begins at Åknes, 1½ hours by bus from Kristiansand (five hours by train from Oslo; ferry connection with Hirtshals, Denmark). Passes through the Rogaland-Setesdal Highlands, Hardangervidda, Finse-Bygdin, Jotunheimen, Rondane, Østerdal-Femund and Sylene Mountains. Ends at Storlien, just inside the Swedish border (trains to Stockholm; buses to Trondheim).

Can be continued on trails through Jämtland in Sweden. Gives you an unfolding panorama of everything Norway has to offer.
Walking Time: 7 weeks, minimum. **Difficulty:** Moderately difficult overall, with several difficult sections. The walk should be attempted only by experienced mountain walkers. **Path Markings:** Cairned for the most part. Roads—along which there is bus service—must be followed between Gjendesheim in the Jotunheimen and Mysuseter in Rondane, and between Vauldalen in Østerdal-Femund and Jamtvoll in the Sylene Mountains. Several seter roads are also followed for short distances and may or may not be cairned.
Trail Lodgings: All the lodgings located along the path have been listed below to help you trace its route on the DNT planning maps. Further information on each of the lodgings is contained in *Mountain Touring Holidays in Norway* (see the section on *Where to Get Walking Information*). The lodgings and walking times between them are:

Rogaland-Setesdal Highlands
Gaukheihytta, staffed hut, 9 hours from Åknes;
Øyuvsbu, self-service hut, 7 hours;
Svartenuthytta, self-service hut, 5 hours;
Bossbu, self-service hut, 3 hours;
Bykle, several hotels, youth hostel, 9 hours;
Hovdehytta, staffed hut, 12 hours;
Sloaroshytta, self-service hut, 5 hours;
Holmevasshytta, self-service hut, 5 hours;
Haukeliseter Fjellstue, staffed hut, 6 hours;

Hardangervidda Mountain Plateau
Hellevassbu, self-service hut, 7 hours;
Litlos, staffed hut, 5 hours;
Hadlaskar Turisthytte, private staffed hut, 6 hours;
Hedlo, private staffed hut, 2 hours;
Viveli Fjellstove, private staffed hut, 1½ hours;
Fossli/Liset, hotels, 4 hours;
Kjeldebu, self-service hut, 5 hours;
Finsehytta, staffed hut, 7 to 8 hours;

Finse-Bygdin Ranges
Geiterygghytta, staffed hut, 5 hours;
Iungsdalhytta, staffed hut, 8 hours;
Bjordalsbu, self-service hut, 6 hours;
Breidstølen, mountain chalet, 4 hours;
Sulebu, self-service hut, 6 hours;

Jotunheimen
Sletningsbu, self-service hut, 7 hours;
Eidsbugarden, hotel, 7 hours;
Gjendebu, staffed hut, 4½ hours;
Leirvassbu, private staffed hut, 6 hours;
Spiterstulen, private staffed hut, (daily excursions with guide to Svellnosbreen glacier), 5 hours;

Glitterheim, staffed hut, 7 hours;
Gjendesheim, staffed hut, 7 hours;
Rondane
Mysuseter (by bus from Gjendesheim), hotel;
Rondvassbu, staffed hut, 8 hours;
Bjørnhollia, staffed hut, 4 hours;
Straumbu, hotel, 2 hours;
Breisjøseter, private staffed hut, 5 hours;
Kvislåseter, private staffed hut, 3 hours;
Alvdal (along a seter road from Kvislåseter), youth hostel, 5½ hours;
Tronsvangen, hotel, 1 hour;
Østerdal-Femund
Knausen Seter, seter farm with self-service accommodation, 8 hours;
Rausjødalseter, seter accommodation, 5 hours;
Ellefsplass Gård, farm lodgings, 6 hours;
Sæter Gård, farm accommodation, 6 hours;
Svukuriset, staffed hut (across Lake Femund from Sæter Gård), 3 hours;
Røvollen, self-service hut, 5 hours;
Ljøsvåvollen, seter accommodation, 7 hours;
Vauldalen, tourist hotel, 7 hours;
Sylene Mountains
Jamtvoll (by bus from Vauldalen to Lake Aursunden and a pleasant walk
    around the lake on a seter road), hotel, 7 hours;
Kjøli, self-service hut, 7 hours;
Nedalshytta, staffed hut, 8 hours;
Storerikvollen, staffed hut, 6 to 7 hours;
Blåhammarstugan, staffed mountain station inside Sweden operated by
    Svenska turistföreningen, 5 hours;
Storlien, hotel, train and bus connections, 5 hours.
Maps:
• DNT planning maps, sheets *Setesdal-Ryfylke Heiane, Hardangervidda,
  Finse-Bygdin, Jotunheimen-Breheimen, Rondane* and *Østerdal-Femund,*
  and Trondhjems Turistforening planning map, sheet *Sylene.*
• Norges Geografiske Oppmåling Gradteigskart (Serie M 711) 1:50,000,
  sheets 1412/I, 1412/IV, 1413/III, 1413/IV, 1414/III, 1414/IV, 1415/I,
  1415/III, 1415/IV, 1619/II, 1619/III, 1718/I, 1718/IV, 1719/I, 1719/II,
  1719/III, 1720/I, 1720/II, 1720/III, 1720/IV, 1721/I, 1721/II, 1818/I and
  1818/IV.
• Norges Geografiske Oppmåling Gradteigskart 1:100,000, sheets D-33 V
  Hardangerjøkulen, D-32 V *Aurlandsdalen,* D-32 A *Djup,* D-31 A
  Fillefjell, E-31 V *Vangsmjøsi,* E-30 V *Gjende,* E-30 A *Sjodalen* and E-29 A
  Vågå.
• Norges Geografiske Oppmåling Turistkart 1:100,000, sheet 29 *Rondane*
  (optional).
Guidebooks:
• *Til Fots i Setesdal- og Rogalandsheiene* (in Norwegian).
• *Til Fots på Hardangervidda* (in Norwegian).

- *Til Fots i Jotunheimen* (in Norwegian).
- *Till Fots i Rondane—Dovrefjell—Trollheimen* (in Norwegian).
- *Til Fots i Femundsmarka og Sylane* (in Norwegian).
- *Mountain Touring Holidays in Norway* (in English; also available in German).

Available From: The DNT (see *Address Directory*).

Blefjell Trail

From Bolkesjø to Uvdal. Follows Blefjell, the southernmost part of a mountain range that runs between Numedal and Telemark in South Norway. Winds between tarns, through forests and up treeless ridges of quartzite. Steep descents alternate with easy stretches across open country and moors. **Walking Time:** 6 days. **Difficulty:** Moderately difficult. **Path Markings:** Cairned and marked for most of its length. There are a few sections, however, where there is no path (between Øvre Fjellstøl and Spjeldsetfjell, for instance); a knowledge of map reading is necessary.

Trail Lodgings: There are two self-service and three unstaffed mountain huts along the trail. In addition, there are hotels in Bolkesjø and Uvdal and on Blefjell (Ble Mountain), and a youth hostel in Uvdal. All of the huts are secured with standard locks. A key which fits the locks is available—to members only—from the DNT's Oslo office and the Kongsberg tourist office. For further information on the huts, refer to *Mountain Touring Holidays in Norway*.

Maps:
- DNT planning map, sheet *Hardanger + Vidda—Blefjell*.
- Norges Geografiske Oppmåling Gradteigskart 1:100,000, sheets E-34 V *Mår*, E-34 A *Nore* and 3-35 A *Tinnisjø*.

Guidebook:
- *Mountain Touring Holidays in Norway* (in English; also available in German).

Lillehammer—Rondane Trail

From Nordseter (30 minutes by bus from Lillehammer) to Lake Rondavtnet. Crosses a mountain plateau covered with heather, reindeer moss and lush grass which provides pastures for cattle, sheep, reindeer and elk. Climbs several ridges. **Walking Time:** 6 days. **Difficulty:** Easy to moderately difficult. **Path Markings:** Cairned throughout.

Trail Lodgings: There are two staffed huts and four self-service huts along the path. In addition, there are youth hostels and hotels in nearby towns. Details are given in *Mountain Touring Holidays in Norway*.

Maps:
- DNT planning map, *Rondane—Lillehammer*.

- Norges Geografiske Oppmåling Gradteigskart (Serie M711) 1:50,000, sheets 1718/I, 1817/I, 1818/II, 1818/III and 1818/IV. Also:
- Norges Geografiske Oppmåling Turistkart 1:50,000, sheet 48 *Lillehammer Omland.*

Guidebook:
- *Mountain Touring Holidays in Norway.*

Synnfjell—Jotunheimen Trail

From Liomseter to Gjendesheim. Crosses the Synnfjellvidda Mountain Plateau. Through birch forests and meadows. Winds gently up to the Flatstranda Plateau, then leads onto the Vangstulkampen Ridge, where there is a sweeping view of the Hiemdalen and Sikilsdalen valleys. Passes several lakes, one of which is the site of King Olav's mountain lodge— Prinsehytta. Later, from the summit of Sikilsdalshø (1,783 meters), you can see Rondane and the array of peaks and glaciers in the Jotunheimen. **Walking Time:** 6 days. **Difficulty:** Moderately difficult. **Path Markings:** Cairned throughout.

Trail Lodgings: There are two staffed huts, two self-service huts and two private staffed huts along the trail. Details are given in *Mountain Touring Holidays in Norway.*

Maps:
- Norges Geografiske Oppmåling Gradteigskart 1:100,000, sheets F-31 A *Nordre Etnedalen,* F-30 A *Vinstra* and E-30 A *Sjodalen.*

Guidebook:
- *Mountain Touring Holidays in Norway.*

Troms Border Trail

Along the Norwegian-Swedish border from Galgojavrre to Innset. There are daily buses from Tromsø via Nordkjosbotn and Skibotndalen to Finland. Get off the bus one kilometer before the Finnish border and pick up the cairns. The route passes through a wilderness region of rocky peaks (up to 1,532 meters), high mountain plateaus, lakes, marshes, and rushing torrents with numerous waterfalls and rapids. **Walking Time:** 8 days. **Difficulty:** Moderately difficult. **Path Markings:** Cairned throughout, except for the last stretch of trail which follows first a reindeer track, then a cart track and finally a road that takes you to Innset, where buses can be caught (though not too frequently) to Setermoen.

Trail Lodgings: Eight unstaffed huts are located along the trail within a day's walk of each other. Keys are available from Andresens Vaabenfor-retning (see *Address Directory*). Further details on the huts—and places where keys can be obtained—is contained in *Mountain Touring Holidays in Norway.*

Maps:
- DNT planning map, sheet *Indre—Troms*.
- Norges Geografiske Oppmåling Gradteigskart (Serie M711) 1:50,000, sheets 1532/I, 1532/II, 1632/III, 1632/IV, 1633/II and 1633/III.

Guidebook:
- *Mountain Touring Holidays in Norway*.

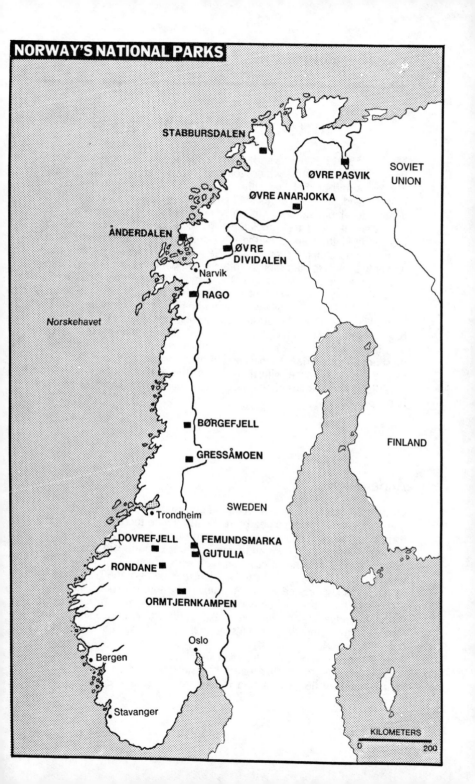

NORWAY'S NATIONAL PARKS

STABBURSDALEN

ØVRE PASVIK

SOVIET UNION

ØVRE ANARJOKKA

ÅNDERDALEN

ØVRE DIVIDALEN

Narvik

RAGO

Norskehavet

BØRGEFJELL

GRESSÅMOEN

FINLAND

SWEDEN

Trondheim

DOVREFJELL

FEMUNDSMARKA

GUTULIA

RONDANE

ORMTJERNKAMPEN

Oslo

Bergen

Stavanger

KILOMETERS
0   200

Norway's National Parks

Norway has 13 national parks. These are large, untouched or mainly untouched natural areas which, for the most part, are owned by the state. The plant and animal life within each park, as well as its natural and cultural landmarks, are protected by the Nature Conservation Act of 1970 against development, construction work and other encroachments.

Several of the parks—including Rondane and Femundsmarka—are crossed by paths marked by the DNT and have mountain huts in which you can stay. Others—such as Børgefjell—have no marked paths or roads and only a few, isolated shelters, often run-down reindeer herders' cabins.

The protection of the parks is the responsibility of every visitor. The flora—including trees—cannot be disturbed, although berry picking is allowed. Wildflowers, however, cannot be picked and branches may not be broken from trees. In forested parks open fires cannot be lit from the beginning of May until the end of September. In mountain parks dry wood may be gathered for use as fuel, but hollow trees suitable for birds' nests must not be touched. Mammals and birds are protected year round. Only fishing—in accordance with the rules for the district—is allowed. Also, new plants and animals (including domesticated pets) must not be brought into the parks.

Ånderdalen

Located on Senja, Norway's second largest island, southwest of Tromsø. The park is small, dominated by rounded, granite mountains up to 852 meters in height and forested with a mixture of pine and birch. The mountains are mostly bare and large, moraine deposits are found in the valleys, particularly at the east and west ends of Lake Åndervatnet. The wildest part of the park is the canyon-like Trolldalen—or the Troll Valley—which is thickly forested with virgin pine trees, some of which are nearly 500 years old. The Ånderelva River bisects the park, rushing down waterfalls and rapids and pausing in lakes bordered by gnarled and twisted pines. Elk and reindeer are often seen in the park, as well as the red fox, otter and weasel.

Area: 53 square kilometers (20.5 square miles).
Access: Senja Island can be reached by steamer from Tromsø in 3 to 4 hours. Highway 86, with a bridge between Finnsnes and Silsand, also

links Senja with the mainland and E6 at Bardufoss. No roads go into the park, although you can drive to within walking distance of its boundaries.
Footpaths: There are no marked paths in the park nor, for that matter, on Senja.
Lodgings: On the south shore of Åndervatnet is a turf hut that was restored in 1964. It is open and can be freely used by visitors. There are no mountain huts on the island. The nearest guesthouse is Senja Turistatasjon at Svanelvmo on Highway 86. There are also hotels in Finnsnes and park huts can be rented in Tranøybotn (Storjord) south of the park.
Maps:
• Norges Geografiske Oppmåling Gradteigskart 1:100,000, sheets M-7 Bjarkøy and N-7 Tranøy.
Publications: Norges Nasjonalparker Ånderdalen, a leaflet available in Norwegian and English from the Ministry of Environment (see Address Directory).

Børgefjell

Børgefjell, located about halfway between Trondheim and Bodø on the boundary between Northern Trøndelag and Nordland, extends partway into Sweden. The majority of the park is alpine, with peaks rising to 1,703 meters, glacial cirques and deep valleys strewn with moraines and talus. The rocky slopes of the Raines Mountains completely lack vegetation. But in other parts of the park, the sloping terrain is characterized by low hills and broad valleys with fertile hillsides and marshes. There are numerous lakes and rivers, many of which are large, torrential and difficult to cross. Dense birch forests cover parts of the park. Elsewhere, heath vegetation dominates and you can walk for hours through stiff sedge grass and bilberry bushes. Up to 295 species of vascular plants have been registered in the park. It has a rich bird life which includes several kinds of waders and ducks, the rather scarce bean goose, plus the temminck's stint, snow bunting, ptarmigan, rough-legged buzzard, golden eagle, osprey and various types of falcons. The most common mammals are the hare, red fox, moose and reindeer. Wolves, lynx and bears wander through the area once in awhile. Mountain foxes are also to be found in Børgefjell, and in some places their old dens remain as green mounds in the moraine landscape.
Area: 1,000 square kilometers (386 square miles).
Access: No motor roads lead into the park. Visitors usually walk in from Majavatn, Susendalen or Fiplingdalen. An excellent starting point is the Lapp camp at Fagerneset, on Namsvatnet, but this will depend upon your being taken by boat across the lake.
Footpaths: There are no marked paths in the park. Bridges, however, cross

some of the rivers, including the Orvass (above its mouth), the Namsen and Vierma at Namsvatnet, the Vierma and Sapman in the Vierma Valley, and the Storelva ("Big River") in Namskroken, north of the Orrek River.

Lodgings: The only shelters are three reindeer herders' cabins—one in Lotter Valley, one at the mouth of the Guikare, and one on the lower Båttjern southwest of Tiplingen. They are open but in poor condition. The cabin at Kjukkel River, east of Jengelvatn, is locked. The other cabins marked on the maps no longer exist. For long trips, complete camping equipment is necessary.

Maps:
- Norges Geografiske Oppmåling Gradteigskart 1:100,000, sheets J-19 *Børgfjell*, K-19 *Ranseren* and 57-B *Namsvatnet*. All the maps are from around the turn of the century and were last revised in the early 1950s. Hence, they are not very accurate.

Publications: *Norges Nasjonalparker Børgefjell*, a leaflet available in Norwegian and English from the Ministry of Environment (see *Address Directory*).

Dovrefjell

Dovrefjell National Park encompasses 265 square kilometers (102 square miles) within the Dovre-Romsdal Ranges (described in detail in the descriptions of *Norway's Mountain Regions* later in this chapter). A network of cairned paths, mountain huts and, in winter, ski tracks allows you to easily explore the park.

Maps:
- Norges Geografiske Oppmåling Gradteigskart (Serie M711) 1:50,000, sheets 1419/I, 1519/I, 1519/II and 1519/IV.

Publications: *Norges Nasjonalparker Dovrefjell*, available in Norwegian and English from the Ministry of Environment (see *Address Directory*).

Femundsmarka

Femundsmarka is located along the Swedish border within the Østerdal-Femund Area (see the descriptions of *Norway's Mountain Regions* later in this chapter) southeast of Trondheim. It is a wilderness of pine forests, rock-strewn clearings, numerous lakes and gentle heights. Mount Svuku with its three conical tops—the highest of which rises to 1,415 meters—is the dominant landmark.

More than half the park is made up of bare mountains and plateaus. The terrain is often uneven and rough, strewn with large boulders. In some areas there are open pine woods with sparse vegetation. In others the landscape is clad with heather. The most luxuriant plant life is found in Rødalen and on the mountain sides above Muggsjølia. The vegetation here includes plants that more naturally belong in meadows, such as moonwort and many species of lady's mantle and dew cup. Many rare plants—such as *Carex appropinquata, Eriphorum brachyantherum* and *Carex parallela*—also grow in the park.

Twenty settlements from the Stone Age have been found in the park as well as a system of reindeer pit traps on the south bank of River Røa and, in other places, remnants of several ember pits. There are also many 18th century charcoal kilns and the ruins of charcoal-burner's huts.

Animal life in the park includes reindeer, a few wolverine and lynx, and around the lakes, mink, marten and beaver. The meadow tit and wheatear are common. Other birds include the three-toed woodpecker, crane, merlin, golden plover, ptarmigan and arctic tern.

Area: 385 square kilometers (147 square miles).

Access: There are no roads into the park, although it is possible to drive to suitable points of approach such as Langen, Sørvika, Feragen, Elgå and Jonasvollen.

Footpaths: Several of the DNT's cairned paths cross the park, and are shown on the DNT planning map *Østerdal—Femund.*

Lodgings: The DNT has two cabins inside the park. Lodgings are also available in towns outside the boundaries of the park.

Maps:
• Norges Geografiske Oppmåling Gradteigskart (Serie M711) 1:50,000, sheets 1719/I, 1719/II, 1819/III, and 1819/IV.

Publications: *Norges Nasjonalparker Femundsmarka,* available in Norwegian and English from the Ministry of Environment (see *Address Directory*).

Gressåmoen

Located in the county of Nord-Trøndelag, northeast of Trondheim, Gressåmoen National Park contains large stands of virgin spruce forest at Gamastuhaugane and in the southern part of the park. The average age of the trees is in excess of 150 years, while some of the oldest specimens are more than 500 years old.

The park also includes the Luru, a broad and peaceful river in an open valley, numerous lakes and marshes and a scattering of glacial moraines. Highest points in the park are the reddish granite peaks of Finnhuva (1,005 meters) and Lurusneisen (992 meters). Tame reindeer graze in the park. In addition, there are lynx, red fox, pine marten and numerous birds, including the golden eagle and gyrfalcon.

Area: 180 square kilometers (69.5 square miles).

Access: The easiest way to reach the national park is by the forestry road from Myrset, north of Agle train station on the Nordland Line.

Footpaths and Lodgings: There are no marked paths in the park and no accommodation is available. The nearest lodgings are the guesthouses at Snasa and the Snasa youth hostel (52 beds, open June 1 to October 1, meals served).

Maps:
• Norge Geografiske Oppmåling Gradteigskart 1:100,000, sheets 54-A *Sanddøla* and 51-C *Jævsjø*.
Publications: *Norges Nasjonalparker Gressåmoen,* available in Norwegian and English from the Ministry of Environment (see *Address Directory*).

Gutulia

Gutulia is the second of the two national parks located in the Østerdal-Femund Area (see the descriptions of *Norway's Mountain Regions*). One of the smallest of Norway's national parks, it was established to protect a virgin pine and spruce forest. With a few exceptions, the forest has been allowed to grow untouched, and includes 300-year-old spruce and pine trees over 400 years old. The landscape is flat, with rough, open forests, stretches of swampland and small lakes. A total of 230 vascular plants have been registered in the park. Nearly 60 different species of birds have been observed. There are also reindeer, beaver and badger.
Area: 19 square kilometers (7.3 square miles).
Access: A forest road that turns off at Brenna (with a roadsign to Gutulia) goes down to Gutulia Lake. From there a path leads eastward along the lake and into the park.
Footpaths: There are no marked paths in the park.
Lodgings: Several old dairy cabins at Gutulivollen are open, but not in very good condition. The nearest places to overnight are at Valdalen Farm, on Highway 221, the Femund Hotel and the Femundsvike Guesthouse at Femundsenden.
Maps:
• Norges Geografiske Oppmåling Gradteigskart (Serie M711) 1:50,000, sheets 1719/II and 2018/I.
Publications: *Norges Nasjonalparker Gutulia,* available in Norwegian and English from the Ministry of Environment (see *Address Directory*).

Ormtjernkampen

Ormtjernkampen is located west and slightly north of Lillehammer. It is dominated by the 1,127-meter peak by the same name and by the summits of Snæreskampen and Dokkampen, which are almost as high. Most of the park is a forest area of spruce, some pine and birch. The remnants of the pine forest are old trees, many of which are attacked by fungus. Wildflowers carpet the park in colorful profusion in the early summer, especially on the south sides of Dokkampen and Snæreskampen. Cloudberries grow in the park's boggy areas. There are also wild strawberries, and one of Norway's rarer plants—*Campanula barbata*—which, in Norway, is confined to this district.
Area: 9 square kilometers (3.5 square miles).

Access: The park is a 10- to 15-minute walk from the public road linking Lillehammer and Fagnernes. A private road which leaves the public road from Vestre Gausdal to Nordre Etnedal, 1 kilometer west of Holsbru, takes you closer to the park. Upon payment of a fee, the key to the toll-bar across the road can be borrowed at a cafe in Holsbru.
Footpaths: There are no marked paths in the park.
Lodgings: There are no buildings in the park. The nearest accommodation is at Kittilsbu, about five kilometers east of Holsbru.
Maps:
• Norges Geografiske Oppmåling Gradteigskart 1:100,000, sheet F-31 A *Synnfjell,* or 1:50,000, sheet 1717/II.
Publications: *Norges Nasjonalparker Ormtjernkampen,* available in Norwegian and English from the Ministry of Environment (see *Address Directory*).

Øvre Anarjåkka

Øvre Anarjåkka adjoins Lemmonjoki National Park in Finland (see description under *Finland's National Parks* in the chapter on Finland). The two areas encompass a large, varied wilderness which has remained virtually untouched by the effects of civilization. Access is difficult and there are neither roads nor accommodation, although the Lapps have roamed here from time immemorial, and as early as the 9th century taxes were collected from their nomadic ancestors. North of the park, in the Lappuluobbal area, tools dating from the Stone Age have also been found.
   Most of the park is a gently undulating plateau with many low hill tops, bogs and forest. Deposits of gold are scattered over the plateau, and many of the rivers are gold-bearing, although the deposits are so finely dispersed that profitable working is not possible. The park contains nearly 700 large and small lakes and several large rivers. The forest is mostly birch, with some pure or mixed Scots pine and a few isolated stands of Norway spruce. In the open parts of the forest, one finds crowberry, ling, bilberry, juniper, reindeer moss and willow scrub, which covers large boggy plains and the banks of streams and rivers, and often grows along with red currant bushes. The fauna includes the Norway lemming, several varieties of vole, blue hare, elk, wolverine, an occasional wolf, reindeer and, in summer—clouds of *mosquitoes.*
Area: 1,390 square kilometers (536.5 square miles).
Access: There is a road from Karasjok southwards to Is'kuras by the border, and a forestry road further along the Anarjåkka River to Caskenjåkka. From there, it is about a 10-kilometer walk to the park.
Footpaths: There are no marked paths in the park.
Lodgings: Some of the Lapps' huts and reindeer herders' cabins are open and available in summer. At Jorbbaluobbal by Skierc'canjåkka there is an old forestry hut with a stove and straw beds. There are also two locked state mountain cabins (in Basevuov'di and Gaevnie). The nearest guesthouse is in Karasjok.

Maps:
- Norges Geografiske Oppmåling Gradteigskart 1:100,000, sheets U-8 *Lavvoaivve*, V-7 *Baeivasgiedde*, V-8 *Noarvas*, V-9 *Njullas*, W-7 *Iskuras* and W-8 *Hugstfjeld*. Also, 1:50,000, sheets 1932/I and 1932/II.

Publications: *Norges Nasjonalparker Øvre Anarjåkka*, available in Norwegian and English from the Ministry of Environment (see *Address Directory*).

Øvre Dividal

This national park, located on the Swedish border between Troms and Narvik, has extensive plateaus with broad valleys, rounded mountain ridges and peaks, and many large and small lakes. On several of the highest summits, one can find boulders which the ice brought from Sweden (on the 1,428-meter summit of Jerta, for instance, there is a boulder of red granite, a type of rock not found elsewhere in the park). Nearly four-fifths of the park has alpine vegetation, made up of 315 species of vascular plants. The coniferous forest is sparse and made up mostly of pine, while birch is the dominant deciduous tree. Predators such as lynx, wolverine and bear still roam here. The gnat must also be mentioned: it is large and blood-thirsty!

Area: 750 kilometers (289.5 square miles) including 100 square kilometers in the Hav'gavuobmi area which has been made into a more restricted "nature park."

Access: The easiest access is by the motor road through Dividalen, and then by the forestry road to Gambekken. From there, a path leads into the park.

Footpaths: There are several marked paths in the park which have been laid out by Troms Turlag (see *Address Directory*). These are shown on the sketch map in the Ministry of Environment leaflet listed below.

Lodgings: Troms Turlag has three self-service huts inside the national park and two huts outside its northern and southern boundaries. Rooms are also kept open in a military cabin at Cievcasjav'ri and a cabin owned by the Council of Lapps at Hav'gavuobmi.

Maps:
- Norges Geografiske Oppmåling Gradteigskart (Serie M711) 1:50,000, sheets 1532/I, 1532/II, 1632/III and 1632/IV.

Publications: *Norges Nasjonalparker Øvre Dividal*, available in Norwegian and English from the Ministry of Environment.

Øvre Pasvik

This is the largest virgin forest in Finnmark, and one of the most valuable areas of scientific study in Norway. Located in the southwest corner of Øvre Pasvik near the Finnish and Russian borders, the park forms a transitional zone between western and eastern plants. The sub-Arctic pine that covers more than half the park is the westernmost representative of the Siberian taiga. The oldest pine is about 420 years, but the majority are about half this age. The flora includes 192 vascular plants, many of which are eastern species that are otherwise rare in Norway, but are found in large quantities here: *Ledum Palustre, Carex tenuiflora, Eriphorum russeolum, Moehringia lateriflora* and *Ranunculus lapponicus*. Typical alpine plants are also found within the park's forests—an unusual occurrence.

Most of the park is flat and strewn with boulders, although there are a few ridges and hills, as well as numerous swamps, marshes, lakes and rivers (one-quarter of the park is covered with water). Traces have been found of the Komsa culture (several thousand years B.C.) and of other hunting cultures covering all phases of the Stone Age. Pit traps and traces of Lapp culture date back to the 6th century A.D.

Area: 63 square kilometers (24 square miles).

Access: A forest road leads into the park at Gjøkåsen from Highway 885. At Gjøkvatn the road divides and one branch takes you to Vinterfiskvatn, almost at the boundary of the park. From there a reindeer path leads into the park.

Lodgings: There are three reindeer herders' cabins inside the park boundaries in which you can overnight. All three are open.

Map:
• Norges Geografiske Oppmåling Gradteigskart 1:100,000, sheet Z-7 *Krokfjell*. On the map, several lakes have the wrong contours and the mountains are incorrectly located. The flat terrain of the park further complicates matters, making it easy to get lost. A compass is an absolute must.

Publications: *Norges Nasjonalparker Øvre Pasvik,* available in Norwegian and English from the Ministry of Environment (see *Address Directory*).

Rago

Rago lies northeast of Bodø on the Swedish border. While small, it is adjacent to Europe's largest national parks: Padjelanta, Sarek and Stora Sjöfallet in Sweden which, together, cover 5,000 square kilometers (1,930 square miles). Access to the park is difficult and strenuous, but its wild scenery makes the trip worthwhile. Deep ravines, which cut across the park between Storskogvatnet (Storskog Lake) and Ragoplatået (the Rago Plateau), are ancient drainage channels for the water melting from the glaciers that once covered the area. The glaciers are now greatly reduced, although several large ones still remain, the largest of which is Lappfjellet/Flatkjølen in the south. At the east end of Storskogvatnet there is luxuriant vegetation which includes the blue sow-thistle, globe flower and whorled Solomon's seal. In other places bog plants such as purple moor-grass and cotton-grass grow—uncharacteristically—on bare rock. The forest is sparse, made up of pine, together with a little birch, rowan and alder, and lacks the willow belt which generally grows immediately above the tree limit (located at 400 to 450 meters in the park). Several scarce mountain plants also grow in the southeast corner of the park, such as Whitlow grass, arctic mouse-ears, chickweed and a species of cat's foot. Because much of the park consists of high mountains, the bird life is sparse. Beavers, however, thrive in Bevervatn (Beaver Lake). There are also otter and mink, fox, pine marten, stoat and ermine.

Area: 170 square kilometers (66 square miles).

Access: From Trengsel bridge on E6 one must take the boat into Nordfjord. From there, it is 2½ kilometers by road to Lakshålen, where a path leads into the park.

Footpaths: A marked path leads from Lakshålen via Nordskaret to Storskogvatnet (about three hours). From Steinbakken in Megården a path leads to the outlet from Little Vaerivatnet. Suspension bridges have been built over the river at the outlet from Storskogvatnet and at the outlet from Little Vaerivatnet. There is a boat at the outlet from Storskogvatnet. The key to the boat may be obtained from the warden.

Lodgings: There is an old cabin at the outlet from Storskogvatnet. It is jointly owned by the Forest Administration and the Council of Lapps, and is kept locked. Another nearby cabin, built in 1973, is open. An old dilapidated cabin near the border (indicated on maps as Gamme) has recently been restored and may be used for shelter. By Vaerifossen, about one kilometer outside the park, is a small cabin in the forest which can be hired on application from the warden.

Maps:
• Norges Geografiske Oppmåling Gradteigskart 1:100,000, sheet L 12 *Sørfold.* An old, but fairly accurate map. The glaciers, however, are smaller than indicated.

Publications: *Norges Nasjonalparker Rago,* available in Norwegian and English from the Ministry of Environment (see *Addess Directory*).

Rondane

Rondane National Park encompasses 572 square kilometers (221 square miles) within the Rondane Mountain Ranges (see the descriptions of *Norway's Mountain Regions* later in this chapter). The DNT has marked several paths in the park. There are also two huts in the park, plus 8 to 10 old stone huts that can be used for shelter during bad weather.

Maps:
• Norges Geografiske Oppmåling Gradteigskart 1:100,000, sheet 29 *Rondane.* Also, 1:50,000, sheets 1519/II, 1519/III, 1718/I, 1918/IV and 1818/IV.

Publications: *Norges Nasjonalparker Rondane,* available in Norwegian and English from the Ministry of Environment (see *Address Directory*).

Stabbursdalen

Located on the outskirts of the Finnmark Mountain Plateau, Stabbursdalen is the site of the world's northernmost pine forest (70° 10' North). The valley for which the park is named is broad and flat at its lower end, gradually narrows into a steep-sided chasm with rock-strewn slopes and then widens out to merge with the mountain plateau of Finnmarksvidda. The Stabburselv River, which runs through the bottom of the valley, is studded with waterfalls, quiet pools, small inlets and islands. The pine forest, which covers about 10 percent of the park, stands on both sides of the river. Some of the trees are 500 years old. There are also birch trees and willows, as well as 233 species of vascular plants in the park. Birds are numerous.

Area: 96 square kilometers (37 square miles).

Access: A road in poor condition leads toward the park from Highway 6 about two kilometers south of the Stabburselv bridge. A path leads down to the Stabburselv River from an improvised parking place at the end of the road. You must ford the river (best place is 200 meters below Vuolleluobbal) to enter the park.

Footpaths: A marked path leads from Vuolleluobbal across Haldde to Sennalandet on Highway 6.

Lodgings: An open cabin owned by the National Tele Services is located near the telephone line which forms the boundary between Badnalas and Læktojokka.

Maps:
• Norges Geografiske Oppmåling Gradteigskart 1:100,000, sheet V-4 *Stabbursdalen.* Generally accurate. However, the *Haldde* on the map is called *Ganicokka* by the locals. Haldde is the hill south of Lake 219 farther west.

Publications: Norges Nasjonalparker Stabbursdalen, available in Norwegian and English from the Ministry of Environment (see *Address Directory*).

Further Information

Further information on the national parks can be obtained from the DNT, local tourist offices or the:

> **Miljøverndepartementet** (Ministry of Environment). See *Address Directory*.

Leaflets in both Norwegian and English describing the terrain, climate, flora and fauna, cultural history, maps, access, marked paths and lodgings in each of the national parks are free on request from the Ministry of Environment. Each of the *Norges Nasjonalparker* leaflets includes color photographs and a sketch map of the parks.

Norway's Mountain Regions

The following descriptions have been adapted from *Mountain Touring Holidays in Norway* with the permission of Den Norsk Turistforening (DNT). They are presented here to give you an idea of the hiking possibilities in Norway and—hopefully—to help you choose the areas where you think you might most want to walk. Information has also been included here on the DNT planning maps, Norges Geografiske Oppmåling topographical maps and Norwegian-language guide books that cover each area, as well as on some of the possibilities for cross-country skiing. For full details on the lodgings in each area, information on access and route descriptions for nearly 30 suggested 5- to 10-day hikes throughout Norway, you should refer to *Mountain Touring Holidays in Norway* (see the section on *Where to Get Walking Information*).

The descriptions of the mountain regions have been arranged geographically, from south to north, as follows:

South Norway
   Rogaland-Setesdal Highlands
   Hardangervidda Mountain Plateau
   Voss-Mjølfjell Ranges
   Finse-Filefjell Ranges
   Stølsheimen Area
   Synnfjellvidda Mountain Plateau
   Jotunheimen
   Jostedal Glacier & Breheimen Area
   Rondane Mountain Ranges
   Østerdal-Femund Area
   Sunnmøre Area
   Dovre-Romsdal Ranges
   Trollheimen-Nordmøre Ranges
   Sylene Mountains

North Norway
   Okstindan Mountain Range
   Svartisen & Mo i Rana Area
   Sulitjelma & Saltfjellet Mountain Ranges
   Bodø & Tysfjord Area
   Lofoten & Vesterålen Isles
   Narvik Region
   Troms Border Area
   Lyngen Peninsula
   Finnmark Mountain Plateau

Rogaland-Setesdal Highlands

Rogaland is the most southerly county in West Norway. It straddles the Bokna Fjord, rising in the east to a land of mountain and moorland. From the Bokna Fjord, the Ryfylke Fjords—a network of thin, rock-bound tentacles of water—extend inland. In the Lyse Fjord and and Jøsen Fjord, deep clefts in the mountains, often with precipitous sides of gray, polished rock, plunge into the sea, with no foothold for vegetation. In others, clumps of pine grow on rocky knolls, and small, trim villages nestle in green creeks and bays. East of the fjords are the Ryfylke and Setesdal Highlands, which rise to peaks in excess of 1,500 meters. On both sides of the Setesdal Valley the land is creviced and indented—a blend of valley, mountain, lake and fjord where large herds of reindeer roam, and from May to October sheep graze near scattered farms.

Tourist Information

See *Address Directory*:

Turisttrafikkomiteen for Rogaland.
Reisetrafikkforeningen for Haugesund.
Reisetrafikklaget for Kristiansand distrikt.

Trail Lodgings

Altogether, there are 43 mountain huts in the Rogaland-Setesdal Highlands. In addition, there are 5 youth hostels, as well as hotels and guesthouses in the surrounding towns and villages. The mountain huts are open from June 25 to August 20. They are operated by:

See *Address Directory*:

Stavanger Tourist Association. Operates 5 staffed huts, 10 self-service huts and 7 unstaffed huts in the Rogaland Highlands, to the west of the Setesdal Valley. Self-service and unstaffed huts are left unlocked during the summer season. Off-season, you must obtain keys from the tourist association.

Kristiansand and Oppland Tourist Association. Operates 4 staffed huts, 4 self-service huts and 4 unstaffed huts in the Setesdal Highlands. Self-service and unstaffed huts are left unlocked during the summer season.

Arendal and Oppland Tourist Association. Operates 7 self-service huts and 2 unstaffed huts in Austheiene, to the east of the Setesdal Valley. Self-service huts are left unlocked during the summer season; unstaffed huts are locked and keys must be obtained from the tourist association.

Further information on each hut can be obtained from the tourist associations. *Mountain Touring Holidays in Norway* also includes a list of the huts, giving their locations and number of beds, and a list of youth hostels, with the dates they are open. Details on hotels and guesthouses are given in the Norway Travel Association's lodging list, *Where to Stay in Norway* (see the section on *Trail Lodgings* earlier in this chapter). Information on the hotels and guesthouses can also be obtained from the appropriate tourist associations.

Maps

All the information you need to plan hikes is shown on the DNT's planning map, *Setesdal—Ryfylke—Heiane* (published by the Stavanger Turistforening; available from either the tourist association or DNT). It shows the names and sheet numbers of 1:50,000 topographical maps covering the area, the locations of lodgings and shelters, and the routes of both marked and unmarked tracks. Once you have determined your final itinerary on the DNT planning map, you can then order the appropriate topographical maps. The planning map is free on request from the DNT (see *Address Directory*). Topographical maps also can be purchased from the DNT.

Guidebooks

- *Til Fots i Setesdal- og Rogalandsheiene* (in Norwegian), available from the DNT (see *Address Directory*).
- *Mountain Touring Holidays in Norway,* available in English and German from the DNT (see description in the section on *Where to Get Walking Information*).

Suggested Walks

From Ådneram chalet in the Upper Sirdal to Kvilldal. Through the Sirdal, Lyse and Suldal Highlands. Numerous tarns and lakes enroute, as well as lush pastures and fields that contrast with the forbidding mountainsides. **Walking Time:** 8 days. **Difficulty:** Moderately difficult. Several steep ascents and descents. **Path Markings:** Marked throughout with cairns.
Maps:
* Norges Geografiske Oppmåling Gradteigskart (Serie M711) 1:50,000, sheets 1313/II, 1413/III, 1413/IV and 1313/I.
Guidebook:
* *Mountain Touring Holidays in Norway.*

From Haukeliseter to Kvilldal in the Suldal Valley. Along ridges, through mountain pastures and across marshes and grassy knolls above the Sandvassåna River. Also passes through birch woods in the Vallargjuvet Gorge and across the Veneheia Plateau with its myriad of lakes and tarns. **Walking Time:** 7 to 8 days. **Difficulty:** Moderately difficult. **Path Markings:** Most of the route is cairned, although some sections follow old cattle tracks, which are not cairned.
Maps:
* Norges Geografiske Oppmåling Gradteigskart (Serie M711) 1:50,000, sheets 1414/IV, 1414/III, 1314/II and 1313/I.
Guidebook:
* *Mountain Touring Holidays in Norway.*

From Ljoslandshytta to Bykle village near Lyngtveit. Through woods and marshes, along ridges and across plateaus with many lakes and tarns, and scattered hamlets and farms. **Walking Time:** 6 to 7 days. **Difficulty:** Moderately difficult. Several stiff climbs. **Path Markings:** Marked with cairns, except betwen Sloaros and Holmevashytte.
Special Note: The path is not shown on the Rjuven map (sheet 1413/III) between the Buhedder tarns and along the Risani River to Lake Kolsvatn. The path, however, is cairned.
Maps:
* Norges Geografiske Oppmåling Gradteigskart (Serie M711) 1:50,000, sheets 1412/I, 1412/IV, 1413/III and 1413/IV.
Guidebooks:
* *Til Fots i Setesdal–og Rogalandsheiene.*
* *Mountain Touring Holidays in Norway.*

From Hovden to Vindilhytta near Åmli. Through birch woods, across marshes and past lakes. A climb up the bare slopes of Brattestølsheii is rewarded with a sweeping view from the summit. There is also an impressive view of the Setesdal Valley at Berdalsbu. Highest point on the route is the Tjørnebroti Gap (1,300 meters). **Walking Time:** 9 days.

Difficulty: Moderately difficult. **Path Markings:** Cairned for most of the route. Not cairned between Berdalsbu and Bjørnevasshytta.

Special Note: The path is not shown on the Dalen and Grøssae maps (sheets 1513/IV and 1513/III) between Hovstøyl and Nystøyl and between Nutevashytta and Granbustøyl.

Maps:
• Norges Geografiske Oppmåling Gradteigskart (Serie M711) 1:50,000, sheets 1414/II, 1413/I, 1513/IV, 1513/III and 1512/IV.

Guidebook:
• *Mountain Touring Holidays in Norway.*

Cross-Country Skiing

Among the areas where you can ski tour in the Setesdal Valley area are:

Byglandsfjord: Located at the southern end of Lake Byglandsfjord. Surrounded by wooded hills. 1½ hours by bus from Kristiansand. Marked trails glide through easy country up to the tree limit. Access is by a chairlift with an upper terminal at 460 meters. There is also a lighted ski trail near the village.

Hovden: Located in the mountains at the head of the Setesdal Valley. One of Norway's eight alpine centers. Six hours by bus from Kristiansand. Marked trails from the Hovden Ski Centre lift lead off into the mountains, where the terrain varies from easy to fairly demanding. The Ski Centre organizes guided tours for parties and offers cross-country instruction. There are also facilities for equipment rental.

Åseral: Ski resort in Vest-Agder, west of Setesdal. Two hours by bus from Kristiansand. Undulating wooded and mountain country with marked trails climbing to an altitude of about 1,000 meters. Organized ski trips with guide.

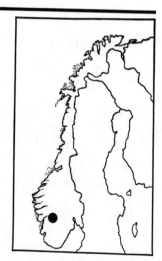

The Hardangervidda Mountain Plateau

This is one of Europe's largest mountain plateaus. Lying east of the Hardangerfjord and south of the Bergen Railway, the vast expanse of Hardangervidda covers an area of more than 7,500 square kilometers. Strewn with lakes, and interlaced by rivers, its high, windswept moors are above the timberline and lack the fertile valleys that usually traverse the mountain ranges of Norway. Only on its outer fringes are there small valleys and wooded hills.

The flora of Hardangervidda contains some 450 plants and, between Litlos and Hadlaskar in the Viersdalen, more than 200 different species of flowers grow along the path. There are also large herds of wild reindeer (especially between Sandhaug and Haukeli) and prehistoric animal pits. Archeologists have discovered hunting grounds with Stone-Age weapons and 7,000-year-old dwelling places. Paths often follow the old trails—the *slepene*—across the plateau along which cattle drivers, horse dealers and soldiers once traveled between East and West Norway. The old trails are still visible, particularly on moraines, where they have made deep furrows. In some places small stone heaps are found in the middle of the old trails, some of which are *varps* on which travelers threw stones to ensure a safe crossing of the mountain plateau. There are also remnants of primitive shelters and of marketplaces where peddlers met farmers from surrounding parishes.

The DNT built its first hut, Krækja, on the plateau in 1879. Bergen Turlag (BT), Drammen og Opplands Turistforening (DOT) and Skien-Telemark Turistforening (STT) have also built huts and marked routes. Together they maintain some 1,200 kilometers of cairned routes as well as 40 footbridges and 19 tourist huts with more than 1,000 beds.

Tourist Information

Turisttrafikkomiteen for Bergen og Vest-Norge (see *Address Directory*).

Trail Lodgings

Altogether, there are 33 mountain huts in the Hardangervidda Mountain area. In addition, there are 5 youth hostels, as well as hotels and pensions in the surrounding towns and villages. The mountain huts are operated by:

See *Address Directory*:

Den Norske Turistforening. Operates 4 staffed huts and 7 self-service huts.

Bergen Turlag. Operates 2 self-service huts and 1 unstaffed hut. The unstaffed hut is not locked during the season.

Drammen og Opplands Turistforening. Operates 2 staffed huts, one on Lake Mårvatn and one on Lake Langesjøen.

Skien-Telemarks Tourist Association. Operates 2 staffed huts.

Stavanger Tourist Association. Operates 1 staffed hut.

In addition, there are 24 private staffed huts. All self-service huts are secured with standard locks. Keys are available from DNT's Oslo office, local tourist associations and neighboring staffed huts. Further information on each hut can be obtained from the tourist associations. *Mountain Touring Holidays in Norway* also includes a list of the huts and youth hostels.

Details on hotels—which are located in Eidfjord, Dagali, Geilo, Kinsarvik, Lofthus, Haukelifjell, Odda, Rjukan, Røldal, Seljestad, Tyssedal, Ustaoset and Uvdal—are given in the Norway Travel Association's lodging list, *Where to Stay in Norway*.

Maps

All the information you need to plan hikes is shown on the DNT's planning map, *Hardangervidda*: the names and sheet numbers of 1:50,000 and 1:100,000 topographical maps covering the area, the locations of lodgings and shelters, and the routes of: 1) marked paths, with walking times between points along the path in hours, 2) unmarked tracks, and 3) routes across glaciers, for which a guide is necessary. Once you have determined your final itinerary on the DNT planning map, you can then order the appropriate topographical maps. The planning map is free on request from the DNT (see *Address Directory*).

Guidebooks

- *Til Fots på Hardangervidda* (in Norwegian), available from the DNT (see *Address Directory*).
- *Mountain Touring Holidays in Norway*, available in English and German from the DNT.

Suggested Walks

From Mogen on Lake Møsvatn to Kinsarvik village on the Hardangerfjord. Through woods and rolling country. Sweeping view of the mountain plateau near Lågaros. Easy ascent near Langebuåni with a fine view of Lake Bjornesfjord—the largest of the Hardangervidda lakes. The path continues past rapids and across extensive marshes with a range of peaks looming into view. There is a climb to the top of Hårteigen up a narrow gorge filled with scree (where at one point, a fixed rope serves as a hand rail). Wonderful view from the top across Hardangervidda. The path then skirts steep mountain bluffs and gradually enters rougher country. From Stavali there is an impressive hike down a beautiful, wild and almost untouched valley where the path twists its way among firs to Nykkjesøy Waterfall. **Walking Time:** 7 days. **Difficulty:** Moderately difficult. Some difficult sections. **Path Markings:** Cairned throughout.
Maps:
- Norges Geografiske Oppmåling Gradteigskart (Serie M711) 1:50,000, sheets 1315/I, 1415/II 1415/III, and 1515/III. The Norske Geografiske Oppmåling Turistkart 1:200,000, sheet 13 *Hardangervidda*, also covers the area and is reliable enough for hikers.
Guidebook:
- *Mountain Touring Holidays in Norway*.

Finse to Haukeliseter. Ascent to the Krobuhalsen gap past a stone-lined reindeer pit. From Fossli there is a view of the magnificent Vøringfoss (waterfall), with a vertical drop of 182 meters. Through birch forest to a mountain plateau east of Høloksli; the path then skirts marshes and continues across moraine ridges, where several more reindeer pits are seen enroute. **Walking Time:** 9 days. **Difficulty:** Moderately difficult. **Path Markings:** Cairned throughout.
Maps:
- Norges Geografiske Oppmåling Gradteigskart (Serie M711) 1:50,000, sheets 1414/IV, 1415/I, II, III and IV, or: 1:100,000, sheet D-33A *Hardangerjøkulen*.
Guidebook:
- *Mountain Touring Holidays in Norway*.

Cross-Country Skiing

Among the areas where you can ski tour in Hardangervidda are:

Rjukan and District: Located deep in the Vestfjord Valley at the southern edge of Hardangervidda, 2¾ hours by bus from Kongsberg. More than 250 kilometers of marked trails traverse the mountains around Rjukan. From the center of the town skiers are carried up to the skiing grounds by telecabine (top terminal 890 meters). From Rjukan Mountain Lodge they are taken up by a T-bar tow, which also serves the slalom slope. Skinnarbu has its own local network of trails in easy mountain terrain. Gaustablikk and Kvitåvatn boast a network of marked trails running through the woods and across the mountain moors. Nearer Mount Gausta the terrain is more rugged. A map of the Rjukan area showing the touring trails is on sale locally. Information: Rjukan Tourist Office (see *Address Directory*).

Haukelifjell: A long, narrow winter-sports region sandwiched between Haukeligrend and Haukeliseter at the southern end of Hardangervidda in Telemark, with mountains up to 1,700 meters. 3½ hours by bus from Oslo, 2½ hours from Bø. Varied mountain country extends from the tree limit (about 800 meters) to the bare mountain plateau. The DNT maintains a wide network of trails radiating from Haukeliseter. A popular goal for skiers setting out from Vågslid, south of Haukeliseter, is Sæsnuten (8 kilometers, 1,400 meters).

Finse—Bergen Railway: The highest railway station in Norway. The winter season extends from early February to well into May. Three hours by train from Bergen, four hours from Oslo. In the immediate vicinity there is plenty of open mountain country suitable even for the novice, but the area as a whole is best for experienced skiers. In the south a popular destination is the Hardanger glacier (about 10 kilometers, 1,876 meters), and in the north St. Pål (about 6 kilometers, 1,697 meters). The Finse Cabin is the starting point of the treks, with dog sled trips organized by the DNT.

Seljestad: Located south of Odda in Hardanger with more than 300 chalets. Three floodlit trails for ski touring. Well marked touring trails to Botnvatn, Steinvatn, Bordalsnuten, Kirkenuten, Odda-varden. Thirty kilometers of marked trails, much of it prepared.

The DNT publishes a sketch map, *Hytter og Kvistruter*, to cross-country ski trails in the area.

Voss-Mjølfjell
Ranges

The Voss-Mjølfjell ranges stretch between the Hardangerfjord and the Sognefjord, encompassing some of the finest scenery in West Norway. In the south, they are divided by the Bergen Railway. They do not form a continuous hiking area, although hikes of several days duration easily can be planned. There are several self-service and unstaffed huts in the ranges, and a few youth hostels, but for the most part, hikers must be prepared to overnight at hotels and guesthouses. Because the region is a constant juxtaposition between mountain and fjord, climbs and descents are often long and steep. Most of the routes are cairned, but some are only partly marked. Thus a knowledge of map-reading and orienteering is useful. Short day and overnight hikes from holiday centers such as Voss or Mjølfjell can be undertaken by most people who are physically fit, but longer hikes should be undertaken only by strong walkers with mountain experience.

Mjølfjell is the site of one of the finest youth hostels in Norway. It is also a splendid center for day excursions—to Mount Skora (1,583 meters), to the Vosseskavl Glacier (1,579 meters) or to Øykjafonn Mountain (1,604 meters) for instance, all of which can be done in 7 to 9 hours. Walks can also be combined with trail and bus journeys: to Flåm, for instance, or to Ulvik and Stalheim, with the return on foot—or vice versa. Similar tours and excursions are possible from Voss and other holiday centers.

A network of trails and huts connect the Voss-Mjølfjell ranges with the Hardangervidda Mountain plateau, the Bergen-Railway-Filefjell ranges and the Stølsheimen area. Consequently, hikes in these areas can be combined with walks in the more restricted Voss-Mjølfjell ranges.

Tourist Information

See *Address Directory*:

Turisttrafikkomiteen for Bergen og Vest-Norge.
Voss Turistkontor.

Trail Lodgings

There are five mountain huts in the Voss-Mjølfjell area. In addition, there are two youth hostels, as well as hotels and guesthouses in the surrounding towns and villages. DNT operates only two huts (both self-service huts) in the area. The rest (all unstaffed) are operated by:

Voss Utferdslag (see *Address Directory*).

All the huts are secured with DNT standard locks. Keys are available from the DNT's Oslo office and the Voss tourist office. Further information on the huts can be obtained from the tourist associations or from *Mountain Touring Holidays in Norway.*

Details on hotels—which are located in Aurland, Bulken, Mjølfjell, Oppheim, Ulvik, Voss and Vossestrand (Myrkdalen)—are given in the Norway Travel Association's lodging list, *Where to Stay in Norway.*

Maps

Two DNT planning maps, *Stølsheimen—Bergsdalen—Kvamskogen— Folgefonni,* and *Finse-Bygdin,* are recommended for planning hikes in the Voss-Mjølfjell ranges. Once you have determined your final itinerary on the planning maps, you can then order the appropriate topographical maps from their indexes. The planning maps are free on request from the DNT (see *Address Directory*). Topographical maps also can be purchased from the DNT.

Guidebooks

- *Til Fots på Hardangervidda og Tilgrensende Områder* (in Norwegian), available from the DNT (see *Address Directory*).
- *Mountain Touring Holidays in Norway,* available in English and German from the DNT.

Suggested Walk

A circular walk from Mjølfjell via Ulvik, Hallingskeid, Upsete and Grindaflet. Among steep mountains scoured by ice, past lakes, across small glaciers and over scree slopes. Many wonderful views. Climbs and

descents are steep and strenuous. **Walking Time:** 5 days. **Difficulty:** Recommended for experienced mountain walkers only. **Path Markings:** Cairned for most of the route. Not cairned between Hallingskeid and Kaldevatn.
Maps:
• Norges Geografiske Oppmåling Gradteigskart 1:100,000, sheets C-32 A *Flåmsdalen* and C-33 A *Ulvik*. Also D-33 *Hardangerjøkulen* and D-32 *Aurlandsdalen* (optional).
Guidebook:
• *Mountain Touring Holidays in Norway.*

Cross-Country Skiing

Among the areas where you can ski tour in the Voss-Mjølfjell ranges are:

Mjølfjell/Bergen Railway: Mjølfjell is located in a snow-filled dip on the Bergen Railway, ringed by magnificent mountain peaks. 2½ hours by train from Bergen, 5 hours from Oslo. Hilly touring country. The trails run through birchwoods and along the floor of the valley, but higher up the country is more alpine in character and trips may be made to peaks such as Mount Skåra (about 15 kilometers, 1,583 meters) and Vossaskavlen (about 20 kilometers, 1,597 meters).

Vatnahalsen—Bergen Railway. Vatnahalsen Station, on the Flåm Line, is close to Myrdal Station on the Bergen Line. 2½ hours by train from Bergen, 5½ hours from Oslo. No motor road. Easy touring country nearby, but comparatively demanding mountain terrain higher up, with correspondingly good downhill runs. Popular objectives are Vossaskavlen (18 kilometers, 1,600 meters) and Storskavlen (29 kilometers, 1,730 meters). Altogether, there are about 60 kilometers of marked and prepared trails.

Voss—Bergen Railway. Norway's leading alpine center, with a teleferique which carries skiers up to a mountain realm served by a whole network of lifts. It also has about 30 kilometers of marked and prepared ski touring trails, which start from the top terminal station of the cable car. 1½ hours by train from Bergen, 5½ hours from Oslo. Voss Ski School provides instruction in cross-country technique. Skiing equipment may be rented at the ski school and from the local sports shops. Information: Voss Tourist Office (see *Address Directory*).

Oppheim—Myrkdal: Oppheim is located north of Voss on the E68 highway, 5 kilometers east of Vinje. Myrkdal, on National Highway 13, is about 8 kilometers north of Vinje. Oppheim is 40 minutes by bus from Voss; Myrkdal, one hour. Varied wooded and mountain country with summits rising to 1,000 and 1,200 meters. The downhill runs are comparatively difficult.

Kvamskogen: Located between Samnanger and Hardanger, east of Bergen. Two hours by bus from Bergen. Hilly wooded and mountain country in the immediate vicinity, with exacting trails up in the mountains. Popular objectives include Tveitskvitingen (about 10 kilometers, 1,299 meters).

Finse-Filefjell Ranges

This area straddles the great divide between the Bergen Railway and Jotunheimen. It encompasses the Aurlandsdal Valley, which is surrounded by precipitous mountains with waterfalls, high plateaus and a myriad of lakes.

The Hallingskarvet Ridge (1933 meters), which stretches between Finse and Geilo along the Bergen Railway, dominates the southern part of these ranges. Its top is almost flat, with a few dwindling glaciers and snowdrifts, steep sides and huge gaps, through which trails climb. Inland the Hemsedal Valley is surrounded by fine mountains including the stately Skogshorn (1,728 meters), the Storehorn (1,478 meters) and Veslehorn (1,338 meters). Some of these mountains offer challenging rock climbs, and the Norsk Alpincenter (see *Address Directory*) is in Hemsedal.

Tourist Information

Turisttrafikkomiteen for Bergen og Vest-Norge (see *Address Directory*).

Trail Lodgings

The DNT operates six mountain huts in the Finse-Filefjell ranges. These include three staffed huts and three self-service huts. Keys to the self-service huts are available from the wardens at nearby staffed huts, as well as from the DNT's Oslo office.

In addition to the DNT huts, there are six private staffed huts, four youth hostels and hotels in the surrounding towns—Ål, Aurland, Flåm, Geilo, Gol, Grindaheim, Hemsedal, Maristova, Nystova, Nøsen, Tyin, Ustaoset and Vatnahalsen. Details on the hotels are included in the Norway Travel Association's lodging list, *Where to Stay in Norway*. Further information on the mountain huts and youth hostels is included in *Mountain Touring Holidays in Norway*.

Maps

The Finse-Filefjell ranges are covered by the DNT planning map: *Finse-Bygdin* (free on request from the DNT; see *Address Directory*). Once you have plotted out your route on the planning map and made your choice of the appropriate 1:100,000 topographical maps, the maps can be purchased from the DNT.

Guidebooks

* *Til Fots på Hardangervidda* (in Norwegian), available from the DNT (see *Address Directory*).
* *Mountain Touring Holidays in Norway*, available in English and German from the DNT.

Suggested Walks

From Finse to Aurland village on the Aurlandsfjord. Begins with a stiff climb up the slope of St. Paul. Extensive view including Mount Gausta, the Hardangerjøkulen Glacier and parts of Jotunheimen. Crosses the Storefonn Glacier (no crevices; easy walk) and a precipice above Lake Nesbøvatn where the path has been blasted in the rock face. A short detour to the Little Hell Cave (Veslehelvete) is recommended—large dome inside a colossal block of gneiss. Ends with a descent to Aurland with its farms and interesting old houses. **Walking Time:** 4 days. **Difficulty:** Moderately difficult. **Path Markings:** Cairned throughout.
Maps:
* Norges Geografiske Oppmåling Gradteigskart 1:100,000, sheets D-33 V *Hardangerjøkulen* and D-32 V *Aurlandsdalen*.
Guidebook:
* *Mountain Touring Holidays in Norway*.

From Haugastøl to Nystova. Lord Garvagh and his son, who came to Norway to hunt reindeer, had several stone huts built in this area. Crosses a high mountain plateau with numerous ridges and lakes. Several steep ascents and descents. Highest point enroute is reached near the Gråhyrnerane (nearly 1,700 meters). View of Jotunheimen with overhanging

snowdrifts. Through scree and across snowdrifts to Bjordalsbu. Steep descent to Nystova through birches and across marshy ground. **Walking Time:** 7 days. **Difficulty:** Moderately difficult. **Path Markings:** Cairned throughout.
Maps:
- Norges Geografiske Oppmåling Gradteigskart 1:100,000, sheets D-33 A *Hallingskarvet,* D-32 A *Djup* and D-31 A *Fillefjell.*
Guidebook:
- *Mountain Touring Holidays In Norway.*

Cross-Country Skiing

Among the areas you can ski tour in the Finse-Filefjell ranges and their nearby surroundings are:

Geilo—Ustaoset: Geilo is the principal winter sports center in the Hallingdal Valley. The chalet community at Ustaoset is on the Bergen Railway, 11 kilometers west of Geilo. Four hours by train from either Oslo or Bergen. Geilo has 10 ski lifts and 17 prepared runs as well as a network of 100 kilometers of ski touring routes. In the northwest and southwest, popular trails running via Prestholt and Ustetind link Geilo and Ustaoset. Popular objectives for ski tourers setting out from Geilo are Ustetind (about 15 kilometers, 1,376 meters) and Prestholt (about 10 kilometers, 1,300 meters). Touring and alpine ski equipment may be hired at the local sports shops. There are cafes and kiosks near the ski tows and at convenient points along the trails. Information: Geilo Tourist Office (see *Address Directory*).

Gol: A lively winter-sports resort with a wide selection of hotels, guesthouses and shops located in the Hallingdal Valley. The mountain touring terrain is easily accessible by ski lift and car. Three hours by train from Oslo, five hours from Bergen. From the top of the longest ski tow some 30 kilometers of marked and prepared trails run through the woods to mountain peaks such as Feten (4 kilometers, 1,000 meters) and Syningen (8 kilometers, 1,090 meters). Maps of the trails are available free of charge. There is a lighted trail near the village. Information: Gol Tourist Office (see *Address Directory*).

Hemsedal: The mountain village of Hemsedal is ringed by peaks up to 1,800 meters in height. It has grown into an alpine ski center billed as one of the best in Scandinavia and has been the site of several international championships. Thirty-five minutes by bus from Gol. In addition to international slalom and giant slalom courses, there are 30 kilometers of marked and prepared touring trails that radiate from the upper terminal above the ski center. These lead through varied terrain to peaks such as Såta (7 kilometers, 1,623 meters). There are also 6 kilometers of trails leading from the upper terminal in Grøndalen (a smaller valley branching off from Hemsedal at Tuv), where Veslebotnskarvet Ridge (about 8 kilometers, 1,778 meters) is a popular objective. Information: Hemsedal Tourist Office (see *Address Directory*).

Hol—Hovet—Sudndalen: A ski touring center at the head of the Hallingdal valley on the north side of the Hallingskarvet Ridge. One hour by bus from Ål. Wooded mountain country of medium difficulty. Sudndalen makes a fine base for long, exacting tours in a mountain area dominated by 1,933-meter Hallingskarvet Ridge. The ground is gentler around Lake Strandavatn and in the direction of Geiteryggen. There is a network of 1,000 kilometers of marked and, in some cases, prepared trails. Trail maps may be purchased locally. Information: Geilo Tourist Office (see *Address Directory*).

Nesbyen—Nesfjellet: A ski touring center located southeast of the Finse—Filefjell ranges in the Hallingdal Valley. Three hours by train from Oslo, five hours from Bergen. Good choice of hotels, guesthouses and floodlit ski trails. Nesfjell offers superb ski touring with a large network of marked trails in terrain 1,000 to 1,100 meters above sea level. Ideal for family outings. In addition to good mountain lodges, Nesbyen has an unusually wide choice of generously equipped chalets in the mountains. Most ski touring fans head into the hills, where a network of marked and prepared runs, covering a total of about 140 kilometers, links the chalet centers with the resort at Myking. Popular objectives include Dyna (8 kilometers, 1,212 meters), conveniently reached from Myking, and Hallingnatten (13 kilometers, 1,315 meters) reached from Bøgåset, 12 kilometers from Nesbyen. The network of trails also links up with nearly 100 kilometers of marked runs in the Eggedal mountains. A free touring map is available on request. Information: Nesbyen Tourist Office (see *Address Directory*).

Ål—Ålsfjellet: Located on the Bergen Railway in rural surroundings, with hotels and mountain lodges. Facilities include a ski jump and floodlit touring trail. Excellent touring country on nearby Veståsen. 3½ hours by train from Oslo, 4 hours from Bergen. From Ål there is easy access by car to good touring country up among the mountain farms of Upper Ål and Liatoppen. Vats and Leveld are surrounded by peaks up to 1,200 meters in height. Marked trails are numerous. Bergsjø alone has 121 kilometers of marked trails. Information: Ål Tourist Office (see *Address Directory*).

Tyinkrysset and District: Located between the Filefjell Mountains and the Jotunheimen Range. Two hours by bus from Fagernes. Touring trails fan out from the top station across Filefjell. From the hotel, there are trails through pleasant wooded country. Tyin Cross, Nystova, and Tyin all offer varied touring country. Toward the end of the winter skiers often take the bus or drive up to Tyin Cross, where they have a choice of about 50 kilometers of marked and prepared trails.

Stølsheimen

The Stølsheimen ranges rise steeply from the Sognefjord to form a huge, creased mountainous region stretching south to the Eksingedal Valley. The area is cut by several deep valleys and has many *seter* paths connecting old mountain summer farms or *støler,* as they are known in the Fjord Country. The local mountain touring association—Bergen Turlag—has built several self-service huts, cairned routes between them and made Stølsheimen popular with hikers in the Bergen district. Apart from the huts owned by Bergen Turlag and affiliated clubs, there are a number of seters—or mountain summer farms—offering simple accommodation.

Tourist Information

> **Turisttrafikkomiteen for Bergen og Vest-Norge** (see *Address Directory).*

Trail Lodgings

There are five self-service huts and one unstaffed hut in the Stølsheimen region. In addition, there are three youth hostels, as well as seters such as Brydalseter in Ortnevik and Nordalshytta. Rooms can be rented in Ortnevik on the Sognefjord and in Øvstedal. The self-service huts are operated by:

> **Bergen Turlag** (see *Address Directory).*

All the self-service huts are left open year round. The unstaffed hut is locked and the key must be obtained from the tourist association in Voss.

Further information on each hut can be obtained from the tourist associations or from the list of trail lodgings in *Mountain Touring Holidays in Norway.*

Details on hotels—which are located in Oppheim, Vik, Voss and Vossestrand (Myrkdalen)—are included in the Norway Travel Association's lodging list, *Where to Stay in Norway.* For information on local guesthouses, you should contact the local tourist associations.

Maps

The Stølsheimen is covered by DNT's planning map: *Stølsheimen— Bergsdalen—Kvamskogen—Folgefonni* (free on request from the DNT; see *Address Directory*). Once you have plotted out your route on the planning map and made your choice of the appropriate 1:100,000 topographical maps, the maps can be purchased from the DNT.

Guidebooks

- *Til Fots på Hardangervidda* (in Norwegian), available from the DNT (see *Address Directory*).
- *Mountain Touring Holidays in Norway,* available in English and German from the DNT.

Suggested Walk

From Sjelingavatn to Modalen. Begins with an easy walk along a string of small lakes. Then the terrain becomes rough: across boulders and snow, along steep ridges and across a few small glaciers. Superb view from the top of Rundehaug towards the Sognefjord. Ends with a descent on a steep and winding seter path into the Hellandsdalen cirque and a walk through a wild and beautiful valley to the Helland farms. **Walking Time:** 6 days. **Difficulty:** Moderately difficult. Several difficult sections. **Path Markings:** Cairned throughout.
Maps:
- Norges Geografiske Oppmåling Gradteigskart 1:100,000, sheets B-31 A, *Kyrkjebø,* B-32 A *Modalen* and C-32 V *Vossestrand.*
Guidebook:
- *Mountain Touring Holidays in Norway.*

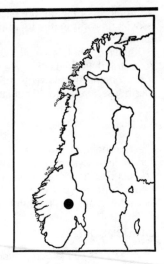

Synnfjellvidda
Mountain Plateau

The mountain plateau between Gudbrandsdal and Valdres with its gently undulating moors, wide vistas and serene heights is typical of East Norway. It was traversed by the pioneers in the 19th century in their search for Jotunheimen—the "Home of the Giants." The sources of the Etna and Dokka rivers are near Mount Skåget (1,686 meters), perhaps the most prominent peak in these mountains. Another dominant peak is Spåtind (1,414 meters), the highest crest on the Synnfjell skyline.

When you cross the Vinstra River you enter the "anteroom" of Jotunheimen and approach wilder country. South of Lake Dokvatnet is Norway's smallest national park—Ormtjernkampen—with an area of only 9 square kilometers and virgin forest in mountainous surroundings.

Tourist Information

See *Address Directory*:

Turisttrafikkomiteen for Oppland fylke.
Reisetrafikkforeningen for Valdres og Jotunheimen.
Lillehammer og Omland Reiselivslag.
Nord-Gudbrandsdal Turist- og Tiltakskontor.
Midt-Gudbrandsdal Reiselivslag.

Trail Lodgings

The DNT operates five mountain huts on the Synnfjellvidda Mountain Plateau. These include one staffed hut, four self-service huts and one unstaffed hut. Keys to the self-service and unstaffed huts are available from the wardens at nearby staffed huts (Liomseter, Sikilsdalseter and Storhøliseter), as well as from the DNT's Oslo office.

In addition to the DNT huts, there are three private staffed huts on the plateau, as well as three youth hostels and hotels in the surrounding towns—Bygdin, Beitostølen, Espedalen, Fagernes, Nord-Torpa and Skåbu. Details on the hotels are included in the Norway Travel Association's lodging list, *Where to Stay in Norway,* while information on the mountain huts and youth hostels is given in *Mountain Touring Holidays in Norway.*

Maps

DNT's planning map, *Gausdal Vestfjell,* is recommended for planning hikes. The planning map is free on request from the DNT (see *Address Directory*). Once you have made your choice of topographical maps they also can be purchased from the DNT.

Guidebooks

- *Til Fots i Jotunheimen* (in Norwegian), available from the DNT (see *Address Directory*).
- *Mountain Touring Holidays in Norway,* available in English and German from the DNT.

Suggested Walk

The Synnfjell-Jotunheimen Trail (see description in the section on *Norway's Long-Distance Footpaths*).

Cross-Country Skiing

There are numerous ski touring centers around the Synnfjellvidda Plateau, both in Valdres and the Gudbrandsdal Valley. Among these are:

Aurdal/Tonsåsen: Located in the Fagernes area. Seven kilometers north of the small village of Aurdal is the community of Danebu (990 meters), and about 15 kilometers to the east is Tonsåsen (700 meters). Tonsåsen is 3½ hours by train from Oslo; Aurdal is 4 hours by train from Oslo. Gentle wooded country both at Danebu and at Tonsåsen. In the mountains the ski touring varies in difficulty from easy to fairly demanding. Radiating from Danebu are about 60 kilometers of marked and prepared trails.

Fagernes and the Nordfjell Mountains: Fagernes is the main ski center in Valdres. The winter resorts in the northern part of the mountains are strung out along the road to Etnedal. They include Nythun (Kruk), Skaråsen (on a side road), and Valdres Mountain Lodge (Steinsetbygda), all located from

15 to 20 kilometers from Fagernes. 4½ hours by train from Oslo, 5 hours by bus from Oslo. The ski tow leads to a stretch of wooded and mountainous country extending eastwards in the direction of Kruk. Skaråsen (1,072 meters) is a popular destination with touring skiers from Kruk. Other trails head south toward Mount Smørlifjell through terrain of medium difficulty. There are about 40 kilometers of marked and prepared trails, plus a lighted trail. Maps showing the local trails are available in Fagernes. Skiing equipment can also be rented from the sports shops in Fagernes. Information: Fagernes Tourist Office (see *Address Directory*).

Fjellstølen: Fjellstølen is located in the hilly countryside to the west of Bagn. Three hours by bus from Hønefoss, four hours from Oslo. Visitors to Fjellstølen are met by hotel car at Bagn and at Bjørgo Station. The ski area can also be reached by train from Oslo in four hours. About 50 kilometers of easy, marked and prepared trails pass through wooded country and across mountain moors toward such peaks as Bødalsfjell and Hollastøls-fjell.

Hovda/Sanderstølen: Located between the Finse-Fifefjell ranges and Synnfjellvidda. Hovda and Sanderstølen (22 and 27 kilometers respectively from Fagernes) rise to an altitude of 800 to 850 meters on the plateau linking Valdres and Hallingdal. Forty minutes by bus from Gol, 1 hour from Fagernes; 5½ hours from Oslo by airbus. The surrounding mountain plateau is wonderfully suitable for ski touring. A popular objective near Hovda is Mount Gribba (about 7 kilometers, 1,057 meters) and—south of Sanderstølen—Nystølfjellet (about 20 kilometers, 1,295 meters). Nearly 30 kilometers of marked and prepared trails traverse the area.

Synnfjell: A winter resort on the Synnfjord at the foot of the Synnfjell Ridge, of which the highest point is Spåtind (1,414 meters). Three hours by train from Oslo to Dokka; a car from Spåtind will fetch visitors at Dokka Station. Open, gentle countryside near the hotel and on the moors to the north toward Fjelldokka. Ski trek near hotel.

Vaset-Gomobu-Nøsen: Located in the mountains about 25 kilometers west of Fagernes. 4½ hours by train from Oslo to Fagernes. Visitors to Vaset and Gomobu are met by a hotel car at Fagernes. Three hours by train from Oslo to Gol; visitors to Nøsen are met by hotel car at Gol. Easy trails pass through wooded country and across mountain moors in the Vaset area, where Mount Ålfjell (1,137 meters) and Mount Grønsetknipen (1,368 meters) are popular goals; they are about 8 kilometers from Lake Vasetvatn. Varied touring terrain from the top of the tow stretches away to such points as Krististølen and Valkjednstølen. There are some 50 kilometers of marked and prepared trails in the area.

Espedal-Skåbu. Skåbu and the villages in the Espedal Valley form a fairly concentrated winter-sports area accessible from both Vinstra and

Lillehammer. 2½ hours by bus from Lillehammer to Strand, ½ hour from Vinstra to Skåbu. 2¾ hours by train from Oslo to Lillehammer, from Oslo to Vinstra 4 hours. The hotels in Espedal are linked by a network of well-marked and prepared trails—about 175 kilometers in all—running through sheltered wooded country and across mountain moors. Popular objectives are: Ruten (7 kilometers, 1,513 meters) and Storhø (9 kilometers, 1,417 meters). At Skåbu, gentle, wooded mountain terrain stretches away to high mountains such as Saukampen (15 kilometers, 1,655 meters) and Heidalsmuen (20 kilometers, 1,743 meters). Trail maps are on sale locally.

Jotunheimen

The Jotunheimen is an enormous expanse of jagged peaks, narrow valleys, large lakes and waterfalls. There are open moors and heaths, 60-plus glaciers and more than 250 peaks in excess of 1,900 meters (6,000 feet), the highest of which is 2,469-meter Galdhøppigen, Norway's highest peak. Northern Europe's largest and Norway's wildest mountain range, the Jotunheimen is the best developed touring area in the country, with a series of mountain lodges connected by marked trails—ideal for walking tours, rock climbs and glacier walks.

Jotunheimen is easily reached in one day from either Bergen or Oslo. From Bergen you may go by boat to Leikanger and catch a bus via Sogndal to huts and lodges along the Sognefjell road. Or you may go by boat to Årdalstangen and catch a bus to Øvre Årdal, where the Vetti—Skogadalsbøen route begins. From Oslo you can either take a train to Otta in the Gudbrandsdal or to Fagernes in Valdres where buses will take you into the Jotunheimen.

Rock Climbs in Jotunheimen

Within the Hurrungane area are icecaps, glaciers and needlesharp ridges. Turtagrø Høyfjellshotell on the Sognefjell road is a popular starting point. The best climbing season is from July 15 to August 15. A guidebook (with international signs and abbreviations) to rock climbs in Hurrungane is available from the DNT (see *Address Directory*).

Tourist Information

See *Address Directory*:

Turisttrafikkomiteen for Oppland fylke.
Reisetrafikkforeningen for Valdres og Jotunheimen.
Lillehammer og Omland Reiselivslag.
Nord-Gudbrandsdal Turist- og Tiltakskontor.
Midt-Gudbrandsdal Reiselivslag.

Trail Lodgings

There are 16 mountain huts in the Jotunheimen, including 6 private staffed huts. In addition, there are five youth hostels, as well as hotels and guesthouses in the surrounding towns and villages. The DNT operates six staffed huts, two self-service huts and two unstaffed huts. One self-service hut (Olavsbu) and one unstaffed hut (Skagastølsbu) are locked. Keys are available from nearby staffed huts and hotels, or from DNT's Oslo office.

Further information on each hut can be obtained from the DNT or from the list of huts and youth hostels in *Mountain Touring Holidays in Norway*.

Details on hotels—which are located in Bessheim, Bygdin, Beitostølen, Bøverdalen, Eidsbugarden, Lom, Skjolden, Tyin and Tyinholmen, Vang and Vågå—are given in the Norway Travel Association's lodging list, *Where to Stay in Norway*. The local tourist associations also can provide information on hotels, as well as on small guesthouses in their areas.

Maps

DNT's planning map, *Jotunheimen—Breheimen,* shows the names and sheet numbers of 1:50,000 and 1:100,000 topographical maps covering the Jotunheimen, the locations of lodgings and shelters, and the routes of: 1) marked paths, with walking times between points along the path in hours, 2) unmarked tracks, and 3) routes across glaciers for which a guide is necessary. The planning map is free on request from the DNT (see *Address Directory*). Once you have made your choice of topographical maps they also can be purchased from the DNT.

Guidebooks

- *Til Fots i Jotunheimen* (in Norwegian), available from the DNT (see *Address Directory*).
- *Mountain Touring Holidays in Norway,* available in English and German from the DNT.

Suggested Walk

From Gjendesheim to Øvre Årdal. One of the finest routes in Jotunheimen. Begins with a steep ascent up gorges to a ridge between Lake Gjende and Lake Bessvatn, the precipitous walls of which were immortalized by Henrik Ibsen when he described Peer Gynt's wild ride on reindeer across the ridge. The path then follows the bank of a turbulent river up the Memurudal, climbs a series of ledges, each offering a more rewarding view than its predecessor (railings are provided in exposed places, but don't leave the cairned path), leads up and down Mount Glittertind, with a superb panorama from the summit (should not be attempted in strong wind or uncertain weather). Then, following a series of scree-filled gorges and boulder-strewn summits, the route takes you across snow and rock to Spiterstulen, where there is an easy ascent to the summit of Galdhøppigen (2,469 meters), Norway's highest mountain. The view embraces some 35,000 square kilometers. The stretch from Leirvassbu to Sognefjellshytta is a guided tour with a rope and ice axe across the Smørstabreen Glacier. (Daily tours in both directions during the summer season.) There are also guided tours with a rope and ice axe from Krossbu and Sognefjell to Fannaråkhytta. Beautiful landscape at Utladal with serrated peaks, hanging valleys and crevassed glaciers. Norway's highest waterfall, the Vettisfoss, with a vertical drop of 275 meters, can be seen at Vetti-Hjelle. The trails end in the aluminium town of Øvre Årdal. **Walking Time:** 12 to 13 days. **Difficulty:** For experienced mountain walkers only. **Path Markings:** Cairned throughout, except where the route crosses a glacier, and on the last stretch from Vetti-Hjelle to Øvre Årdal where a pack trail is followed.
Maps:
- Norges Geografiske Oppmåling Gradteigskart 1:100,000, E-30V *Gjende,* E-30A *Sjodalen* and D-30A *Sygnefjell.* A small-scale map, 1:250,000 *Jotunheimen* No. 2105, may also be used, but the 1:100,000 maps are recommended.
Guidebook:
- *Mountain Touring Holidays in Norway.*

Cross-Country Skiing

Among the areas you can ski in the Jotunheimen are:

Bøverdal: The mountainous terrain of the Bøverdal Valley includes 1,400-meter Leirvassbu and 1,106-meter Spiterstulen. The skiing season begins in February/March and extends to the end of April. Three hours by bus from Otta (Otta is 3¾ hours by train from Oslo). With Norway's highest mountains close by, the area offers a variety of touring routes to challenge experienced mountain skiers, as well as less demanding tours in the mountain valleys.

Lom: Lom has limited opportunities for winter sports, although it is easily accessible to the mountain lodges of Soleggen (970 meters) and Brimi (880 meters), which are set in the midst of magnificent mountain country. 1½ hours by bus from Otta. Guests staying at Soleggen are met by hotel car at Graffer. Brimi's guests take the bus from Otta to Randsverk where they are met by hotel car at Fluguhaugen. 3¾ hours by train from Oslo to Otta.

Sjodalen: The Sjodal Valley carves its way into the heart of the Jotunheimen Mountains, where Hindsæter (950 meters) and Bessheim (964 meters) are ringed about by soaring peaks. From here, experienced mountain skiers can make their way up a series of 2,000-meter summits. Close to the lodges the terrain is gentle. There are about 25 kilometers of prepared trails in the immediate vicinity. The skiing season extends from February to the end of April. Two hours by bus from Otta to Hindsæter, 2½ hours from Otta to Bessheim; 3¾ hours by train from Oslo to Otta.

Vågå: Vågåmo. A beautiful resort on the shores of Lake Vågåvatn, with easy access to the mountains. Forty-five minutes by bus from Otta (the train from Oslo to Otta takes 3¾ hours). Vågåmo T-bar tow makes it easy to reach the higher mountain country where there are 40 kilometers of marked and prepared trails. A popular objective is Mount Blåhø (10 kilometers, 1,618 meters). Trail maps are available free of charge. There is a ski school and facilities for ski rental at Vågåmo.

Beitostølen and District: Beitostølen, in Øystre Slidre, on the southern threshold of the Jotunheimen range, is the best-developed winter sports resort in Valdres. Bygdin (1,065 meters) is located in the Jotunheimen Mountains about 14 kilometers north of the resort. Beito and Øyang (both about 700 meters) are located in the foothills, 3 kilometers from Beitostølen and Heggenes. Yddin (990 meters) is situated in the mountains to the east, about 7 kilometers from Heggenes. One hour by bus from Fagernes, 4½ hours by air bus from Oslo. With its lifts and ski school, Beitostølen is the area's skiing center. Nearly 80 kilometers of marked and prepared trails fan out from the center, linking it with such places as Bygdin, Yddin and Øyang. Ski tows enable ski tourers to reach the area north of Beitostølen. From the top terminal in Rauddalen, touring trails go across Slettefjell, and through superb mountain terrain toward Tyin/Eidsbugarden. Beitostølen Ski School offers cross-country instruction. Touring equipment can be rented from Beitostølen Sports Shop.

Eidsbugarden: Eidsbugarden, at the western end of Lake Bygdin (1,060 meters), is located in the heart of the Jotunheimen Mountains. The skiing season extends from early February to early May. Access: Snowmobile from Tyin. The area has exacting touring country for skiers prepared for stiff climbs and long downhill runs. Popular objectives include Galdeberg (2,075 meters) and the Mjølkedal Glacier (about 1,800 meters). Skiing is easier nearer the hotel. A popular outing is to fly from the hotel up to the Uranos Glacier (a snowfield in winter) and ski back (about 1½ hours).

A sketch map of ski trails in the Jotunheimen, *Hytter og Kvistruter*, is available on request from the DNT.

Jostedal Glacier & Breheimen Area

West of Jotunheimen, between the Sognefjord and the Nordfjord, is Breheimen, with Norway's largest icefield, Jostedalsbreen. From the fjords, canyonlike valleys extend toward the large icefield, their innermost cirques surrounded by towering peaks. Jostedalsbreen technically covers an area of 475 square kilometers, but geographers usually lump all the glaciers in the inner Sogn and Nordfjord into the Jostedalsbreen icefield. Thus Jostedalsbreen becomes Europe's largest glacier. Whereas the Jotunheimen glaciers are located among peaks, the Jostedalsbreen spreads out above the peaks to form a plateau such as is found in Iceland or Greenland. The main icecap lies at about 2,000 meters and is believed to be more than 300 meters thick. There are 24 glacial tongues, each of which thrusts into the valleys at varying speeds. Bøyabreen, for instance, moves at the rapid rate of about half a meter every 24 hours.

Guides for a trek across the glacier are available at Fjaerland, Oppstryn, Loen, Åmot i Jølster, Byrkjelo, Stryn and Oldedalen. (For details, write the DNT; see *Address Directory*).

A trek across the glacier is strenuous, but seldom exceeds four to six hours. Most of the routes to the icecap are marked and cairned, but navigation across the glacier requires a map and compass. Crossings without guides must only be attempted by experienced mountaineers properly equipped with a rope and an ice axe.

Starting points for tours in the area include Grotli and Sota in the Ottadal Valley, which can be reached by bus from Otta. In the fjord country, you can start from Veitastrond, Jostedalen and Skjolden, which can be reached by bus from Leikanger or Kaupanger.

Tourist Information

Turisttrafikkomiteen for Bergen og Vest-Norge (see *Address Directory*).

Trail Lodgings

The DNT operates eight mountain huts in the Jostedal and Breheimen area. These include one staffed hut and seven self-service huts. Keys to the self-service huts are available from the wardens at nearby staffed huts and hostels, as well as from the DNT's Oslo office.

In addition to the DNT huts, there are two private self-service huts and two private staffed huts, as well as three youth hostels and several hotels in the surrounding towns—Fjaerland, Grotli, Jølster, Jostedal, Loen, Olden, Skjolden and Skjåk. Details on the hotels are included in the Norway Travel Association's lodging list, *Where to Stay in Norway*. For information on guesthouses—such as those in Jølster and Jostedalen—you should contact the local tourist associations.

Maps

The Jostedal Glacier and the Breheimen area are covered by DNT's planning map: *Jotunheimen—Breheimen* (free on request from the DNT; see *Address Directory*). Once you have plotted out your route on the planning map, the appropriate 1:50,000 and 1:100,000 topographical maps can be purchased from the DNT.

Guidebooks

- *Til Fots i Jotunheimen* (in Norwegian), available from the DNT (see *Address Directory*).

  mountain Touring Holidays in Norway, available in English and German from the DNT.

Suggested Walk

From Sota Turisthytte to Bøvertun. Among birches up the Surtbyttdal to the Handspikje Gap (1,379 meters), across boulders and ledges, then past a large snowdrift and across the Steindøla River to the Gluggevardsholet Gap west of the Greinbre Glacier. From the slope south of Lake 1175, there is a wonderful view toward Spørteggbreen, with its glacial tongue and the white Kvitadn torrents emerging from it. The path continues along a ledge between the lake and the precipitous Bukkaboth cirque, then up to a ridge extending northeast from Liabrekulen (1,910 meters), with a sweeping view in all directions. From here the path goes down a steep incline to Bøvertun. **Walking Time:** 4 to 5 days. **Difficulty:** Moderately difficult. **Path Markings:** Cairned throughout.
Maps:
- Norges Geografiske Oppmåling Gradteigskart (Serie M711) 1:50,000, sheets 1418/I, 1418/II, and Norges Geografiske Oppmåling Gradteigskart 1·100,000 D-30A *Stygnefjell.*

Guidebook:
- *Mountain Touring Holidays in Norway.*

Cross-Country Skiing

Among the areas you can ski tour in the Jostedal Glacier and the Breheimen area is:

Utvikfjellet: Situated near Highway 60 on Nordfjord. Good parking facilities. Ski tow with ski trails from the top station. Floodlit runs.

Rondane Mountain Ranges

The Rondane Ranges lie between the Gubrandsdal and the Østerdal valleys south of Dovre—a land of high peaks, precipitous cirques and lovely valleys divided in the center by Lake Rondvatnet. West of the lake is the highest of the Rondane summits, 2,178-meter Rondslottet. Here, the ranges are at their wildest, with deep-cut valleys, and the long, serrated ridge of Sagtrindann (the Saw Peaks).

To the north, behind the Rond Castle (Rondslottet), are pyramid-like peaks, undulating hills, mountain pastures and seters (summer farms). Throughout Rondane are signs of geologically recent glaciation—narrow, steep-walled canyons, and large Kame terraces of sand and gravel. South of Dørålseter, so-called "kettle holes" pock the hilly terrain, and in the Uladal below Mysuseter is a curious geological phenomenon: the Kvitskriuprestinn earth-pyramids.

Of the Rondane Ranges, 572 square kilometers are a national park, 170 square kilometers of which are in the high alpine zone. All ten peaks in Rondane that rise above 2,000 meters are inside the park, as is Lake Rondvatnet. The flora is sparse, although 215 vascular plants have been identified and, in a few places, coniferous trees have crept across the park boundaries. As in all mountain areas in Norway dwarf birch is the dominant tree and the lichen popularly called reindeer moss gives large tracts in the ranges a yellowish-white color. Along the watercourses there are otter and mink, and on the periphery of the park one occasionally sees moose. There are also wild reindeer, wolverine, red fox, stoat, weasel and hare. Among the park's birds are the ptarmigan, snow bunting, meadow pipit and wheatear, which nest up to 1,600 meters. In several places, old pit traps have been dug for wild reindeer. There are also remnants of ancient grave mounds and settlements.

For hundreds of years falcons were captured in Rondane for export to the hunting aristocracy in England and on the Continent. It also has a rich tradition of legends. The Norwegian fairy-tale collector, P.C. Asbjørnsen, gathered material for several stories here, and Henrik Ibsen made use of the Peer Gynt legends. According to old Gudbrandsdal tales Gynt came to grips with the "trolls" at Høvringen and met the Bogey ("Bøygen") at Straumbu in the Atnedal.

Accommodation is available in several mountain lodges and tourist huts. DNT has marked several routes in Rondane and from the south, the Lillehammer–Rondane trail crosses into the area.

Tourist Information

See *Address Directory*:

Turisttrafikkomiteen for Oppland fylke.

Reisetrafikkforeningen for Valdres og Jotunheimen.

Lillehammer og Omland Reiselivslag.

Nord-Gudbrandsdal Turist- og Tiltakskontor.

Midt-Gudbrandsdal Reiselivslag.

Trail Lodgings

The DNT operates four mountain huts in the Rondane Mountain Ranges. These include three staffed huts and one self-service hut. A key to the self-service hut is available from the wardens at nearby staffed huts, as well as from the DNT's Oslo office.

In addition to the DNT huts, there are nine private staffed huts; three youth hostels; and hotels and guesthouses in the surrounding towns— Dombås, Folldal, Hjerkinn, Høvringen, Mysuseter, Ringebu and Otta. Details on the mountain huts and youth hostels are included in *Mountain Touring Holidays in Norway*. For information on hotels and guesthouses, you should contact the local tourist associations.

Maps

The locations of lodgings and shelters, and the routes of marked and unmarked tracks, are shown on the DNT's planning map: *Rodane* (free on request from the DNT; see *Address Directory*). Topographical maps also can be purchased from the DNT once you have plotted out your itinerary on the planning map, and made your choice of the appropriate 1:50,000 and 1:100,000 topographical maps from its index.

Guidebooks

- *Til Fots i Rondane—Dovrefjell—Trollheimen* (in Norwegian), available from the DNT (see *Address Directory*).

- *Mountain Touring Holidays in Norway,* available in English and German from the DNT.

Suggested Walk

From Alvdal to Hjerkinn. Across Rondane from east to west. Passes several reindeer pits. Highlights include a lovely ascent among pines towards Musvollkampen; a detour up Sjerdalen, a canyon-like valley with interesting vegetation; and a crossing of a large moraine in the Illmanndal Valley. The path leads up steep, rocky slopes to the summit of Mount Storronden (2,142 meters); across scree and boulders to the south top of the "Rond Castle" (2,042 meters); and along a ridge with a near-vertical drop into the Storboten cirque (view of deep cirques and distant peaks). There is also a wonderful view from Ridge 1869. After a steep descent the path continues across the Storflya moors to the Dørålen Valley. Here, kame terraces, "kettle holes" and glacier deltas give the landscape the appearance of a battlefield scarred by the explosions of large shells. An overnight stop at the Grimsdalhytta is near the site where several Viking graves (9th century A.D.) have been excavated. The final section of the path leads among birches, across the Folla River and along the railway line to Hjerkinn Station. **Walking Time:** 8 days. **Difficulty:** Moderately difficult. **Path Markings:** Cairned throughout.

Maps:
- Norges Geografiske Oppmåling Gradteigskart (Serie M711) 1:50,000, sheets 1619/III, 1818/I, 1818/IV, 1718/I, 1519/II and 1519/III. Most of the area is also covered by the Norges Geografiske Oppmåling Turistkart (Tourist Map), 1:100,000, sheet 29 *Rondane.*

Guidebook:
- *Mountain Touring Holidays in Norway.*

Cross-Country Skiing

Among the areas you can ski tour in the Rondane Mountain Ranges are:

Høvringen: The huddle of mountain farms where Peer Gynt reputedly battled with the trolls is now the biggest winter sports resort in the Rondane Range. Ødegård Mountain Lodge is located 5 kilometers north of Høvringen and may be reached by car from Brennhaug. Two hours by bus from Otta (Otta is 3¾ hours by train from Oslo). Rondane has a network of 150 kilometers of marked and prepared trails linking up with those around Høvringen. Near Høvringen the mountain terrain is gentle and open. Experienced skiers who wish to climb the Rondane Peaks can be towed to the park by snowmobile. Trail maps are on sale locally. Høvringen Ski School provides cross-country instruction and organizes guided day tours.

Mysuseter: This is a collection of old farms at the tree limit that has been turned into a chalet community and tourist resort. Thirty minutes by bus from Otta (3¾ hours by train from Oslo to Otta). Mysuseter is linked with Rondane's 150-kilometer network of marked and prepared trails. Easy, open mountain terrain stretches away to the foothills of the Rondane massif. Popular objectives are the Peer Gynt Cabin and Rondvassbu Cabin. In the south, trails lead through hilly country to Raphamn. Trail maps are on sale locally. Skiers are towed to Rondane National Park by snowmobile.

Otta—Raphamn: The most popular of the ski areas associated with the village of Otta are at Raphamn, 9 kilometers away. 3¾ hours by train from Oslo; 25 minutes by bus from Otta. A 40-kilometer network of marked and prepared trails passes through the hilly, wooded country around Raphamn and links up with the Rondane trail network. Trail maps are on sale locally. There is a lighted ski trail just outside the town. A T-bar tow 5 kilometers from Otta takes skiers up to the Raphamn area.

Folldal: The mountain community of Folldal borders on the Dovre and Rondane ranges. Thirty minutes by bus from Hjerkinn, one hour from Alvdal. (Alvdal is five hours by train from Oslo, Hjerkinn six hours). Popular ski tours include treks to Vollen (900 meters) to the north and Dalhole and Sletten to the west.

A sketch map showing trails and lodgings, *Hytter og Kvistruter,* is available on request from the DNT (see *Address Directory*).

Østerdal–Femund Area

East of Rondane, between the Østerdal Valley and the Swedish border, is a region of conical mountains and open pine moors clad with reindeer moss. Named for Lake Femund, Norway's third largest lake (202 square kilometers), it is an area rarely visited by foreign hikers. Yet it contains two national parks (see the section on *Norway's National Parks*), has numerous accommodation facilities and is easily reached by train from stations such as Hanesdal, Alvadal, Tynset and Røros on the *Oslo—Røros—Trondheim* line, where you can pick up cairned paths and begin your walk almost as soon as you leave the train platform.

Tourist Information

See *Address Directory*:

> **Østerdalene Reisetrafikklag.**
> **Trysil Reiselivslag.**
> **Reiselivslaget for Hamar og Hedemarken.**
> **Elverum Turistservice.**
> **Rendalen Reisetrafikklag.**
> **Tolga Reisetrafikklag.**

Trail Lodgings

The DNT operates two mountain huts in the Østerdal–Femund area; one is a staffed hut and the other is a self-service hut. The key to the self-service hut is available from the wardens of nearby staffed huts, as well as from the DNT's Oslo office.

In addition to the DNT huts, there are tourist huts on the Swedish side of the border, which are linked to the Norwegian huts by marked trails. The huts are operated by:

Svenska Turistföreningen (Swedish Mountain Touring Association), see *Address Directory*.

There are also five private staffed huts in the region which offer farm or seter accommodation by agreement with DNT; two youth hostels and hotels in the surrounding towns, Alvdal, Engerdal, Os, Rendal, Røros, Tolga and Tynset. Further information on the huts and youth hostels is included in *Mountain Touring Holidays in Norway*. Hotels are listed in the Norway Travel Association's lodging list, *Where to Stay in Norway*.

Maps

The Østerdal–Femund Area is covered by the planning map: *Østerdal–Femund* (free on request from the DNT; see *Address Directory*). All the information you need to plan hikes—areas covered by 1:50,000 topographical sheets, and the locations of lodging and walking routes—is shown.

Guidebooks

- *Til Fots i Femundsmarka og Sylane* (in Norwegian), available from the DNT (see *Address Directory*).
- *Mountain Touring Holidays in Norway*, available in English and German from the DNT.

Suggested Walk

From Tynset to Vauldalen. Through forests and across marshes, moors and mountain pastures. The country becomes barren and boulder strewn near the Røveltjørna Lakes, then is graced by birch-clad slopes and slender moraine ridges between tarns. At one point the path crosses the Swedish border, shortly before reaching Vauldalen. Some fine views. **Walking Time:** 7-8 days. **Difficulty:** Easy to moderately difficult. **Path Markings:** Cairned throughout.
Maps:
- Norges Geografiske Oppmåling Gradteigskart (Serie M711) 1:50,000, sheets 1619/II, 1719/III, 1719/II, 1719/I and 1720/II.
Guidebook:
- *Mountain Touring Holidays in Norway*.

Cross-Country Skiing

Among the areas where you can ski tour in the Østerdal–Femund region are:

Atna—Skjæringfjell: Skjæringfjell is a ski center in the mountains between the Østerdal and Gudbrandsdal valleys. Three hours by train from Atna. Guests are met at the station by hotel car. Wooded mountain terrain of medium difficulty, with nearly 40 kilometers of marked and prepared trails. Popular objectives are Mounta Storkletten 4 kilometers away, and Mount Storvola 11 kilometers away. Trail maps are available locally.

Engerdal—Femund: The rural community of Engerdal is located at the southern edge of the Østerdal–Femund region. Femund is about 25 kilometers north of the center of Engerdal. 3½ hours by bus from Rena to Engerdal; 4 hours by bus from Rena to Femund (3 hours by train from Oslo to Rena). From the village, touring skiers can go up into the mountains by chairlift. There are some 30 kilometers of marked and prepared trails. Popular objectives are Mount Kvitvola, 2 kilometers away, and Mount Hogna, 10 kilometers away. The wooded terrain has peaks between 700 and 1,400 meters in height. There are lighted trails at Drevsje, SLEN AND Hylleråsen.

Os—Narbuvoll: The small village of Os is situated at an altitude of 600 meters to the north of the Hummelfjell Mountains. Narbuvoll is located to the east of the Hummelfjell Range on National Highway 26, about 26 kilometers away. Thirty minutes by bus from Trondheim. The Hummelfjell Mountains and Mount Gråhøgda (1,541 meters) loom above the two mountain communities. There is a network of about 50 kilometers of marked and, in some cases, prepared trails. Lighted trails at Os.

Rendal: The villages of the Rendal Valley are located in the heart of the Østerdal system of valleys. Rendal Mountain Lodge (610 meters) is situated on National Highway 217. About 12 kilometers to the east a 2-kilometer toll road leads up to the Grøndal area. Down in the valley is Øiseth Mote, beside Lake Storsjø. One hour by bus from Koppang to Rendal Mountain Lodge (4 hours by train from Oslo to Koppang). The Rendal Valley is dominated by the bulk of Mount Rendalssøln (1,751 meters). Other popular destinations for touring skiers are Lake Harsjø and Søvollen. Easy wooded and mountain terrain with marked and prepared trails. Trail maps are available free of charge. Lighted ski trails.

Tynset—Savalen: The village of Tynset is situated at an altitude of 500 meters in a beautiful mountain setting. Savalen is about 20 kilometers to the west. 5½ hours by train from Oslo to Tynset; 30 minutes by bus from Tynset to Savalen. From the ski lodge at the upper end of the skilift a network of 50 kilometers of marked and, in some cases, prepared trails spreads out through woods and across the mountains. From Tron Youth Center a difficult, unmarked trail leads to Mount Tronfjell, five kilometers away. There is a lighted trail close to the town. Savalen has a variety of trails in wooded and mountain country, including one to Mount Rødalshø about 8 kilometers away. Trail maps available locally. Information: Østerdalene Reisetrafikklag (see *Address Directory*).

Sunnmøre Area

Ask Norwegians to choose the finest fjord landscape in the country and many will pick Sunnmøre. The Storfjord, with its branches Voldafjord, Hjørundfjord, Sunnylvsfjord, Geirangerfjord, Norddalsfjord and Tafjord, cut into Sunnmøre's mountainous terrain. Hjørundfjord has been compared with the nave of a Gothic cathedral. Geirangerfjord—often seen on Norwegian travel brochures—is the epitome of a Norwegian fjord with its steep, winding mountainsides, tumbling waterfalls and deserted farms on ledges high above the water. Everything is close: the fjords, the valleys, the wild array of peaks; even the ocean is not far away. The Sunnmøre Alps are noted for their absence of high connecting ridges. Almost every peak has a magnificent view, and there is a feeling of isolation about every summit.

Geologically, the Sunnmøre Mountains are old. They were formed in Cambrian or pre-Cambrian times by folding and volcanic action which produced a striped granite-gneiss with quartz, feldspar and mica. When the volcanic period came to an end, abrasive forces took over. Valleys and fjords were formed along faulted zones. During the glacial periods the ice carried on the sculptural work. Peaks, cirques and moraines were created and V-valleys were turned into U-valleys with numerous side valleys on the mountainsides—known as "hanging valleys"—high above the fjords.

Although Sunnmøre's peaks challenge rock climbers, most of the summits can be reached by ordinary hikers along safe routes without a rope and ice axe. Many one- to two-day mountain hikes are possible. Longer mountain hikes, however, can only be undertaken in the Tafjord Mountains, where Ålesund og Sunnmøre Turistforening (ÅST) operates several huts and has marked trails.

Tourist Information

Ålesund og Sunnmøre Turistforening (see *Address Directory*).

Trail Lodgings

There are nine mountain huts in the Sunnmøre area; two staffed, four self-service and three unstaffed. In addition, there are three youth hostels, as well as hotels and guesthouses in Geiranger, Grotli, Lesjaverk, Skjåk, Stordal, Volda and Ørsta. Details on the hotels are given in the Norway Travel Association's lodging list, *Where to Stay in Norway*.

Of the mountain huts, only one—a self-service hut on Lake Torsvatn—is operated by the DNT. The rest are operated by Ålesund og Sunnmøre Turistforening (see *Address Directory*). All the self-service and unstaffed huts are secured with standard locks. A key which fits all the locks is available to DNT members from the DNT's Oslo office and the Ålesund Tourist office. For further information on the huts, see *Mountain Touring Holidays in Norway*.

Maps

The Sunnmøre area is covered by the following maps:

- Norges Geografiske Oppmåling Gradteigskart (Serie M711) 1:50,000, sheets 1319/I, II, III and IV.

Guidebooks

- *Climbers' Book* by mountaineers—many of them British—who have entered reports of ascents in the area. Can be seen at Union Hotel in Øye.
- *Sunnmøre* (in Norwegian) by Kristofer Randers. Describes routes of varying grades to 50 different peaks. Available from the DNT (see *Address Directory*).
- *Mountain Touring Holidays in Norway*, available in English and German from the DNT.

Suggested Walk

From Valldal to Billingen. Across moors and ridges, to the brink of the precipice above Lake Onilsavatn (stupendous view) and below the Reindalsfoss—considered to be the finest waterfall in Sunnmøre. The last stretch goes across the Torsflya moors, a wide expanse which evokes a "top of the world" feeling. **Walking Time:** 6 days. **Difficulty:** Moderately difficult. **Path Markings:** Cairned throughout.
Maps:
• Norges Geografiske Oppmåling Gradteigskart (Serie M 711) 1:50,000, sheets 1319 I, II, III and IV.
Guidebook:
• *Mountain Touring Holidays in Norway.*

Cross-Country Skiing

Among the areas where you can ski tour in the Sunnmøre region are:

Stranda: Stranda Ski Center is situated 7 kilometers west of the village center on Geirangerfjord. Reached via Ålesund (57 kilometers) and Andalsnes (120 kilometers). By bus: 1½ hours. Touring trails in mountain terrain of varying degrees of difficulty from the top station. Ski school at the ski center. Touring guide available. Skis and accessories can be rented.

Sykkylven: Located near Fjellsetra. Reached from Ålesund (54 kilometers) 1½ hours by bus. Touring country of varying degrees of difficulty from the top station. Many easy runs in the valley bottom and along Lake Nysaetervann. Trails mechanically prepared.

Ørsta: Ørsta Ski Center, at Bondalseidet, is located 15 kilometers east of the village. Two hours by bus from Ålesund (59 kilometers). Marked touring trails radiate out across exacting mountain terrain; a popular destination is Verhaldet (5 kilometers away).

Dovre–Romsdal Ranges

The Dovre-Romsdal ranges are a region of lofty mountains—serene and undulating in the south and east, steep and serrated in the west. They are situated between the Romsdal, Drivdal and Sunndal valleys and the innermost branches of the Romsdal and Sunndal fjords. On the Dovrefjell there are wide, open spaces with moors and marshes and rounded ridges, and, in the northwest, high mountains with glaciers. These include the largest concentration of high peaks outside Rondane and Jotunheimen— Snøhetta (2,278 meters), Store Svånåtind (2,215 meters) and Larstind (2,106 meters)—and above the Romsdalen, some of Norway's wildest pinnacles. This valley and its mountains are said to be worthy rivals of America's Yosemite, and the Romsdalshorn has been compared with the Matterhorn. The east wall of the Trolltindane Ranges is the highest overhang in Europe, and is considered one of the world's six most difficult rock climbs. Rock climbs in Romsdalen and neighboring Eikesdalen are for experts only. (A booklet in English has been published on routes and ascents in Romsdalen and is available from the DNT, see *Address Directory*.) There is, however, no reason for non-climbers to be afraid of the Romsdal Mountains. Strenuous but safe routes lead to the top of most peaks. But before starting off, you should always seek the advice of local mountaineers and hikers. Guides might be available through Åndalsnes tourist office.

There is a rich flora and fauna in the eastern part of the Dovrefjell Plateau. The Knutshø Mountains east of Kongsvoll have been called the cradle of Norwegian plant geography, and rare plants that survived the last ice age have been found here. The district was made a national preserve in 1911. In the Snøhetta region there are herds of wild reindeer, and the Fokstumyrene marshes are rich in bird life, especially during the nesting season (April 25 to July 8).

Tourist Information

Åndalsnes og Romsdals Reiselivslag (see *Address Directory*).

Trail Lodgings

There are 15 mountain huts in the Dovre-Romsdal Ranges. In addition, there are five youth hostels, as well as hotels and guesthouses in the surrounding towns and villages. The mountain huts are operated by:

See *Address Directory*:

Den Norske Turistforening. Operates two self-service huts, one in the Stroplsjødal and one near Lake Eikesdalsvatn. The huts are locked. Keys can be obtained from the wardens of nearby staffed huts, from DNT's Oslo office or from Elvsaas & Co., Molde.

Molde og Romsdal Turistforening. Operates two self-service and two unstaffed huts in the region. Self-service and unstaffed huts are kept locked; keys are available from the wardens at nearby staffed huts, from DNT's Oslo office or from Elvsaas & Co., Molde.

Kristiansund og Nordmøre Turistforening (KNT). Operates one staffed hut, three self-service huts and two unstaffed huts in the Dovre-Romsdal area. Self-service and unstaffed huts are left unlocked during the summer season. Off-season, you must obtain keys from the tourist associations.

Trondhjems Turistforening (TT). Operates one self-service hut in the Dindal Valley. The hut is locked; a key must be obtained from the neighboring seter.

Further information on each hut can be obtained from the tourist associations. *Mountain Touring Holidays in Norway* lists the huts and gives their locations and number of beds. It also lists youth hostels and gives the dates they are open and notes whether meals are served.

Details on hotels—which are located in Dombås, Hjerkinn, Lesjaverk, Oppdal, Sunndalen and Åndalsnes—are given in the Norway Travel Association's lodging list, *Where to Stay in Norway*. The lodging list does not include several small guesthouses—such as those at Eikesdalen and one between Hjerkinn and Kongsvoll. For information on these, you should contact the respective tourist associations.

Maps

DNT's planning map, *Dovrefjell—Trollheimen—Møre Romsdal* (free on request from the DNT; see *Address Directory*), is recommended for planning hikes in the Dovre–Romsdal Ranges. Once you have determined your final itinerary on the DNT planning map, you can then order the appropriate 1:50,000 topographical maps from the DNT.

Guidebooks

- *Walks and Climbs in Romsdal Norway* (in English) by Tony Howard, Cicerone Press, Manchester, England. Available from the DNT (see *Address Directory*).
- *Til Fots i Rondane—Dovrefjell—Trollheimen* (in Norwegian), also available from the DNT.
- *Mountain Touring Holidays in Norway*, available in English and German from the DNT.

Suggested Walk

From Kongsvoll to Grøvdal. Into the Åmotsdal Valley, across the Leirsjutelet moors, and through the Grøvudal with its fantastic terraces, remnants of old deserted farms and numerous rare plants, such as the Dovre poppy and the Norwegian wormwood. The path also takes you past Lake Eikesdalsvatn, where mountains rise almost vertically on both sides. The path then continues across the Gjuvskard Glacier before the descent to Grøvdal. **Walking Time:** 8 to 9 days. **Difficulty:** Moderately difficult. **Path Markings:** Cairned, except between Reinheim and Åmotsdalhytta, where the path is partly cairned and partly marked.

Maps:
- Norges Geografiske Oppmåling Gradteigskart (Serie M711) 1:50,000, sheets 1519/IV, 1419/I, 1419/IV, 1420/III and 1320/II.

Guidebook:
- *Mountain Touring Holidays in Norway.*

Cross-Country Skiing

Among the areas where you can ski tour in the Dovre–Romsdal ranges are:

Bjorli–Lesja: This resort is six hours by train from Oslo. It hosted the Norwegian Alpine Skiing Championships in 1972 and 1975. There are 20 kilometers of marked, prepared touring trails winding through the nearby woods and mountain moors. Popular destinations for experienced skiers are Mount Storhø, Mount Odolshø and Mount Merratind.

Dombas–Dovre: Dombas is the winter-sports center of the Dovrefjell Mountains; it is also the site of the Norwegian Athletic Association's training center and Dombas Mountaineering School. Skiers staying in Dovre, 13 kilometers south of the center, ski in the terrain around Dombas. 4½ hours by train from Oslo; 3½ hours from Trondheim. From Dombas and the upper terminal of the T-bar tow a network of 100 kilometers of marked and prepared trails stretches away across the moors to the bare mountains. Popular destinations are Hardbakken and Grønhø. The Dombas T-bar tow serves a giant run suitable for touring skiers. Trail maps are on sale locally. Touring skis, boots and poles may be hired from the Holum Sports Shop. There is also a ski school at Dombas.

Hjerkinn: This is a tiny village on the railway set amid the Dovre Mountains. Six hours by train from Oslo; two hours by train from Trondheim. There are wide expanses of mountain moorland rising to the mountain peaks within range of a good touring skier. The highest mountain is Snøhetta (about 25 kilometers away, 2,286 meters in altitude). Nearer the lodge the terrain is gentler.

A sketch map to ski trails, *Hytter og Kvistruter,* is available from the DNT.

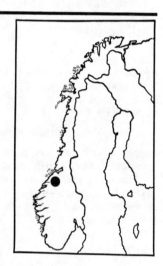

Trollheimen & Nordmøre Ranges

Trollheimen—or the "home of the Trolls"—lies south of Trondheim. The ranges are crisscrossed by glens and nearly split in two by the cleft made by the pine-forested Folldal and its continuation, the Hyttdal, which runs towards Lake Gjevilvatn, the largest of the Trollheimen Lakes. Innerdalen with its tributary, the Giklingdal, is surrounded by majestic peaks that rise up to more than 1,800 meters and makes a wonderful entrance to Trollheimen from the fjord country. In the Innerdal Valley, rock climbing courses are arranged during the summer. (A booklet with international signs and abbreviations on rock climbs in Innerdalen has been published by Norsk Tindeklubb and is available from the DNT.)

The Trollheimen Mountains have regular, conical forms as well as ridges, cirques and crests resulting from glacial erosion. Grass, bracken, herbs, even nettles grow to a height of nearly two meters in the Svartadal. In the luxuriant forest near Trollheimshytta, dead pines stand like skeleton trolls.

Trondhjems Turistforening, assisted by Kristiansund og Nordmøre Turistforening, has built huts and marked routes. For hikers who arrive on the Oslo–Trondheim train (Dovre Line), Oppdal and Ulsberg are the best starting points. Other starting points are Storfale in Sunndalen; Innerdalen; Rindal in Surnadal; and Grindal in Orkladal.

Tourist Information

See *Address Directory*:

Reiselivsforeningen for Kristiansund og Nordmøre.
Reisetrafikkforeningen for Trondheim og Trøndelag.

Trail Lodgings

There are seven staffed mountain huts in Trollheimen and Nordmøre. In addition, there are two youth hostels, as well as hotels and guesthouses in the surrounding towns and villages. The mountain huts are open from June 25 to August 20. Three of the staffed huts are private, the others are operated by:

Trondhjems Turistforening (see *Address Directory*).

Further information on each hut can be obtained from the tourist association. *Mountain Touring Holidays in Norway* also includes a list of the huts and youth hostels in the mountain region.

Details on hotels—which are located in Berkåk, Oppdal, Sunndalen and Surnadal—are given in the Norway Travel Association's lodging list, *Where to Stay in Norway*.

Maps

All the information you need to plan hikes is shown on the DNT's planning map: *Dovrefjell—Trollheimen—Møre Romsdal* (free on request from the DNT; see *Address Directory*). Once you have determined your final itinerary on the planning map, you can then purchase the appropriate topographical maps from the DNT.

Guidebooks

- *Til Fots i Rondane—Dovrefjell—Trollheimen* (in Norwegian), available from the DNT (see *Address Directory*).
- *Mountain Touring Holidays in Norway*, available in English and German from the DNT.

Suggested Walk

From Oppdal to Storfale. Along the edge of a deep cirque, across scree, and high above the glittering, blue-green Trollauget (Troll's Eye) tarn. After a steep descent through forest, the path climbs alongside the torrent at Skjerdingfjell, until it reaches the Brona Gap where you are rewarded with a sweeping view of the Innerdalen and its mountains. The path then takes you along a precipice and down numerous loops into Sunndalen, a few kilometers from Storfale. **Walking Time:** 6 days. **Difficulty:** Moderately difficult. **Path Markings:** Cairned throughout.

Maps:
• Norges Geografiske Oppmåling Gradteigskart (Serie M711) 1:50,000, sheets 1520/III, 1520/IV, 1420/I and 1420/II.

Guidebook:
• *Mountain Touring Holidays in Norway.*

Cross-Country Skiing

Among the areas where you can ski tour in the Trollheimen is:

Oppdal: Located on highway E-6, 150 kilometers south of Trondheim. Railway town with a population of about 3,000, surrounded by mountains up to 1,600 meters in height. Oppdal offers excellent facilities for alpine and cross-country skiing. The national championships in all skiing events are often staged here. It is 6 hours by train from Oslo, 1½ hours from Trondheim. Lifts take touring skiers up into the mountains, where there is good touring country and about 70 kilometers of marked and prepared trails leading to the nearby mountains. Ski school for cross-country technique. Skiing equipment may be hired. Information: Oppdal Tourist Office (see *Address Directory*).

Sylene Mountains

Until the Norwegian-Swedish border was finally determined in 1929, it was uncertain to what country some of the Sylene summits belonged. Storsola (1,710 meters) was one of three peaks that went to Norway. The peak was considered inaccessible, but the summit was easily scaled the same year by a group of masons who were carrying stones for the frontier cairn.

The name Sylene is also used to designate the mountain plateau to the west, between the Stjørdal and Gauldal valleys. In the south this moorland region merges with the Røros Plateau, which forms part of the same hiking region. The mountain plateau, planed down by ice, with no great differences in height, is ideal for people who are looking for comfortable walks.

Access to the area is easy from the Haltdalen and Reitan train stations on the Røros line, and from the Meråker and Storlien (Sweden) stations on the Meråker Line.

Tourist Information

> **Reisetrafikkforeningen for Trondheim og Trøndelag** (see *Address Directory*).

Trail Lodgings

There are nine mountain huts in Sylene (not including those on the Swedish side). In addition, there are hotels and guesthouses in the surrounding towns and villages. Two of these huts are private farms offering accommodation by TT-agreement. The others are operated by:

Trondhjems Turistforening (see *Address Directory*). Operates three staffed huts and four self-service huts. The self-service huts are locked; keys must be obtained at neighboring staffed huts and from TT's Trondheim office. Further information on each hut can be obtained from the tourist association or from the hut list in *Mountain Touring Holidays in Norway*.

Details on hotels—which are located in Meråker and Tydal—are given in the Norway Travel Association's lodging list, *Where to Stay in Norway*. The lodging list does not include several small guesthouses such as the one in Selbu. For information on these, you should contact the respective tourist associations.

Maps

The Sylene Mountains are covered by the following maps:

- Norges Geografiske Oppmåling Gradteigskart (serie M711) 1:50,000, sheets 1720/II, 1720/IV, 1721/II and 1720/III.
- The locations of lodgings and shelters, and the routes of marked and unmarked tracks are also shown on the planning map: *Sylene* (free on request from the DNT; see *Address Directory*).

Guidebooks

- *Til Fots i Femundsmarka og Sylene* (in Norwegian), available from the DNT (see *Address Directory*).
- *Mountain Touring Holidays in Norway*, available in English and German from the DNT.

Suggested Walk

From Nordpå to Stugudal. Gentle ascent to Hilmobola with a fine view into Sweden. The path leads among birches down to marshy ground and continues to Stormoen seter. At Sankadalsvoll there is an interesting, old open-hearth hut. The rest of the path leads through birches, over bare mountains and along the foot of Mount Skardøra where there is an extensive view of Nedalen and Stugusjøen. You can catch a bus at the Vektarhaugvoll seter to Stugudal. **Walking Time:** 6 to 7 days. **Difficulty:** Easy to moderately difficult. **Path Markings:** Cairned throughout.
Maps:
- Norges Geografiske Oppmåling Gradteigskart 1:50,000, sheets 1720/II, 1720/IV, 1721/II and 1721/III.
Guidebook:
- *Mountain Touring Holidays in Norway*.

Cross-Country Skiing

Among the areas where you can ski tour in the Sylene Mountains is:

Tydal: Site of Vektarstua Lodge, located beside Lake Stugusjø, beneath the Sylene Mountains. The Skardørsfjell area in the east (1,500 meters and above) is suitable for experienced skiers, while the rolling expanses to the west and south of Lake Stugusjø are suited for the less experienced.

North Norway

The mountains of North Norway are not as easily accessible as those in South Norway. From Oslo, for instance, the trip to Tromsø takes two and a half days by bus. The facilities for hikers are also less developed. Only a handful of mountain regions have a sufficient network of cairned paths and huts to make hikes of more than three days' duration possible.

Trip planning is also more difficult. Only six of the mountain areas are covered by the DNT's planning maps. Guidebooks are few, limited primarily to *Mountain Touring Holidays in Norway* and *Fiske og Ferie Nordpå* (both available from the DNT) and the Norwegian National Park leaflets published by the Ministry of Environment (see "Further Information" at the end of the section on *Norway's National Parks*). In addition, a good, strong insect repellent (such as the kind that can be bought in Norway) is a must during the summer.

But the effort is more than worthwhile. For those who are prepared to bring their own sleeping bag, tent and cooking gear, don't mind carrying most—or in some cases, all—of their food, and can navigate skillfully with a map and compass, North Norway is filled with opportunity. It is the enclave of some of the finest mountain scenery in Norway. And its very remoteness has helped keep it wild and lightly traveled. The Lofoten and Lyngen areas are also considered to be among the best in Norway for rock climbing.

Okstindan Mountain Range

This is a wonderful, ice-carved mountain region southeast of Mo i Rana near the Swedish border. Rugged peaks composed of slated mica rise up to 1,915 meters above icefields and glaciers, and white-foam torrents rush down the mountainsides. In the valleys are lakes, marshes and forests of pine and birch. The countryside is wild and isolated. Nonetheless, rock climbers have long been drawn to its heights. Rock walls on the region's 12 peaks, which include North Norway's highest—Oksskolten—challenge even experienced climbers. Glacial traverses are also strenuous, and suited only for well-equipped and experienced mountaineers. For the general hiker, the possibilities are limited. Cross-country travel is difficult, cairned routes are few, and there are only four unstaffed huts in the area.

Tourist Information

See *Address Directory*:

Nordland Turisttrafikkomite.
Rana Reisetrafikklag.

Trail Lodgings

The four unstaffed huts in the Okstindan Mountains—Kjennsvasshytta, Grådfjellhytta, Leirbotnhytta and Steinbaua—are owned by the Hemnes Turistforening in Korgen. They are left open during the summer season. At other times of the year, keys may be obtained from the tourist association. Be sparing with the firewood in these huts. Getting it there is an expensive business.

Hotels are located in Mo i Rana. In addition, there are youth hostels in Mo i Rana and Umbukta.

Maps

The Okstindan Mountains are covered by the following maps:

* Norges Geografiske Oppmåling Gradteigskart 1:100,000, sheets J-16 *Rana,* J-17 *Røsvatn,* K-16 *Umbugten* and K-17 *Krutfjell,* as well as the 1:100,000 Turistkart, sheet 26 *Okstindan.*

Guidebooks

* *Fiske og Ferie Nordpå* (in Norwegian), available from the DNT (see *Address Directory*).
* *Mountain Touring Holidays in Norway.*

Suggested Walk

From Umbukta to Korgen. Stiff climbs and steep descents alternate with easy walks along lakes and up valleys. Passes near the Austisen icefield, from which both Oksskolten (1,915 meters) and Okshornet (1,907 meters) can be climbed by experienced mountaineers with the proper equipment. Also takes you near the Vestisen icefield. Umbukta can be reached by bus in one hour from Mo i Rana. **Walking Time:** 4 to 5 days. **Difficulty:** Moderately difficult; some difficult sections. **Path Markings:** The first day's walk is on an uncairned route, although the path is generally clear. The remainder of the route is cairned. **Trail Lodgings:** The route links the four unstaffed huts in the Okstindan region. Details are given in *Mountain Touring Holidays in Norway.*
Maps:
* Norges Geografiske Oppmåling Gradteigskart 1:100,000, sheets J-16 *Rana,* J-17 *Røsvatn* and K-16 *Umbugten.*
Guidebook:
* *Mountain Touring Holidays in Norway.*

Svartisen Glacier
& Mo i Rana Area

Astride the Arctic Circle, within the Rana and Beiarn districts, is a wild and rugged landscape of limestone caves, sharp peaks and glaciated valleys dominated by the Svartisen icecap.

Svartisen—the Black Ice—lies near the coast north of Mo i Rana. It is the largest icefield in North Norway, covering about 400 square kilometers. Svartisen is heavily crevassed and only properly trained and equipped mountaineers—or guided parties—should attempt to cross it. Hikers, however, can reach the numerous glacial tongues which project from the two parts of the icefield—Østisen and Vestisen. The best known of these glaciers is Østerdalsisen, which has numerous ice caves and crevasses. It can be reached on a short path following a 20-minute boat ride across Lake Svartisvatn (32 kilometers by road from Mo i Rana). There are two small, unstaffed huts in the Svartisvatn area—one with bedding and one without—both owned by the Rana Tourist Association. One of the huts is located at the east end of Lake Svartisvatn and is accessible by car from Mo i Rana. A cairned path links the two huts—Svartishytta and Blakkådalshytta—and continues to Staupåmoen in the Beiardal Valley, providing access to the Østisen icefield for mountaineers who wish to explore it.

Limestone Caves. The six major cave areas in the Rana district—Røvassdal, Reingardslivatn, Glomdal, Plurdal, Dunderlandsdal and the north side of Langvatn—can be reached on local bus services from Mo i Rana. More than 100 caves have been located within the district, six of which have a surveyed length in excess of two kilometers. The district also includes *Larshullet* which, at 326 meters, is the deepest cave in Norway and was the world's sixteenth deepest cave when it was explored in 1951 by the Cave Research Group of Great Britain.

The larger cave systems are normally found below tree line in the lower parts of the valleys, which are covered with thick pine forests and dense birch scrub. This sometimes makes the location of entrances difficult without local assistance. Also, because bus service is generally infrequent and the caves are a several-kilometer walk from where the buses stop, it is often necessary to camp in the vicinity of the caves if you wish to explore them.

Advice and information for planning caving trips can be obtained from the Rana Reisetrafikklag (see *Address Directory*) which publishes a leaflet with details on the caves and the equipment required to explore them. The tourist office also can put you into contact with the Rana Grotteklubb, the local Norwegian caving association.

Tourist Information

See *Address Directory*:

Nordland Turisttrafikkomite.
Rana Reisetrafikklag.

Maps

- **The Svartisen icecap:** Norges Geografiske Oppmåling Gradteigskart 1:100,000, sheets J-14 *Meløy,* J-15 *Svartisen,* K-14 *Beiardalen* and K-15 *Dunderlandsdalen.*
- **The Rana Cave District:** Norges Geografiske Oppmåling Gradteigskart 1:100,000, sheets J-15 *Svartisen,* J-16 *Rana,* K-14 *Beiardalen,* K-15 *Dunderlandsdalen* and K-16 *Umbungten.* The Rana cave district is also covered by the DNT planning map: *Rana* (free on request from the DNT; see *Address Directory*).

Guidebooks

- *Fiske og Ferie Nordpå* (in Norwegian), available from the DNT (see *Address Directory*).
- *Mountain Touring Holidays in Norway.*

Sulitjelma & Saltfjellet Mountain Ranges

Sulitjelma is a region of glaciers and ice-girded peaks which lies at the end of the Saltfjord, east of Bodø. Deposits of copper ore in the mountains are mined by the Sulitjelma Mining Company in a desolate area along Lake Langvatn. But elsewhere, the area is hardly touched—a place where solitude can easily be found among gabbro peaks which rise up to 1,913 meters above the 40-square-kilometer Sulitjelma Glacier and the 124-square-kilometer Blåmannsisen icecap.

To the south, impressive peaks rise above the bare undulating moors of the Saltfjellet Mountain Plateau and its wildly beautiful valleys. In the Junkerdalen, which forms the divide between the Sulitjelma and Saltfjell ranges, wild strawberries grow in profusion, and lowland plants such as the sea buckthorn are found further north than anywhere else on earth. Botanists will also notice the *Carex scirpoides,* a sedge normally found only in Greenland, North America and northeast Asia. To the west is another luxuriant valley, Beiardalen, which has numerous limestone caves.

Unstaffed huts and marked trails have been established by the Bodø og Omegns Turistforening (BOT) and Sulitjelma Turistforening. None of the huts are supplied with provisions, so you must carry your own food. Several of the paths lead into Swedish Lappland and the Padjelanta National Park. The Swedish huts are open and usually supplied with firewood. Boats will be found on lakes and unfordable rivers in Sweden, and there must always be one on each side. This means that, if you use one of the boats, you must row across, get the boat on the other side, row back, tie up the other boat and then row across again before continuing on your way.

Tourist Information

See *Address Directory*:

Nordland Turisttrafikkomite.
Salten Reiselivslag.

Trail Lodgings

There are 13 unstaffed huts in the Sulitjelma and Saltfjellet mountain ranges. These are maintained by:

See *Address Directory*:

Bodø og Omegns Turistforening. Operates eight unstaffed huts, three of which are open during the summer season. Keys for the rest may be obtained from BOT's office and neighboring farms.

Sulitjelma Turistforening. Operates five unstaffed huts, all of which are locked. Keys are available only from ST's secretary/chairman in Sulitjelma, who will also arrange for boats to take you across Lake Balvatn.

In addition to the huts, there are youth hostels in Bleiknesmo and Skjerstad, hotels in Fauske and Lønsdal and guesthouses in Sulitjelma, Misvær, Beiarn and Finneid. Details on the huts and hostels are given in *Mountain Touring Holidays in Norway*. For information on the hotels and guesthouses, you should refer to the Norway Travel Association's lodging list, *Where to Stay in Norway*, or contact the local tourist offices.

Maps

The two mountain ranges are covered by the DNT planning maps: *Saltfjellet—Sulitjelma* (free on request from the DNT; see *Address Directory*). All the information you need to plan hikes—areas covered by 1:100,000 topographical sheets, and the locations of lodgings and walking routes—is shown.

Guidebooks

fiske og Ferie Nordpå (in Norwegian), available from the DNT (see *Address Directory*).

• *Mountain Touring Holidays in Norway.*

Suggested Walk

From Sulitjelma to Beiarn. Both settlements are accessible by bus from Fauske. The route skirts the edge of Lake Balvatn, follows rivers, occasionally crossing them on suspension bridges, and climbs ridges with rewarding views over the surrounding countryside. A portion of the route passes through the Junkerdalen. **Walking Time:** 6 to 7 days. **Difficulty:** Moderately difficult. **Path Markings:** Cairned, except between Sulitjelma and Tjorvihytta (where, as an alternative, you can walk along a road).

Trail Lodgings: Unstaffed huts are located within a 6- to 8-hour walk of each other along the route.

Maps:

* Norges Geografiske Oppmåling Gradteigskart 1:100,000, sheets K-14 *Beiardalen,* L-13 *Saltdal* and L-14 *Junkerdalen.*

Guidebooks:

* *Fiske og Ferie Nordpå.*
* *Mountain Touring Holidays in Norway.*

Cross-Country Skiing

Among the areas where you can cross-country ski in the two ranges is:

Lønsdal: Located on the Nordland Railway and E 6 Highway in the Saltfjell Mountains, 146 kilometers south of Bodø and 105 kilometers north of Mo i Rana. 2½ hours by train from Bodø and 1½ hours from Mo i Rana. Wooded mountain terrain with 40 kilometers of marked trails in the immediate vicinity. Open, rolling moorland is suitable for the lesser-experienced while experienced skiers can tackle rugged mountain terrain. Popular destinations are Kjemågtind (5 kilometers, 1,501 meters), Flatviskis (7 kilometers, 820 meters) and Rundhaugen (10 kilometers, 1,111 meters).

Bodø—Tysfjord Area

This is a wild, ruggedly beautiful mountain region deeply indented with fjords between Bodø and Narvik. Two large fjord basins—Sørfolda and Nordfolda—lie directly north of Bodø. Above the fjords, imposing mountain ranges rear into the sky, offering numerous challenges to rock climbers—the walls of the Strandåtind, the monolith of the Husbyviktind, plus many opportunities to explore unclimbed routes.

Tysfjord is the narrow part of Norway between Nordfolda and Narvik, which includes Rago National Park (see the section on *Norway's National Parks*), the Stetind pyramid—said to be the most remarkable natural obelisk in the world—the Frostisen icefield and the Storsteinsfjell rock massif on the frontier with Sweden.

There are only a few marked trails in the area and no mountain huts. Access, however, is easy and the possibilities for exploration are numerous for those who carry their own equipment, have mountaineering experience and are competent orienteers. The fjords in the Folda region are served either by boats from Bodø or by a combination of buses and ferries. The Arctic Highway between Fauske and Narvik and its branches also provide excellent access. Highway 81 from Bodø, for instance, takes rock climbers directly to the Strandåtind.

There are marked foot trails in Rago National Park. There is also a marked trail from Hellmobotn, where Norway is at its narrowest, to Ritsemjokk and Vaisaluokta, which lie 50 kilometers inside Sweden.

Tourist Information

See *Address Directory:*

Nordland Turisttrafikkomite.

Bodø Reiselivslag.
Narvik Turistkontor.

Trail Lodgings

There are several camping sites with huts and a few guesthouses along the Arctic Highway (E 6). In addition, there is a youth hostel at Kråkmo. Some of these lodgings are listed in the Norway Travel Association's lodging list, *Where to Stay in Norway*. Information on the others may be obtained from the local tourist offices. There are no lodgings in the mountains.

Maps

The region is covered by:

- Norges Geografiske Oppmåling Gradteigskart 1:100,000, sheets K-11 *Steigen*, K-12 *Kjerringrøy*, L-10 *Hamarøy*, L-11 *Nordfold*, L12 *Sørfold*, M-10 *Tysfjord*, M-11 *Hellemobotn* and M-12 *Linnajavrre*. Also, Svenska Fjällkarten No. 3 (also available from the DNT).

Guidebooks

- *Fiske og Ferie Nordpå* (in Norwegian), available from the DNT (see *Address Directory*).
- *Mountain Touring Holidays in Norway*.

The Lofoten &
Vesterålen Isles

Lofoten is primarily an area for mountaineers and rock climbers. There are no marked trails nor mountain huts in the area and the terrain is extremely rugged—something like the Chamonix Aiguilles surrounded by water. From the mainland, the Lofoten island group appears to be one continuous mountain range, stretching for 100 kilometers between Raftsundet and Lofotodden on the tip of Moskenesøy, where the sea is churned by the Moskenesstraum tide-race—known as the *Malstrøm*—which inspired stories by Edgar Allan Poe and Jules Verne.

The island group is made up of 6 large islands, plus 76 other inhabited islands and countless small islets which jut 190 kilometers into the sea southwest of Narvik. The mountains, composed of granite and volcanic rocks, have been ice-scoured up to 600 meters above the sea and many rock faces are unclimbable because the smooth, glacier-worn slabs are devoid of hand- and foot-holds. Ascents and descents are generally made by the same route, and it is helpful to build a string of two-stone cairns on the way up, which you should then knock down on the return journey.

The Vesterålen Archipelago, which lies to the north of Lofoten, is more suitable for hikers. There are no marked routes or mountain huts, but the terrain between its needle-sharp peaks is less severe, especially along the coastal plains on the eastern side of the islands. For climbers, there are the Higravstindan ranges, the Trollfjord or Trolltindan peaks and the mountains on Hinnøy, as well as one of the most remarkable peaks in North Norway, located on the island of Langøy—the 607-meter obelisk of Reka, with its steep, smooth-rock sides and its knife-edge summit, which is 36.5 meters long and barely a meter wide.

Tourist Information

See *Address Directory*:

Nordland Turisttrafikkomite.
Narvik Turistkontor.

Climbing Information

Magnar Pettersen and **Arne Randers Heen** (see *Address Directory*). Both men are local mountaineers who have extensive knowledge of the Lofoten ranges, including both winter and summer ascents. Information on how to contact the two men can be obtained from the Narvik tourist office.

Trail Lodgings

In the Lofoten fishing villages you can rent shanties—known as *rorbuer*—which have electric light outlets for radios and electric shavers, wood burning stoves and a kitchenette which is usually provided with an electric hot plate, running water and a sink. The shanties were used by fishermen when their boats were too small to sleep aboard. No linen is provided, so you must bring your own sleeping bag. You must also provide your own cooking utensils. Information on the "Shanty Holidays" can be obtained from either of the tourist offices listed above.

In addition to the shanties, there are hotels, guesthouses and camping huts scattered around the islands, as well as youth hostels in Stamsund, Svolvær, Andenes, Bø, Kleiva and Melbu. Information on these lodgings can be obtained from the tourist offices. Several are also listed in the Norway Travel Association's lodging list, *Where to Stay in Norway*.

Maps

The Lofoten and Vesterålen Isles are covered by the following maps:

- Norges Geografiske Oppmåling. Gradteigskart 1:100,000, sheets I-10 *Moskenesøy*, I-II *Lofotodden*, J-10 *Vestvågøy*, K-8 *Økhes*, K-9 *Hadsel*, K-10 *Svolvær*, L-7 *Andøy*, L-8 *Kvæfjord*, L-9 *Lødingen*, M-8 *Harstad* and M-9 *Ofoten*.

Part of the region is covered by the DNT planning map: *Harstad* (free on request from the DNT; see *Address Directory*).

Guidebooks

- *Fiske og Ferie Nordpå* (in Norwegian), available from the DNT (see *Address Directory*).

- *Camps and Climbs in Arctic Norway* (in English) by Thomas Weir, Cassel & Company, London, 1953.

Cross-Country Skiing

One area where you can ski in the Lofoten Isles is:

Svolvær: The largest urban center in the Lofoten (population: about 5,000). Half an hour by air from Bodø; 6 hours by boat. Has facilities for alpine skiing, as well as superb ski touring. Facilities include a five-kilometer floodlit touring trail, a ski trek at Kongstinden, floodlit nursery slopes, heated shelters adjoining the ski slopes, ski rentals and ski instruction. It is also possible to ice fish when you aren't skiing.

Narvik Region

Several peaks near the town of Narvik can be ascended by hikers without climbing. These include Fagernestoppen (1,270 meters), which has a path from the terminus of its cable railway to a ridge that leads to the summit; Rombakstøtta (1,243 meters), which has a good path up to Isvatnet and cairns the rest of the way to the top; and *Den sovende Dronning* (the Sleeping Queen), or Kongsbakktind (1,576 meters), which has a marked path to the summit from Lake Nedstevatn (accessible by bus from Narvik).

Elsewhere around Narvik, there is plenty of hard rock for climbers. To reach the climbs, wide, fast flowing rivers often must be crossed and a rope is usually necessary to ford them. Paths are often hopelessly overgrown and thick birch scrub makes the going difficult below treeline. Expanses of rock slab and scree also slow down ascents. In addition, there are mosquitoes to contend with. Insect repellents are necessary for both hikers and climbers. And it is best to use the local varieties since they are likely to be more effective.

Tourist Information

Narvik Turistkontor (see *Address Directory*).

Trail Lodgings

Narvik og Omegn Turistforening (NOT) operates five unstaffed huts in the mountains surrounding Narvik and Troms Turlag (TT) operates one unstaffed hut. All the huts are locked. Keys to the NOT huts are available from the Narvik Rådhus (Town Hall) caretaker. Keys to the TT's Stordalsstua hut are available from Arne Værum (see *Address Directory*).

There are several hotels and guesthouses in Narvik listed in the Norway Travel Association's lodging list, *Where to Stay in Norway*. In addition, there is a youth hostel in Narvik (Nordkalotten) and a campground which is well provided with huts.

Maps

The region surrounding Narvik is covered by the DNT planning map: *Narvikfjella* (free upon request from the DNT; see *Address Directory*). Once you have plotted out your route on the planning map, the appropriate 1:100,000 topographical maps can be purchased from the DNT.

Guidebooks

- *Fiske og Ferie Nordpå* (in Norwegian), available from the DNT (see *Address Directory*).
- *Mountain Touring Holidays in Norway*.

Suggested Walk

From the Ofoten Railway to Skjomen. Take the train from Narvik to the Katterat Station. From the station, the route passes through the Hunndal Valley, Sørdalen, across Djevlepass, up the Oallavagge Valley past Lake Sälkajokka, through Norddalen and the Caihnavagge Valley, across a gap east of Mount Caihnacokka (1,596 meters) and down the Sørdal Valley to the Skjomdalen Turisthytte, where a bus can be caught back to Narvik. The walk also can be extended by starting from Bones in the Salangsdal (accessible by bus from Narvik via Lund on E 6, where you can either get local transportation or walk up the road to Bones). **Walking Time:** 3 days.

Difficulty: Moderately difficult. **Path Markings:** Partially cairned.
Trail Lodgings: Unstaffed huts are located along the route within about an eight hour walk of each other.
Maps:
• Norges Geografiske Oppmåling Gradteigskart 1:100,000, sheets N-9 *Narvik* and N-10 *Skjomen.*
Guidebooks:
• *Fiske og Ferie Nordpå.*
• *Mountain Touring Holidays in Norway.*

Cross-Country Skiing

Narvik: This is North Norway's leading winter sports center, with good ski touring and alpine skiing facilities close to the town center. Located 927 kilometers north of Trondheim. Accessible by train from Bjørnfjell (50 minutes), Kiruna (3 hours) and Stockholm (21 hours). Flights from Oslo take two hours and land at Evenes, 1½ hours by bus from Narvik. In the Fagernes Mountains, just above Narvik, are downhill and giant slalom courses, as well as less demanding runs, accessible by a télécabine. Narvik skilift is located at Ankenes Ski Center, five kilometers from the town. This serves pisted slalom and giant slalom courses and takes touring skiers up to an expanse of mountain moorland crossed by marked and prepared trails. At Bjørnfjell, close to the Swedish border, there is good mountain skiing country. Skiing equipment can be hired at the Ankenes Ski Center. Halvor Malm's Ski School at the center offers instruction in cross-country ski techniques.

Troms Border Area

This is a region of rocky peaks, fjords, lakes, high plateaus and forests where torrents pour forth from glaciers and tumble down the mountain-sides through a series of waterfalls and rapids. Both the Troms Border Trail (see the section on *Norway's Long-Distance Footpaths*) and Øvre Dividal National Park (see the section on *Norway's National Parks*) lie within this region. Fishing is excellent. And for those with a tent and all their food, there are numerous possibilities for cross-country hikes. Access is easy via the E 6 highway and its branch roads.

Tourist Information

See *Address Directory*:

> **Turisttrafikkomiteen for Troms.**
> **Tromsø Turistkontor.**

Trail Lodgings

There are 14 unstaffed mountain huts in the Troms Border Area, 8 of which are located along the Troms Border Trail. Six of the huts belong to the DNT. The rest are run by:

> **Troms Turlag** (see *Address Directory*).

All the huts are secured with DNT standard locks. Keys are available from Andresens Vaabenforretning in Tromsø, as well as from local contacts (listed in *Mountain Touring Holidays in Norway*). A deposit is required on the keys, which is returned when the key is handed back to one of the contacts. The huts are equipped with kitchen utensils and bedding, but hikers must bring their own sheet sleeping bags and provisions. You are also asked to bring your own Butane gas container (No. 2202), which can be fitted to burners in all huts, and to *carry it back out when it is empty*. Firewood is often provided in the huts, but getting it to the huts is difficult and expensive, so please be sparing.

Several hotels near the Border Trail are listed in *Mountain Touring Holidays in Norway*. In addition, there is a youth hostel in Helligskogen.

Maps

All the information you need to plan walks in the Troms Border Area is shown on the DNT planning map: *Indre—Troms* (free on request from the DNT; see *Address Directory*). Once you have determined your final itinerary on the planning map, you can then order the appropriate 1:100,000 and 1:50,000 topographical maps from the DNT.

Guidebooks

- *Fiske og Ferie Nordpå* (in Norwegian), available from the DNT (see *Address Directory*).
- Annual pamphlet from Troms Turlag.
- *Mountain Touring Holidays in Norway*.

Suggested Walk

See the description of the Troms Border Trail in the section on *Norway's Long-Distance Footpaths*.

Cross-Country Skiing

Among the areas where you can cross-country ski in the Troms Border Area are:

Bardu: A resort on the E 6 highway in Inner Troms. Ski trek and downhill runs. Touring terrain is reached from the upper terminal of the ski lift.

Gratangen: A resort north of Narvik surrounded by 1,200 to 1,400-meter mountains. One hour by bus from Narvik. Flights from Oslo take three hours and land at Bardufoss, 1½ hours by bus from Gratangen. A ski tow leads up to marked touring trails in wooded terrain and across the mountain plateau.

Tromsø: A colorful town on the Arctic Ocean backed by a range of mountains. Two hours by airplane from Oslo; 6½ hours from Narvik by bus. Easy access by télécabine to Mount Storsteinen (421 meters), from which marked trails fan out into the surrounding terrain, leading to such peaks as Bønntua (5 kilometers, 778 meters), Sollitind (7 kilometers, 788 meters) and Tromsdalstind (12 kilometers, 1,238 meters). There are runs back to the town suitable for touring skiers. A ski store is located at the upper terminal of the télécabine. Krokem Ski Center, 6 kilometers from the town, has a T-bar tow with pisted slalom, giant slalom and downhill courses, plus a run for touring skiers. The upper terminal station is the starting point of several trails that cross the mountain plateau. There are lighted trails at Tromsøya and in Tromsdalen.

Lyngen Peninsula

The Lyngen Peninsula, east of Tromsø, is a turmoil of peaks, glaciers and cirques which divide the Ullsfjord from the Lyngen fjord—one of the most beautiful in Norway. Because of a lack of trails and huts, the area is of little interest to the hiker. Rock climbers, however, have been coming to the peninsula since William C. Slingsby first climbed Store Jaegervasstind (1,668 meters) in 1898, and many new routes still remain to be explored.

The region is accessible by bus and ferry from Tromsø. Local roads also lead off of Highway 91 to suitable starting points for rock climbs. Because most of the area is uninhabited, camping is essential. Information on climbing in the area can be obtained from the climbing club at Tromsø University.

Tourist Information

See *Address Directory*:

Turisttrafikkomiteen for Troms.
Tromsø Turistkontor.

Maps

The Lyngen Peninsula and the surrounding region is covered by the following maps:

- Norges Geografiske Oppmåling Gradteigskart (Serie M711) 1:50,000, sheets 1633/I, 1633/IV, 1634/I, 1634/II, 1634/III, 1634/IV, 1635/II and 1635/III.

Guidebooks

- *Fiske og Ferie Nordpå* (in Norwegian), available from the DNT (see *Address Directory*).
- *Camps and Climbs in Arctic Norway* (in English) by Thomas Weir, Cassel & Company, London, 1953.

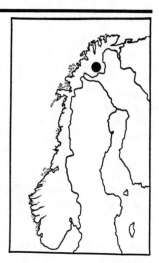

The Finnmark Mountain Plateau

This undulating plateau in northernmost Norway is where the majority of the reindeer-herding Lapps live. The region is studded with large and small lakes, rich in fish, and numerous rivers and streams, along which the Lapp hamlets and villages are scattered. The average height of the plateau—known as *Finnmarksvidda* in Norway—is 300 to 400 meters. Heather turf carpets much of the plateau, growing among open birch forest, brushwood and stunted bushes.

Soft marsh, rivers and thick brush sometimes hamper progress, but walking is generally easy. Many of the Lapp mountain lodges—or *fjellstuer*—are not obliged to serve meals, although they have provisions for sale and usually will serve a simple meal on request.

There is continuous daylight on the plateau from about the middle of April until late August. The best hiking time is in August and the first part of September. Before that, mosquitoes are a major nuisance. Even in August, they are bad enough, and one of the local repellents is a must. After the middle of September, sleet and snow storms are likely.

Rubber boots are a necessity on the plateau's marshy ground. Numerous rivers and streams also must be forded. You should carry a stick to support you when wading, and always walk diagonally upstream against the current. In addition, you should always carry (and use) a map and compass and, before starting each day's hike, consult with the local people.

Tourist Information

Turisttrafikkomiteen for Finnmark (see *Address Directory*).

Trail Lodgings

There are 14 *fjellstuer* which serve as youth hostels between June 15 and September 15. Most of the *fjellstuer* have eight beds set aside for this purpose. Kitchen utensils and mattresses are provided, but you must bring your own sleeping bag and sheet sleeping bag. Youth hostels are also located in Alta, Kautokeino, Karasjok, Lakselv, Rustefjelbma, Skaidi and Neiden. In addition, there are several hotels and guesthouses on the plateau, many of which are listed in the Norway Travel Association's lodging list, *Where to Stay in Norway.*

Maps

DNT's planning map, *Fjellruter i Finnmark,* provides all the information you need to plan hikes on Finnmarksvidda—the names and sheet numbers of 1:50,000 topographical maps which cover the region, the locations of lodgings and shelters, and the routes of marked and unmarked hiking routes. The planning map is free on request from the DNT (see *Address Directory*).

Guidebooks

- *Fiske og Ferie Nordpå* (in Norwegian), available from the DNT (see *Address Directory*).
- *Mountain Touring Holidays in Norway.*

Suggested Walk

From Karasjok to Alta. A winding route through forests, across open plateaus and past numerous lakes. Many fine views across the undulating Finnmarksvidda. **Walking Time:** 4 days. **Difficulty:** Easy to moderately difficult. **Path Markings:** Cairned throughout, except along a cart track which is followed from Karasjok to Ravnastua.
Trail Lodgings: *Fjellstuer* are located within a 9 to 10 hour walk of each other.
Maps:
- Norges Geografiske Oppmåling Gradteigskart 1:100,000, sheets U-5 *Alta,* U-6 *Masi* and V-6 *Jiesjokka.*
Guidebook:
- *Mountain Touring Holidays in Norway.*

Cross-Country Skiing

Among the places where you can ski tour on the Finnmarksvidda are:

Alta: Located close to the Finnmark moors. Four hours by air from Oslo; 3½ hours by bus from Hammerfest. Gentle terrain with floodlight trails near the town. Access to the Finnmark moors is from the road to Kautokeino.

Karasjok: "Capital of the Lapps." Ideal for those who wish to meet the Lapplanders in their own setting, travel by reindeer-drawn sled, or ski in the light of the Midnight Sun in May. January to February are harsh months. March, April and May are recommended for holidays. Accessible in 1½ hours by bus from Lakselv. Flights from Oslo to Lakselv take four hours. A climb of 200 to 250 meters from the village brings you out onto the rolling mountain plateau of Finnmarksvidda, with the unlimited opportunities it offers for experienced mountain touring skiers. A lighted trail is located near the village.

autokeino: This small Lapp town is the center of Norway's largest and most thinly populated municipality. Half of the town's population gain their livelihood from raising reindeer. Best time to visit the town is early spring, before winter completely releases its grip. Three hours by bus from Alta. Alta can be reached from Oslo in four hours by air. A climb through birch woods brings skiers out onto the plateau, where mountains range between 400 and 600 meters in height. Skiing here means launching off into trackless country, and one must be an experienced mountain skier to embark on ambitious tours. Easter festivities in the town include reindeer racing on the Kautokeino River.

Kirkenes: Sør-Varanger, of which Kirkenes is the urban center, is the only municipality in Norway which borders on the Soviet Union. Accessible in 4½ hours by air from Oslo. Facilities include marked ski trails, lighted trails and a skating rink. There are also guided excursions to the Russian border.

Address Directory

A

- *Ål Tourist Office,* N-3570 Ål. Tel. (067) 82 100 or 82 60.
- *Ålesund og Sunnmøre Turistforening,* Postboks 300, N-6001 Ålesund. Tel. (071) 21 202.
- *Åndalsnes og Romsdals Reiselivslag,* N-6300 Åndalsnes. Tel. (072) 21 622.
- *Andresens Vaabenforretning,* Storgaten 53, N-9001 Tromsø.
- *Arendal and Oppland Tourist Association,* N. Tyholmsveg 2, Postboks 400, N-4801 Arendal. Tel. (041) 23 2 14.

- *Arne Randers Heen*, see *Heen, Arne Randers*.
- *Arne Værum*, see *Værum, Arne*.

B

- *Bergen Turlag*, C. Sundsgaten 3, N-5000 Bergen. Tel. (05) 21 46 46.
- *Bodø og Omegns Turistforening*, Storgaten 30, N-8001 Bodø. Tel. (081) 25 095.
- *Bodø Reiselivslag*, Dronningensgaten 1, N-8000 Bodø. Tel. (081) 21 240.

C

- *Cicerone Press*, 16 Briarfield Road, Worsley, Manchester, England.

D

- *DNT*, see *Den Norsk Turistforening*.
- *Den Norsk Turistforening*, Stortingsgaten 28 III, Oslo 1. Tel. (02) 33 42 90.
- *Deutscher Wanderverlag*, Haussmannstrasse 66, D-7000 Stuttgart 1, Germany.
- *Drannem og Opplands Turistforening*, N-3000 Drammen. No telephone.

E

- *Edward Stanford Ltd.*, The International Map Centre, 12-14 Long Acre, London WC2E 9LP, England. Tel. (01) 836 1321.
- *Elverum Turistservice*, N-2400 Elverum. Tel. (064) 10 300.

F

- *Fagernes Tourist Office*, Fagernes Railway Station. Tel. 1538.
- *Foreningen til Ski-Idrettens Fremme*, Storgaten 2, Oslo 1. Tel. (02) 33 37 70.

G

- *Geilo Tourist Office*, N-3580 Geilo. Tel. (067) 86 100 or 41 206.
- *GEO CENTER*, Internationales Landkartenhaus, Honigwiesenstrasse 25, Postfach 80 08 30, D-7000 Stuttgart 80, Germany. Tel. (0711) 73 50 31.

- *Gol Tourist Office,* N-3550 Gol. Tel. (067) 76 100 or 76 400.

H

- *Heen, Arne Randers,* N-6300 Åndalsnes.
- *Hemsedal Tourist Office,* N-3560 Hemsedal. Tel. (067) 7600 or 76 156.

K

- *Kristiansand and Oppland Tourist Association,* Henrik Wergelands GT 36, N-4600 Kristiansand S. Tel. (042) 25 263.
- *Kristiansund og Nordmøre Turistforening (KNT),* N-6500 Kristiansund.

L

- *Landslaget for Norske Ungdomsherberger,* Dronningensgate 26, Olso 1. Tel. (02) 33 11 92.
- *Landslaget for Reiselivet i Norge* (Norway Travel Association), H. Heverdahlsgate 1, Oslo 1. Tel. (02) 42 70 44.
- *Lillehammer og Omland Reiselivslag,* Storgaten 56, N-2600 Lillehammer. Tel. (062) 51 098.

M

- *Magnar Pettersen,* see *Pettersen, Magnar.*
- *Meterologisk Institutt,* Niels Henrik Abels V. 40, Oslo 3. Tel. (02) 50 50 90.
- *Midt-Gudbrandsdal Reiselivslag,* N-2640 Vinstra. Tel. Vinstra 329.
- *Miljøverndepartementet (Ministry of Environment),* Postboks 8013, Oslo-Dep, Oslo 1. Tel. (02) 11 90 90.
- *Ministry of Environment,* see *Miljøverndepartementet.*
- *Molde og Romsdal Turistforening,* N-6400 Molde.

N

- *Narvik Turistkontor,* Kongensgaten 66, N-8500 Narvik. Tel. (082) 43 309.
- *Nesbyen Tourist Office,* N-3540 Nesbyen. Tel. (067) 72 100 or 72 249.
- *Nord-Gudbrandsdal Turist- og Tiltakskontor,* N-2670 Otta. Tel. Otta 335.

- *Nordland Turisttrafikkomite,* Norrøna Hotel, Postboks 128, N-8001 Bodø. Tel. (081) 24 406.
- *Norges Geografiske Oppmåling,* Postboks 8153 Oslo-Dep., Oslo 1. Tel. (02) 20 01 10.
- *Norsk Alpincenter,* N-3560 Hemsedal. Tel. (067) 78 306.
- *Norway Travel Association,* see *Landslaget for Reiselivet i Norge.*
- *Norwegian National Tourist Office, London,* 20 Pall Mall, London SW1Y 5 NE, England. Tel. (01) 839 6255.

O

- *Oppdal Tourist Office,* N-7400 Oppdal. Tel. (074) 21 760.
- *Østerdalene Reisetrafikklag,* N-2501 Tynset. Tel. (063) 61 100.

P

- *Pettersen, Magnar,* N-8300 Svolvaer.

R

- *Rana Reisetrafikklag,* Postboks 225, N-8601 Mo i Rana. Tel. (078) 50 421.
- *Reiselivsforeningen for Kristiansund og Nordmøre,* Fosnagatan 12, N-6500 Kristiansund. Tel. (073) 72 156.
- *Reiselivslaget for Hamar og Hedemarken,* Brygga, N-2300 Hamar. Tel. (065) 21 217.
- *Reisetrafikkforeningen for Haugesund,* Smedesundet 90, N-5500 Haugesund. Tel. (047) 26 180.
- *Reisetrafikkforeningen for Trondheim og Trøndelag,* Dronning-ensgatan 12, N-7000 Trondheim. Tel. (075) 25 890.
- *Reisetrafikkforeningen for Valdres og Jotunheimen,* N-2900 Fagernes. Tel. (061) 52 900.
- *Reisetrafikklaget for Kristiansand distrikt,* Vestre Strandgaten 16, N-4600 Kristiansand. Tel. (042) 26 065.
- *Rendalen Reisetrafikklag,* N-2482 Storsjøen. Tel. Ytre Rendal 4972.
- *Rjukan Tourist Office,* N-3600 Rjukan. Tel. (036) 91 290.

S

- *Salten Reiselivslag,* N-8200 Fauske. Tel. (081) 43 303.
- *Scandinavian National Tourist Offices, New York,* 75 Rockefeller Plaza, New York, New York 10019, U.S.A. Tel. (212) 582-2802.
- *Skien-Telemarks Tourist Association,* N-3700 Skien. No telephone.

- *Sport Co A/S,* Roald Armundsensgaten 6, Oslo 1. Tel. (02) 11 03 63 or 44 73 81.
- *Statens Ungdoms- og Idrettskontor (S.T.U.I),* Osterhausgaten 9, Postboks 8172-Dep., Oslo 1. Tel. (02) 11 90 90.
- *Stavanger Tourist Association,* Turistpaviljongen, N-4000 Stavanger. Tel. (045) 28 437.
- *Sulitjelma Turistforening,* N-8230 Sulitjelma. No telephone.
- *Svenska Turistföreningen* (Swedish Mountain Touring Association), Box 7615, S-103 94 Stockholm, Sweden. Tel. (08) 22 72 00.

T

- *Tolga Reisetrafikklag,* N-2540 Tolga. Tel. Tolga 39.
- *Troms Turlag,* Postboks 284, N-9001 Tromsø. No telephone.
- *Tromsø Turistkontor,* Postboks 312, N-9001 Tromsø. Tel. (083) 84 776.
- *Trondhjems Turistforening,* Hans Hagerupsgaten 1, N-7000 Trondheim. Tel. (075) 31 863 or 23 808.
- *Trysil Reiselivslag,* N-2420 Trysil. Tel. (064) 70 900.
- *Turisttrafikkomiteen for Bergen og Vest-Norge,* Bryggen 4, N-5000 Bergen. Tel. (05) 21 51 10.
- *Turisttrafikkomiteen for Finnmark,* N-9510 Elvebakken (Alta). Tel. (084) 37 426.
- *Turisttrafikkomiteen for Oppland Fylke,* Kirkegatan 74, N-2600 Lillehammer. Tel. (062) 53 580.
- *Turisttrafikkomiteen for Rogaland,* Turistpaviljongen, N-4000 Stavanger. Tel. (045) 28 437.
- *Turisttrafikkomiteen for Troms,* Postboks 1077, N-9001 Tromsø. Tel. (083) 82 169.

V

- *Værum, Arne,* Bones, N-9250 Bardu. Tel. Bardu 423 A.
- *Voss Turistkontor,* Postboks 57, N-5701 Voss. Tel. (055) 11 7 15 or 11 7 16.
- *Voss Utferdslag,* N-5700 Voss. No telephone.

W

- *Weather Forecasts, Recorded Weather Forecasts:* Tel. 016. *Weather Service:* Tel. 018. *Meterologisk Institutt,* Niels Henrik Abels V. 40, Oslo 3. Tel. (02) 50 50 90.

A Quick Reference

In a hurry? Turn to the pages listed below. They will give you the most important information on walking in Norway.

Search & rescue, page 189.

Weather Forecasts, page 175.

Associations to Contact for Information:
    On walking, page 176.
    On Climbing, page 185.
    On Cross-Country Skiing, page 186.
    Tourist information, page 188.

Maps, page 177.

Guidebooks, page 179.

Equipment, page 183.

Address Directory, page 275.

Sweden

SWEDEN CONTAINS THE LARGEST EXPANSE of trackless wilds and lake-spangled forests of any European country except Russia. In Swedish Lappland, mountains rise to 2,117 meters along the border with Norway, towering above narrow valleys and deep glacial basins with fast-flowing streams, lakes, marshes, dense willow thickets and tundra-like heaths. Within this region is Europe's largest preserved wilderness—an area comprised of three national parks and several adjacent nature reserves which together cover 5,330 square kilometers (2,057 square miles).

Forests cover 225,390 square kilometers (87,000 square miles), slightly more than half the country. In addition, Sweden has 96,000 lakes, 7,000 kilometers of coastline and more than 150,000 islands.

Conditions in the Swedish highlands vary greatly from those in most other European mountains. The walking season is short, lasting only from the end of June until the middle of September. Temperatures average only 15° C. (59° F.) in mid-July. And storms can arise explosively, bringing snow and torrential downpours that swell streams and turn mountainsides into cascades.

The *Statens Naturvårdsverk* (National Environmental Protection Board) maintains more than 4,500 kilometers of marked hiking and skiing tracks in the Lappland highlands and the mountainous areas of Jämtland, Härjedalen and Dalarna. Nearly 2,300 kilometers of these routes were marked by the *Svenska turistföreningen* (Swedish Touring Club). The STF has also established 80 mountain huts along these routes, built bridges and made it possible to cross waterways.

Elsewhere in the highlands facilities are few. The Swedish mountains are practically uninhabited, with long distances between communications and settlements. Even some of the huts maintained by the STF do not have telephones. And areas such as Sarek National Park, the single largest remaining wild area in Europe, are virtually without tracks, bridges or buildings of any kind. As a result, walkers who venture into the Swedish highlands must be in good physical condition, experienced in mountain and wilderness travel, and properly equipped. You must also be prepared to ford fast-flowing streams and walk on wet ground. Those not accustomed to these conditions will do best to join one of the hiking tours

281

conducted by the STF (see the section on *Walking & Skiing Tours* later in this chapter).

Numerous less demanding walking opportunities exist in central Sweden's Lake District and the undulating country of southern Sweden where marked footpaths lead you through forests and meadows, alongside streams, and across fertile plains alternating with open farmlands and beech-wooded hills. Here, access is easy, the weather milder and facilities for food and lodging readily available in small towns along the way.

The majority of Sweden's 16 national parks and many of its forest reserves have marked trails maintained by the *Domänverket* (Swedish Forest Service). Or you can walk on one of Sweden's coastal islands, such as Öland with its windmills, wild orchids and bird sanctuaries; or Gotland, an old Viking center with high cliffs, sunny beaches, Stone Age artifacts and medieval churches covered with wild, rambling roses.

In winter, prepared cross-country ski tracks lead through forests, across frozen lakes and over barren moors from more than 30 major winter sports centers, as well as from hundreds of towns and villages. Many skiing routes have also been marked in the highlands with red crosses affixed to long posts driven into the ground. These routes are shown on the *Nya Fjällkartan* (mountain maps) available from the STF.

Sweden is the largest country in Scandinavia and the fourth largest in Europe (after Russia, France and Spain). It occupies 449,793 square kilometers (173,654 square miles) and extends 1,574 kilometers from north to south. Apart from the mountain regions along the border with Norway, elevations are relatively low. The eastern part of northern Sweden is typified by undulating forests cut by large rivers flowing in a southeastern direction. Much of southern Sweden is a plain, broken here and there by outcroppings of low hills, woods and the ever-present lakes and rivers.

Only 10 percent of the country is cultivated. Most of the rest is given over to forests, lakes, meadows and, above tree line, vivid mountain heath communities. In fact, Finland is the only country in Western Europe with more forest. Sweden also has one of the most extensive networks of footpaths in Scandinavia. Many of the paths in southern Sweden are suitable for families with small children. Others, such as Kungsleden—the Royal Route—will challenge even experienced mountaineers. And for the truly experienced, there are the vast, untracked wilds of the far north.

More than 90 percent of Sweden's 8.3 million people live in the southern half of the country, and nearly 20 percent of these live in the cities of Stockholm, Göteborg and Malmö. In the far north, there are some 8,500 Lapps—about 2,000 of whom are engaged in raising reindeer—and nearly 35,000 Finnish-speaking farmers, fishermen and lumberjacks living along the Finnish border.

A vast number of Swedes speak English, and many speak at least some German. Nonetheless, it is helpful to learn the proper pronunciation of place names, since even a Swede who speaks good English may find it difficult to understand a foreigner who mispronounces the name of the place to which he or she wants to go. A Swedish-English pocket dictionary is useful for this purpose. You will also need the dictionary to help translate guidebooks and map legends, nearly all of which are written only in Swedish.

Everyman's Right

A centuries-old tradition known as *allemansträtten*—or Everyman's Right—gives everybody in Sweden (including foreign visitors) the right to wander freely virtually everywhere in the country—even on private land which is hedged or fenced in. *Allemansträtten* is not embodied in any law; instead, it is a *privilege* based upon mutual consideration and the belief that each and every person is aware of his or her responsibility to ensure that neither the countryside nor others' property is abused.

Few countries grant you so much freedom. But *allemansträtten* also requires a high degree of individual responsibility. Here's a set of guidelines to help you enjoy this unique freedom without overstepping its bounds.

You are allowed:

- To enter somebody else's land—but not land which may be damaged as a result. For instance, you should *never* tramp across a cultivated field.
- To camp for *one* night without asking the landowner's permission—but only at a reasonable distance from a dwelling. This generally means you should remain out of earshot and sight. If you stay more than one night, you should ask permission of the property owner. (In fact, it is a good habit whenever possible to *always* ask permission, even if you plan to remain on a person's land for only a few hours.)
- To climb over fences—but not fences enclosing land on which a house or other private building stands.
- To walk through areas which are hedged or fenced in—providing you do no damage and take special care to properly close all gates after you.
- To draw water from natural wells or lakes—but not from a privately owned well or reservoir before you have asked permission from its owner.
- To pick wild berries, mushrooms and flowers—but not flowers which are protected *(fridlyst)*. These flowers are so rare they are in danger of extinction.
- To light a fire—but only if there is no risk of its spreading. *Never*

light a fire on bare rock; the heat might crack it. In some municipalities you cannot light a fire anywhere outdoors without permission from the Chief Fire Office. It is advisable to check on this with the local tourist office.

- To row, sail or canoe across waters belonging to someone else.
- To moor a boat temporarily, swim and go ashore everywhere—but not at someone else's jetty or on the private land surrounding a dwelling.
- To cycle, ride and ski everywhere—but not too close to dwelling houses.

You must not:

- Enter the private land surrounding a house *(privat tomt)* unless you have business with the owner. You must not climb over a fence surrounding this type of private land, and you must not trespass on it in any other way. *Private tomt* is defined as the area which immediately surrounds a dwelling house and within which the person owning or using the house has a justifiable claim to be left in peace. This area is not always fenced in.
- Camp for more than one night without asking permission from the landowner.
- Enter newly planted woodlands, fields of growing crops or other land which is likely to suffer damage through your presence.
- Pull down or damage a fence.
- Leave gates open after you.
- Pick plants on someone else's property.
- Light a fire during a drought or in places where the undergrowth is likely to catch fire.
- Cut growing trees, break off twigs of branches, or take bark, leaves, acorns, nuts or resin from growing trees. If you do so, this is considered either willful damage or theft.
- Fish in other people's fishing waters without permission and a fishing license. Before you start fishing, you should find out what regulations apply to the fishing water. Local tourist offices can usually help you here.
- Go ashore on nature reserves or areas where animals are breeding in the spring and summer. Signposts to this effect are displayed in all such areas.
- Hunt on other people's land. Hunting, moreover, is limited to certain periods of the year.
- Take birds' nests or eggs; this counts as hunting.
- Drive a car or ride a motorcycle off the public highway. Private

roads are marked with a sign reading: *Förbud mot trafik med motordrivet fordon.*

- Leave litter in the countryside. If you do, you can be fined or sent to prison for up to six months. You should always be sure to take all bottles, tins, plastic bags and paper with you when you leave, and to dispose of them properly.

- Some areas are restricted to use by the armed forces and are not open to the general public. These areas are marked by special signs.

Flora & Fauna

Because of Sweden's long north-south length and range of elevations, the country has a wide diversity of vegetation. The sunny west coast and the province of Skåne—which produces a large part of what Sweden eats and drinks—are a patchwork of cultivated fields and deciduous forests of beech with mixed elements of ash, oak, hornbeam, alder and hazel. In some areas of the central Lake District, yew trees can be found on chalky soil along with broad helleborine. Berries and mushrooms are found growing practically everywhere. And hundreds of species of wildflowers speckle meadows, the banks of streams and rivers, and the edges of fields.

In the mountains, graceful stands of silver birch, interspersed with rowan, alder and aspen, march up to the tree line. One also finds mountain ash, bird cherry and several species of willow. The greater part of Sweden's forest cover, however, consists of conifers—spruce, pine and some juniper.

The coniferous forest extends from the south far into the mountain ranges of Lappland. The makeup of the forests varies greatly, depending upon soil type and the activities of human beings. In some places the forests open up into luxuriant meadows. In others the ground cover consists mainly of mosses and bilberry, crowberry or cowberry. Bogs and marshes—covered with various species of mosses, sedges and grasses—are also common.

Fine stands of conifers are occasionally found in places close to the tree line, but as a rule the mixture of birch, aspen and rowan becomes greater toward the mountains, until the birch gradually becomes dominant.

Many plants typical of coniferous forests accompany the pine and spruce up the mountains. In low-lying swampy ground, sedge, cotton grass, goldilocks, selfheal, knotted pearlwort and marsh bedstraw grow. In rocky areas, one finds the Lappland rhododendron, saxifrages and mountain avens.

Within the birch belt, great beds of yellow globe flowers grow in damp meadows along with kingcups and mountain violets. Alpine lettuce—of which bears are very fond—is seen swaying on tall stalks almost everywhere in the Lappland highlands. Another easily noticed plant appreciated by bears is the great angelica, which sometimes grows two or three meters high. There are several species of grass and strikingly rich growths of tall ferns. Dogwood also occupies a prominent place in the mountain undergrowth, and in spring forms white carpets which become bright red in late summer.

Around lakes and deltas and along some valleys and winding streams, willows form almost impenetrable thickets. The bushes often grow to a height of two or three meters, cutting off visibility entirely from inside the thickets. When you have to push your way through one, it can sometimes take you two hours to go half a kilometer.

Above the limit of the birch forest, vast expanses of heath, covered with willow, shrubs, mosses and lichens, stretch upward toward the horizon. The most common types of heath are formed of carpets of crowberry. Different kinds of heather, alpine clubmoss and black bearberry grow on these heaths, which are not particularly attractive in spring, but become vivid cascades of color in autumn. The mountain campion, Lappland lousewort, wavy hair grass and some species of sedge break the monotony of the scrub heath. Bilberry heaths are also found in areas which become free from snow early.

At higher altitudes, lichen-covered stones lie scattered everywhere, providing shelter for pockets of hardy, flowering plants. Below melting snowfields, the ground is damp and spongy. There are also stony holes, dark brown earth ridges and raised tussocks of peat caused by the repeated freezing and thawing of the water in the surface layer of soil.

In the mountains, elk can be seen wandering out from the forest region. One occasionally sees bears grazing on the great angelica and alpine lettuce, and wolverines scampering, with a rolling gait, over the mountain heaths. Reindeer are common, as are lemmings, particularly during so-called lemming years, when these small mice experience population explosions. The polar fox is seldom seen, except during lemming years.

Forest animals include the moose, mountain hare, fox, lynx, otter, marten, squirrel and several species of shrews. Among the typical birds in the alpine belt are the dotterel, golden plover, long-tailed skua, ptarmigan and the rare snowy owl and purple sandpiper. The Lappland bunting may be seen in the willow thickets; the meadow pipit, snow bunting, and wheatear are common on the mountain heaths; and the red-necked phalarope and Temminck's stint are seen near small tarns and marshes. The trumpeting of cranes and the call of wood sandpipers are heard throughout Lappland, and the alarm note of the wood sandpiper and the neighing tone of the snipe are often heard over highland marshes. Other birds include the rough-legged buzzard, golden eagle, gyrfalcon and numerous common small birds such as the brambling, red poll, garden warbler, willow warbler, reed bunting and bluethroat. Numerous species of waders abound in the marshes of south and central Sweden. There are also several bird sanctuaries on the islands off the east and south coasts, which lie along the migratory routes of several bird species which summer in Sweden.

The only dangerous snake is the viper, which is occasionally found in south and central Sweden. You are unlikely to encounter one. Nonetheless, a bite should receive immediate medical attention. Mosquitoes, gnats and gadflies are a major nuisance in the mountain areas during midsummer. They can also be bothersome near bogs and marshes in central Sweden. A good, strong insect repellent (such as those which can be bought in Sweden) is essential. Tightly knit insect netting to protect your face is also advisable in Lappland.

Climate

Sweden has a relatively mild, dry climate. Prevailing west winds and the Gulf Stream make it possible to grow grain and potatoes even in the northern parts of Sweden and to cultivate forests profitably at latitudes which, in countries outside of Scandinavia, are covered with tundra or glaciers. Sweden is also sheltered from the west by the mountain frontier with Norway, and is consequently less affected by Atlantic than by Continental conditions to which it is open on the east.

Average temperatures in July range from 15° to 17° C. (59° to 62° F.) in most of Sweden. Maximum temperatures for the month seldom exceed 20° C. (68° F.) in the mountains, but often climb as high as 26° C. (78° F.)—or more—on the southern coasts. On the other hand, freezing temperatures are not uncommon in the mountains in summer.

In January, average temperatures vary from *minus* 1° C. (30° F.) in southern Sweden to *minus* 14° C. (7° F.) in the far north, while the average in some of the mountain areas plunges as low as *minus* 24° C. (*minus* 11° F.).

Spring is the driest season throughout most of Sweden. In the short space of a month or so, the sunshine gains in intensity and soon brings about the thaw of river and lake ice and the budding of trees and wild flowers. In the north, the change is so sudden that full summer follows in a matter of weeks.

Summer is short—June, July and August in the south; even shorter in the north. The sunlight, however, is intense. The Midnight Sun remains above the horizon for several weeks beyond the Arctic Circle, while the south has short summer nights which resemble a twilight.

Most summer rain falls quickly, and sometimes heavily, usually following thunder. Quite different weather, however, may prevail simultaneously in neighboring areas. When the sun is shining out of blue skies in the western parts of Sarvesvagge in Sarek, for example, heavy rain clouds or mist may cover the eastern parts.

Autumn, the wettest season in most of Sweden, brings superb colorings to both the sky and landscape, especially in the north.

The wettest season in some of the mountain regions, however, is summer. In Sarek, 150 mm to 200 mm (6 to 10 inches) of precipitation may fall during the month of August. The corresponding figure for Stockholm is 76 mm (3 inches). The annual mean precipitation in Sarek varies locally, but the average is more than 2000 mm (79 inches); in Stockholm it is 500 mm (20 inches).

Snow begins accumulating in the mountains as early as September. As a rule, however, no lasting layer of snow collects in the lower regions before October or November. Winter days are so short in the far north that artificial light must be used almost continuously in homes. Nevertheless, the weather is often crisp and clear—ideal for skiing and sleigh riding.

As late as the beginning of June large parts of the lower mountain regions are still covered with snow. At a higher altitude the snow does not melt until July, and on the highest mountain summits the snow is perennial.

Those who plan to walk in the highlands during the summer must be prepared for virtually any contingency—swift weather changes, freezing temperatures, ice and snow storms, lightning, swollen streams and wet, soggy terrain. After mid-September, when the weather can become even more violent, only the most experienced mountain hikers should venture into the highlands. On trails elsewhere in Sweden, one need only worry about occasional thunder showers, a cool, windy day or two and damp terrain. You can also walk trails in central and southern Sweden from early May into October.

Weather Forecasts

Because weather conditions change so quickly in the Swedish highlands and can vary greatly over relatively short distances, weather forecasts for this part of Sweden are of limited value. Nevertheless, they can warn you about a low pressure system which is going to drench northern Lappland in a week of rain, and thus allow you to change plans before leaving Stockholm for the long trip north. But at best they can only give you a very general, and sometimes imprecise, idea of what to expect from day to day, and from valley to valley. Also, once you are in the north, you will not find many telephones from which to obtain weather forecasts.

The weather forecasts are more useful for the rest of Sweden. They can tell you which areas are going to be sunny and which rainy, what temperatures and wind speeds to expect, and whether the small puffy clouds on the horizon mean you should stay put in the comfort of your guesthouse, don shorts, or pack a rain parka and sweater (which, of course, you should do anyway).

The most reliable weather forecasts can be obtained by telephoning:

Sveriges Meteorologiska och Hydrologiska Institut (Swedish Meteorological and Hydrological Institute). Tel. (011) 17 01 03. Forecasts are in Swedish.

Where to Get Walking Information

Information on virtually any outdoor activity in Sweden can be obtained from:

> **Svenska turistföreningen (STF).** For its address and telephone number, see the *Address Directory* at the back of this chapter. Located in the Marmorhallarna building off Stureplan, at the intersection of Sturegatan and Birger Jarlsgatan (Underground stop: Östermalmstorg). Staff speaks English, French and German. Very helpful.

The Swedish Touring Club is an extremely active touring association with 250,000 members. Founded in 1885, it operates Sweden's youth hostels; owns and runs 80 mountain stations, chalets and huts along the footpaths in northern Sweden; runs more than 360 guest harbors along the coast and in larger lakes; and handles rentals for more than 450 private cottages and holiday village chalets throughout Sweden. It operates a boat service on several lakes in Lappland and provides boats at strategic places for crossing other large waterways. The STF also publishes an annual Swedish-language guide to mountain walking, with information on all the huts and marked trails in northern Sweden; sells large-scale maps to the Swedish highlands, on which all mountain tracks and skiing routes are shown; and distributes free information sheets and Swedish-language booklets with information on its summer and winter tours. In addition, it runs a complete travel service which:

- Provides travel information;
- Arranges group tours and individual package tours for walking, skiing, cycling, canoeing and horseback riding;
- Conducts mountaineering courses for individuals and groups and for leaders of walking and skiing tours;
- Provides assistance in renting accommodation at its guest harbors, in private cottages and chalets and in chalets in other Nordic countries; and
- Operates Club Young Sweden, which arranges group travel in Sweden and abroad for Swedish youth, and arranges tailor-made tours in Sweden for foreign groups.

The STF's only limitation is that it cannot always provide full details on the marked footpaths in southern Sweden, and in Sweden's national parks and forests. Nonetheless, it is best to always contact the STF first for information on hiking and skiing. Then, if you need additional details on the footpaths outside the mountain regions, you can contact one of the following organizations:

Friluftsfrämjandet (see *Address Directory*). A large, extremely active outdoor activities organization with a central office in Stockholm and branch offices in southern Sweden. Can provide information on footpaths in southern Sweden. Also offers instruction in cross-country skiing. Staff speaks English and German.

Sverek (see *Address Directory*). Staff speaks English, French and German. Most publications are also available in translation.

Sverek is a subsidiary of the Swedish Forest Service responsible for recreation. It organizes hiking tours and canoe trips in Sweden's forests, mountains and wilderness areas (which can also be booked through STF); conducts nature outings, some of which combine short forest rambles with visits to historic castles; sells fishing permits and arranges fishing holidays throughout Sweden's forests; grants limited hunting rights on Forest Service lands; and handles bookings for the more than 400 cottages it maintains throughout Sweden. In addition, Sverek can provide free leaflets on each of Sweden's national parks and forest reserves. The leaflets describe flora, fauna, terrain and recreational facilities, and include sketch maps showing marked footpaths and other facilities.

Many provincial tourist offices, such as those listed in the regional descriptions later in this chapter, can also provide information on footpaths in their areas.

Sweden's Walking & Climbing Clubs

The STF is by far the largest walking club in Sweden. It has 40 local sections scattered around the country and, in addition to its central office in Stockholm—which is staffed by more than 70 people—operates offices in Göteborg and Malmö. It also cooperates closely with Sweden's other walking and climbing clubs and has been working with Friluftsfrämjandet and the Statens Naturvårdsverk in the development of a network of long-distance footpaths in southern Sweden.

Foreign hikers are welcome to join the STF (and, in fact, should do so to take advantage of its member benefits). As a member, you receive:

1. Reduced rates on overnight stays in STF tourist stations, mountain stations, mountain huts and youth hostels;
2. Reduced prices on STF-conducted tours;
3. Reduced prices on all publications issued by the STF;
4. Free travel information and services from all STF offices;
5. A hard-cover copy of the STF year book (in Swedish);
6. The STF member magazine, *Turist* (also in Swedish), which is issued six times a year.

The STF maintains reciprocal membership agreements with the mountain touring and travel associations in Finland and Norway, which allows members to stay in the mountain huts in these countries at reduced rates. Reciprocal membership agreements do not exist between the STF and other walking and alpine clubs in Europe. Hence, to take advantage of the member services and reductions, you must join the STF, unless you are already a member of Den Norske Turistforening or Suomen Matkailuliitto. Full details on membership in the STF and a membership application will be sent on request. Or you can join up at the STF office in Stockholm.

In addition to the STF, there are three other principal walking and climbing clubs in Sweden. These are:

Friluftsfrämjandet (see *Address Directory*). An organization with 70,000 centrally registered members and 130,000 locally registered children belonging to 450 local sections in 23 districts throughout Sweden. Organizes member outings in Sweden, offers instruction in downhill and cross-country skiing and conducts courses in various aspects of outdoor life. Publishes a member magazine, *I alla väder*, six times a year as well as several educational and outdoor-oriented publications. Works intensively with children. One district, in cooperation with the Södermanlands County Council, oversees Sweden's longest marked footpath—500-kilometer Sörmlandsleden—which it helped establish from the outskirts of Stockholm to Nyköping. The organization publishes a Swedish-language guide to the path, plus a brief route outline and sells 1:50,000 maps covering its route. Its central office can also provide information on other footpaths in southern Sweden, as well as on its walking and skiing activities.

Svenska Fjällklubben (see *Address Directory*). The Swedish Mountain Club has 850 members. It is devoted to both mountain hiking and climbing and is affiliated with the UIAA (Union Internationale des Associations d'Alpinisme), to which most of the world's alpine clubs belong. Members participate in mountain hikes, wilderness treks, rock and ice climbs, and ski mountaineering trips organized by the club in Sweden and abroad. It also cooperates with other alpine organizations on international mountaineering expeditions. The club maintains a mountaineering library in Stockholm which is open every Tuesday from 7 to 9 p.m. Foreigners may join the club, but must be experienced climbers and know the Swedish mountains. Members receive the club magazine, *Fjällklubbsnytt*, and its year book, *Till fjälls*.

Svenska Klätterförbundet (see *Address Directory*). The Swedish Climbing Association has 500 members and 9 sections in southern, central and northern Sweden. It offers instruction in rock climbing to both members and non-members, organizes climbs in Scandinavia and abroad, conducts weekend climbs and member activities through its local sections and reports climbing news to its members. It also publishes a quarterly member magazine, *Bergsport.*

Maps

A series of four-color 1:50,000 topographical maps cover nearly all of Sweden, except the northwest, which is covered by 1:100,000 topographical maps. The Swedish mountains are covered by a series of five-color mountain maps—or *Fjällkartan*—on which marked walking and skiing routes are shown in red. Several other topographical maps showing walking routes are also available to some areas in central and southern Sweden. All the maps are published by:

> **LiberKartor** (see *Address Directory*). A free catalog, map indexes and price list are available upon request. Staff speaks English, German, French, Danish and Norwegian.

The map series you choose will depend largely upon where you intend to hike in Sweden. Those which are suitable for walking and skiing include:

Topografiska kartan. A series of 649 sheets in a scale of 1:50,000 and 42 sheets in a scale of 1:100,000 covering all of Sweden. These four-color topographical maps form the basis for the *Nya Fjällkartan* and *Sörmlandsleden* map series and are well-suited for hiking in Sweden outside the mountain areas. Footpaths are shown by means of a series of black dots. Skiing routes are not always shown. When they are, they are indicated by a solid black line with a row of black dots on each side—a symbol which gives the impression of a single ski track bordered by a series of pole marks. Contours are shown at 5-meter intervals on the 1:50,000 sheets and at 20-meter intervals on the 1:100,000 sheets. About 30 of the sheets have not been updated since 1954. The rest have been revised within the last 10 years.

Nya Fjällkartan. Due to be completed early in 1980, this five-color map series provides the most complete, up-to-date coverage of the Swedish mountains. The series is comprised of 32 sheets in a scale of 1:100,000 and 8 special sheets in a scale of 1:50,000, covering selected areas within the mountains. All features of interest to walkers and skiers—such as marked walking and skiing tracks, tourist and mountain huts, wind shelters, reindeer enclosures, the locations of telephones and bridges—are shown in red. Contours are shown at 20-meter intervals on the 1:100,000 sheets and at 5-meter intervals on the 1:50,000 sheets. The maps also have a dual set of index contour lines—darker lines at 40-meter intervals and still darker lines at 200-meter intervals on the 1:100,000 sheets, for instance. Information on the maps is in Swedish, English and German. For walking and skiing in the Swedish mountains, these are the best maps available. Produced by LiberKartor in collaboration with the STF.

Svenska Fjällkartan. An old series of three-color maps covering the Swedish mountains which are being replaced by the newer, more detailed Nya Fjällkartan. The 1:100,000 and 1:200,000 sheets show all topographical features in black and white, with water areas in blue and facilities of interest to walkers and skiers in red. A few sheets may still be around. When you have a choice, however, use the Nya Fjällkartan.

Sörmlandsleden. A series of 6 five-color topopographical maps, in a scale of 1:50,000, covering the 500-kilometer Sörmlandsleden long-distance footpath in southern Sweden. In addition to the footpath, the maps show service facilities along the route and provide tourist information. All information on the maps is in Swedish. Produced by LiberKartor in collaboration with Friluftsfrämjandet.

Resekartor. A series of 11 maps; 10 in a scale of 1:250,000 and 1 in a scale of 1:200,000. These six-color topographical maps cover virtually all of central and southern Sweden and part of northeastern Sweden. While their small scale does not make them suitable for use on the trail, they are useful planning aids. For instance, the newest map, *Svealand östra delen,* the only 1:200,000 sheet in the series, shows hiking routes, gives tourist information and indicates road distances between towns in eastern Svealand, which encompasses much of Sweden's Lake District. Also, all information on the maps is translated into English and German. Contours are indicated by layer tints.

All maps may be purchased by mail from Liber Grafiska. The maps covering Sörmandsleden may also be purchased from Friluftsfrämjandent. The STF provides free indexes to the Nya Fjällkartan. You can also order the Fjällkartan by mail from the STF or buy them from any of its offices.

Guidebooks

Sweden has very few guidebooks. Moreover, most of those available are written in Swedish. The STF, however, distributes several free leaflets in English and German which are useful to the hiker and skier. These include:

- *Hiking in the Swedish Highlands.* Provides an overview of the walking opportunities in the Swedish mountains. Gives a brief description of Lappland, Dalarna, Jämtland and Härjedalen, as well as of Sweden's five best-known national parks. Also includes descriptions of nine two- to five-day walks, information on boat and bus routes in northern Lappland, suggestions for equipment and food, plus a list of emergency provisions which should be carried. Published by the Swedish Tourist Board in cooperation with the STF. Recommended.

- *Mountain Maps 1981*. Gives up-to-date information on the maps covering the Swedish mountains. Includes an index and current prices. Issued annually.

- *Mountain Holidays in Sweden*. Gives a brief description of the walking tours organized each summer by the STF, along with information on how to book space. Includes the dates, length, cost and booking number for several tours to popular mountain hiking areas.

- *Kungsleden: The Royal Route*. Gives a brief description of Sweden's most popular walking route in northern Lappland. Provides information on the map sheets needed to hike the 430-kilometer route, hut facilities enroute and access. Includes a sketch map.

The Swedish Tourist Board (see *Address Directory*) also issues several Travel Fact sheets in English, German and French that provide information on a variety of outdoor activities. Of these, one of the most useful for hikers is:

- *Youth-travels in Sweden: Travel Facts No. 7*. Among other information, this fact sheet gives a brief description of 13 hiking routes in southern Sweden (including Sörmlandsleden) with the addresses where further information and maps can be obtained for each. The fact sheet also includes information on cycling and cycling tours, canoeing, yachting, horseback riding and skiing. Free upon request.

Swedish-Language Guidebooks

Even if you do not read Swedish the guidebooks published by the STF and Friluftsfrämjandet can be extremely useful in helping you plan hikes and follow hiking routes. Information on the locations of lodgings, the names of locales through which the routes pass, daily hiking distances, elevations and the sheet numbers of the required maps can all be understood without any knowledge of Swedish. In fact, the guides are worth the investment simply for their lists of addresses and telephone numbers of local lodgings and transportation services. And with the help of a Swedish-English dictionary (or an amiable Swede), you can get even more out of them. The available guidebooks are listed below. For the addresses of their mail-order outlets, see the *Address Directory*.

- *Fjäll '81.* If you purchase no other guidebook in Sweden, you should at least buy this one. Revised and updated by the STF each year, this is the only guide available that covers all the Swedish mountain districts. (Next year, the book will be entitled *Fjäll '82,* and so on each year.) It includes: 1) the addresses and telephone numbers of all the STF offices; 2) directions on how to reach each of the mountain districts by road, by bus (with the telephone numbers to call for schedules) and by air; 3) information on boat services on larger lakes in the Swedish mountains; 4) a list of youth hostels in the mountain districts, with their opening and closing dates, number of beds, addresses and telephones, and the sheet numbers of the Nya Fjällkartan on which their locations are indicated; 5) the locations and telephone numbers of mountain stations, tourist hotels, pensions, camping sites and other lodgings, with the map sheet reference number for each; 6) a list of the places where emergency telephones are located in each mountain district and the sheet numbers of maps on which they are shown; 7) full details on all the STF's mountain huts and shelters; 8) a list of the maps and guidebooks covering the Swedish mountains; and 9) route descriptions for more than 40 two- to six-day mountain walks and ski tours. The book is also packed with advice on trip preparation, equipment, clothing, food, mountain safety and winter travel. And more. At the back is a sketch map in a scale of 1:300,000 showing the locations of all roads, lodgings and the principal hiking routes in the mountain regions. Available from the STF. Highly recommended.

- *Vandra i Sverige: Låglandsleder* (Walking in Sweden: Low Country Tracks). Jointly published by the STF and Friluftsfrämjandet. A booklet with one-page descriptions of 32 long-distance footpaths outside the mountains. Each description includes information on the path's location and length, the type of terrain it crosses and how you can get to it; the telephone numbers to call for bus schedule information; a list of overnight accommodation and other service facilities on or near its route; and the telephone numbers to call for further information on the path. The sheet numbers of maps covering each path and the titles of leaflets or guidebooks with route descriptions are also listed. Even if you do not read Swedish, you can use the telephone numbers to obtain information on the paths. A map in the middle of the booklet shows the locations of all the footpaths. Available from the STF or Friluftsfrämjandet. Recommended.

- *Kungsleden och 13 angränsande turer* (The Royal Route and 13 Adjoining Tours). Published by the Generalstabens Lithografiska Anstalts Förlag in cooperation with the STF, revised 1978. Describes 14 possible walking tours in northern Sweden, including a full description of 430-kilometer Kungsleden. Also provides advice on how to cross streams, gives information on access and lists full details on shelters and lodgings. The book may be difficult to understand for those who do not read Swedish. Available from most large bookstores and the STF.

- *Sörmlandsleden*. Published by Friluftsfrämjandet. Gives a full description of Sweden's longest footpath, with details on access, lodgings and points of interest along its route. Available from most large bookstores and Friluftsfrämjandet.

- *Guiden över Skåneleden från kust till kust* (From Coast to Coast: A Walking Guide to the Skåneleden). Gives a full description of the most recent addition to Sweden's long-distance footpath network— 220-kilometer Skåneleden, stretching from coast to coast across the southern tip of Sweden. Provides details on access, lodgings and points of interest. Available from most local bookstores in Skåne, the Kristianstadts Turistbyrå in Kristianstad, and the Karlshamns Turistbyrå in Karlshamn.

- *Vandringsguiden över Ostkustleden* (Walking Guide to the East Coast Route), published by Döderhults naturskyddsförening, Döderhult, 1979. Gives a full description of the 152-kilometer Ostkustleden circling through the countryside near Oskarshamn in the province of Småland on Sweden's east coast. Provides details on access, lodgings and points of interest. Available from most local bookstores, and from the Döderhults naturskyddsförening and the Oskarshamns Turistbyrå in Oskarshamn.

- *Vandringsguiden över Siljansleden* (Walking Guide to the Lake Siljan Route). A 15-page guide to the 340-kilometer Siljansleden encircling Lake Siljan and Lake Orsasjön in the province of Dalarna. Includes provisional maps and brief details on lodgings and access. Free upon request from the Mora Turistbyrå. A detailed guide to Siljansleden is in preparation.

- *Vandra i Sarek* (Walking in Sarek) by Svante Lundgren, Norstedts, Stockholm, revised 1979. Describes cross-country walking possibilities in Sarek National Park, Europe's single largest remaining wilderness area. Also provides information on the park's flora and fauna, terrain, geology and climate. Recommended only for experienced mountaineers who are intimately familiar with conditions in the Swedish mountains. The book may be difficult to understand for those who do not read Swedish. Available from the STF.

- *Detta är Sarek* (This is Sarek) by Tore Abrahamsson, Raben & Sjögren, Stockholm. A guide for the experienced mountaineer who plans to walk in the valleys, walk on glaciers or climb in Sarek National Park. Includes sketch maps. Available from most large bookstores and the STF.

With few exceptions, most of the remaining guidebooks do not include route descriptions, but instead concentrate on discussions of summer and winter walking techniques, orienteering, mountain safety, equipment, clothing and the flora, fauna, topography and climate of the regions they cover. Of these, a few may be useful to those who are able to read at least some Swedish. All the following guidebooks can be obtained from most large bookstores, as well as from the STF:

- *Kebnekaise* by Tore Abrahamsson, Norstedts, Stockholm. Describes the mountain region north of Sarek National Park. Kebnekaise is traversed by the Kungsleden long-distance footpath.
- *Växter och djur i fjällen* (Plants and Animals in the Mountains) by Ingmar Holmåsen, Aldus/Bonniers, Stockholm.
- *De vilda djurens Sarek* (The Wild Animals in Sarek) by Edvin Nilsson, Bonniers, Stockholm.
- *Sarek* by Edvin Nilsson, Bonniers, Stockholm.

English-Language Guidebooks

- *Wandering: A Walker's Guide to the Mountain Trails of Europe* by Ruth Rudner, Dial Press (see *Address Directory*), 1972. Describes two-week hikes in six European countries, including a two-week hike along the Kungsleden in Sweden. Contains some inaccuracies. Available from most bookstores in North America or by mail from the publisher.
- *Sarek, Stora Sjöfallet, Padjelanta: Three National Parks in Swedish Lapland* by Kai Curry-Lindahl, Rabén & Sjögren, Stockholm, 1968. Describes the geology, topography, climate, flora and fauna of Sweden's three largest national parks. No information on walking or skiing in the parks is given. Nonetheless, if you plan to visit the parks, the book provides excellent background. Available from the STF.

German-Language Guidebooks

- *Wandern unter der Mitternachtssonne* (Walking under the Midnight Sun), Alex Verlag. Describes walking and camping trips in northern Sweden, Norway and Finland. Available from GEO CENTER (see *Address Directory*).
- *Sarek, Stora Sjöfallet, Padjelanta: Drei Nationalparke in Schwedisch Lappland* by Kai Curry-Lindahl, Rabén & Sjögren, Stockholm, 1968. See description above. Available from the STF.

Trailside Lodgings

There is a wide choice of lodgings from which to choose near paths in central and southern Sweden—youth hostels, hotels, manor houses, farm houses and Sweden's ubiquitous holiday cottages. Many holiday cottages are available in parts of northern Sweden, and lodgings usually can be found in the region's far-flung settlements. The STF also operates 10 mountain stations, plus 80 mountain huts and *kåtor* (Lapp-style huts) situated at 10- to 25-kilometer intervals along hiking routes in the Swedish highlands. Several other mountain huts are operated by the Statens Naturvårdstverk (principally in Padjelanta National Park) and the Domän-verket. Elsewhere in northern Sweden lodgings are very sparse. If you plan to venture off marked routes, you must carry everything with you and camp.

Many lodgings in popular holiday areas become booked during July and August, and reservations are almost essential to ensure you have a place to sleep. Because of this, and the sparseness of lodgings in the far north, it is advisable to obtain at least one of the available lodging lists described below and plan out where you are going to stay before you get on the path. In the mountain huts you will never be turned away, even if all the beds are taken; but quarters can sometimes become cramped, and there occasionally may not be enough spare mattresses and blankets to accommodate everyone on the floor. A sleeping bag is therefore useful—especially on popular walking routes such as the Kungsleden.

Mountain Stations

The STF's *fjällstationer*—or mountain stations—are large, staffed mountain refuges. They are designed to enable walkers to spend their nights in comfort and, in most, substantial meals are served. Some of the mountain stations even have hobby rooms, bathtubs and showers with hot and cold running water, saunas, central heating, and small shops where you can buy provisions. Most of the *fjällstationer* have rooms with two beds, but most of the rooms have four to six beds. Prices are less if you bring your own sheet sleeping bag. If you wish, however, you can get crisp clean sheets for an additional charge.

The mountain stations are generally open from mid-June to mid-September, as well as during part of the ski season (usually March-April). Several of the *fjällstationer* are located near roads; the rest can be reached only on foot. They are located at Abisko, Kebnekaise, Saltoluokta, Ritjemjokk, and Kvikkjokk in Lapland; at Storulvån, Blåhammaren, Helags and Sylarna in Jämtland; and at Grövelsjön in Dalarna. Reservations in the mountain stations can be made through the STF.

Mountain Huts

Sweden's *fjällstugor* and *kåtor* are smaller and simpler than the mountain stations. All are equipped with bedding, stoves, cooking utensils, pails for carrying water and dishes. Cutlery normally is not provided. In a few you can buy food (see *Fjäll '81*, described in the section on *Guidebooks*). Most of the huts also have wardens to welcome you when you arrive and look after the maintenance of the buildings. Nonetheless, you are expected to do everything on your own: cooking, cleaning up, shaking out and folding blankets each morning, and sweeping the floor and wiping it down with a damp cloth before you leave. Some of the huts have rooms with four to six beds, wash basins, mirrors and individual wood-burning stoves. Others have a single communal dormitory.

The huts are intended for a maximum stay of two nights. There is a nominal visiting charge for use of the huts during the day. You can also camp near the huts for a small charge, which entitles you to the use of all hut facilities, except a bed. It is not possible to reserve space at the mountain huts, but no one is ever turned away. In the unstaffed huts you are expected to sign the guest book and mail the overnight fee to the STF. The huts are generally open from the beginning of July to mid-September. Some are open during March and April. All the huts also have at least one room which is kept unlocked year round, and some have rescue telephones so you can contact the police.

Youth Hostels

Sweden has 200 youth hostels—or *vandrarhem*—scattered the length of the country, all of which are operated by the STF. They offer informal, inexpensive accommodation and are open to people of all ages. The hostels vary in standards, but most are modern and have rooms with two to four beds, and generally have free showers and hot and cold running water. To stay in the youth hostels you must have either a youth hostel card or an STF membership card.

Most of the *vandrarhem* have self-cooking facilities and rooms for families (which should be booked well in advance if you want one during the summer). Cooking utensils usually are provided, but generally not dishes or cutlery. Sheets and towels can be rented at the *vandrarhem,* and some sell non-woven sheet sleeping bags. In the long run, however, it is much cheaper to bring your own.

Some of the *vandrarhem* remain open all year. Most, however, are open only from June until September. The STF does not handle reservations for the *vandrarhem*. Instead, you should make reservations directly to the *vandrarhem* in which you wish to stay.

Cottage Holidays

Sweden has more than 20,000 private cottages, chalets and log cabins available for summer and winter rental. Situated along the coast, on lakes, in forests and in some of the mountain valleys, they are an ideal base for those who want to spend time in one spot and take exploratory day hikes and ski tours into the surrounding countryside. More than half of Sweden's 500 camping sites have special holiday villages with about 3,000 chalets. Each of the specially built chalets has a living room, two bedrooms, kitchen and toilet. Cooking utensils, dishes, cutlery, blankets and pillows are provided. You only have to supply bed linen and towels. Log cabins and renovated cottages and farm buildings are generally simpler, more rustic and situated in more isolated places. Blankets, pillows and dishes are provided, but you have to bring your own bed linen, towels and, in some cases, your own cutlery.

The cottages and chalets can be rented for periods as short as a week. Prices include heating, but electricity is sometimes extra. The cottages should be booked well in advance for the peak season (mid-June to mid-August), and during Christmas, Easter and the winter sport weeks (mid-February through the beginning of March) in the mountains. Off-season rentals—early June and late August, for instance—cost less (in some cases, half the peak-season price), the selection of locations is better and reservations are easier to make. And even in the mountains, the weather often remains mild well into September.

Cottages can be rented through travel agents, Sweden's local tourist offices and principal holiday cottage rental agents in Sweden, such as the STF and Sverek. A complete list of the principal agents in Sweden is available upon request from the Swedish Tourist Board.

Lodging Discounts

Numerous low-cost arrangements, such as go-as-you-please hotel vouchers, bonus passports and budget-priced package coupons, can save you money on overnight stays in hotels. Some even grant you generous discounts on admissions to main tourist attractions and sightseeing tours. Information on the various low-cost arrangements is contained in a free fact sheet published by the Swedish Tourist Board:

- *Budget Price Accommodation in Sweden: Travel Facts No. 6* (in English; also available in German and French).

Lodging Lists

Details on each of Sweden's lodgings are contained in the following books and pamphlets:

- *Fjäll '81* (in Swedish), published annually by the STF (see description under the section on *Guidebooks*). This is the most complete lodging list available to the Swedish mountains. Recommended.
- *Youth Hostels, Hiking Tours, Mountain-Stations* (in English; also available in German), published by the STF. A pamphlet with brief information on the STF's hiking tours, travel services and lodgings. Includes a list with the names, locations, opening and closing dates, and telephone numbers of about 80 youth hostels. Also includes a sketch map showing the locations of all STF lodgings. Free upon request.
- *Vandrarhem '81* (in Swedish; some text in English, French, German and Finnish), issued annually by the STF. Gives full details on all the youth hostels in Sweden. Includes a sketch map showing locations. Available from the STF for a nominal charge. Recommended.
- *Hotell och pensionat i Sverige '81* (in Swedish), issued annually by the STF. Gives details on hotels, pensions and motels throughout Sweden. Information is included on nearby sport facilities and outdoor activities. Available for a moderate charge from the STF.
- *Stugsemestrar* (in Swedish), published by the STF. Provides full information on the private cottages and holiday chalets rented by the STF, as well as how to book space. Free upon request.
- *Färdiga Semestrar i natur & vildmark* (in Swedish), published annually by Sverek. Gives full details on the canoeing trips, mountain walks and fishing holidays organized by Sverek, plus full information on the 400-plus holiday cottages rented by Sverek. The cottage descriptions include photographs, floor plans and a series of symbols indicating distances to the nearest stores, restaurants and telephones as well as which outdoor activities can be enjoyed in the vicinity. Booking information and seasonal prices are also given. Free upon request.
- *Country and Mountain Package Holidays* (in English; also available in German), published annually by Sverek. A 12-page summary of *Färdiga Semestrar i natur & vildmark*. Gives more generalized information. Only briefly describes Sverek's cottages and the general areas in which they are located. Does not include specifics on any of the individual cottages. Free upon request.
- *Gästhamn '81/82* (in Swedish; some text in English, Finnish and German). Useful only if you plan to boat in Sweden. Gives information on all the STF's 360-plus guest harbors—locations, telephone numbers, mooring facilities, average depth of water, fuel facilities, lodging possibilities, land transportation and other services. Includes sketch maps showing locations. Free on request.
- *Hotels in Sweden* (in English, with explanatory information and introductions in Swedish, French and German), published annually

by the Swedish Tourist Board. Gives all essential details on hotels, pensions and motels throughout Sweden. Also indicates which hotels accept low-cost vouchers. Free upon request. Recommended.

Information on other lodging possibilities in Sweden, such as manor house and farm house accommodation and holiday cottage rentals, can be obtained upon request from the Swedish Tourist Board (see *Address Directory*) and its branch offices.

Camping

Sweden has fewer restrictions on camping than practically any other country (see the section on *Everyman's Right*). Once you are out of earshot and sight of private dwellings, the countryside is pretty much yours. Nonetheless, you should always follow environmentally sound camping practices. Also, if you are on somebody else's land, it is always a good practice to ask the landowner for permission before you set up your tent, even though you are not always required to do so. You may just earn a friend instead of simply a spot to pitch your tent for the night.

More than 500 commercial campsites are available throughout Sweden. Many of these have showers with hot and cold water, hot plates for cooking, laundry facilities, food shops and facilities for swimming, boating and fishing. Nearly half the campsites have holiday chalets for rent. To stay in many of the campsites you must have an International Camping Carnet or a Swedish camping card, which can be purchased from the first campsite you visit. Sweden also has a camping voucher system which, like its hotel vouchers, can save you money on overnight stays in more than half the country's campsites. Information on the vouchers can be obtained from local tourist information offices, as well as from the branch offices of the Swedish Tourist Board (see *Address Directory*).

Details on commercial campsites in the Swedish mountains is contained in STF's *Fjäll '81* (see the section on *Guidebooks*). Other useful camping guides include:

- *Svensk Camping Guide* (in Swedish, with a key to symbols and introductions in English, German and French). A series of nine regional camping guides covering all of Sweden. Each contains detailed information on all the campsites in one of the nine camping regions. Aerial photographs of each site show the surrounding countryside. Sketch maps showing locations are also included. Available from all campsites. Free when you purchase a Swedish camping card.

- *Campingplatser i Sverige* (in Swedish, with a key to symbols in English, German, Finnish and French), published by the Swedish Tourist Board. Gives full details on all the campsites in Sweden. Includes a 1:300,000 road map of Sweden showing the locations of, among other things, all of Sweden's campsites (with symbols keyed according to their classification), touring club lodges and youth hostels, mountain stations, mountain huts, marked mountain trails and guest harbors. Available for a nominal charge from most bookstores, as well as by mail from the Swedish Tourist Board and STF. Recommended.

Crossing Swedish Waterways

Boat service is available on most of the large lakes in Sweden, including several lakes in the Lappland mountains. The STF, for instance, operates boat services during the summer on the large lakes crossed by the Kungsleden. Foot bridges have also been built across streams on many marked hiking routes. Nonetheless, many streams must be forded, especially in the highlands of Lappland. In addition, the walker must often cross marshy areas and bogs. And even on higher slopes, the ground is often spongy and water-soaked.

Water, in fact, is a characteristic aspect of walking in the Swedish highlands and wilderness areas. If it isn't coming down out of the sky, it is underfoot or rushing in a torrent between you and the opposite bank of a stream.

As a result, leather hiking boots are highly impractical in the Swedish highlands. Instead, you should wear knee-high rubber boots. That's the only way your feet will stay dry.

You should also know how to ford streams in cold, waist-deep water against swift currents. For such crossings, a pair of light canvas shoes, a walking staff (or sturdy branch) to help you maintain balance and, in some cases, a rope are necessities. So is a companion or two to help you should you get in trouble. Heavy-gauge plastic bags to keep your gear dry during stream crossings are also useful.

Some streams, of course, can be crossed by simply stepping from one stone to another. But many crossings in Lappland can only be made by hiking up and down the bank to find a suitable crossing point; stripping down; hanging boots, socks and pants on your pack; loosening shoulder straps and completely undoing the waist belt to ensure you can jettison your pack—quickly—should you slip or be swept off your feet; donning canvas shoes to protect your feet (note: cork soles have less of a tendency to slip on rocks in the stream bed than rubber soles); facing upstream with your walking staff held firmly in front of you in both hands; carefully lifting and placing each foot a few centimeters ahead of you while bracing yourself with the staff; and heading diagonally up and across the current toward the opposite bank. The faster and deeper the water, the more sharply upstream you must angle.

Experience is the only way in which you can learn to do this properly. If you haven't done it before, Lappland is no place to learn. Instead, you should join one of the STF's mountain hikes or pick a marked route to hike outside of Lappland.

On some lakes and unfordable rivers in the highlands, the STF has placed boats on both sides of waterways along marked hiking routes. There must always be one boat left on each bank. This means that, if you use one of the boats, you must row across the waterway three times: first, to get the boat on the other side; second, to bring the second boat back and tie it up; and third, to make your crossing of the waterway and tie up your boat on the opposite bank. This may seem like a lot of extra rowing, but it is the only way you—and every other hiker—can be assured that you won't arrive at a river only to see two boats tied up on the opposite bank and none on your side.

Water

With so much water in Sweden, you are unlikely to ever have a problem finding enough to drink. Lakes, streams and rivers are everywhere pure in Sweden's mountain and wilderness areas. It is advisable to avoid drinking water from bogs and marshes, especially those on peat soil, which can give water a brackish taste. Generally, there will be a nearby stream or other water source from which you can drink anyway.

Normal precautions should be taken to avoid possibly contaminated water sources near populous settlements and farms and downstream from mountain stations and villages. Lakes near industrial areas or with towns strung around their shores should, of course, be avoided. The Swedes have been very careful to minimize the pollution of their waterways, but it is not unknown, and there is no sense taking chances.

In those places where you might be in doubt, you will always be able to obtain water from wells, a farmer or from a tap.

Equipment Notes

A pair of higher rubber boots with lug soles are either necessary or highly advisable for walking virtually anywhere in Sweden. On footpaths in central and southern Sweden, the rest of your equipment needs differ little from those for most other lowland footpaths in Europe. Light clothing (and, if you wish, shorts) should be packed for the long, warm summer days, along with a sweater, jacket and raingear. You'll also need food for lunches and snacks on the trail, a sheet sleeping bag and towel for staying in youth hostels, a light pair of shoes to change into at the end of the day and, of course, a map and compass.

Mountain walkers, on the other hand, must be prepared for a wide range of contingencies, any one of which can cause a delay—or a complete change—in plans.

On marked routes in the mountain regions, you should have a sheet sleeping bag, towel and your own cutlery for staying in the mountain huts. A good, strong insect repellent, such as can be bought in Sweden, is essential from mid-June to mid-August. In Lappland, you may also want to wear a hat draped with insect netting to protect your face. A pair of sunglasses is another necessity, especially in early summer and at higher elevations, where snowfields will be encountered.

You must also plan on carrying most of your food. Provisions can be bought in some of the mountain huts, but you may have to walk for several days before you reach another hut where food can be purchased. And then, there is always the chance that its supply has run low. The huts which sell provisions are indicated in the STF's annual guide *Fjäll '81* (look for the word *proviant* in the hut listings).

Very few of the mountain tracks pass through villages or towns, except at their beginning and end points. Freeze-dried food can be bought in some of these settlements. But the selection of food suitable for carrying on the trail is sometimes very restricted. For this reason, it is advisable to buy all your provisions in a large town before you head off into the mountains.

In addition to your normal provisions, you must always carry sufficient emergency provisions to sustain you for at least one and preferably for two days—smoked ham or bacon, dried fruit, instant macaroni, bread, cheese, oatmeal, sugar, coffee and chocolate bars, for instance.

Away from the marked mountain tracks and in Sweden's wilderness areas, walkers must be entirely self-reliant. You must have a sturdy tent able to stand up to gale-force winds, preferably with a dark-colored fabric to cut out the Midnight Sun, tightly sealing insect netting and enough room to accommodate you—and your gear—comfortably should you become weather-bound; a warm sleeping bag; ground insulation; all your cooking gear and utensils; plenty of fuel for your stove; all your food; a rope for stream crossings; sufficient clothing to keep you warm and dry in a wide range of weather conditions; the proper medical supplies and equipment to cope with possible emergencies; plus all your personal items.

Most important of all, however, is experience. To safely venture into the Swedish wilderness, you must be at home with the weather conditions and terrain that is peculiar to the far north. You must be prepared for delays due to bad weather, impassable terrain and unfordable streams. And you must be able to accurately navigate through the wilds with Swedish maps. There is no margin for error. If you are lost or injured, it may take several days before you are missed—or for a companion to walk out and get assistance—and several more days before help arrives.

For these reasons, the STF recommends that foreign walkers who are visiting Sweden for the first time walk one of the major trails. Then as you become accustomed to conditions in the Swedish highlands, you can venture farther afield, first onto the less-traveled mountain tracks, then on short excursions into the wilds, and finally on a cross-country trek. Or, as an alternative, you can join one of the STF's wilderness treks the first time around—just as a precaution.

After mid-September, when mountain huts are closed and weather conditions can become fierce, only the most experienced mountain travelers—properly equipped for winter travel—should venture into the highlands.

Caution in the Mountains

To everyone who ventures into the Swedish highlands, the STF offers the following advice:

- Never walk alone in the mountains.
- Leave details of your planned route with your hotel or host, even for short day trips.
- For mountain tours, one family member at home should know the route.
- Report your return immediately, especially if plans have been changed or there has been a delay.
- A map and compass should always be carried, even on short tours; visibility can deteriorate rapidly.
- Acquaint yourself in advance with the route, either by reading the appropriate literature or consulting the local tourist office or residents.
- Maps are not always precise regarding route selection, difficulties, huts, bridges, boat-ferrying places and so on; changes may have occurred since the map was printed.
- Consider and plan your tour so the difficulties and stages correspond to your fitness and mountaineering experience.
- Turn back or seek shelter if, in continuing your journey, there is the slightest danger to anyone in the party.
- The weather, even in summer, can change suddenly; be prepared.
- It is very dangerous to wade through swift running and deep water; select shallow, wide crossings.
- Do not walk barefoot.
- Try to use the walking-stick upstream to find support.
- Use a rope at dangerous crossings.

Crowded Trails

In much of northern Sweden, solitude is considerably easier to find than companionship. Even in southern Sweden, you can find paths leading into the woods from youth hostels which, with less than half a kilometer of walking, will lead you into a forested alcove where you can be alone with the sounds of the wind and rushing water, the smells of meadow grass and resin, and the soft earth beneath your feet.

Nonetheless, some paths are heavily used and mountain huts along the more popular hiking routes in the Swedish highlands can be crowded during July and August. The most popular hiking route is Kungsleden, which stretches south through Lappland from Abisko to Ammarnäs. Most other marked mountain tracks are also heavily traveled in July and August.

The STF, however, recommends that walkers who are coming to Sweden for the first time not only walk the major trails, but do so during midsummer. The hiking routes most often recommended by the STF are: first, Kungsleden and second, from the Storulvån mountain station to Lungdalen in Jämtland. For easier tours in southern Sweden, Sörmlandsleden is often recommended.

Normally, walking clubs try to steer walkers away from heavily traveled routes to prevent excessive overuse which, in turn, promotes path erosion, and to avoid overtaxing lodging facilities, both of which can diminish the experience of walking a path. But in Sweden, the overriding concern is safety. If you get into trouble on one of the major trails during the summer, there will always be another walker who can provide assistance. And given the highland's penchant for unpredictable, fierce weather and the long distances between communications, this is no small concern in selecting a route.

Walking & Skiing Tours

More than 150 guided mountain walks, spanning all grades of difficulty and lasting from one to two weeks, are organized by the STF each summer to the mountain regions of Lappland, Jämtland, Härjedalen and Dalarna. Some of the walks are geared for novices who want to experience both walking and the Swedish mountains for the first time. Others are wilderness treks for the experienced which take you into the hinterlands of Sarek, Padjelanta and Stora Sjöfallet national parks—Europe's largest preserved wilderness.

The STF also arranges individual package tours. These allow you to go off on your own with one or two companions on a tailor-made walk. On these tours, the STF helps you select a route, provides advice on walking it, makes your travel and lodging arrangements, provides you with tickets for food and lodging in the huts and advises you on all the maps and literature necessary for your trip.

Guided walks are also arranged by four other organizations to the vast river-laced forests of Norrbotten, the moors and marshes of the Blaiken wilderness in Västerbotten, the forest and lake regions of central and southern Sweden and along Sweden's sunny west coast. Most of these tours can be booked through the STF.

In addition, several tourist hotels, holiday villages and camping sites arrange easy, day-long excursions with and without guides into the Swedish mountains.

In the winter and spring, guided ski tours into the Swedish mountains are arranged for both novices and experienced mountain skiers by the STF, as well as by Sweden's winter sport centers. Some of these are day-long tours from a single base; others are overnight tours with accommodation in mountain huts.

Accommodation on the mountain walks is usually in mountain stations and huts. Participants are expected to carry their own provisions and, in the huts, to help bring in water, cook and clean. Some of the walks into wilderness regions utilize tents (which are provided, but again, must be carried by participants). A few of the walks, especially those for novices, are based at a single hut, from which day hikes into the surrounding area are taken. The maximum group size on most tours ranges from 12 to 15 people.

Several one- and two-day nature expeditions into the countryside surrounding Stockholm are organized by Sverek. Sverek also organizes short hikes on Sörmlandsleden in southern Sweden.

Full details on the tours can be obtained from the following organizations:

Walking Tours

See *Address Directory*:

Svenska turistföreningen/STF. Organizes the largest number of mountain walks in Sweden. Also organizes tours for canoeing, cycling and horseback riding, as well as more than 100 mountain tours to Norway, Finland, Greenland, Switzerland and the Faeroe Islands of Denmark. Can provide information and make bookings for walking tours conducted by other organizations in Sweden. Details on the STF mountain tours is contained in two publications, both of which are free on request:

- *STF-resor sommaren och hösten* (in Swedish). Summer and autumn tours. Issued annually in March. Gives full details on each of the STF's mountain walks in Sweden and abroad, as well as on its canoeing, cycling and horseback riding trips. Includes dates, costs, equipment requirements, difficulties and booking terms. Illustrated with color photographs.

- *Mountain Holidays in Sweden* (in English; also available in German). A mimeographed information sheet with a brief overview of the STF's mountain tours. Gives the dates and costs of principal tours.

Sverek. Organizes one-week walks to Padjelanta National Park in Lappland, Sonfjället National Park in Härjedalen, and to the Blaiken wilderness and Kittelfjäll Mountains in Västerbotten. Also organizes three-day tours where groups of four people walk on their own along marked paths in the Nirra wilderness region above the Arctic Circle. Tours are geared for both novices and more experienced walkers. One of the tours—in Padjelanta National Park—consists of guided day-excursions from a base camp. Several one-week tours combining forest walks with visits to historic castles, manor houses and areas of local color are organized in the provinces of Skåne, Småland and Dalarna. Five different one- and two-day nature expeditions are also organized on a weekly basis from Stockholm during the summer. Details are given in three free publications:

- *Färdiga semestrar i natur & vildmark* (in Swedish). Issued annually. Gives full information on each of Sverek's walking tours, nature expeditions, canoeing trips and fishing holidays. Also includes full information on each of its 400-plus holiday cottages. Liberally illustrated with color photographs.
- *Country and Mountain Package Holidays* (in English; also available in German). Issued annually. Contains an overview of the information presented in *Färdiga semestra i natur & vildmark*. Gives tour dates, but not prices. Contains sufficient information for you to decide which tour appeals to you. Includes color photographs.
- *Nature Expeditions* (in English, Swedish and German). Issued annually. Gives full details on each of Sverek's one- and two-day nature expeditions from Stockholm. Includes dates, departure times, prices and booking information. Illustrated with color photographs.

Västkustens Turisttrafikförbund. Handles bookings for nearly 30 walking tours over heathland, past dramatic rock formations, through forests and past lakes in the west coast provinces of Halland and Västergötland. The tours include weekend family walks, as well as individual walks of varying length and difficulty which are taken on footpaths in the countryside surrounding a single base. The longest walk is the 86-kilometer Salmon March, held in the vicinity of Falkenberg during the last week of May each year, which concludes with a salmon party. Many of the other hikes can be taken throughout the year. Full details are available upon request. Staff speaks English, German and French.

Til Fjälls Resor AB. Organizes walking tours into the mountains of Jämtland. Full details are available upon request. Staff speaks English and German.

Nordkalottresor AB. Organizes walking tours in the forest and river regions of Norrbotten, as well as in the mountains of Northern Lappland. Full details are available upon request. Staff speaks English, German and Finnish.

Among the numerous tourist hotels which offer guided day-excursions into the Swedish mountain areas are:

Hemavans Högfjällshotel. Located in the mountains of Southern Lappland, about 75 kilometers from Ammarfjället at the southern terminus of the Kungsleden.

Lapplandia Sporthotel. Sweden's northernmost mountain hotel. Located about 30 kilometers from both Narvik, Norway and Abisko at the northern terminus of Kungsleden.

Storliens Högfjällshotell. Located on the Norwegian-Swedish border in Jämtland. Sweden's largest mountain hotel.

Guided excursions are also conducted from the STF's mountain stations. Information on other tourist hotels, holiday villages and camping sites which offer guided day-excursions is available from the STF.

Ski Tours

Svenska turistföreningen/STF (see *Address Directory*). Organizes the largest number of mountain ski tours in Sweden. Also organizes mountain ski tours to Norway in cooperation with the Norwegian Mountain Touring Association. Can provide information and make bookings for ski tours conducted by other organizations in Sweden. Details on the STF's winter and spring tours is contained in:

• *Fjällsemester med STF resor: vintern och våren 1980-81* (in Swedish). Issued annually in October. Gives full details on all the STF's mountain ski tours and winter camping trips. Includes dates, costs, equipment requirements, difficulties and booking terms. Illustrated with color photographs. Free upon request.

Mountain Guides

There is no system in Sweden for hiring guides. Even Sweden's two climbing clubs—Svenska Klätterförbundet and Svenska Fjällklubben—do not provide guide services. There is, however, no lack of guides. Most hotels and tourist stations in the mountains have their own guides to lead groups of hotel guests on short walking and skiing tours. All organized hikes are also led by experienced guides. If you want to hire a guide on your own, you can probably find one. But you will have to contact the guide yourself and make all arrangements with him directly.

For walkers or skiers who feel they want—or need—a guide, it is best to join one of the guided tours. Cheaper, too.

Because guides are not readily available, those who wish to climb in the Swedish mountains should already be experienced, capable climbers able to climb on their own—and able to cope with the conditions in the Swedish mountains. Experienced climbers who wish to obtain information on climbing routes and advice on approaches, weather and difficulties on specific routes may contact either the Svenska Klätterförbundet or Svenska Fjällklubben (see *Address Directory*).

Mountaineering & Ski Touring Courses

Two organizations in Sweden offer instruction in basic and advanced rock climbing—the STF and Svenska Klätterförbundet. The STF and Friluftsfrämjandet also conduct special courses to train the leaders of walking and skiing tours. In addition, the STF offers courses in first aid, mountain navigation and ski mountaineering.

Those who wish to learn—or improve—their cross-country skiing skills can take part in one of the courses offered by Friluftsfrämjandet (see *Address Directory*). Several of Sweden's winter sport centers also offer instruction in cross-country skiing.

Requests for information on the specific courses offered and the dates they are available should be addressed to the STF, Svenska Klätterförbundet or Friluftsfrämjandet. Generally, the cross-country skiing courses at the winter sports centers are available throughout the winter and do not require prior sign ups.

All the courses, with the exception of the STF's leadership training courses, are open to both individuals and groups.

Cross-Country Skiing

Skiing in Sweden starts as soon as the first snow falls, usually in November. Much of the country is blanketed with snow through March or April and in the far north the skiing season extends until the middle of June. The four weeks from mid-February to mid-March are the Swedish schools' winter sports weeks, and both lodgings and ski facilities near Sweden's winter sports centers are crowded. Easter is also a peak skiing time.

Prepared ski tracks, many of which are illuminated, are found in the vicinity of virtually every town and large village in Sweden. Cross-country ski tracks also fan out from all of Sweden's winter sports centers, and many centers offer guided ski touring trips into the surrounding mountains.

Ski touring routes have been marked in the Swedish highlands with red crossed boards affixed to long posts, and are shown on the 1:100,000 Nya Fjällkartan. Thirteen ski tours on these routes, ranging up to 154 kilometers in length, are described in the STF's annual guide *Fjäll '81* (see the section on *Guidebooks*). Information is also given in the guide on lodging possibilities along the routes and the dates they are open. Because of the severity of weather conditions in the mountains at this time of year—and the possibility of avalanches—these routes should be followed only by groups of experienced mountain skiers.

Details on the winter sports centers can be obtained from the Swedish Tourist Board (see *Address Directory*), which publishes a useful fact sheet entitled:

- *Winter Sports in Sweden: Travel Facts No. 5* (in English; also available in German). Describes lodging and ski facilities at winter sports centers located in Dalarna, Härjedalen, Jämtland and Lappland. Notes which sports centers have ski instructors, rent ski equipment and offer guided ski touring trips. Also provides information on access by automobile, train and bus, and gives the addresses of organizations which arrange package ski tours. Free upon request.

Information on marked and illuminated ski tracks near Swedish towns can be obtained from the local and provincial tourist information offices in the regions you wish to visit. Several of the provincial tourist associations publish maps of their provinces showing the locations of towns with marked and illuminated ski tracks (several of these maps are listed in the regional descriptions later in this chapter). Many of the local tourist offices also publish sketch maps showing marked and illuminated ski tracks in their areas.

The format and quality of the tourist office maps and winter sports brochures vary widely. But for the time being they are the best source of information available on the possibilities for cross-country skiing outside the Swedish mountains. As yet, no comprehensive booklet exists listing all the towns in Sweden—nor even all the towns in a single province—which have marked and illuminated ski tracks, or giving specifics on the lengths of the ski tracks and the places where ski equipment can be rented.

Even the provincial tourist associations cannot always give you specific information on the ski tracks and facilities in local areas. They can, however, steer you to the appropriate local tourist offices where this information can be obtained. The addresses and telephone numbers of both the provincial tourist associations and local tourist information offices are listed on the following fact sheet:

- *Tourist Information offices in Sweden: Travel Facts No. 10* (in English; also available in German). Free upon request from the Swedish Tourist Board.

Information on the cross-country skiing possibilities in southern Sweden can also be obtained from Friluftsfrämjandet. Friluftsfrämjandet cannot provide specific information on individual ski tracks, but it can tell you where the principal ski touring centers are located and give you information on its ski touring activities.

Transportation in Sweden

There are several ways in which to travel from, say Stockholm, to the Swedish mountain districts—airplane, train, bus and even boat. Often, you must travel on a combination of transport facilities before you can set foot on a mountain trail—train and bus, for instance. Also, because distances are long in Sweden, it can take considerable time (and money) to get to some of the mountain districts.

From airports in Lappland connections can be made by mail coach—or, to some areas, by boat—to reach the walking areas. From Stockholm, regularly scheduled flights go to Kiruna and Gällivare in Northern Lappland; to Östersund at the doorway to the mountains of Jämtland; and to Luleå, Skelleftea and Umeå at the edges of the forest and wilderness regions of Norrbotten and Västerbotten in northeastern Sweden.

A less expensive way to travel is by train. Train lines in Sweden reach clear up to Abisko at the northern end of Kungsleden—farther north than in any other country. Trains will also take you within striking distance of the mountain regions of Jämtland, Härjedalen and Dalarna, and directly to towns in central and southern Sweden where you can easily find footpaths in the surrounding countryside.

Many of the smaller towns and villages in northern Sweden are connected by exceedingly comfortable mail buses which, in addition to the mail, deliver newspapers, milk and groceries along their routes. Often, the mail buses are waiting right outside the train station when you arrive or, if not, will be along shortly. Between the trains and mail buses there will be few walking areas you cannot reach in Sweden. In many cases, the buses drive right up the STF's mountain stations or drop you off in a village at the foot of a mountain track that leads up to one.

To reach a few walking areas, you may also have to take a boat. Generally, schedules are such that connections can easily be made with the mail buses and trains.

Travel tickets for the mail buses may be obtained directly from the drivers or from most travel agents. At all main railway stations in Sweden it is possible to buy direct travel tickets and book your walking gear to selected places along the mail bus and boat routes. Timetables for the mail bus and boat routes are contained in *Tidtabellen* (the Official Swedish

Railway Timetable), which is sold at all main railway stations. Information on joint travel connections and ticket prices for the mail buses can be obtained from:

Postverkets Diligenstrafik (see *Address Directory*).

or from:

Poststyrelsen (see *Address Directory*).

Information on flights to Lappland, and on train, mail bus and boat connections can also be obtained from the STF. In addition, the STF can provide a schedule of transport facilities in the mountains, entitled:

- *Turisttrafik i Tjūllen* (in Swedish). Issued annually. Free upon request.

Special Train & Bus Fares

A series of special discount tickets are available which can save you money on train and, in some cases, on mail bus travel in Sweden. Many of these special fares, however, come and go and are replaced by new money-saving schemes.

The Eurail, Eurail Youth and InterRail passes are honored on all train lines (but not mail bus and boat lines) in Sweden. For current information on other special discount fares, it is advisable to contact a travel agent, one of the branch offices of the Swedish Tourist Board (see below), the mail bus company or the information offices at one of Sweden's main train stations.

Useful Addresses & Telephone Numbers

General Tourist Information

In Sweden:

Sveriges Turistråd (see *Address Directory*). Staff speaks English, German and French. Can provide general information on all aspects of travel in Sweden. Publishes numerous tourist information booklets, including a series of free Travel Fact sheets. The fact sheets include:

- *Sweden Ferry Connections: Travel Facts No. 1*

- *Sweden Coming Events: Travel Facts No. 2*
- *Golf in Sweden: Travel Facts No. 3*
- *Cycling in Sweden: Travel Facts No. 4*
- *Winter Sports in Sweden: Travel Facts No. 5*
- *Budget Price Accommodation in Sweden: Travel Facts No. 6*
- *Youth-travels in Sweden: Travel Facts No. 7*
- *"Allemansrätten": Travel Facts No. 8*
- *Boat-hire in Sweden: Travel Facts No. 9*
- *Tourist Information Offices in Sweden: Travel Facts No. 10*
- *Holidays on Swedish Waterways: Travel Facts No. 11*
- *Chalets in Sweden during Winter: Travel Facts No. 13*
- *Angling in Sweden: Travel Facts No. 14*
- *Hiking in the Swedish Highlands: Travel Facts No. 16*
- *Game Shooting in Sweden: Travel Facts No. 17*

All the Swedish Tourist Board publications can be obtained from its branch offices.

Abroad:

Branch offices of the Swedish Tourist Board are located in EUROPE: Amsterdam, Copenhagen, Hamburg, Helsinki, London, Oslo, Paris, Rome and Zurich; and in the U.S.A.: Los Angeles and New York.

London: Swedish National Tourist Office, 3 Cork Street, London W1X 1HA. Tel. (01) 437 5816.

New York: Swedish National Tourist Office, 75 Rockefeller Plaza, New York, New York 10019. Tel. (212) 582-2802.

Sport Shops

There are several sport shops in large towns in Sweden where you can purchase—or replace—walking and skiing equipment. Many large department stores even have freeze-dried food, stoves and other equipment. If you are heading to the Swedish highlands, however, it is advisable to purchase everything you need *before* you take off to the mountains. You will have no difficulty finding good equipment in towns like Kiruna, Gällivare and Östersund. But, as with everything else in the far north, sport shops are few and far between. The best shop in Stockholm from which to buy walking, mountaineering and ski touring equipment is:

Friluftsmagasinet (see *Address Directory*). Two locations in Stockholm. Carries a full range of mountain clothing, footwear (including a large selection of rubber boots), raingear, frame packs, rucksacks, sleeping bags, tents, climbing gear and hardware, stoves, cooking equipment and other accessories. Also sells hiking maps and guidebooks. A free mail order catalog is available on request.

Friluftsmagasinet also has stores located in Göteborg and Malmö (see *Address Directory*).

Search & Rescue

In an emergency: Find the nearest telephone and dial: Tel. 90 000.

Some mountain huts (but not all) have emergency telephones which connect you directly with the police in the nearest town or village. With these telephones you do not have to dial a number; simply lift up the receiver. The huts with emergency telephones are indicated in the STF's annual guide *Fjäll '81* (look for the word *Hjälptelefon* in the hut listings). The locations of emergency telephones in the Swedish mountains are also shown in red on the *Nya Fjällkartan*.

Search and rescue in the Swedish mountains is carried out by an organization known as *Fjällräddningen* (mountain rescue squad), which consists of the police and local people living in the villages near the mountains. Elsewhere, the chief police officer in each district is responsible for search and rescue operations. All search and rescue operations are carried out under the auspices of the *Rikspolisstyrelsen* (National Police Board) in Stockholm and are financed by Swedish taxes. There is also a reciprocal agreement between Sweden and Great Britain whereby British citizens are entitled to the same medical services as Swedes. Hence, if you are British or Swedish and are injured or become ill in Sweden, the only costs you will incur are a nominal hospital visit charge, plus the cost for any prescribed medication. If you have to stay in the hospital, it will not cost you anything. Visitors to Sweden of other nationalities will be charged for medical care and for hospital stays. Nonetheless, search and rescue operations are still provided free of charge if you are lost or injured.

Walkers and skiers who venture into the Swedish mountains—and especially Sweden's wilderness areas—should keep in mind that distances between communications are great and, in some remote areas, it may take several days before the police or *Fjällräddningen* can be alerted. Also, because poor weather conditions can seriously hamper air operations, it can sometimes take several days for rescuers to reach you, even after they have been alerted. Your best insurance in these areas *always* is prevention—proper trip preparation, proper physical conditioning and proper equipment.

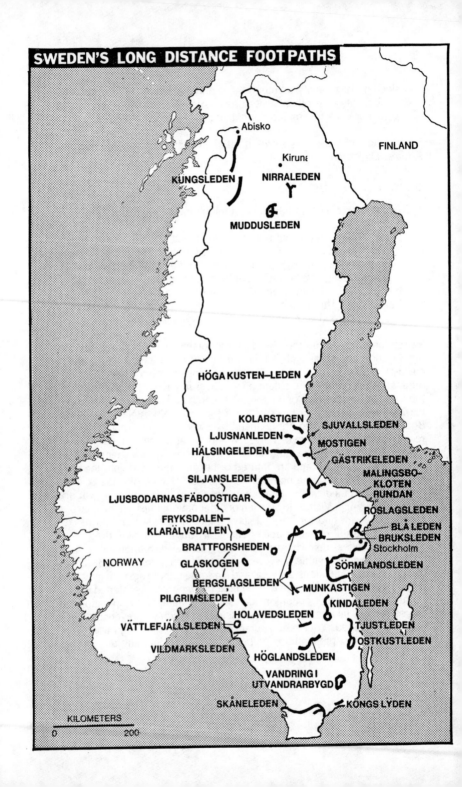

SWEDEN'S LONG DISTANCE FOOT PATHS

FINLAND

Abisko

Kiruna

KUNGSLEDEN

NIRRALEDEN

MUDDUSLEDEN

HÖGA KUSTEN—LEDEN

KOLARSTIGEN

SJUVALLSLEDEN

LJUSNANLEDEN

MOSTIGEN

HÄLSINGELEDEN

GÄSTRIKELEDEN

SILJANSLEDEN

MALINGSBO-KLOTEN RUNDAN

LJUSBODARNAS FÄBODSTIGAR

ROSLAGSLEDEN

FRYKSDALEN—KLARÄLVSDALEN

BLÅ LEDEN

BRUKSLEDEN

BRATTFORSHEDEN

Stockholm

NORWAY

GLASKOGEN

SÖRMLANDSLEDEN

BERGSLAGSLEDEN

MUNKASTIGEN

PILGRIMSLEDEN

KINDALEDEN

HOLAVEDSLEDEN

VÄTTLEFJÄLLSLEDEN

TJUSTLEDEN

OSTKUSTLEDEN

VILDMARKSLEDEN

HÖGLANDSLEDEN

VANDRING I UTVANDRARBYGD

SKÅNELEDEN

KÖNGS LYDEN

KILOMETERS

0   200

Sweden's Long-Distance Footpaths

Sweden has two major long-distance footpaths exceeding 400 kilometers (250 miles)—430-kilometer Kungsleden in the mountains of Lappland, and 500-kilometer Sörmlandsleden, which circles through the wooded hill and lake region south of Stockholm. Another 31 long-distance footpaths—many of which can be skied in winter—currently offer nearly 2,600 kilometers of walking opportunities in central and southern Sweden, and in the forests of Gästrikland, Hälsingland and Ångermanland.

Numerous long distance walks are also possible on the marked routes in the Swedish mountains, although only one of these routes—Kungsleden—is considered part of Sweden's long-distance footpath network. All the rest of the existing long-distance footpaths lie outside the mountains.

Most of the footpaths have lodgings within relatively close proximity to each other and can easily be divided into sections to allow a choice of routes of varying lengths and degrees of difficulty. Many sections of the paths are suitable for families with children. On some of the paths, however, it is necessary to camp. A few also have some strenuous sections.

Guidebooks currently exist for only five of the long distance footpaths—Sörmlandsleden, Skåneleden, Siljansleden, Oskustleden and Kungsleden (see "Swedish-language Guidebooks" under the section on *Guidebooks*). A series of Swedish-language leaflets, sketch maps and provisional route descriptions cover the other paths. The leaflets are published by and are generally available only from the tourist associations for the regions in which the paths are located. Route descriptions—when they are included in the leaflets—tend to be sketchy. Nonetheless, the leaflets are worth obtaining for their sketch maps and lodging information. They should, however, be supplemented with the appropriate 1:50,000 topographical maps. Local advice on walking the paths should also be sought, since several are not yet shown on the topographical maps.

The tourist offices which publish the footpath leaflets are usually quite good about helping you plan walks and ski trips on the paths, and can assist you with making arrangements for lodgings. General information on the paths can also be obtained from the STF and Friluftsfrämjandet or:

> **Statens Naturvårdsverk** (National Environmental Protection Board). See *Address Directory*. Oversees the planning of long-distance footpaths outside the mountains in conjunction with Sweden's region-al administrations, walking clubs and local tourist associations. Staff speaks Swedish and English.

All the long-distance footpaths outside the mountains are also briefly described in a booklet published jointly by the STF and Friluftsfrämjandet:

- *Vandra i Sverige: Låglandsleder* (in Swedish). See description under the section on *Guidebooks*). Available for a nominal charge from the STF. Recommended.

Most of the long-distance footpaths are marked with orange bands painted on trees (or lacking trees, on anything else that is handy) and have blue signposts located at strategic points indicating the direction and distance to the next locale. In the following descriptions the path markings have been mentioned only when they differ from the orange-band/blue-signpost norm.

Berglagsleden

From Kloten to Tiveden in the provinces of Närke and Västmanland west of Stockholm. Stretches between two forest reserves—Malingsbo-Kloten and Tiveden—in Örebro County. Also passes through Garphyttan National Park, a region of meadows, former farmlands and mixed deciduous and coniferous forest. Lovely rolling countryside with numerous lakes, large forests and traditional red-painted farmhouses and cottages. Passes near Svea Falls with its huge water-carved stone blocks, fall channels, boulders and witches' cauldrons—a dry waterfall that was once three times the size of Niagara. Several sections can be skied in winter. The path links up with both the Malingsbo-Kloten rundan and the Munkastigen long-distance footpaths. **Length:** When completed, 274 kilometers. About two-thirds of the path can currently be walked. **Walking Time:** For the completed sections, 7 to 8 days. The path is divided into 17 shorter sections for day hikes. There are also numerous local footpaths, some of which lead off from Bergslagsleden. **Difficulty:** Easy to moderately difficult.

Lodgings: Available in most towns and villages along the way. Longest distance between lodgings is 22 kilometers. Timbered wind shelters with stone fire pits, refuse bins and access to drinking water have also been constructed in the middle of each section.

Maps:
- Topografiska kartan 1:50,000, sheets 9E *Askersund* NO and SO; 10E *Karlskoga* NO and SO; 11E *Filipstad* NO (optional); 10F *Örebro* NV: and 11F *Lindesberg* NV, NO AND SV.

Path Descriptions:
- *Bergslagsleden: Allmän Beskrivning* (in Swedish). Provides an overview of the entire path and its development. Gives information on lodgings, rest places, the lengths of each section, the possibilities for skiing the path in winter and group walks. Includes a sketch map showing the location of lodgings and the sheet numbers of topographical maps covering the path. Free from the Örebro läns Turistnämnd (see *Address Directory*).
- *Bergslagsleden: Etappbeskrivning* (in Swedish). A folder and series of

route descriptions covering each section of the path. Gives information on transportation to and from the path, the telephone numbers of local tourist offices and the names and telephone numbers of lodgings in towns and villages at each end of the path section. On the back side is a black and white reproduction of the 1:50,000 topografiska kartan covering the path section, on which Bergslagsleden is shown along with the routes of local footpaths and the locations of bus stops, lodgings and wind shelters. Free from the Örebro läns Turistnämnd.

- *Tourist Guide: Örebro County Sweden* (in English). A general tourist guide packed with useful information for traveling in the county. Includes a brief description of the principal marked footpaths in the county, including Bergslagsleden. Free from the Örebro läns Turistnämnd.

Further Information: Contact the Örebro läns Turistnämnd (see *Address Directory*). Staff speaks Swedish, English and German.

Blå leden

From Domarudden in the fertile, rolling countryside of Uppland to Vaxholm on the coast northeast of Stockholm. Passes near several historical sites, some dating back to prehistoric times. Links up with the Roslagsleden long-distance footpath in Domarudden. **Length:** 31 kilometers. **Walking Time:** 1 to 2 days. **Difficulty:** Easy.

Lodgings: Available in Domarudden, Ellboda and Vaxholm. There is also one hut located along the path. A sleeping bag is necessary to stay in the hut.

Maps:
- Topografiska kartan 1:50,000, sheets 10I *Stockholm* NO and 11I *Uppsala* SO.

Path Description:
- A booklet in Swedish with a route description, topographical map and information on lodgings and points of interest along the path is available for a nominal charge from the Vaxholms Turistbyrå. When ordering the booklet, ask for the *"vandringsguiden över Blå leden."*

Further Information: Contact the Vaxholms Turistbyrå (see *Address Directory*).

Brattforsheden

A circular path in the Brattforsheden Nature Reserve, 15 kilometers southwest of Filipstad in the province of Värmland. The nature reserve encompasses a region of moors broken by a series of ridges formed during the last Ice Age. In the nearby village of Brattfors is a 16th century smeltery, one of the oldest is Värmland. **Length:** 20 kilometers. **Walking Time:** 1 day. **Difficulty:** Easy to moderately difficult.

Lodgings: There is a campsite with cottages at Mangenbaden, outside the nature reserve to the west, and three wind shelters inside the nature reserve.
Map:
• Topografiska kartan 1:50,000, sheet 11D *Munkfors* SO.
Path Description:
• A brochure in Swedish and sketch map covering the Brattforsheden Nature Reserve can be obtained upon request from the Filipstads Turistbyrå. When ordering, ask for the *"stencilerad broschyr över Brattforsheden."*
Further Information: Contact the Filipstads Turistbyrå (see *Address Directory*).

Bruksleden

A circular path from Västerås on the shores of island-studded Lake Mälaren to the village of Ramnäs in eastern Västmanland. Västeras is accessible by train from Stockholm. Several circular routes of varying lengths are possible on the path. The path can also be skied in winter. Passes through rolling, wooded country, past peaceful, tree-trimmed ponds, and along the shores of several lakes. In Hallstahammar, you can see the Strömsholms Canal with its numerous sluices, built in the 18th century to transport ore and iron to the Mälaren harbors. **Length:** 100 kilometers. **Walking Time:** 4 to 5 days. A one-day loop trip from Ramnäs or Surahammar is also possible. **Difficulty:** Easy.
Lodgings: Available in Ramnäs, Surahammar, Hallstahammar, Västerås and Skultuna. Three overnight cottages are also located on the path, as well as five rest places and five wind shelters.
Maps:
• Topografiska kartan 1:50,000, sheets 11G *Västerås* NV, SO, SV and SO.
Path Description:
• *Bruksleden: Vandringsled i Västmanlands län* (in Swedish). A leaflet with a brief description of the path. Gives the numbers of bus lines for reaching the path from various points, the telephone numbers of bus companies for schedule information, and the telephone numbers to call for tourist and lodging information. Includes a sketch map showing the locations of bus stops, tourist information offices, rest places, refuse bins, viewpoints, wind shelters, overnight cottages and places where drinking water can be obtained. Free from the Västmanlands länsstyrelse.
Further Information: Contact the Västmanlands länsstyrelse (see *Address Directory*).

Fryksdalen-Klarälvsdalen

From Rattsjöberg in the Fryksdalen Valley to Segenäs in the Klarälvsdalen Valley, in northern Värmland. Can also be skied in winter. The Fryksdalen encompasses an 80-kilometer string of lakes, famed by Nobel laureate Selma Lagerlöf's writings. Scattered throughout the valley, particularly between Torsby and Rattsjöberg, are numerous historic reminders of the valley's 16th century Finnish settlers. The forested Klarälvsdalen cradles the serpentine River Klaräven, followed by the ancient Pilgrim's Way, which stretches to St. Olov's grave in Trondheim, Norway, and was in use between 1050 and 1550 A.D. Numerous cottage industries, such as ceramic, birch-bark and textile design, flourish in the valley villages. **Length:** 51 kilometers. **Walking Time:** 2 days. **Difficulty:** Easy to moderately difficult.
Lodgings: Available in Vägsjöfors (at the recreation center). Simple lodgings are also available at Hovfjället and Ladtjänstorpet. There is a wind shelter along the path in which it is possible to overnight if you have a sleeping bag and food.
Maps:
* Topografiska kartan 1:50,000, sheets 12C *Torsby* nr 401, 12C *Torsby* NO and 12D *Uddeholm* NV.
Path Description:
* A folder in Swedish with a route description, sketch map and lodging information is available upon request from the Vägsjöfors friluftscenter. When ordering, ask for the *"vandringsledsbeskrivning över Fryksdalen-Klarälvsdalen."*
Further Information: Contact the Vägsjöfors friluftscenter (see *Address Directory*).

Gästrikeleden

From Hemlingby to Hofors in the province of Gästrikland, 2½ hours north of Stockholm. A region of lake-spangled forests where you can pitch your tent in the middle of nowhere and hear nothing but the birds and the plopping of the fish. The province comprises part of Sweden's "folklore regions" where summer brings village plays, peasant auctions and numerous folk festivals with singing, dancing and colorful costumes. The port of Gävle, near Hemlingby, has an interesting old town with narrow streets of red and white cottages and the *Silvanum* forestry museum, the only one of its kind in Europe. Highest points enroute are 306 meters in the Kungsberget Nature Reserve and 310 meters at Åsen. **Length:** 130 kilometers. **Walking Time:** 5 to 6 days. **Difficulty:** Easy to moderately difficult.
Lodgings: Available in Gävle and Hemlingby. There are also five huts and five wind shelters along the path. Camping is a good alternative.
Maps:

- Topografiska kartan 1:50,000, utmärkta Kartor Gästrikeleden, *blad 1,*
  Hemlingby-Rönnåsen and *blad 2, Rönnåsen-Hofors.* Two special sheets
  on which the footpath has been indicated. Available for a nominal
  charge from the Gävle Turistbyrå.

Path Descriptions:

- *Vandra i Hälsingland och Gästrikland* (in Swedish). A pamphlet with a
  brief description and sketch maps of the Gästrikeleden, Hälsingeleden,
  Ljusnanleden, Sjuvallsleden and Mostigen long-distance footpaths.
  Provides some information on lodgings near the paths, along with the
  telephone numbers of tourist offices. Free upon request from the
  Kommungruppen för fritid i Gävleborgs län (see *Address Directory*).
- *Värt att veta för Dig som går Gästrikeleden* (in Swedish). A provisional
  route description. Available for a nominal charge from the Gävle
  Turistbyrå.

Further Information: Contact Friluftsfrämjandet in Gävle or the Gävle
Turistbyrå (see *Address Directory*).

Glaskogen

A network of paths wandering through the Glaskogen Nature Reserve, a
forest region encompassing 30,000 hectares (77,721 acres) and two large
lakes—Övre Gla and Stora Gla—in the hills of western Värmland.
Numerous side trips are possible. **Length:** Altogether, the nature reserve
contains nearly 250 kilometers of footpaths. **Walking Time:** Many itineraries are possible, up to 10 days duration. **Difficulty:** Easy to moderately
difficult. **Path Markings:** Yellow rings painted on trees and rocks.

Lodgings: There are 10 rest places, 15 wind shelters and 4 huts in which
you can overnight inside the nature reserve. A sleeping bag is necessary to
stay in the huts.

Maps:

- Topografiska kartan 1:50,000, sheets 10B *Årjäng* NO, 10C *Åmål* NV,
  and 11C *Arvika* SV.

Path Description:

- *Naturreservat Glaskogen* (in Swedish). A folder describing the Glaskogen
  Nature Reserve. Includes a topographical map showing walking and
  canoeing routes. Available for a small charge from the Arvika Turistbyrå
  and Skogsvårdsstyrelsen i Värmlands län.

Further Information: Contact the Arvika Turistbyrå or the
Skogsvårdsstyrelsen i Värmlands län (see *Address Directory*).

Hälsingeleden

From Bollnäs to Los in the province of Hälsingland. Heavily wooded
region with many lakes and rivers. Comprises part of Sweden's "folklore

regions." **Length:** 120 kilometers. **Walking Time:** 4 to 5 days. **Difficulty:** Easy to moderately difficult.

Lodgings: Available in cottages and recreation centers located along the path at Bolleberget, Orbaden and Harsa. Lodgings are also available in several villages near the path. In addition, several wind shelters and rest places have been built on the path.

Maps:

• Topografiska kartan 1:50,000, two special sheets: *Harsa-Bollnäs* and *Harsa-Los*. Available for a nominal charge from the Bollnäs Turistbyrå.

Path Descriptions:

• *Vandra i Halsingland och Gästrikland* (in Swedish). See description under the Gästrikleden, above. Free upon request from the Kommungruppen för fritid i Gävleborgs län.

• A detailed route description of the section of path from Bollnäs to Harsa (51 kilometers) is included with the 1:50,000 *Harsa-Bollnäs* map listed above.

Further Information: Contact the Bollnäs Turistbyrå (see *Address Directory*).

Höga Kusten-leden

From Veda to Örnsköldsvik along the fjord-like coast of Ångermanland. Through a region of steep cliffs and low mountains, deeply cleft streams and rivers, small fishing villages, fertile agricultural districts and the Skule Forest wilderness. Sweden's most rugged coastal region. **Length:** When completed, more than 100 kilometers; about 50 kilometers can now be walked. **Walking Time:** For the completed section, 2 to 3 days. **Difficulty:** Moderately difficult.

Lodgings: Several rest places—normally with possibilities to overnight in nearby houses—are located along the path. Distances between lodgings are generally about 15 kilometers or less.

Maps:

• Topografiska kartan 1:50,000, sheets 18I *Kramfors* NV, NO, SV and SO; and 19I *Örnsköldsvik* NO, SV and SO.

Path Description:

• *Höga Kusten-leden: Delsträcka 3-4* (in Swedish). A black and white 1:50,000 map showing the path's route from Lappudden to Fjärdbotten (about 25 kilometers). Includes a list of lodgings and rest places, with the facilities available at each, keyed to numbers on the map. The map is not suitable for use on the path. Map folders are in preparation for other completed sections *(delsträcka)*. Free upon request from the Västernorrlands läns Landsting and Kramfors Turistbyrå.

Further Information: Contact the Västernorrlands läns Landsting or the Kramfors Turistbyrå (see *Address Directory*).

Höglandsleden

From Eksjö to Hooks Herrgård in the province of Småland. Through the "South Swedish Highlands" in the county of Jönköping. Numerous Iron Age and Bronze Age remains. The route takes you across rolling fields; past an Iron Age graveyard with ancient Torsa stones; through Vikskvarn, a wooded area with waterfalls, old brickworks and numerous rock formations exposing different sedimentary bedrocks; and over Tomtabacken with an elevation of 377 meters (1,237 feet), the highest point in the South Swedish Highlands. The path can also be skied in winter. **Length:** 84 kilometers. **Walking Time:** 4 days. **Difficulty:** Easy to moderately difficult. **Lodgings:** Available in Lövhult and Hok. Camping is possible along the rest of the route. Rest places have been constructed at Vikskvarn, Huluberget, Tomtabacken and Malmbäcksån.
Maps:
- Topografiska kartan 1:50,000, sheets 6E *Nässjö* NO and NV.

Path Descriptions:
- *Höglandsleden: vandringsled Lövhult-Hok* (in Swedish). A sketch map with brief general information. Describes places of interest enroute which are keyed to numbers on the map. Free upon request from the Nässjö Turistbyrå.
- *Nässjö on the Highlands of Småland* (in English). A panorama map of the region surrounding Nässjö. Artist sketches show objects of interest and the route of Höglandsleden. Information in the margin describes points of interest. Other tourist information, and a brief history of the region, is also given. Free from the Nässjö Turistbyrå.

Further Information: Contact the Nässjö Turistbyrå (see *Address Directory*).

Holavedsleden

From Tranås to Gränna, on the shore of Lake Vättern, in Småland's Jönköping County. Passes through a lovely region of meadows, forests and lakes, with wide views over the surrounding countryside from the tops of ridges and hills. **Length:** 59 kilometers. **Walking Time:** 2 to 3 days. **Difficulty:** Easy to moderately difficult.
Lodgings: Available in Tranås and Örsbäcken. There is a campsite at Hättebaden, as well as three rest places with wind shelters in which it is possible to overnight along the path. A sleeping bag and food are necessary.
Maps:
- Topografiska kartan 1:50,000, sheets 7E *Jönköping* NV and NO, and 7F *Tranås* NV and SV.

Path Description:
- A folder in Swedish with a sketch map, route description and information on lodging possibilities is available upon request from the Gränna Turistbyrå. When ordering, ask for the *"foldern över Holavedsleden."*

Further Information: Contact the Gränna Turistbyrå (see *Address Directory*).

Kindaleden

From Tolvmannabacken, outside the town of Kisa, to Rimforsa in the province of Östergötland; forests, peaceful lakes, fertile farmlands, graceful manor houses and numerous ancient relics. **Length:** 57 kilometers, including a 12-kilometer loop trail around Lake Pinnarp from Tolvmannabacken. **Walking Time:** 2 days. **Difficulty:** Easy. **Path Markings:** Red bands and circles on trees and rocks.
Lodgings: Available in Kisa and Rimforsa. There is a hut and campsite at Pinnarpsbaden, as well as a wind shelter in which it is possible to overnight at Lake Ösjön. A sleeping bag and food are necessary.
Maps:
• Topografiska kartan 1:50,000, sheets 7F *Tranås* NO and 8F *Linköping* SO.
Path Description:
• *Kindaleden: vandrings- och kanotleder i Kinda* (in Swedish). A 1:100,000 sketch map showing walking and canoeing routes in the region surrounding the town of Kisa. Brief information is given on various points along the path. Free upon request from the Östergötlands Länsturistnämnd.
Further Information: Contact the Östergötlands Länsturistnämnd or Kisa Turistbyrå (see *Address Directory*).

Kolarstigen

From Hallboviken to Sörgimma in the province of Hälsingland, paralleling the northeast shore of Lake Norr-Dellen. Begins about 15 kilometers northwest of the coastal town of Hudiksvall. **Length:** 32 kilometers. **Walking Time:** 1 to 2 days. **Difficulty:** Easy.
Lodgings: Closest lodgings are in Hudiksvall. Several rest places and a wind shelter are located along the path. Camping is possible.
Maps:
• A special 1:50,000 topographical strip map covering the path is available from the Hudiksvalls Fritidskontor. When ordering ask for the "särtryck ur topografisa kartan."
• Topografiska kartan 1:50,000, sheets 16G *Ljusdal* SO and 16H *Bergsjö* SV.
Path Description:
• *Kolarstigen och Sjuvallsleden* (in Swedish). A brochure with a route description of both the Kolarstigen and Sjuvallsleden outside Hudiksvall. Includes information on access and points of interest enroute. Free upon request from the Hudiksvalls Fritidskontor and Hudiksvalls Turistbyrå.

Further Information: Contact the Hudiksvalls Fritidskontor or Hudiksvalls Turistbyrå (see *Address Directory*).

Kongs Lÿden

A short footpath from Ronneby to Bräkne-Hoby in the province of Blekinge. Winds through beech forests and meadows past several small lakes, following an ancient King's road. First recorded reference to the road was made in 1296. **Length:** 15 kilometers. **Walking Time:** 1 day. **Difficulty:** Easy.
Lodgings: Available in Ronneby.
Map:
• Topografiska kartan 1:50,000, sheet 3F *Karlskrona* NV.
Path Descriptions:
• *Ronneby visar vägen in naturen* (in Swedish). A folder with a brief route description and sketch map. Free upon request from the Ronneby Turistybrå.
• *Gambal landzväg, Kongs Lÿden kallad* (in Swedish). Describes the historical sites and artifacts along the path. Also available from the Ronneby Turistbyrå.
Further Information: Contact the Ronneby Turistbyrå (see *Address Directory*).

Kungsleden

This is Sweden's best-known long-distance footpath. Stretching from Abisko to Ammarnäs in the mountains of Lappland, Kungsleden takes you through birch woods, across high mountain heaths and up valleys hemmed in by high, snow-capped peaks. Much of the route passes through wide valleys above tree limit and—on clear days—provides striking views of the central part of the Kebnekaise Massif, the glacier-draped peaks of Sarek National Park and the delta land of the Rapa Valley. Bridges have been built over most streams, and boats are available for crossing lakes. There are also planks on some areas of wet ground. Nonetheless, long stretches of wet ground must be crossed and several streams must be forded. There are also several strenuous sections. One of these is the 24-kilometer section from Alesjaure to Sälka, which takes you over a 1,150-meter pass—Tjäktjapasset—the highest point on Kungsleden. The hiking season is short. Snow remains on parts of Kungsleden late into June and reappears in September. The best time to hike the path is July and August. During July, however, gnats and mosquitoes abound, and not everyone can learn to live with them. Daylight hours, on the other hand, are long; at Abisko the midnight sun is visible from June 13 to July 4. **Length:** 430 kilometers. Several shorter routes are possible. For instance, you can take the train to Abisko, finish the walk 187 kilometers later at Kvikkjokk, and bus to Jokkmokk or Murjek where you can catch the train south. An even shorter route (104 kilometers) is from Abisko to Singi, thence to the mountain station at Kebnekaise, and from there to Nikkaluokta, where you can catch a bus to Kiruna for the train south. The walk can also be started at Nikkaluokta. From there, you can go to Kebnekaise, then to Singi and south on Kungsleden to Kvikkjokk. This allows you to avoid the most difficult section of trail—and the most treacherous stream crossing—between Alesjuare and Sälka. The length of this route is 143 kilometers. Several other routes are also possible, such as from Kvikkjokk to Peljekaise and from Peljekaise to Ammarnäs. The most popular section is from Abisko to Kvikkjokk, which is outlined below.

Walking Time: For the entire path, 22 to 26 days *without rests;* for the section from Abisko to Kvikkjokk, 10 to 12 days *without rests;* for the route from Abisko to Nikkaluokta, 6 days *without rests;* and for the route from Nikkaluokta to Kvikkjokk, 8 to 10 days *without rests.* **Difficulty:** For experienced walkers, moderately difficult; some difficult sections. The path should not be walked by those who have not previously forded cold, swift-flowing streams. **Path Markings:** Most of the path is marked with cairns; some sections are marked with red bars or orange bands painted on trees. Markings are intermittent south of Kvikkjokk.

Special Notes: The entire path crosses uninhabited country a long way from roads or dwellings. It is essential that you be physically fit, experienced in mountain travel and well equipped. Food for several days at a time must be carried along with a two-day emergency ration. Hot meals and other amenities are available at the mountain stations in Abisko, Saltoluokta and Kvikkjokk. Food can also be purchased in the mountain huts at Alesjaure, Sälka, Kaitumjaure and Aktse. South of Kvikkjokk, you must camp; there are only five huts between Kvikkjokk and Ammanäs, none of which sell food. The 15-kilometer detour to the mountain station at Kebnekaise is worthwhile. It is a great place for a rest day. Nearby is 2,117-meter Mt. Kebnekaise, Sweden's highest peak. A hut at 1,880 meters claims to be the highest dwelling in Sweden.

Lodgings: Hot meals, showers, saunas and lodgings are available in the mountain stations at Abisko, Saltoluokta and Kvikkjokk. Mountain huts are located at Abiskojaure, Alesjaure, Sälka, Singi, Kaitumjaure, Teusajaure, Vakkotavare, Sitojaure, Aktse and Pårte. South of Kvikkjokk, there is a mountain hut at Tsielekjakk, and simple lodgings at Västerfjäll, Vuonatjviken, Jäckvik and Adolfström. Hotels and pensions are available in Abisko and Ammarnäs. There is also a camping site in Ammarnäs. Lodgings along the path are often crowded during July and August.

Maps:
* Nya Fjällkartan 1:100,000, sheets BD 6, BD 8 and BD 11 cover the route from Abisko to Kvikkjokk; sheets BD 14 and BD 16 cover the route from Kvikkjokk to Ammarnäs. Kebnekaise is shown on both sheets BD 8 and BD 6.

Path Descriptions:
* *Kungsleden och 13 angränsande turer* (in Swedish). A comprehensive

guidebook published by and available from the STF (see *Address Directory*). Last revised in 1978.

• *Fjäll '81* (in Swedish with English leaflet), also available from the STF. See description, under the section on *Guidebooks* earlier in this chapter.

Further Information: Contact the STF.

Route Outline—Abisko to Kvikkjokk

Approach: Take the train to Abisko. There are two train stations in Abisko. Get off at the *Abisko Turist* station. The mountain station is visible from the train station. From the mountain station, there are signs which say "Kungsleden."

Day 1: To Abiskojaure, 15 kilometers, 4 to 5 hours. Alongside a brook through a birch forest. The hut is situated at the south side of Lake Abiskojaure.

Day 2: To Alesjaure, 22 kilometers, 6 to 8 hours. Through the last remnants of the birch forest. The rest of the day's walk is above tree limit. Food is available at Alesjaure.

Day 3: To Sälka, 24 kilometers, 6 to 9 hours. The most strenuous section. A stream must be forded south of the Alesjaure hut. You also cross a 1,150-meter pass. Food is available at the Sälka hut.

Day 4: To Singi, 13 kilometers, 3 to 5 hours. The trail runs through the Tjäktjavagge Valley. If the weather is clear, you can see the central part of the Kebnekaise Massif, where Sweden's highest peak, 2,117-meter Kebnekaise, is located. Detour possible to the Kebnekaise mountain station, 15 kilometers, 3 to 4 hours. Another 15 kilometers beyond Kebnekaise, Nikkaluokta is reached, where you can catch a bus to Kiruna (hotels, youth hostel, camping site, airfield, trains to Stockholm and Narvik).

Day 5: To Kaitumjaure, 13 kilometers, 3 to 5 hours. Food available.

Day 6: To Teusajaure, 9 kilometers, 2 to 3 hours. This hut is situated in a birch forest on the shores of the mountain-ringed lake of Teusajaure.

Day 7: To Vakkatavare, 15 kilometers, 3 to 4 hours. Across the lake of Teusajaure by boat. You must either row yourself or, if you are lucky, someone will be available to ferry you across. From Vakkotavare, you go by bus to Kebnats and then by boat to the Saltoluokta mountain station, a charming old mountain station built in 1916. Sauna, hot meals, showers and lodgings are available. From Kebnats you can take a bus to Gällivare (hotels, youth hostel, camping site, trains to Stockholm and Narvik).

Day 8: To Sitojaure, 22 kilometers, 5 to 7 hours. Birch woods at the beginning and end of the day. The Sitojaure huts are situated at the north end of the lake.

Day 9: To Aktse, 13 kilometers, 3 to 4 hours. The Lapps who live in Sitojaure take you over the lake (ask at the STF hut). You can also row yourself, being sure to row across three times so one boat is left on each side of the lake. Before descending to Aktse you should make a detour to Mt. Skierfe, where you will have a spectacular view over the Rapa Valley leading into Sarek National Park. Food available at Aktse.

Day 10: To Pårte, 24 kilometers, 6 to 8 hours. By ferry across the lake and into Sarek National Park (or, again, you can row yourself). To the west, the park's peaks and glaciers can be seen. No other marked trails exist in the park.

Day 11: To Kvikkjokk, 17 kilometers, 4 to 5 hours. Through a pine forest. The mosquitoes are especially fierce here in July. From the mountain station at Kvikkjokk, you can go by bus to Jokkmokk (hotels, youth hostel, camping site, trains to Stockholm and Narvik), or you can continue south for another 10 or 11 days to Ammarnäs, at the terminus of Kungsleden.

Days 12 through 22: From Kvikkjokk, the distances between lodgings are as follows: to Tsielekjåkk, 15 kilometers, 3 to 4 hours; to Västerfjäll, 23 kilometers, 6 to 8 hours; to Vuonatjviken, 34 kilometers, 9 to 12 hours; to Jäckvik, 29 kilometers, 8 to 10 hours; to Adolfström, 22 kilometers, 5 to 7 hours; and to Ammarnäs, 57 kilometers, 15 to 19 hours.

Ljusbodarnas fäbodstigar

A circular path south of Lake Siljan in the province of Dalarna. Leads through an undulating countryside with many rivers and lakes, peaks as high as 500 meters, small villages and several mountain dairy farms which are still in use. Logical starting place is Ljusbodarnas fäbodar, 3 kilometers southwest of Lake Djursjön. **Length:** 70 kilometers. **Walking Time:** 3 days. **Difficulty:** Easy to moderately difficult.

Lodgings: Available in Ljusbodarnas fäbod. There are also hotels, pensions and a youth hostel in Leksand, about 20 kilometers northeast of the path on the southern shore of Lake Siljan. Along the path it is necessary to camp.

Map:
• Topografiska kartan 1:50,000, sheet 13E *Vansbro* SO.

Path Description:
• A sketch map and other information to aid you in walking the path can be obtained upon request from the Leksands Turistbyrå. When ordering the sketch map, you should ask for the *"stencilerad blad över Ljusbodarnas fäbodområde."*

Further Information: Contact the Leksands Turistbyrå (see *Address Directory*).

Ljusnanleden

From Nore, near the town of Ljusdal, to Vallåsen, near the town of Färila. Located in the province of Hälsingland, one of Sweden's "folklore regions." Follows the banks of the Ljusnan River up a lovely, wooded valley. Eventually the path will be extended to Laforsen to link up with the Hälsingeleden long-distance footpath. It will also eventually link up at Ljusdal with the Sjuvallsleden. **Length:** When completed, 40 kilometers; 15 kilometers can currently be walked. **Walking Time:** For the completed section, 1 day. **Difficulty:** Easy.

Lodgings: Available in Ljusdal and Färila. A campsite is located in Nore.
Maps:
- Topografiska kartan 1:50,000, sheet 16G *Ljusdal* SV.
- A 1:40,000 topographical map showing the path is also available (see below).

Path Descriptions:
- *Vandra i Hälsingland och Gästrikland* (in Swedish). See description under the "Path Descriptions" for the Gästrikleden.
- *Ljusdals informationsfolder* (in Swedish). Includes a 1:40,000 map showing the Ljusnanleden. Free upon request from the Ljusdals Turistbyrå.

Further Information: Contact the Ljusdals Turistbyrå (see *Address Directory*).

Malingsbo-Kloten rundan

A circular path in the Malingsbo-Kloten Forest, in the province of Dalarna. The path winds past tree-rimmed lakes, alongside streams and over low hills from Malingsbo through Björsjö and Nyfors to Kloten, where it intersects with the Bergslagsleden, which stretches south to the Tiveden Forest on the shores of Lake Vättern. **Length:** 45 kilometers. **Walking Time:** 2 to 3 days. **Difficulty:** Easy. **Path Markings:** Yellow rings painted on trees and rocks.

Lodgings: Available in Kloten and Björsjö. There is also a campsite near Malingsbo and two huts located along the path—one between Malingsbo and Björsjö, and the other between Björsjö and Nyfors.

Maps:
- *Topografiska kartan över Malingsbo-Klotens friluftsområde,* sheet 11F *Lindesberg* nr 301. A special sheet showing footpaths and other recreational facilities. Available for a nominal charge from the Domänverket in Björsjö and the Malingsbo-Klotens Turistbyrå.

Path Description:
- *Malingsbo-Kloten* (available in Swedish, French, German and English). A forest service pamphlet describing the forest. Includes a sketch map showing marked footpaths, huts and other recreational facilities. Free upon request from the Domänverket in Björsjö and the Malingsbo-Klotens Turistbyrå.

Further Information: Contact the Domänverket i Björsjö nyttjandeförvaltning or the Malingsbo-Klotens Turistbyrå (see *Address Directory*).

Mostigen

From Söderhamn to Bocksjön in the province of Hälsingland. Through a lake-spangled forest. Eventually, the path will link up with the Hälsingeleden at Bollnäs. **Length:** 17 kilometers. **Walking Time:** 1 day. **Difficulty:** Easy to moderately difficult.

Lodgings: Available in Söderhamn and Bocksjön.
Maps:
• Topografiska kartan 1:50,000, sheets 14H *Soderhamn* NV and 15H *Hudiksvall* SV.
Path Description:
• *Vandra i Hälsingland och Gästrikland* (in Swedish). See description under the "Path Descriptions" for the Gästrikleden.
Further Information: Contact the Söderhamns Turistbyrå (see *Address Directory*).

Muddusleden

A circular route with an intersecting spur trail in Muddus National Park in Northern Lappland. Leads through virgin forest and marsh, past several lakes and along the edge of the rocky Muddusjokk Canyon, where the Muddus Waterfall plunges 42 meters in two stages. The park can be reached by taking the train to either Liggadammen/Jokkmokk or Nattavara, where local buses will take you to the outskirts of the park. **Length:** 50 kilometers. **Walking Time:** 2 days. **Difficulty:** Easy to moderately difficult. **Lodgings:** Four huts and one shelter are located along the path. The huts are open from the beginning of May until the beginning of October. To stay in the huts, you must have a sleeping bag and all your provisions.
Maps:
• Topografiska kartan 1:50,000, sheets 27J *Porjus* NO and SO, and 27K *Nattavara* NV and SV.
Path Description:
• *Muddus* (available in Swedish, French, German and English). A forest service pamphlet describing the park with a sketch map showing the locations of footpaths, huts and shelters. Free upon request from the Domänverket in Jokkmokk or the Jokkmokks Turistbyrå.
Further Information: Contact the Domänverket in Jokkmokk or the Jokkmokks Turistbyrå (see *Address Directory*).

Munkastigen

From Ramundeboda to Olshammar, on the shore of Lake Vättern, Sweden's second-largest lake. Passes through Tiveden Forest in Örebro County. Links up with the Bergslagsleden at Ramundeboda. **Length:** 50 kilometers. **Walking Time:** 2 to 3 days. **Difficulty:** Easy to moderately difficult.
Lodgings: Available in Laxå, 5 kilometers east of Ramundeboda. No lodgings are located along the path. Camping is necessary.
Maps:
• Topografiska kartan 1:50,000, one special sheet from 9E *Askersund: Karta över Laxå kommun*. Also sheets 10E *Karlstoga* SV and SO.
Path Description:
• A sketch map and brief route description in Swedish are available upon

request from the Laxå Kommuns fritidskontor. When ordering, ask for the *"stencil med översiktskarta"* and *"kort färdbeskrivning över Munkastigen."*
* *Tiveden* (available in Swedish, French, German and English). A forest service pamphlet describing the forest with a sketch map showing footpaths and other recreational facilities. Also available from the Laxå Kommuns fritidskontor.

Further Information: Contact the Laxå Kommuns fritidskontor (see *Address Directory*).

Nirraleden

From Gällivare to Nirra through an isolated region of forest and marsh laced with numerous streams in Northern Lappland. Altitudes are moderate, ranging between 360 and 550 meters. **Length:** 30 kilometers. **Walking Time:** 1 to 2 days. **Difficulty:** Easy to moderately difficult.

Lodgings: Huts are located in Gällivare and Nirra. There are also two huts along the path—Toppojärvistugan, 8 kilometers from Nirra, and Kojsjöstugan, 12 kilometers from Nirra—as well as hotels, a youth hostel and campsite in Gällivare.

Maps:
* *Topografiska kartan över Nirra fritidsområde/Leipir vildmark,* 1:50,000. A special sheet showing the Nirraleden and other nearby footpaths. Available for a nominal charge from the Gällivare Turistbyrå.

Path Description:
* In preparation. Information to aid you in walking the path can be obtained upon request from the Gällivare Turistbyrå.

Further Information: Contact the Gällivare Turistbyrå (see *Address Directory*).

Ostkustleden

A circular route beginning in Döderhult, a woodcarving center outside Oskarshamn on the east coast of Småland. The path is divided into eight sections of about 20 kilometers each. Overnight huts, which you can use for free, are located at the end of each section. Passes through a lovely, undulating region of forests, small villages and farms with numerous lakes and streams. Part of the route also follows the coast. The last day of the walk you pass through the 17th century village of Stensjö with its red-painted buildings, which is now owned by the Royal Society of Letters, History and Antiquities. The long-distance footpath Tjustleden intersects with the Ostkustleden at Mörtfors. From Oskarshamn, boats leave daily during the summer for the rocky island comprising Blå Jungfrun National Park, which can be explored only on foot. You can also go by boat from Oskarshamn to the island of Öland, noted for its picturesque windmills,

fragrant wildflowers, Viking burial sites and prehistoric forts. **Length:** 152 kilometers. **Walking Time:** 8 days. **Difficulty:** Easy.
Lodgings: Forest cottages are located along the route every 16 to 21 kilometers. The use of the cottages is free. Cooking facilities are provided in the cottages. You must, however, bring your own sleeping bag and food.
Maps:
• Topografiska kartan 1:50,000, sheets 6G *Vimmerby* SO, SV and NO; and 6H *Kråkelund* SV and SO.
Path Descriptions:
• *Kort information om Ostkustleden* (in Swedish). A small booklet with information on overnight lodgings, path markings, transportation, places where food can be bought and a list of useful telephone numbers. Includes brief route descriptions of each day's walk and a 1:200,000 sketch map showing the locations of forest cottages along the path as well as the locations of lakes, villages and other features of interest. Free upon request from the Oskarshamns Turistbyrå.
• *Vandringsguiden över Ostkustleden* (in Swedish). A 155-page guidebook with detailed route descriptions. Includes information on lodgings, transportation and points of interest enroute. Available for a nominal charge from the Döderhults naturskyddsförening.
Further Information: Contact the Oskarshamns Turistbyrå or the Döderhults naturskyddsförening (see *Address Directory*).

Pilgrimsleden

From Mellerud to Edsleskog in the province of Dalsland. Follows a portion of the ancient Pilgrim's Way, which stretches to Trondheim, Norway, through one of the most beautiful parts of Dalsland. Pine- and spruce-forested valleys scattered with lakes rise up to rocky highland plateaus where, in places, you can look out over Lake Vänern, Sweden's largest, and to the tree-clad shores of the Dalsland Canal. Can also be skied in winter. **Length:** 51 kilometers. **Walking Time:** 2 to 3 days. **Difficulty:** Easy to moderately difficult.
Lodgings: Available in Mellerud, Upperud and Håverud (off the path). No lodgings between Håverud and Edsleskog (34 kilometers). Rest places, however, are located every 5 to 10 kilometers along the path. Camping is possible.
Maps:
• Topografiska kartan 1:50,000, sheets 9C *Mellerud* SV and NV; and 10C *Åmål* SV.
Path Description:
• *Pilgrimsleden: Vandringsled genom norra Dalsland* (in Swedish). Gives brief information on the history, flora and points of interest along the path. Also gives brief information on hikes organized on the path each

year by Friluftsfrämjandet. Includes a 1:70,000 four-color sketch map with topographical contours showing the locations of telephones, restaurants, lodgings, rest places and ruins along the path. Free upon request from the Dalslands Turisttrafikförening.
Further Information: Contact the Dalslands Turisttrafikförening (see *Address Directory*).

Roslagsleden

From the northern suburbs of Stockholm to Domarudden in the province of Uppland; rich farming country with numerous historical sites, red-painted soldier's cottages, rune stones and quiet country churches, many with superb murals dating from the 15th century. Links up with the Blå leden long-distance footpath at Domarruden. **Length:** 56 kilometers. **Walking Time:** 2 to 3 days. **Difficulty:** Easy.
Lodgings: Available at Domarudden. There are also three wind shelters along the path. Camping is possible.
Map:
• Topografiska kartan 1:50,000, one special sheet: *Roslagsleden*. Available for a nominal charge from the Danderyds fritidskontor and Vaxholms fritidskontor.
Path Description:
• *Vandringsguiden över Roslagsleden* (in Swedish). A 10-page booklet with a route description and other information on the path. Comes with the 1:50,000 *Roslagsleden* map. Available for a nominal charge from the Danderyds fritidskontor and Vaxholms fritidskontor.
Further Information: Contact the Danderyds fritidskontor or the Vaxholms fritidskontor (see *Address Directory*).

Siljansleden

A long, meandering footpath encircling Lake Siljan and Lake Orsasjön in the Province of Dalarna. Can be started in Leksand, Rättvik, Mora or Orsa. Passes through a beautiful, wooded region with rocky gorges, waterfalls and old weathered farms. In Dalarna every parish has its own folk costumes, which also vary at specific times in the church year. At midsummer, flower-entwined maypoles are raised on every village green and the costumed villagers dance around them through the twilight night to the centuries-old music of the Dalecarlian fiddlers. On certain Sundays at Midsummer, people still row to church across Lake Siljan in the old church boats, direct descendants of the Viking longships. Numerous local footpaths fan out from towns enroute, such as Orsa and Rättvik. **Length:** 340 kilometers. **Walking Time:** 14 to 20 days. **Difficulty:** Easy to moderately difficult.
Lodgings: Available in Leksand, Rättvik, Mora and Orsa. There are also 26

wind shelters, 3 overnight huts, 6 campsites and 4 youth hostels along the path.
Maps:
* Topografiska kartan 1:50,000, five special sheets: *Siljansleden*, blad 1, blad 2, blad 3, blad 4 and blad 5. Available for a nominal charge from the Mora Turistbyrå.
Path Description:
* *Vandringsguiden över Siljansleden* (in Swedish). A 15-page guide with route descriptions and information on lodgings and access. Free upon request from the Mora Turistbyrå. A detailed guidebook is in preparation.
Further Information: Contact the Mora Turistbyrå (see *Address Directory*). Information on other footpaths in the area can be obtained from the Leksands Turistbyrå, Orsa Turistbyrå and the Rättviks Turistbyrå (see *Address Directory*).

Sjuvallsleden

From Delsbo to the coastal town of Hudiksvall in the province of Hälsingland. Through small villages and forests, across meadows and alongside small lakes. The path will eventually link up with the Ljusnanleden in Ljusdal. For now, it can be walked between Delsbo and Storberget. **Length:** When completed, 54 kilometers; 32 kilometers can currently be walked. **Walking Time:** For the completed section, 2 days. **Difficulty:** Easy to moderately difficult. **Path Markings:** Solid blue circles painted on trees.
Lodgings: Available in Hudiksvall and Deslbo. There are also five huts and two wind shelters along the path.
Map:
* Topografiska kartan 1:50,000, special sheet: *Sjuvallsleden*. Available for a nominal charge from the Hudiksvall Turistbyrå.
Path Descriptions:
* *Vandra i Hälsingland och Gästrikland* (in Swedish). See description under the "Path Descriptions" for the Gästrikleden.
* *Kolarstigen och Sjuvallsleden* (in Swedish). A brochure describing both the Kolarstigen and Sjuvallsleden outside Hudiksvall. Free upon request from the Hudiksvall Turistbyrå.
Further Information: Contact the Hudiksvall Turistbyrå (see *Address Directory*).

Skåneleden

From coast to coast across the province of Skåne in southernmost Sweden. The path stretches through orchards, golden fields and lake-spangled beech forests from Sölvesborg, a lovely old-world port city on the Baltic coast, to Torekov on the west coast. Opened in November, 1979, this is one of the most recent additions to Sweden's long-distance footpath network. It is divided into 17 sections of about 10 to 15 kilometers each. **Length:** 220 kilometers. **Walking Time:** 8 to 10 days. **Difficulty:** Easy. **Lodgings:** Available in most towns enroute. There are also several rest places and overnight shelters along the path. Details are contained in the *från kust till kust* folder listed below.

Maps:
* Topografiska kartan 1:50,000, sheets 3C *Helsingborg* NO; 3D *Kristianstad* NV and NO; 3D *Karlshamn* NV, SV and SO; and 4C *Halmstad* SV and SO.
* A series of six 1:100,000 topographical maps showing the path are included in the *från kust till kust* folder. These are sufficient to follow the path, although you may wish to supplement them with the 1:50,000 topografiska kartan which show greater detail.

Path Descriptions:
* *Från kust till kust* (in Swedish). A folder giving a brief description of Skåneleden. Includes information on access and lodgings, as well as six topographical map sheets showing the path. Free upon request from the tourist bureaus in Hässleholm, Kristianstad and Karlshamn.
* A Swedish-language guidebook to the footpath, with detailed route descriptions, maps and information on lodgings, access and points of interest enroute, was to have been published in November 1979. The guidebook may be purchased from most large bookstores, as well as from the tourist bureaus in Hässleholm, Kristianstad and Karlshamn. When ordering, ask for the *"Guiden över Skåneleden."*

Further Information: Contact the Hässleholms Turistbyrå, Kristianstads Turistbyrå or Karlshamns Turistbyrå (see *Address Directory*).

Sörmlandsleden

This is Sweden's longest footpath outside the mountains, arcing from Björkhagen, on the outskirts of Stockholm, to the town of Nyköping on the Södermanland coast. Passes through birch and pine forests, along the rocky shores of tree-rimmed lakes, over meadows rife with wildflowers and along ridges with sweeping views over the surrounding countryside. Enroute are several picturesque villages, the remains of Iron Age battlements, ancient burial cairns, rune stones and old iron ore mines. The path is divided into 41 sections. Portions of the path can also be skied in winter. **Length:** About 500 kilometers. **Walking Time:** 18 to 22 days. Day hikes are also possible on the path. **Difficulty:** Generally easy; some easy to moderately difficult sections.
Lodgings: Available in Tyresta, Paradiset, Lida, Tveta (youth hostel), Vattgruvan, St. Envättern, Fredriksberg, Skottvång, Finnsjön, Ånhammar, Malmköping, Hagtorp, Hälleforsnäs, Svalboviken, Vallmotorp, Strångsjö, Viggaren, Fagerön, Åbo, Stavsjö, Lövsjön, Brytsebo, Nävsjön, Nyköping

and Eskilstuna Vilsta (youth hostel). Longest distances between lodgings are between Björkhagen and Tyresta (27 kilometers), Lida and Tveta (27 kilometers), Svalboviken and Lundsjön (25 kilometers), Vallmotorp and Strångsjö (26 kilometers), and Nävsjön and Nyköping (27 kilometers). Other lodgings are located within 6 to 20 kilometers of each other. Details are given in the guidebook (listed below).

Maps:
* Sörmlandsleden topografiska kartor 1:50,000, sheets 1, 2, 3, 4, 5 and 6. Available from Liber Grafiska or Friluftsfrämjandet.

Path Descriptions:
* *Sörmlandsleden* (in Swedish). A comprehensive guidebook. Gives a full route description of the path, along with information on access, lodgings and points of interest. Available for a nominal charge from Friluftsfrämjandet.
* *Sörmlandsleden* (in Swedish). A pamphlet with a brief description of the path. Includes a list of locales on the path with the walking distances between each, information on transportation connections to and from each locale, the telephone numbers to call for bus schedule information, a notation of the type of lodgings found on or near the path (and, for some, the telephone numbers to call for reservations) and information on other facilities along the path. Also includes a sketch map and the addresses and telephone numbers of local tourist offices. Free upon request from the Södermanlands läns Landsting Turist- och Friluftsnämnd.

Further Information: Contact Friluftsfrämjandet or the Södermanlands läns Landsting Turist- och Friluftsnämnd (see *Address Directory*).

Tjustleden

From Mörtfors to Galdhammar through the northern part of Kalmar County in the province of Småland. The path links the long-distance footpath Ostkustleden, with the lovely Tjust archipelago, which encompasses almost 5,000 islands, islets and skerries on the Swedish coast north of Västervik. **Length:** About 160 kilometers. **Walking Time:** 6 to 8 days. **Difficulty:** Easy.

Lodgings: Rest places and storm shelters accommodating from 6 to 8 people are located at intervals of about 12 to 20 kilometers along the path. A sleeping bag and food are necessary to stay in the shelters.

Maps:
* Topografiska kartan 1:50,000, sheets 6G *Vimmerby* NO and 7G *Västervik* SO.

Path Description:
* A sketch map showing the path, access points and lodging possibilities is available free of charge from the Västerviks Turistbyrå. When ordering, ask for the *"siktskarta över Tjustleden."*

Further Information: Contact the Västerviks Turistbyrå (see *Address Directory*).

Vandring i utvandrarbygd

A circular footpath south of Lessebo in the province of Småland, beginning at Ljuder. The path winds through lake-spangled forests in the counties of Kronoberg and Kalmar, passing near several glassworks, some of the best known of which—Johansfors, Boda and Åfors—are located in the commune of Emmaboda. **Length:** 96 kilometers. **Walking Time:** 4 days. **Difficulty:** Easy.

Lodgings: Youth hostels are located in Ljuder, Korrö and Långasjö. There is also a pension at Sofielund.

Maps:
- Topografiska kartan 1:50,000, sheets 4F *Lessebo* NO, SV and SO.
- A 1:40,000 topographical map covering the path is included in the path description available from the Turism och Fritid i Kronoberg.

Path Description:
- *Vandring i utvandrarbygd* (in Swedish). A folder with a route description and information on access and lodgings. Includes a 1:40,000 topographical map showing the footpath. Free upon request from the Turism och Fritid i Kronoberg.

Further Information: Contact the Turism och Fritid i Kronoberg (see *Address Directory*).

Vättlefjällsleden

A circular path lying between the Göta älv canal and Lake Mjörn in the gently undulating countryside of Bohuslän, 15 kilometers from the center of Göteborg on Sweden's west coast. The path circles through Dammekärr, Jennylund, Vallarne and Lövgärdet in a region of beech forest and heathland. **Length:** 29 kilometers. **Walking Time:** 1 to 2 days. **Difficulty:** Easy.

Lodgings: Huts with showers are located in Dammekärr and Jennylund. A sleeping bag is necessary to stay in the huts.

Maps:
- An orienteering map in a scale of 1:20,000, published by OK Alehof, a local orienteering club, covers the path. The map can be purchased from Kartcentrum in Göteborg (see *Address Directory*). When ordering, ask for the "*orienteringskarta i skala 1:20,000 över vandringsleder i Vättlefjäll.*"

Path Descriptions:
- *Vandra i Vättlefjäll* and *Vandringsleder i Ale* (both in Swedish). Two folders describing walking opportunities in the region between the Göta älv canal and Lake Mjörn. Free upon request from the Västkustens Turistråd and the Ale Fritidsnämnd.

Further Information: Contact the Ale Fritidsnämnd (see *Address Directory*).

Vildmarksleden

From Skatås to Hindås outside the city of Göteborg on Sweden's west coast. Passes through virgin forest and heathland amid a varying scenery of granite rock formations, beech woods and lakes. **Length:** 44 kilometers. **Walking Time:** 2 days. **Difficulty:** Easy.

Lodgings: Available in Hindås. There are also two wind shelters located along the path. Camping is possible.

Maps:

• Topografiska kartan 1:50,000, sheets 7B *Göteborg* NV and NO, and 7C *Borås* NV.

Path Description:

• A folder in Swedish with a brief route description and 1:15,000 and 1:25,000 topographical maps covering the path is available for a nominal charge from the Västkustens Turistråd and the two organizations listed below. When ordering, ask for the *"foldern över Vildmarksleden."*

Further Information: Contact the Upplysningar lämnas även av Fritid Centrum or Göteborgs Fritidsförvaltning (see *Address Directory*).

Sweden's National Parks

Sweden's 16 national parks were created to preserve large areas in their natural state for research and recreation. Together, the parks cover an area of 6,150 square kilometers (2,374 square miles) and encompass areas as vastly different from each other as coastal islands, former farmlands and untracked wilds with jagged peaks and extensive glaciers. Many of the parks have marked footpaths and shelters which are maintained by the *Domänverket*—the Swedish Forest Service. But some, such as Sarek, are completely isolated and difficult to both reach and cross.

A series of brochures with a description of the geology, flora, fauna and recreation opportunities in each park are published by the Forest Service and Statens Naturvårdstverk. These include maps showing the routes of footpaths, principal topographical features and the locations of huts and other shelters within the parks. Many of the brochures have been translated into English, French and German, although some are only available in Swedish. The brochures, plus additional information on Sweden's national parks, can be obtained from:

Domänverkets naturvårdssektion (Swedish Forest Service, Nature Conservation Section). See *Address Directory*.

or:

Statens Naturvårdsverk (National Environmental Protection Board). See *Address Directory*.

Abisko

Located south of Lake Torneträsk in Northern Lappland, the gateway to the mountains and the starting point for the Kungsleden. The park encompasses the valley of the Abiskojåkka with its rocky canyon, as well as part of Lake Torneträsk and the island of Abiskosuolo. About one-third of the park is barren rock, but the greater part is characterized by vegetation typical of the birchwood belt. The highest peak within the park is 1,174-meter Slåttatjåkka, although the best known is 1,163-meter Njulla, from the top of which the Midnight Sun is visible from the first night of June until the middle of July. It is light in the park from the beginning of May to the middle of August, while the arctic night, when the sun never rises above

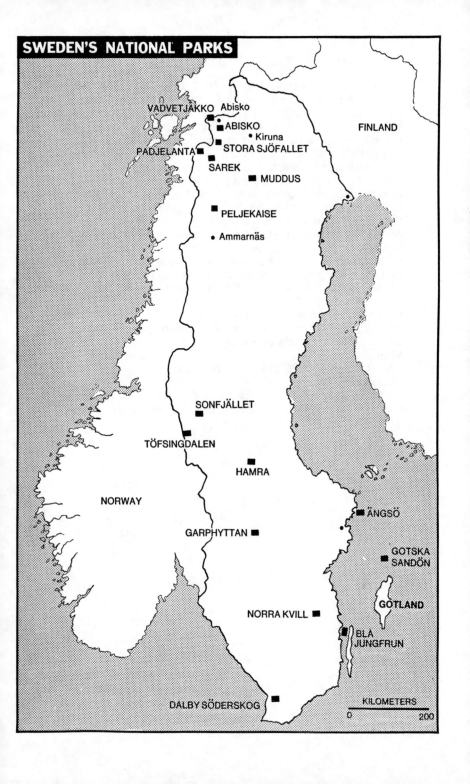

the horizon, lasts from about December 5 to January 9. The arctic night, however, is by no means pitch dark; the snow lights up the landscape, and the twilight, the moon and stars and the flaming, vividly colored northern lights shine with a strange brilliance from typically clear skies. Lying in a rain shadow, Abisko has the lowest annual precipitation in Sweden—only 298 mm (12 inches). Birch woods, with some pines, cover the valley along with a rich mountain vegetation, the rarest species of which is *Platanthera parvula*. Among the many species of birds in the park are the arctic warbler which comes from India and Indonesia by way of China to its breeding grounds on the north slope of Njulla.

Area: 7,500 hectares (18,532 acres).

Access: By train to Abisko station from either Stockholm or Narvik, Norway.

Footpaths: In addition to the Kungsleden, several other paths run through the park, leading along the shores of Lake Torneträsk, up both sides of the Abiskojokk canyon, alongside the Pallenjåkka brook, and to several mountain regions outside the park.

Lodgings: The Abisko mountain section is located on the northern edge of the park in sight of the train station. A mountain hut is also located at the southern edge of the lake of Abiskojaure.

Maps:
• Nya Fjällkartan 1:100,000, sheets BD 5 and BD 6.

Guidebooks:
• *Fjäll '81* (in Swedish). Published annually by the STF.
• *Kungsleden och 13 angränsande turer* (in Swedish). Also published by the STF.

Ängsö

A small island located off the coast of Uppland, northeast of Stockholm. The park consists of green, flowering meadows surrounded by copses of leafy decidous trees, conifer woodland, bare grassland and a cottage with farm buildings and some cultivated land. There are also two lakes on the island. Red deer, martens and foxes live on the island, and the gryfalcon occasionally visits the island. The most notable floral species is the elderflowered orchid.

Area: 75 hectares (185 acres).
Access: By boat from Stockholm.
Footpaths: The entire island can be explored on foot. Several well-established tracks crisscross the island, leading past its lakes, across meadows and through forests to inlets and bays on its shore. No motorized vehicles are allowed on the island.
Lodgings: None.
Map:
• Topografiska kartan 1:50,000, sheet 11J *Norrtälje* SV.
Guidebook:
• Forest Service pamphlet, *Ängsö.*

Blå Jungfrun

A red granite island located between Oskarshamm and the northern tip of Öland off the coast of Småland. Most of the park is bare rock, in the cracks of which spring pasque flowers bloom. Huge boulders are scattered throughout the southern part of the island. Pine, spruce and birch grow in crevices, and the southern slope of Toppen (86.5 meters) is covered with dense oak woods. Numerous species of mosses and lichens are found on the rocks. The island also has several caves.

Area: 66 hectares (163 acres).
Access: By boat from Oskarshamn.
Footpaths: Several footpaths loop around the shore of the island, winding between boulders, over Toppen and through wooded areas.
Lodgings: None.
Map:
• Topografiska kartan 1:50,000, sheet 5H *Borgholm* NV.
Guidebook:
• Forest Service pamphlet, *Blå Jungfrun.*

Dalby Söderskog

Located near Lund in Skåne, Sweden's southernmost province. The park encompasses a beautiful stand of mixed deciduous trees. During the

spring, the ground is covered with numerous flowers, chief among these being the early purple orchids, wood anemone, yellow anemone and *Corydalis cava*.
Area: 36 hectares (89 acres).
Access: By bus from Lund to the village of Dalby. The park is a short walk from the town.
Footpaths: Several short footpaths lead through the park.
Lodgings: Nearest lodgings are in Dalby.
Maps:
• Topografiska kartan 1:50,000, sheets 2C *Malmö* NO or SO.
Guidebook:
• Forest Service pamphlet, *Dalby Söderskog*.

Garphyttan

Located in the Province of Närke, about 20 kilometers west of the town of Örebro. The park was established to preserve an area of cultivated land and consists of old holdings belonging to iron masters' houses on the south slopes of Mount Kilsbergen. Copses of deciduous and coniferous trees alternate with old hayfields, small gardens, common grazing lands and charcoal woods.
Area: 108 hectares (276 acres).
Access: By bus from Örebro to the village of Garphyttan. The park is about a 5-kilometer walk from the village.
Footpaths: Several short footpaths lead through the park's woodlands and fields. A portion of the long-distance footpath Bergslagsleden also passes through the edge of the park.
Lodgings: Available in Suttarboda, a small settlement about one kilometer north of the park on Bergslagsleden.
Map:
• Topografiska kartan 1:50,000, sheet 10E *Karlskoga* SO.
Guidebooks:
• Forest Service pamphlet, *Garphyttan*.
• *Bergslagsleden: Etapp 10 Ånnaboda—Suttarboda* (in Swedish). A route description and black and white reproduction of the 1:50,000 topografiska kartan covering the 7-kilometer section of Bergslagsled which passes through the park. Free upon request from the Örebro läns Turistnämnd (see *Address Directory*).

Gotska Sandön

An isolated island in the Baltic Sea north of Gotland. The island consists primarily of sand dunes bounded by practically untouched pine woods. Owing to the island's extreme climate and the wealth of dry and dying trees, the beetle fauna is richer here than anywhere else in Sweden. Several species of orchids grow on the island. Old rusting cannons, an ancient mausoleum and old burial stones are also found on the island. Swedish groups must obtain special permission to visit the island. Foreign visitors are not allowed entry.

Area: 3,640 hectares (8,944 acres).

Guidebook:
• Forest Service pamphlet, *Gotska Sandön* (only available in Swedish).

Hamra

Located in the province of Dalarna in the region known as Orsa Finnmark. Although this is one of Sweden's smallest national parks, it is surrounded by extensive forest reserves which contain remarkable stands of virgin forest. The park encompasses the oldest pines, which grew up after a great forest fire in the 1690s. Spruce trees did not survive the fire, but have reappeared and are now competing with the pines.

Area: 27 hectares (67 acres).

Access: Highway 81, leading from Orsa on Lake Orsasjön to Sveg in the province of Härjedalen, passes the park. The nearest settlement is Tandsjöborg, located halfway between Orsa and Sveg. Buses run regularly between the two towns.

Footpaths: The park contains several short, local paths.

Lodgings: None.

Map:
• Topografiska kartan 1:50,000, sheet 15E *Älvho* NO.

Guidebook:
• Forest Service pamphlet, *Hamra*.

Muddus

Located east of Porjus (between the towns of Jokkmokk and Gällivare) in Northern Lappland. The park encompasses a large, uninterrupted area of virgin forest and marsh, several lakes and rocky canyons. In the canyon of the Muddusjokk, the Muddus waterfall plunges 42 meters (138 feet) in two stages. In the center of the park is a bird sanctuary, to which entrance is forbidden from March 15 to July 31. The large Sjaunja Bird Sanctuary lies outside the park to the west. Bears, martens, reindeer, otters and moose are seen in the park, as well as golden eagles, capercaillies, whooper swans, ospreys and bean geese.

Area: 49,200 hectares (121,573 acres).

Access: By train to Liggadammen/Jokkmokk or Nattavara. Local buses take you to within walking distance of the park.

Footpaths: There are several marked paths in the southern part of the park, including the long-distance footpath Muddusleden, which leads up the western side of the Muddusjokk canyon. Another footpath leads over several streams above the shores of Lake St. Luleäv. Altitudes are moderate, ranging between 250 and 660 meters.

Lodgings: Five huts and two shelters are located along paths in the southern part of the park.

Maps:
- Topografiska kartan 1:50,000, sheets 27J *Porjus* SO and NO, and 27K *Nattavara* SV and NV.

Guidebook:
- Forest Service pamphlet, *Muddus.*

Norra Kvill

Located in the province of Östergötland at the eastern edge of Småland highlands, about 10 kilometers from the village of Österbymo. The park encompasses a stretch of primeval coniferous forest, which includes numerous 200- to 300-year-old pine trees. The most impressive approach to the park is from the north through the steep country northwest of Idegölen.

Area: 27 hectares (67 acres).

Access: By train to Tranås. By bus to Österbymo and the outskirts of the park.

Footpaths: Several short, local paths lead through the park.

Lodgings: None. A youth hostel is located in Österbymo.

Map:
- Topografiska kartan 1:50,000, sheet 7F *Tranås* SO.

Guidebook:
- Forest Service pamphlet, *Norra Kvill.*

Padjelanta

Located in the mountains of Northern Lappland between Sarek National Park and the Swedish-Norwegian border. This is the largest national park in Europe. It is a wide open mountain plain with large lakes and occasional high mountains. Only in two places does the park extend down into the birch forest. Botanically, it is regarded as one of the most valuable in Sweden, with species of plants not found anywhere else in Sweden— the creeping sandwort, arctic cinquefoil and the pale gentian, for instance. Padjelanta has been used for centuries as summer pasture for reindeer, and Lapps have their summer quarters in several places in the park. Other animals found in the park include bear, lemming, polar fox and wolverine. Bird life includes the gyrfalcon, hooded crow, song thrush, dunnock, garden warbler and grey shrike. Mountaineering skill is not essential for a visit to the park, but first-class equipment, including all your provisions, should be carried. Some waters in the park may be fished for food, but a license is required. No fish may be taken out of the park.

Area: 201,000 hectares (496,671 acres).

Access: By train to Gällivare, then by bus to the Ritsen mountain station and by boat to Vaisaluokta or Änonjalme. A marked footpath leads from the Vaisaluokta mountain hut into the park.

Footpaths: The footpath from Vaisaluokta leads south through Staloluokta to Staddajåkk. From Staddajåkk, the path can be followed into the Sulitjelma mountain region of Norway. A second path branches off to the east from Staloluokta, leading eventually to Kvikkjokk. From Vaisaluokta, it takes about seven days to walk to Sulitjelma in Norway and about 10 days to walk to Kvikkjokk.

Lodgings: Mountain huts and shelters operated by the STF and Naturvårdsverk are located at regular intervals along the paths between Vaisaluokta and the Sulitjelma mountain region in Norway, and between Stalolukta and Kvikkjokk.

Maps:
• Nya Fjällkartan 1:100,000, sheets BD 9 and BD 12.

Guidebooks:
• *Fjäll '81* (in Swedish). Available from the STF (see *Address Directory*).
• *Kungsleden och 13 angränsande turer* (in Swedish). Also available from the STF.
• *Sarek, Stora Sjöfallet, Padjelanta: Three National Parks in Swedish Lappland* (in English; also available in Swedish and German) by Kai Curry-Lindahl. Does not include footpath descriptions. Available from the STF.
• Forest Service pamphlet: *Sarek, Padjelanta, Stora Sjöfallet.*

Pieljekaise

Located just below the Arctic Circle on the south and west slopes of 1,122-meter Mount Peljekaise in Southern Lappland. The park is covered primarily with birch woods and has a rich variety of ground cover ranging from herbs to heaths. It also includes a part of Lake Sädvajaure. Its flora and fauna are typical of most Lappland mountain regions within the birch belt. Mountaineering skill is not required to explore the park, although good equipment should be carried.

Area: 14,600 hectares (36,076 acres).

Access: By train to Arvidsjaure and by bus to Hällbacken, Adolfström or Jäckvik.

Footpaths: A 15-kilometer section of Kungsleden leads through the park between Jäckvik and Adolfström. No other marked footpaths exist in the park, although there are some unmarked tracks.

Lodgings: Available in Hällbacken, Adolfström and Jäckvik. There are no lodgings within the park.

Map:
• Nya Fjällkartan 1:100,000, sheet BD 16.
Guidebooks:
• *Fjäll '81* (in Swedish). Available from the STF (see *Address Directory*).
• *Kungsleden och 13 angränsande turer* (in Swedish). Also available from the STF.
• Forest Service pamphlet, *Peljekaise.*

Sarek

Europe's single largest remaining wild area; located west of Gällivare in the mountains of Northern Lappland. In no other area of Sweden are there so many jagged peaks, wide mountain plateaus or glaciers. From Sarek's mountain slopes one looks out over narrow valleys laced with the winding silver ribbons of mighty rivers, glittering lakes at several levels, and to white peaks with hanging glaciers and innumerable brooks rushing in torrents down their slopes. Veritable jungles of willow make parts of its valleys almost impenetrable, and wide heaths, covered with willow, shrubs, mosses and lichens, spread out in undulating waves above the tree limit. The park contains all the mountain vegetation zones, plus an abundant fauna which includes bear, reindeer, wolverine, lemming, polar fox, mountain elk, moose, lynx, golden eagle, rough-legged buzzard, dotterel, snow bunting, long-tailed skua and snipe. Sarek contains 96 glaciers, the largest of which—Pårtejekna—covers an area of 11 square kilometers. The second largest, 12 square-kilometer Ålmijekna, lies mostly in neighboring Padjelanta National. Eight peaks in the park top 1,850 meters (6,000 feet), and three exceed 2,000 meters (6,560 feet). The highest of these is 2,089-meter Sarektjåkko. There are few facilities of any kind in the park except a few unmarked tracks and bridges and a scattering of Lapp huts, none of which are open to the public. Those who hike in Sarek must be entirely self-sufficient and able to navigate across rough terrain with a map and compass. You must also be experienced in fording cold, swiftly flowing streams and prepared for erratic and sometimes severe weather.
Area: 194,000 hectares (479,374 acres).
Access: Paths lead toward Sarek in several directions from the Kvikkjokk mountain station. One track leads westward along the Tarra Valley to Tarreluobbal and onto Virihaure and Vastenjaure. Another track leads northwest along the Kamajokk—whose extensive delta, Änok, is a congregating spot for migratory birds—to the Tjuolta Valley, where the largest uninterrupted stretch of birch forest, with enormous boulder fields, is found. A third track leads to the north over lakes and marshes to Lake Pårekjaure. Finally, the Kungsleden leads northeast to the mountain hut at Aktse, where the Rapa Valley, with its wide delta lands, runs into the high mountain country, perhaps the most magnificent entrance to the heart of Sarek. Several other access routes are also possible—from the Ritjemokk

mountain station by boat to the Akka mountain hut, then by foot to the northwest corner of the park, or by boat from the Sitojaure mountain hut on the Kungsleden, for instance.

Footpaths: There is only one marked footpath on the southeast edge of the park—the Kungsleden. A few unmarked tracks lead into the park and several wander through its valleys, but these often disappear when they cross marshy or rocky areas. To hike in Sarek you must be prepared to travel cross-country.

Lodgings: None.

Map:
- Nya Fjällkartan 1:100,000, sheet BD 10.

Guidebooks:
- *Detta är Sarek* (in Swedish) by Tore Abrahamsson, Rabén & Sjörgen. Available from the STF (see *Address Directory*).
- *Vandra i Sarek* (in Swedish) by Svante Lindgren, Norstedts, Stockholm. Also available from STF.
- *De vilda djurens Sarek* (in Swedish) by Edvin Nilsson, Bonniers, Stockholm. Available from the STF.
- *Sarek, Stora Sjöfallet, Padjelanta: Three National Parks in Swedish Lappland* (in English; also available in Swedish and German) by Kai Curry-Lindahl, Rabén & Sjögren, Stockholm. Available from the STF.

Sånfjället

Located in the province of Härjedalen, south of the villages of Hede and Hedeviken. The park is one of the most populous bear districts in Sweden. Surrounded on all sides by dense forest, the park has a magnificent canyon and a well-developed system of overflow channels formed by the melting inland glaciers. The highest peak, Sånfjället, rises above the tree limit to 1,277 meters. Small lakes in the park reflect the peak and provide a habitat for several species of waders.

Area: 2,700 hectares (6,672 acres).

Access: By train to Sveg and by bus to Hede or Hedeviken. A road leads south from Hedeviken to Rånddalen, passing within one kilometer of the park. You can hike into the park from the road or on a path from Skärsjövålen.

Footpaths: There are several marked paths in the park.

Lodgings: Available in Hede. There are no lodgings in the park.

Map:
- Nya Fjällkartan 1:50,000, one sheet, *Sånfjallet*.

Guidebook:
- Forest Service Pamphlet, *Sonfjället*.

Stora Sjöfallet

This is the third of three contiguous Lappland national parks that together make up Europe's largest protected wilderness. It consists of high glaciated mountains rising to 2,015 meters around the source lakes of the Stora Lule River. The park stretches across the alpine belt from the upper coniferous forest region in the east, spanning the full range of Sweden's mountain vegetation zones. In the lower reaches of the Vietasvagge Valley is a virgin pine forest considered to be one of the most magnificent of its kind in Sweden. It has existed and developed for about 7,000 years and is a western outpost of the mighty Eurasian taiga, the most extensive forest in the world. The northernmost part of the park was, until 1967, bounded by a chain of lakes which was destroyed by damming. The countryside around the lakes is still attractive, but the remarkable series of aquatic faunas, once different in each lake, was destroyed. The heart of the national park is the Stora Lule River with Stora Sjöfället—the Great Waterfall—and the Vietasvagge Valley between lakes Satisjaure and Langas. The Great Waterfall formerly broke through a remarkable geological formation of so-called Sjöfall sandstone between lakes Kårtjejaure and Langas, stretching across the entire width of the valleys in a series of five falls. The main fall and some of the lateral falls still remain, but they do not compare to the power of the once-free Stora Sjöfället, although the stored waters behind the falls are sometimes released during the summer tourist season and the Great Waterfall is briefly restored to its former grandeur. Below the steep slopes of Mount Nieras is a geologically remarkable glaciofluvial plain, a treeless haunt of whimbrels, golden plovers and short-eared owls. East of the park is the Sjauna Bird Sanctuary, one of the largest wetland areas in Europe, with its sand marshes, lakes, thin spruce woods and low mountains (441 to 1,720 meters). The sanctuary is the breeding area for the bean goose, whooper swan, osprey, white-tailed eagle, golden eagle, jacksnipe, spotted redshank, broad-billed sandpiper, red-throated pipit and rustic bunting. The bear, lynx and very scarce wolf range through the sanctuary and into the primeval forests on the northeastern shore of Lake Satisjaure.

Area: 138,000 hectares (340,998 acres).

Access: By train to Gällivare. Buses take you from Gällivare to Vietas, near the Great Waterfall, and to Ritsen at the western edge of the park. The road opens up a very instructive cross section of the coniferous forest of Lappland as it passes along the shores of Stora Lulevatten, through the Sjaunja Bird Sanctuary and across a magnificent primeval landscape, where the ancient virgin forest along the Lulejaure and Langas rises gently to greater heights, leading finally into the mountains.

Footpaths: Several marked footpaths, including a portion of Kungsleden, lead through the park between the mountain stations and huts inside and on the perimeter of the park. There are also several unmarked tracks which can be followed by experienced walkers.

Lodgings: The Ritsen station is located outside the park and the Saltoluokta mountain station is located on its southeastern edge. There are two mountain huts—Vakkotavare and Sjöfallet—located in the park, and three huts on its perimeter, including the Kisuris mountain hut in Padjelanta National Park.

Maps:
• Nya Fjällkartan 1:100,000, sheets BD 7, BD 8 and BD 10.

Guidebooks:
• *Fjäll '81* (in Swedish). Available from the STF (see *Address Directory*).
• *Kungsleden: vägar och vandrigar* (in Swedish). Also available from the STF.
• *Sarek, Stora Sjöfallet, Padjelanta: Three National Parks in Swedish Lappland* (in English; also available in Swedish and German) by Kai Curry-Lindahl, Rabén & Sjögren, Stockholm. Does not contain footpath descriptions. Available from STF.
• Forest Service pamphlet: *Sarek, Padjelanta, Stora Sjöfallet.*

Töfsingdalen

Located near the Norwegian border in the province of Dalarna. The park consists of virgin forests of spruce and pine growing on bouldery and hummocky terrain formed by the inland ice, in the most southerly part of the Swedish mountains. The stony land which dominates the park constitutes some of the wildest country in Sweden. Beasts of prey roam over the park and birds of prey, such as the golden eagle, glide overhead. Herbs dominate its flora. Next to Sarek and Vådvetjakko, Töfsingdalen is the most difficult park in Sweden to reach and cross. Walkers who do so must be well equipped and physically fit.

Area: 1,365 hectares (3,373 acres).

Access: By train to Mora. By bus via Idre to the mountain station at Grövelsjön. A marked path leads across the Långfjället mountain region to the Forest Service fishing cottage at Hävlingen. The park is located on the opposite shore of Lake Hävingen and Storån River from the fishing cottage. From the cottage you can cross over to the park by bridge.

Footpaths: A marked footpath leads through the northern edge of the park between the Domänverket fishing cottage and the Storrödtjärn mountain hut (10 kilometers). Travel elsewhere in the park must be done cross-country with a map and a compass.

Lodgings: The only lodgings near the park are the Grövelsjön mountain station (12 kilometers distant) and the huts at Hävingen and Storröftjärn, south and north of the park. Neither of the huts sell food; you must carry all your provisions.

Map:
• Nya Fjällkartan 1:100,000, sheet Z 9.

Guidebooks:
- *Fjäll '81* (in Swedish). Available from the STF (see *Address Directory*).
- Forest Service pamphlet, *Töfsingsdalen.*

Vådvetjåkka

Located on the Norwegian border northwest of Lake Torneträsk in Northern Lappland; Sweden's northernmost national park. The park encompasses a wild, untouched Arctic region surrounding Mount Vådvetjåkka. The southern part of the park is a broad plain covered with lakes, willow thickets and mires, the haunt of a rich variety of bird life. Different kinds of heather, alpine clubmoss and black bearberry grow in the park, as well as a variety of scrub heaths and grass heaths, which are studded with melancholy thistles, stitchworts and campions. The park is difficult to reach and cross and should only be entered by experienced mountain walkers who are able to navigate cross-country with a map and compass and are carrying all of their provisions and suitable equipment for camping.

Area: 2,450 hectares (6,054 acres).

Access: By train to the Abisko mountain station and by boat to the Pålnoviken hut, or by train to Tornehamm and by foot along a marked track to the hut (8 kilometers). The park is about five kilometers west of the Pålnoviken hut.

Footpaths: There are no marked tracks in or leading to the park.

Lodgings: Three mountain huts are located within 10 kilometers of the borders of the park—two primitive unstaffed huts in Norway, both of which are kept locked and for which keys must be obtained (see the chapter on Norway), and the Pålnoviken hut, which has six beds and an emergency telephone. There are no lodgings or shelter in the park.

Map:
- Nya Fjällkartan 1:100,000, sheet BD 5.

Guidebooks:
- *Fjäll '81* (in Swedish). Available from STF (see *Address Directory*).
- Forest Service pamphlet, *Vådvetjakko.*

Forest Reserves

Sweden has numerous State Forest Reserves scattered the length and breadth of the country, many of which have marked footpaths and huts maintained by the Domänverket. Pamphlets describing these areas with sketch maps showing the locations of footpaths and huts are available upon request from Sverek and the Domänverkets naturvårdssektion (see *Address Directory*). Local tourist offices can also provide information on the State Forest Reserves and other forest areas with marked footpaths in their vicinities.

Götaland
(Southern Sweden)

This region encompasses the eight southernmost provinces in Sweden plus the Baltic Sea islands of Gotland and Öland. Once the home of the Goths, Götaland is a treasury of archeological remains, small villages, sandy bays and gentle forest-clad heights that look out over the region's glittering array of lakes, fertile agricultural lands and graceful manor houses. Numerous short footpaths fan out into the surrounding countryside from villages and towns. There are also marked footpaths in Götaland's three national parks and 20 Crown Forests, as well as 11 long-distance footpaths ranging in length up to 220 kilometers. In winter, cross-country ski tracks, many of which are illuminated, lead through forests and across frozen lakes from more than 200 localities.

Lodgings are rarely far away. Götaland has more youth hostels than any other part of Sweden, and there are numerous old villages where you can stay in quaint inns and hotels. Or, if you prefer, you can camp.

The Götaland scenery is not as rugged as in the far north, but it is no less appealing and, on the whole, much more varied. Some examples:

Bohuslän & Halland. These two west coast provinces comprise one huge archeological museum. Their coasts are littered with ship burial sites from Viking times, grave fields, cairns and cromlechs, as well as Bronze Age rock carvings, ancient fortresses and quaint little churches. The Bohuslän coastline is characterized by granite rocks and promontories rising above small sandy coves, while the Halland coast has great sweeping bays of silver sand, wind-sculpted dunes and a shallow foreshore. There is only one large town along the coastline—Göteborg. The remaining towns are small, and many are old fishing villages now devoted to yachting. Inland is a gentle countryside of lakes, woods, heathland and small towns where traditional handicrafts are still pursued. One of the most interesting walks in the province is the Lax-marschen—

the Salmon March—held each year at the end of May in the town of Falkenberg. Numerous walking tours are also organized from Göteborg by the Västkustens Turisttrafikförbund (see *Address Directory*), including spring and autumn hikes on the Vildsmarksleden and Vättlefjällsleden long-distance footpaths.

Dalsland. This tiny province, lying between the Norwegian border and Lake Vänern, is often called "Sweden in miniature." It has more than 1,000 lakes, many of which are long, deep and fjord-like. Above the lakes rise wooded hills with rocky plateaus, from which you can look out over the province's winding valleys and waterways and the Dalsbo plains in the south and southeast. The biological borderline between the north and south Swedish landscape crosses Dalsland, and each contributes its characteristic fauna—an aspect that has long attracted biologists to the province. For walkers, two attractions are the Pilgrimsleden (long-distance footpath) and Kroppefjäll Forest, a hilly region of deep forests and tiny fish-filled lakes crisscrossed with paths marked with yellow rings painted on trees and rocks. It was across Kroppefjäll that King Charles XII and his veterans marched on their way to their last campaign in Norway, a route that can still be followed on foot. Despite its history, much of the forest remains wild with areas difficult to penetrate, home of deer and elk. The province is also crossed by the hill-bound Dalsland Canal (said to be one of the world's prettiest by Roger Pilkington, the English canal expert), which connects Lake Vänern with the Norwegian canal and lake system and, eventually, the North Sea.

Gotland & Öland. These two Baltic Sea islands have a warm, sunny climate and a landscape fragrant with wild flowers and alive with bird-song. Öland is a narrow strip of land, 140 kilometers long and 16 kilometers across at its widest point, with a hinterland of treeless, limestone plains carpeted with flowers, including 30 species of wild orchids. Nearly 400 windmills dot the island, and many Viking burial sites, rune stones and 16 prehistoric forts are hidden among its quiet meadows. There are bird sanctuaries all along the coast, the southernmost of which is one of the largest ornithological stations in Europe. Footpaths are few on the island, but you can wander at heart's content on its back roads, over its stone-wall fields and along the coast.

Gotland has nearly 400 kilometers of coastline with small coves, sandy beaches and cliff formations known as *raukar*, which serve as nesting sites for guillemots and razorbills. Like Öland, it has numerous prehistoric remains, plus the ancient Hanseatic city of Visby—the city of ruins and roses—and more than 90 medieval churches with lovely frescoes.

Östergötland. This province is composed of fertile farmlands, rocky seacoast archipelagos and forests where one finds manor estates, castles, tiny cottages and smithies. In its flat country are large farms surrounded by trees and straight rows of wheat, corn, rape and rye, as well as rows of ancient sacrificial stones, Iron Age burial sites and rune stones. Steeper terrain lies to the west, toward Lake Vättern, where Norra Kvill National Park and the Omberg Forest—with its lakeside precipices, flower-strewn meadows and forest paths—are located. Altogether, there are 35,000 registered ancient relics in the province, as well as the Kindaleden long-distance footpath and more than 40 marked cross-country ski tracks, 26 of which are illuminated.

Skåne & Blekinge. Skåne is the most important and most fertile agricultural province in Sweden. Along its coastline (which stretches around the southern tip of Sweden for more than 500 kilometers), clear blue waters lap against white sands. Inland there are rolling hills covered with swaying, golden grain, orchards that burst into a sea of blossoms in spring, wooded ridges and more than 200 chateaus and manor houses with meticulously kept grounds. At local inns you can sample the region's food delicacies: smörgåsbord and eel—smoked, baked, stewed or fixed in any number of a hundred different ways. You might also see a sign in the châteaux gardens which reads *Gå gärna på graset*—please walk on the grass—a good indication of the type of hospitality you are likely to encounter in the province. Numerous country lanes and short footpaths wander through beech forests graced with small lakes and ponds and tree-shrouded cascades in the northern part of the province. For longer walks, there is the 220-kilometer Skåneleden which stretches from coast to coast across the province. Blekinge, snuggling in the southeast corner of Sweden, is of less interest to the walker, although it has several short footpaths leading to lakes and streams in its forests and meadows, including the 15-kilometer Kongs Lÿden.

Småland. The province of Småland is an area of primeval forests, swamps and meadows, glacial moraines, cottage industries and—as might be expected in Sweden—lakes. The province is the center of the Swedish glass industry. The glass works, both large and small, are scattered throughout the woods and produce some of the world's most exquisite handblown glass. Near Nässjö, in the county of Jönköpings (capital of the Swedish match industry), are the Småland Highlands, where rift valleys expose sedimentary bedrocks and 300-year-old pine forests grow, a region traversed by the Höglandsleden long-distance footpath (described in the section on *Sweden's Lond-Distance Foothpaths*). Four other long-distance footpaths—Holavedsleden, Ostkustleden, Tjustleden and Vandring i utvandrarbygd—wind through the Småland countryside. Many other marked woodland paths are also found throughout the province. In addition, there are more than 125 marked cross-country ski tracks, which are used as keep-fit trails during the summer.

Västergötland. More than half this province is made up of flat-topped mountains, wooded country, fens and water. It borders the largest lakes in Sweden—Lake Vänern to the west and Lake Vättern to the east—and has Sweden's densest moose population. Among its hills are remote, inaccessible ravines, swamps and steppe-like heaths rich in vegetation. Numerous marked footpaths wind through its sparsely populated forests, taking you past waterfalls and leafy meadows. And if you are in the province in April, you can go to Lake Hornborga to see the "crane dance," when more than 5,000 cranes alight on the lake in the course of migration. The other half of the province is a gentle, undulating landscape of river valleys rich in prehistoric remains and peaceful old villages. The province is the oldest inhabited area in Sweden and contains no fewer than 290 of the country's 380 chambered tumuli—family graves from the Stone Age—plus more than 500 churches dating back to the 13th century or before, and numerous medieval castles and manor houses. There are also marked cross-country tracks near many villages and towns in winter.

Useful Addresses

See *Address Directory*:

Bohuslan & Halland

Västkustens Turisttrafikförbund. Provides general tourist and hiking information on the Swedish West Coast. Also arranges walking tours. Staff speaks Swedish, English and German. Useful publications available from the office include:

- *What's on on the West Coast of Sweden* (in English). A mimeographed sheet listing activities in Göteborg and organized group hikes on the west coast. More detailed information on each hike, including length, accommodation facilities, dates and cost, is available upon request.
- *Lax-Marschen* (in English). Gives details on the Salmon March in Falkenberg. Free upon request.
- *Hiking Tour in Halmstad, Simlångsdalen* (in English). Gives details on group hikes based in Halmstad, 150 kilometers south of Göteborg. Free upon request.
- *Hiking Tour, Varberg* (in English). Gives details on weekend and week-long hikes based out of Varberg, 80 kilometers south of Göteborg. Free upon request.

Dalsland

Dalslands Turisttrafikförening. Provides general tourist information and some hiking information on the province of Dalsland. Staff speaks Swedish, English and German. Useful publications available from the office include:

- *Pilgrimsleden: vandringsled genom Norra Dalsland* (in Swedish). Gives a brief description of the Pilgrimsleden long-distance footpath. Includes a topographical sketch map. Free upon request.
- *Kronoparken Kroppefjäll* (in Swedish). A Forest Service pamphlet describing the Kroppefjäll Forest. Includes a sketch map. Free upon request.

- *Daisland: Sweden in miniature* (in English: also available in Swedish, German and French). A color brochure describing principal areas of interest in Dalsland. Principal walking areas, for which walking maps are available from the tourist office, are mentioned. Includes a sketch map showing the locations of marked footpaths, lodgings, forest reserves, prehistoric sites and other facilities and points of interest. Free upon request.

Gotland & Öland

Gotlands Turistforening. Provides general tourist information on the island of Gotland. Staff speaks Swedish, English and German. Useful publications available from the office include:

- *Gotland: the summer island in the Baltic* (in English). A magazine-size brochure with general tourist information; a list (and photographs) of hotels, boarding houses, holiday villages, youth hostels and campsites; and information on access to the island. Includes a 1:300,000 color map showing the locations of towns and lodgings, nature reserves, bird sanctuaries, restricted-access areas, historical remains, churches, botanical and geological sites and so on. Walking is not mentioned and no footpaths are shown on the map. Free upon request.

Borgholms Turistbyrå. Provides general tourist information on Öland and its largest town, Borgholm. Staff speaks Swedish, English and German. Useful publications available from the office include:

- *Öland Holiday island in the Baltic* (in English). A general information brochure describing the island's flora and bird life, and listing places of interest, lodgings, campsites and summer markets. Includes a sketch map of the island showing the locations of lodgings. Walking is not mentioned. Free upon request.

Kalmar läns Turisttrafikförbund. Also provides general tourist information and brochures in English on the island of Öland.

Östergötland

Östergötlands Länsturistnämnd. Provides general tourist information on the province of Östergötland. Can also provide information on walking and cross-country skiing. Staff speaks Swedish, English and German. Useful publications available from the office include:

- *Kindaleden: vandrings-och kanotleder i Kinda* (in Swedish). Gives a brief description of the Kindaleden long-distance footpath and of canoe routes in the region west of Lake Åsunden. Includes a sketch map. Free upon request.

- *Vintersport i Östergötland* (in Swedish). A sketch map of the province on which symbols indicate the locations of marked cross-country ski tracks *(märkta skispår)*, illuminated ski tracks *(elbelyst skidspår)*, wind shelters and rest huts, ski lifts, ice skating rinks and other winter facilities. On the back is a list giving the length of ski tracks in each locality, the availability of other winter facilities and the telephone numbers to call for additional information. Free upon request.
- *Östergötland Logi* (in Swedish with English and German keys to symbols). An annual lodging list giving details on the province's hotels, youth hostels, campsites and chalets. Free upon request.

Skåne & Blekinge

Blekinge turist- och fritidskansli. Provides general tourist information on the province of Blekinge. Cannot provide information on walking opportunities. Staff speaks Swedish, English and German.

Skånes Turisttrafikförbund. Provides general tourist information on the province of Skåne. Staff speaks Swedish, English and German. Useful publications available from the office include:

- *Skåne: Turistnytt för Skåne* (in Swedish, with keys to symbols in English, French and German). An annual tourist guide with a complete list of local tourist offices, the facilities and sites in each town and village, and a detailed list of hotels, boardinghouses, youth hostels and camping sites. Free upon request.
- *Från kust till kust* (in Swedish). A provisional guide to the Skåneleden long-distance footpath with six 1:100,000 topographical maps covering its route. Available for a nominal charge.

Småland

Turism och Fritid i Jönköpings län. Provides general tourist information on the county of Jönköping in northwestern Småland. Also provides information on walking and cross-country skiing in the so-called highlands of Småland, south of the town of Jönköping. Staff speaks Swedish, English and German. Useful publications available from the office include:

- *Höglandsleden: vandringsled Eksjö-Hok* (in Swedish). A route description and sketch map of the Höglandsleden long-distance footpath. Free upon request.
- *Come along to the highlands of Småland: Here is beautiful Nässjö* (in English). Gives general information on the highlands of Småland outside the town of Nässjö. Lists points of interest and includes a map with artist sketches showing points of interest and the route of Höglandsleden. Free upon request.

• *Nature i Jönköpings län* (in Swedish, with supplements in English, French and German). A color brochure describing the county's geology, flora, fauna, marshes and nature reserves. Natural phenomena are listed and keyed to numbers on a map. Free upon request.

Kalmar länd Turisttrafikförbund. Provides general tourist information on the county of Kalmar, along the east coast of Småland, the island of Öland and the province of Blekinge. Also provides information on walking in Kalmar County and on cross-country skiing in Småland. Staff speaks Swedish, English and German. Useful publications available from the office include:

• *Kort information om Ostkustleden* (in Swedish). A route description and sketch map of the Ostkustleden long-distance footpath, which circles 150 kilometers through forests and along the coast above the city of Oskarshamn. Free upon request.

• *Småland vinterguide* (in Swedish). A sketch map of the province of Småland with symbols showing the locations of marked cross-country ski tracks *(Elljusspår)*, as well as other winter sports facilities. The lengths of each cross-country ski track are given in the margin beside a list of the localities where they are located. All the cross-country ski tracks (which number more than 125) are illuminated and are used as keep-fit trails in summer. Free upon request.

Turism och Fritid i Kronoberg. Provides general tourist information on the county of Kronoberg in southwestern Småland, the heart of Sweden's glass district. Can only provide brief information on marked woodland paths in the county. A list of local tourist offices, from which more specific information can be obtained, is available upon request. Staff speaks Swedish, English and German.

Västergötland

Västergötlands Turisttrafikförening. Provides general tourist information on the province of Västergötland. Also can provide brief information on walking. Staff speaks Swedish, English and German. Useful publications available from the office include:

• *Västergötland Sweden* (in English). A general information tourist brochure which hints at some of the walking possibilities in the province. Includes a sketch map showing the locations of marked paths, skiing centers, mountain plateaus, lakes, marshes and other points of interest. In the margins of the map is a list of principal points of interest and a description of the various prehistoric remains which can be found in the province—chambered tumuli, cists, cairns, paleoglyphs, ship burials, bauta stones, judge rings and rune stones. More such remains exist in Västergötland than any other province in Sweden. Free upon request.

• *Västergötland Tourist Guide* (in English). Gives more specific information on outdoor recreation opportunities in the province. Also includes a list of lodgings and principal sites. Available for a nominal charge.

Maps

Götaland is covered by the following 1:50,000 Topografiska kartan:

Blekings: sheets 3E *Karlsham* NV, NO and SO; 3F *Karlskrona* NV, NO, SV and SO; 3G *Kristianopel* NV; and 4F *Lessebo* SV and SO.

Bohuslän: sheets 7B *Göteborg* NV, NO, SV and SO; 8A *Lysekil* NO and SO; 8B *Vänesborg* NV, SV and SO; 9A *Strömstad* NO and SO; 9B *Dals-Ed* NV and SV; and 10A *Svinesund* SO.

Dalsland: sheets 8B *Vänersborg* NO and SO; 8C *Lindköping* NV; 9B *Dals-Ed* NV, NO, SV and SO; 9C *Mellerud* NV and SV; 10B *Årjäng* SV and SO; and 10C *Åmål* SV.

Gotland: sheets 5I *Hoburgen* NO and SO; 5J *Hemse* NV and SV; 6I *Visby* NO and SO; 6J *Roma* NV, SV and SO; and 7J *Farösund* NV, SV and SO.

Halland: sheets 4C *Halmstad* NV, NO and SO; 5B *Varberg* NO and SO; 5C *Ullared* NV, NO, SV and SO; and 6B *Kungsbacka* NV, NO, SV and SO.

Öland: sheets 3G *Kristianopel* NO; 4G *Kalmar* NO and SO; 4H *Rusten* NO and SO; 5H *Borgholm* NV and SV; and 6H *Kråkelund* SV and SO.

Östergötland: sheets 7E *Jönköping* NO; 7F *Tranås* NV, NO, SV and SO; 7G *Västervik* NV, NO and SV; 7H *Loftahammar* NV; 8E *Hjo* NO and SO; 8F *Linköping* NV, NO, SV and SO; 8G *Norrköping* NV, NO, SV and SO; 8H *Arkösund* NV and SV; 9F *Finspång* NO, SV and SO; and 9G *Katrineholm* NV, SV and SO.

Skåne: sheets 1C *Trelleborg* NV and NO; 1D *Ystad* NV and NO; 2C *Malmö* NV, NO, SV and SO; 2D *Tomelilla* NV, NO, SV and SO; 2E *Smirishamn* SV; 3B *Höganas* NO; 3C *Helsingborg* NV, NO, SV and SO; 3D *Kristianstad* NV, NO, SV and SO; 3E *Karlshamn* NV and SV; 4D *Markaryd* SV and SO; and 4E *Tingsryd* SV.

Småland—Jönköpings County: sheets 5C *Ullared* NO and SO; 5D *Värnamo* NV, NO and SV; 5E *Växjö* NV and NO; 5F *Åseda* NV; 6D *Gislaved* NO, SV and SO; 6E *Nässjö* NV, NO, SV and SO; 6F *Vetlanda* NV, NO, SV and SO; 7D *Ulricehamn* SO; 7E *Jönköping* NV, NO, SV and SO; and 7F *Tranås* SV.

Småland—Kalmar County: sheets 3G *Kristianopel* NV; 4F *Lessebo* NO and SO; 4G *Kalmar* NV, NO and SV; 5F *Åseda* NO and SO; 5G *Oskarshamn* NV, NO, SV and SO; 6F *Vetlanda* NO and SO; 6G

Vimmerby NV, NO, SV and SO; 7F *Tranås* SO; 7G *Västervik* NV, NO, SV and SO; and 7H *Loftahammar* NV and SV.

Småland—Kronobergs County: sheets 4D *Markaryd* NV, NO, SV and SO; 4E *Tingsryd* NV, NO, SV and SO; 4F *Lessebo* NV, NO and SV; 5D *Värnamo* SV and SO; 5E *Växjö* NV, NO, SV and SO; and 5F *Åseda* NV, NO, SV and SO.

Västergötland: sheets 6B *Kungsbacka* NO and SO; 6C *Kinna* NV, NO, SV and SO; 6D *Gislaved* NV and SV; 7B *Göteborg* NO and SO; 7C *Borås* NV, NO, SV and SO; 7D *Ulricehamn* NV, NO, SV and SO; 7E *Jönköping* NV; 8B *Vänersborg* SO; 8C *Lundköping* NV, NO, SV and SO; 8D *Skara* NV, NO, SV and SO; 8E *Hjo* NV and SV; 9D *Marlestad* NO and SO; and 9E *Askersund* NV, SV and SO.

Guidebooks

In addition to the publications listed under the tourist office addresses for each province above and the various leaflets describing each of Göta-land's 11 long-distance footpaths, three guidebooks exist to walks in Götaland:

- *Vandra i Sverige: Låglandsleder* (in Swedish). Gives a brief description of each of Götaland's long-distance footpaths. Available from the STF or Friluftsfrämjandet.

- *Guiden över Skåneleden: från kust till kust:* (in Swedish). A comprehensive guidebook to the 220-kilometer Skåneleden long-distance footpath. Available from most local bookstores in Skåne, as well as from the tourist offices in Kristianstad, Karlshamn and Hässleholm.

- *Vandringsguiden över Ostkustleden* (in Swedish). A comprehensive guidebook to the 152-kilometer Ostkustleden long-distance foot-path. Available from most local bookstores, as well as from the Döderhults naturskyddsförening and Oskarshamn Turistbyrå.

For more details on these guidebooks, see the section on *Guidebooks* earlier in this chapter.

Suggested Walks

The possibilities are numerous. The most highly recommended walks, however, are on Götaland's 11 long-distance footpaths—the Höglandsleden, Holavedsleden, Ostkustleden, Tjustleden, and Vandring i utvandrarbygd in Småland; the Kindaleden in Östergötland; the Pil-grimsleden in Dalsland; the Kongs Lÿden in Blekinge; the Skåneleden in Skåne; and the Vättlefjällsleden and Vildmarksleden in Bohuslän and Halland. (For further information on these footpaths, see the section on

Sweden's Long-Distance Footpaths.) Other recommended walks are in the Kroppefjäll Forest in Dalsland, in the Omberg Forest in Östergötland, and on the footpaths around Lake Hornboga—particularly in April—Lake Mjörn, Lake Ömmern and in the Tiveden Forest in the province of Västergötland.

Cross-Country Skiing

The principal areas for cross-country skiing in Götaland are in the provinces of Östergötland, Småland and Västergötland. The provincial tourist associations in each province publish winter guides showing the locations of marked and illuminated cross-country ski tracks, and giving the lengths of the tracks, information on other winter sports facilities and the telephone numbers to call in each locality for further information. Two of these guides are listed under *Useful Addresses* above. Once you have decided where you want to cross-country ski, you can often obtain sketch maps of the cross-country ski tracks from local tourist information offices, the addresses of which are available on request from the provincial tourist associations.

Jämtland & Härjedalen

Situated in north-central Sweden between Lappland on the north and Svealand on the south, the wild, sparsely populated provinces of Jämtland and Härjedalen occupy the geographical center of the Scandinavian peninsula. The western half of the region, along the Norwegian border, is dominated by a mountain chain with numerous peaks above 1,000 meters. The mountains fall away toward the east to rolling, forested country cut by broad river valleys and spangled with hundreds of lakes.

Only about 130,000 people live in the two provinces, which are roughly the size of Denmark. Of these, 40,000 or so reside in Östersund, the only town of notable size in the region. The rest of the people live in widely scattered villages. Several areas are entirely uninhabited and accessible only on foot.

Jämtland and Härjedalen offer splendid wilderness walking. Hundreds of kilometers of marked footpaths cross the region, wandering through dense forests of spruce and pine, along rambunctious mountain streams, by quiet glacial lakes, near highland meadows rife with wildflowers and among the dwarf, windswept heaths above timberline.

The mountains of Jämtland and Härjedalen are among the southernmost in Sweden and are therefore readily accessible from nearby population centers. They offer an excellent alternative to those who yearn for solitude amid rugged mountain scenery, but prefer to avoid the harsh climate, rough walking and remoteness of the Lappland ranges. Mountain stations providing food and lodging are more numerous and are situated closer together than in the mountains of Lappland. The network of footpaths is denser. Walking is altogether easier, and in case of emergency help is closer at hand.

Although there are few truly imposing mountain crags in the ranges of Jämtland and Härjedalen, the open, undulating ridgetops offer nearly endless opportunities for roaming and provide sweeping views of forested lowlands stretching toward the east. The southernmost glacier in Sweden lies in a high cirque on 1,796-meter Helagsfjället, the highest peak in the country south of the Arctic Circle. Numerous small tarns scattered among the peaks nestle in rocky basins once quarried by ice.

Great streams tumble toward the valleys through rocky gorges fringed with forest, such as that in Sonfjället National Park in Härjedalen. Waterfalls abound throughout the region, the most notable being Tann-forsen, the largest in Sweden, and Hällingsafallet, which plunges head-long into a spectacular chasm. Numerous large, fjord-like lakes lie in the lowland valleys, dammed by glacial debris. The largest in the region is Storsjön in central Jämtland.

Scattered throughout the region are tokens of the past: rune stones, abandoned Lapp villages, rock carvings and paintings more than 4,000 years old, Iron Age burial mounds and the remains of medieval churches and castles. The mountain pastures are often scattered with old sod-roofed chalets, remnants of a pastoral culture now largely vanished in Sweden. Most of the chalets are abandoned, but a few are still in use. And their inhabitants still tend their animals and make their cheeses in the traditional ways.

Lodging is readily available throughout Jämtland and Härjedalen. There are more than 100 mountain hotels and boarding houses, nearly a dozen youth hostels and numerous mountain stations and huts.

Useful Addresses

See *Address Directory:*

Jämtland-Härjedalens Turistförening. Provides general tourist information for Jämtland and Härjedalen. Staff speaks Swedish and English. Useful publications available from the office include:

• *Jämtland Härjedalen* (in English). Gives a description of the region, general lodging information and a list of campgrounds and youth hostels. Includes a map of the region with symbols indicating the services and facilities available in major towns. It also gives the telephone numbers of local tourist offices, as well as addresses where you can write for more information.

Maps

The mountains of Jämtland and Härjedalen are covered by the following maps:

• Nya Fjällkartan, 1:100,000, sheets Z 1, Z 2, Z 3, Z 4, Z 5, Z 6, Z 7, Z 8 and Z 9.

• Nya Fjällkartan, 1:50,000, five special sheets: *Storlien, Åre, Klövsjö–Vemdalen, Sånfjället* and *Lofsdalen.*

The remainder of Jämtland and Härjedalen are covered by the following Topografiska kartan:

Jämtland: 1:50,000 sheets 17E *Rätan* NO; 17F *Ånge* NV and NO; 18E *Hackås* NV, NO, SV and SO; 18F *Bräcke* NV, NO, SV and SO; 18G *Håsjö* NV, NO, SV and SO; 18H *Graninge* NV; 19E *Östersund* NV, NO, SV and SO; 19F *Häggenås* NV, NO, SV and SO; 19G *Krångede* NV, SV and SO; 20E *Hotagen* NO and SO; 20F *Störmsund* NV, NO, SV and SO; and 20G *Fjällsjo* NV, NO and SV. Also, 1:100,000 sheets 21F *Alanäs* and 21G *Dorotea.*

Härjedalen: 1:50,000 sheets 15D *Särna* NO; 15E *Älvho* NV and NO; 16D *Lofsdalen* NO and SO; 16E *Sveg* NV, NO, SV and SO; 16F *Karböle* NV and SV; 17D *Hede* NV, NO, SV and SO; and 17E *Rätan* NV, NO, SV and SO.

Guidebooks

• *Fjäll '81* (in Swedish). Available from the STF.
• *Hiking in the Swedish Highlands* (in English). Also available from the STF.

Suggested Walks

Numerous walks are possible throughout the region, but the most highly recommended are in the western mountains. The following is but one example:

From Storulvån to Vålådalen. Through meadow, forest, birch woodland and alpine heath in the mountains of southern Jämtland. Passes near the highest peaks in the region, including 1,796-meter Helagsfjället. The route crosses into Norway, where there is a boat crossing of Nesjöen, one of that country's mountain lakes. From Stockholm, you can take the train to Enafors, where there is a taxi service to the Storulvån mountain station. **Length:** 111 kilometers, not including the distance covered by boat. **Walking Time:** 8 days (1 spent traveling by boat). **Difficulty:** Moderately difficult. **Path Markings:** Mostly marked with cairns.

Lodgings: Mountain stations serving food are located at Storulvån, Blåhammaren, Storerikvollen (Norway), Nedalen (Norway), and Vålådalen. There is a self-service station (no food) at Sylarna and self-service huts (no food) at Gåsen Lunndönnen, Anaris, Vålåvalen Stensdalen.

Special Note: The season for walking this route is short. Snow may remain on the ground until the end of June. And after the middle of September, the weather is unpredictable. Only very experienced walkers should attempt the route after this time.

Maps:
• Nya Fjällkartan 1:100,000, sheets Z 6, Z 7 and Z 8.

Path Description:
• Fjäll '81 (in Swedish). Includes descriptions of various segments of the route and of the mountain stations along the way. Available from the STF.

Route Outline:
Day 1: From Storulvån to the Blåhammaren mountain station. 11 kilometers, 4 to 5 hours.
Day 2: To Storerikvollen, Norway, 15 kilometers, 4 to 5 hours.
Day 3: To Nedalen, Norway, by boat across Nesjöen Lake.
Day 4: To Sylarna through the region's highest peaks, 20 kilometers, 5 to 7 hours.
Day 5: To Helags, 19 kilometers, 5 to 6 hours.
Day 6: To Gåsen, 18 kilometers, 5 to 7 hours.
Day 7: To Stensdalen, 15 kilometers, 3 to 4 hours.
Day 8: To Vålådalen, 13 kilometers, 3 to 4 hours. Bus service links the tourist hotel with the train station in Undersåker.

Cross-Country Skiing

Among the principal skiing centers in Jämtland and Härjedalen are:

Åre & Duved. Located 110 kilometers west of Östersund on the train line between Östersund and Storlien. Has more than 100 kilometers of marked cross-country ski tracks, several slalom slopes, facilities for renting ski equipment, a ski school and numerous lodging possibilities.

Bruksvallarna. A mountain village located 15 kilometers north of Funäsdalen. Accessible by bus from the train station at Sveg. Surrounded by nearly 40 peaks in excess of 1,000 meters elevation. Has ski lifts, a ski school, facilities for ski equipment rental and several lodging possibilities.

Edsåsdalen. Located 8 kilometers south of the train station at Untersåker on the Östersund-Storlien railway line. Has numerous marked ski tracks leading to surrounding mountains, slalom slopes, several hotels, a ski school and ski touring guides.

Funäsdalen. Located 35 kilometers from the Norwegian border. Accessible by bus from the train station at Sveg. Has an illuminated cross-country ski track, slalom slopes, facilities for ski rentals, several hotels and ski touring guides for excursions into the surrounding mountains.

Hammarstrand. Located along the River Indal 7 kilometers from the Ragunda railway station. Undulating forest terrain 100 kilometers east of Östersund. Has several marked and illuminated cross-country ski tracks, slalom slopes, hotels with ski equipment for hire and ski touring guides for excursions into the surrounding mountains, which rise up to 416 meters.

Kall. A mountain village on Lake Kallsjön, located 22 kilometers north of the Järpen railway station on the Östersund-Storlien line. Good cross-country terrain. Has illuminated slalom slopes, hotels with ski equipment for hire and ski touring guides for excursions into the surrounding countryside.

Storlien. Located at the end of the rail line leading through Östersund from Stockholm, virtually on the Norwegian border. Has several marked cross-country ski tracks, slalom slopes, a large hotel with ski shop, facilities for equipment rental and a ski school.

Tänndalen. Located 10 kilometers west of Funäsdalen. Accessible by bus from the railway station at Sveg. Has two ski lifts leading up into mountainous terrain and several hotels.

Trillevallen. A mountain village on the southeastern slopes of 1,024-meter Vällistefjället, located 10 kilometers from the train station at Untersåker.

Vemdalsskalet. Located 55 kilometers northwest of the railway station at Sveg. Surrounded by three 1,000-meter mountain peaks. Has marked cross-country ski tracks, slalom slopes, ski equipment rentals, a ski school and several hotels.

In addition to these areas, the STF has marked eight cross-country ski routes in the mountains of Jämtland and Härjedalen. These routes—from 29 to 79 kilometers in length—are marked by red crossed boards affixed to long posts. The routes are described in *Fjäll '81*.

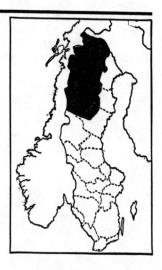

Lappland

Swedish Lappland is a vast, sparsely populated region covering more than 259,000 square kilometers (100,000 square miles) in northwestern Sweden. Lappland accounts for a quarter of the country's total area, yet contains only 1.2 million inhabitants. Kiruna, in northern Lappland, is the region's only town. Elsewhere, its inhabitants are scattered among far-flung villages and outlying farms. There are relatively few roads in Lappland and but a single railway line. Most of Lappland consists of uninhabited wilderness, offering some of the remotest, most challenging walking in Europe.

The region derives its name and identity from the Lapps, a semi-nomadic herding people who were once the only inhabitants in northern Norway, Sweden and Finland. They followed their reindeer herds to the high mountain pastures in the spring and back to the lowlands in the fall. A few still do so, but most Lapps now live in settlements. Even so, they have retained many of their old customs, including their colorful dress and traditional handicrafts. Their abandoned seasonal settlements are scattered throughout Lappland and southward into Jämtland and Härjedalen.

The seasoned wilderness traveler who is prepared to cope with Lappland's rugged terrain and erratic weather can wander for days—or even weeks—among spectacular peaks crowned with glaciers and peren-nial snowfields; across sweeping mountain plateaus, through rocky gorges where rivers leap eastward in countless rapids, cascades and waterfalls; past thousands of lakes strewn across the empty land; and through lonely expanses of forest, marsh and tundra.

Lappland is a paradise for the experienced walker seeking magnificent scenery, challenging routes and solitude. But it is not recommended for the casual or inexperienced visitor or for anyone unfamiliar with local conditions of weather and terrain. The weather is erratic and can be harsh even in midsummer, especially in the western mountains. Even on existing footpaths, you may have to ford raging torrents, cross stretches of difficult bog and marsh or negotiate treacherous mountain passes and rocky defiles.

There are relatively few mountain stations, and these are typically more than a day's journey apart. Walkers in Lappland must therefore be prepared to spend the night far removed from civilization in unstaffed mountain huts—which are from 10 to 24 kilometers apart—or in a tent pitched on open, windswept heights. In cases of emergency, the nearest road or village may be days away.

Inexperienced walkers should limit themselves to short day trips along established, well-marked footpaths, reserving extended trips for other parts of Sweden, where conditions are more congenial. Even experienced walkers are advised to stick to the principal, well-marked routes until they become acquainted with the vagaries of weather and terrain in the region.

Marked footpaths lead through many sections of the western mountains, as well as through various lowland areas. The best known route in Lappland is the 430-kilometer Kungsleden—or Royal Route—from Abisko National Park in the north to Ammarnäs in the south. Providing a grand tour of the Lappland mountains, the Kungsleden is the second-longest and most strenuous long-distance footpath in Sweden. Two other long-distance footpaths—the 50-kilometer Muddusleden and the 30-kilometer Nirraleden—provide easier tours of Muddus National Park and the lowland area southeast of Gällivare.

Lappland contains seven of Sweden's 16 national parks: Abisko, Muddus, Padjelanta (the largest in Europe), Peljekasje, Sarek, Stora Sjöfallet and Vadvetjåkko. All of the national parks in Lappland except Sarek have marked footpaths. Sarek National Park, however, is virtually trackless, accessible only to the seasoned cross-country walker. Sarek, Padjalenta and Stora Sjöfallet national parks form a continuous block that together with the extensive roadless lands around them constitute the largest wilderness in Europe outside Russia—more than 5,300 square kilometers (2,000 square miles). A quick glance at a map of Lappland will also reveal many other, smaller areas of wilderness.

The western portion of Lappland is dominated by mountains that extend along the Norwegian border for some 550 kilometers and continue southward into Jämtland, Härjedalen and Dalarna. Sweden's highest, craggiest summits, however, are found in Lappland, where several peaks exceed 2,000 meters elevation. All of the highest peaks are found north of the Arctic Circle, and many are in Sarek National Park, where eight summits rise above 2,000 meters.

The mountains of Sarek also contain the greatest concentration of glaciers in Sweden. There are 96 ice fields in all, of which the largest—Pårte Glacier—covers 11 square kilometers. Evidences of glaciation abound throughout Lappland, even in the lowlands, in the form of U-shaped canyons, hanging valleys, scoured rock faces, glacial cirques and thousands of lakes, large and small, cupped in sockets quarried by ice from the obdurate rock.

The mountains of Lappland comprise an elevated plateau, one crowned with peaks but offering great expanses of undulating terrain where you can wander endlessly through dense tundra carpets vivid with summer flowers. Because of the mountains' high elevations and situation north of the Arctic Circle, forests are confined to their lower slopes, where stands of birch form a ragged timberline marking the westernmost outpost of the great Eurasian taiga, which sprawls eastward across northern Europe and Siberia to the Pacific.

Eastern Lappland consists of hilly, rather than mountainous, terrain, where elevations seldom exceed 600 meters. Here and in the adjacent northeast coastal provinces are found the bulk of Sweden's remaining forest. There are numerous forest reserves in the region, several of which contain marked footpaths. Eastern Lappland also has extensive areas of tundra, bog and willow thickets, as well as thousands of lakes and streams.

Useful Addresses

See *Address Directory:*

Northern Lappland

Norrbottens Turisttrafikförbund. Provides general tourist information on both Norrbotten and Lappland. Staff speaks Swedish and English. Useful publications available from the office include:

- *Hej Semester Norrbotten* (in English). Describes some of the most beautiful areas in Norrbotten and Northern Lappland. Includes a map of the region, on which symbols indicate points of interest and lodging possibilities. Also gives the times for the midnight sun, as well as the names of other brochures available from the tourist office. These include:
- *Hej Bilist* (in English). Tells motorists where to stay, where to eat and what to see.
- *Hej Kanotist* (in English). Describes canoeing trips featuring walking, fishing and swimming.
- *Hej Turist* (in English). Contains descriptions and photographs of holiday cottages for rent and includes a price list. Also lists campgrounds and has a sketch map.

Southern Lappland

Västerbottens Länsturistnämnd. Provides general tourist information on both Västerbotten and Southern Lappland. Staff speaks Swedish and English. Useful publications available from the office include:

• *Västerbotten Southern Lappland* (in English). Lists hotels, summer cottages, campgrounds, youth hostels, travel bureaus, transportation facilities, and local tourist offices in Västerbotten and Southern Lappland. Also contains a map of the region, on which symbols indicate lodging possibilities, activities and places of special interest.

Maps

The mountains of Lappland are covered by the following maps:

• Nya Fjällkartan 1:100,000, sheets BD 1, BD 2, BD 3, BD 4, BD 5, BD 6, BD 7, BD 8, BD 9, BD 10, BD 11, BD 12, BD 13, BD 14, BD 15, BD 16, AC 1, AC 2, AC 3, AC 4 and AC 5.

The remainder of Lappland is covered by the following Topografiska kartan:

• 1:50,000 sheets 24J *Arvidsjaur* NV, NO, SV and SO; 25J *Moskosel* NV, NO, SV and SO; 26J *Jokkmokk* NV, NO, SV and SO; 26K *Murjek* NV, NO, SV and SO; 27J *Porjus* NV, NO, SV and SO; 27K *Nattavaara* NV, NO, SV and SO; 28J *Fjällåsen* NV, NO, SV and SO; 28K *Gällivare* NV, NO, SV and SO; 29K *Vittangi* NV, NO, SV and SO; 29L *Lainio* NV, NO, SV and SO; 30K *Soppero* NV, NO, SV and SO; 30L *Lannavaara* NV, NO, SV and SO; and 31L *Karesuando* SV and SO.

• 1:100,000 sheets 21G *Dorotea*, 21H *Åsele*, 21I *Fredrika*, 22G *Vilhelmina*, 22H *Järvsjö*, 22I *Lycksele*, 23G *Dikanas*, 23H *Stensele*, 23I *Malå*, 24G *Umnäs*, 24H *Sorsele*, 24I *Storavan*, 25H *Arjeplog*, 25I *Stensund* and 26I *Luvos*.

Guidebooks

Available from the STF:

• *Detta är Sarek* (in Swedish) by Tore Abrahamsson, Raben & Sjögren, Stockholm.

• *De vilda djurens Sarek* (in Swedish) by Edvin Nilsson, Bonniers, Stockholm.

• *Fjäll '81* (in Swedish).

- *Hiking in the Swedish Highlands* (in English.)
- *Kebnekaise* (in Swedish) by Tore Abrahamsson, Norstedts, Stockholm.
- *Kungsleden: The Royal Route* (in English). Swedish Tourist Board and STF.
- *Kungsleden och 13 angränsande turer* (in Swedish), STF.
- *Sarek* (in Swedish) by Edvin Nilsson, Bonniers, Stockholm.
- *Sarek, Stora Sjöfallet, Padjelanta: Drei Nationalparke in Schwedisch Lappland* (in German) by Kai Curry-Lindahl, Raben & Sjögren, Stockholm.
- *Sarek, Stora Sjöfallet, Padjelanta: Three National Parks in Swedish Lappland* (in English) by Kai Curry-Lindahl, Raben & Sjögren, Stockholm.
- *Vandra i Sarek* (in Swedish) by Svante Lundgren, Norstedts, Stockholm, revised 1979.
- *Wandern unter der Mitternachtssonne* (in German), Alex Verlag.

Suggested Walks

One of the finest mountain walks in Lappland is the 430-kilometer Kungsleden, which can be walked in its entirety or broken into five segments ranging in length from 48 to 101 kilometers (see description under the section on *Sweden's Long-Distance Footpaths*). Other routes branch west from the Kungsleden, providing access to Padjelanta National Park and the mountains of Norway. Marked footpaths are also found in Muddus, Abisko, Stora Sjöfallets and Peljekaise national parks, as well as in the forests of Pahakurkkio, Arieplog, Reivoreservalet and Stenbithöjden.
Another possibility is:

From Vaisaluokta to Sulitjelma, Norway. Through the heart of Padjelanta National Park. Wide open mountain plain with large lakes, occasional peaks and wildlife, including Lapp reindeer. Bus service from Gällivare to Ritsen, then by boat across Akkajaure Lake to the STF hut at Vaisaluokta. Lodgings and bus service also available at Sulitjelma, Norway. **Length:** 110 kilometers. **Walking Time:** Six days. **Difficulty:** Moderately difficult. **Path Markings:** Cairns.
Special Notes: Because the entire path crosses remote, uninhabited country, you should observe the same precautions as for walking the Kungsleden (see *Special Notes* under the description for the Kungsleden in the section on *Sweden's Long-Distance Footpaths*). Hot meals and other amenities are available at Ritsen.
Lodgings: Huts are located at Vaisaluokta Akka, Kisuris, Låddejåkk, Arasluokta, Saltoluokta, Staddajåkk and Sårjåsjaure; huts in Norway are located at Sorjushytta and Ny-Sulitjelma.

Maps:
- Nya Fjällkartan 1:100,000, sheets BD 9 and BD 12 cover the entire route. The section of the route from Akka to Saltoluotka is also shown on BD 10.

Path Description:
- Fjäll '81 (in Swedish). Available from the STF.

Cross-Country Skiing

The principal skiing centers in Lappland are:

Abisko. Located on the railway line linking Stockholm and Narvik. Numerous ski tracks are located south of the Abisko mountain station in Abisko National Park.

Ammarnäs. Located at the southern terminus of the Kungsleden, 90 kilometers northwest of the train station at Sorsele. Has several slalom hills, a ski lift, and a snow scooter taxi service for tours into the mountains.

Björkliden. A mountain resort on the Gällivare-Riksgränsen railway line, 7 kilometers west of Abisko. Has slalom slopes, ski lifts, a ski school, ski equipment rentals and hotels.

Borgafjäll. A mountain village located 105 kilometers northwest of the train station at Dorotea. Has a hotel and holiday village. Numerous opportunities for ski tours in the surrounding countryside.

Hemavan. Located near the Norwegian border, 150 kilometers northwest of the train station at Storuman. Has slalom slopes, ski instructors, ski touring guides and several hotels.

Riksgränsen. Located on the Norwegian border on the main railway line linking Stockholm and Narvik. Has a large hotel, slalom slopes, ski equipment for hire and a ski school which also operates during the summer.

Tärnaby. A mountain village located 130 kilometers northwest of the train station at Storuman. Has slalom slopes, ski equipment rentals and several hotels.

The STF has also marked several cross-country ski routes in the mountains of Lappland. These routes—from 49 to 154 kilometers in length—are marked by red crossed boards affixed to long posts. The routes are described in Fjäll '81 (see description under Guidebooks earlier in this chapter).

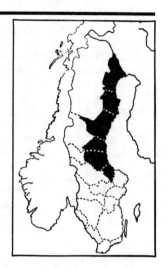

The Northeastern Coast

This region lies along the Gulf of Bothnia, extending northward from Uppland to the Finnish border, a distance of some 750 kilometers (465 miles). It includes the provinces of Gästrikland, Hälsingland, Medelpad and Ångermanland and the coastal portions of the provinces of Västerbotten and Norrbotten. The region is bounded on the west by the mountainous country of Lappland and Jämtland-Härjedalen.

The region contains seven long-distance footpaths that range in length up to 130 kilometers. In addition to the long-distance footpaths, there are marked walking routes in the region's forest reserves and numerous shorter paths radiating from towns and villages.

Lodgings are easily found throughout the region in youth hostels, guesthouses and hotels. Each of the principal walking areas also has one or more campgrounds.

The coastal scenery is splendid, with quaint fishing villages, numerous bays and fjords, rocky cliffs, sandy beaches and hundreds of nearby islands cloaked with woods. Inland the terrain consists largely of rolling, forest-covered hills cradling innumerable lakes. Great river valleys wind through the hills to the sea, their fertile soils supporting small farms strung between rural villages. The uplands between the valleys are sparsely inhabited and largely covered by forest, particularly in the southern provinces. The scenery along the Northeastern Coast is not so rugged as that of the mountainous districts to the west, but the walker will find beauty enough to warrant tarrying in the region. Some examples:

Ångermanland & Medelpad. These two provinces, covering 25,900 square kilometers (10,000 square miles), comprise the region known as Västernorrland. The rocky, hill-bound coast with its cliffs, headlands, fjords, islands and picturesque villages is renowned throughout Sweden for its beauty. Away from the coast, Västernorrland consists mostly of rolling hill country, with pleasant farmlands, vast forest tracts and lakes. Numerous hills and ridges top 500 meters (1,640 feet). Slicing through the hills are three great valleys carved by the Ljungan, Indalsälven and Angermanälven rivers. The estuary at the mouth of the Ljungan is the largest in Sweden. Of special interest to walkers are the Höga Kustenleden long-distance footpath and the Arnäsleden, a 30-kilometer path beginning near Tossböle and passing near Skallbergsgrottan, probably the largest rock cave in Scandinavia. In addition, most municipalities maintain walking paths and cross-country ski routes. There are also numerous short forest walks throughout Västernorrland. Two good areas are the Skule Forest and the nature reserve near 593-meter Solberget, with its extensive network of game trails.

Gästrikland & Hälsingland. Lying just south of Västernorrland, these two provinces comprise the southernmost outpost of the Northeastern Coast region. They are part of Sweden's "Folklore District," where summer festivals, colorful costumes and traditional music, dancing and handicrafts are the rule. Like Västernorrland, Gästrikland and Hälsingland contain rolling, forested countryside with innumerable lakes and streams to lure the walker. The terrain is somewhat lower and gentler than that to the north. And the coast, although still irregular, is not so imposing. These two provinces are for quiet woodland walks alongside purling streams and clear, cold lakes. In addition to many local paths, Gästrikland and Hälsingland together have no less than six long-distance footpaths: the Gästrikleden, Hälsingleden, Kolarstigen, Ljusnanleden, Mostigen and Sjuvallsleden.

Norrbotten & Västerbotten. These are the two northernmost provinces of Sweden, stretching across the northern third of the country from Norway in the west to the Gulf of Bothnia in the east. They encompass not only the coastal region but Lappland. Although there are no marked long-distance footpaths in the coastal region, numerous walks are possible in this rugged hill country with its sprawling forests, broad river valleys, marshes and thousands of lakes. Northward, the forests are less extensive, giving way increasingly to grasslands, tundra, bog and great marshy thickets. The northern half of Norrbotten lies above the Arctic Circle, where you can walk all night in the midnight sun. The coast, with its fishing villages, fjords, cliffs, headlands and hundreds of islands, is especially picturesque. Västerbotten is the more populous of the two provinces, offering easier access to food, lodgings and other amenities, but Norrbotten is the wilder, offering opportunities for cross-country rambles through great tracts of uninhabited country. Of special interest to walkers are the Blaiken wilderness, Kittelfjäll Mountains and the forest reserves of Marjakursu, Pahakurkkio, Räktforsen, Fällforsen, Storforsen, Hällnäs, Kroksjökälen, Käringbergsområdet and Stenbithöjden—all of which have marked footpaths leading through wild woodlands with tumbling streams and remote lakes. In Västerbotten alone forest reserves cover about 1.1 million hectares (2.7 million acres).

Useful Addresses

See *Address Directory:*

Ångermanland & Medelpad

Västernorrlands läns Landsting, Turist- och näringslivssektionen.
Provides general tourist information on Västernorrland. Some leaflets
describing walks are available. Staff speaks Swedish, German and
English. Useful publications available from the office include:

- *Bo och Äta* (in Swedish). Lists hotels, motels, guesthouses, restaurants, touring club lodges, campgrounds, and camping chalets in Västernorrland. Symbols indicate the services and activities provided by hotels, motels and guesthouses. Facilities for other types of accommodation are shown on charts. Gives addresses and phone numbers of local tourist offices.

- *Höga Kusten-leden* (in Swedish). A leaflet with 1:50,000 map of the area through which sections 3 and 4 of this path pass. Numbers indicate rest stops and lodging possibilities. Gives information on path markings.

- *Summer in Medelpad Ångermanland-Winger Västernorrland* (in English). Gives a general description of Västernorrland and its various districts, and provides information on summer and winter activities for visitors. Lists ski areas with illuminated ski tracks. Local tourist offices are listed, as are the names of other tourist information brochures. A map of the region is included. Symbols indicate services and activities available in the region, including viewpoints, lodgings, campgrounds, ski trails and a few walking paths.

Gästrikland & Hälsingland

Kommungruppen för fritid i Gävleborgs län. Provides general tourist
information and walking information for Gästrikland and Hälsingland. Staff speaks Swedish and English. Useful publications available
from the office include:

- *Hälsingland Gästrikland Fritidsvinter* (in Swedish). A map showing ski resorts in the region. Services, facilities and activities, including marked ski tracks, are listed for each resort. The addresses of camping chalets, ski chalets and local tourist offices are also listed.

- *Vandra i Hälsingland och Gästrikland* (in Swedish). Describes five marked footpaths in the region: the Gästrikeleden, Hälsingeleden, Ljusnanleden, Sjuvallsleden and Mostigen. Sketch maps are included for each footpath. There is also a general map of the entire region, showing the location of all five paths.

Maps

The Northeastern Coast is covered by the following 1:50,000 Topografiska kartan:

Ångermanland: sheets 18H *Graninge* NV, NO and SO; 18I *Kramfors* NV, NO and SV; 19G *Krångede* NV, NO and SO; 19H *Sollefteå* NV, NO, SV and SO; 19I *Örnsköldsvik* NV, NO, SV and SO; 19J *Husum* NV and SV; 20G *Fjällsjö* NO, SV and SO; 20H *Junsele* NV, NO, SV and SO; 20I *Björna* NV, NO, SV and SO; and 20J *Vännäs* SV.

Gästrikland: sheets 12G *Avesta* NO; 12H *Söderfors* NV; 13G *Hofors* NO and SO; 13H *Gävle* NV, NO, SV and SO; 14G *Ockelbo* SV and SO; and 14H *Söderhamn* SV and SO.

Hälsingland: sheets 14F *Rättvik* NO; 14G *Okelbo* NV, NO, SV and SO; 14H *Söderhamn* NV and SV; 15F *Voxna* NV, NO, SV and SO; 15G *Bollnäs* NV, NO, SV and SO; 15H *Hudiksvall* NV, NO and SV; 16F *Karböle* NO, SV and SO; 16G *Ljusdal* NV, NO, SV and SO; 16H *Bergsjö* NV, NO, SV and SO; 17F *Ånge* SO; and 17G *Ljungaverk* SV.

Medelpad: sheets 16H *Bergsjö* NV and NO; 17F *Ånge* NV, NO, SV and SO; 17G *Ljungaverk* NV, NO, SV and SO; 17H *Sundsvall* NV, NO, SV and SO; 17I *Härnösand* NV; 18G *Håsjö* SO; 18H *Graninge* NV, SV and SO; and 18I *Kramfors* SV.

Norrbotten: sheets 23K *Boliden* NO; 23L *Byske* NV; 24K *Älvsbyn* NV, NO, SV and SO; 24L *Luleå* NV, NO, SV and SO; 24M *Brändön* NV; 25K *Harads* NV, NO, SV and SO; 25L *Boden* NV, NO, SV and SO; 25M *Kalix* NV, NO, SV and SO; 25N *Haparanda* NV, NO and SV; 26L *Pålkem* NV, NO, SV and SO; 26M *Överkalix* NV, NO, SV and SO; 26N *Karungi* NV and SV; 27L *Lansjärv* NV, NO, SV and SO; 27M *Korpilombolo* NV, NO, SV and SO; 27N *Svanstein* NV and SV; 28L *Tärendö* NV, NO, SV and SO; 28M *Pajala* NV, NO, SV and SO; 29M *Huukl* NV, NO, SV and SO; and 30M *Muonionalusta* NV, SV and SO.

Västerbotten: sheets 20I *Björna* NO; 20J *Vännäs* NV, NO, SV and SO; 20K *Umeå* NV, NO and SV; 21J *Vindeln* NV, NO, SV and SO; 21K *Robertsfors* NV, NO, SV and SO; 21L *Ånäset* NV; 22J *Kalvträsk* NV, NO, SV and SO; 22K *Skellefteå* NV, NO, SV and SO; 22L *Rönnskär* NV and SV; 23J *Norsjö* NV, NO, SV and SO; 23K *Boliden* NV, NO, SV and SO; and 23L *Byske* NV and SV.

Guidebooks

In addition to the publications listed under the tourist office addresses for each province above and the various leaflets describing each of the seven long-distance footpaths in the Northeastern Coast region, only one guidebook exists to walks in the region:

- *Vandra i Sverige: Låglandsleder* (in Swedish). See description under the section on *Guidebooks* earlier in this chapter. Available from the STF.

Suggested Walks

The possibilities are numerous. For instance, you can walk on the Gästrikleden long-distance footpath and in the Grönsinka Forest in Gästrikland; on the Hälsingleden, Kolarstigen, Ljusnanleden, Mostigen, or Sjuvallsleden long-distance footpaths in Hälsingland; in the Gussjö-Paljakka Forest in Medelpad; on the Höga Kusten-leden and in the Anundsjö Forest in Ångermanland; in the forest reserves at Stenbithöjden, Käringberget and Kroksjökälen in Västerbotten; or in the forest reserves at Storforsen, Fällforsen, Räktforsen, Pahakurkkio and Marjakursu in Norrbotten. (For further information on the long-distance footpaths, see the section on *Sweden's Long-Distance Footpaths*.)

Cross-Country Skiing

There are numerous cross-country ski tracks, both long and short, marked and unmarked, scattered throughout the Northeastern Coast region. The region's long-distance footpaths—the Gästrikleden, Hälsingleden, Höga Kusten-leden, Kolarstigen, Ljusanleden, Mostigen and Sjuvallsleden—are all marked and can be used for extended ski tours during the winter. Gästrikland and Hälsingland alone have more than 20 ski centers with marked tracks (see the brochure *Hälsingland Gästrikland Fritidsvinter*, under *Useful Addresses*, above). Västernorrland offers nearly 20 centers that provide some 40 marked, illuminated ski tracks. Opportunities in Västerbotten and Norrbotten are comparable. Local tourist offices throughout the Northeastern Coast region can provide further information on where to cross-country ski.

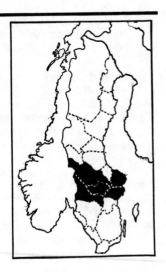

Svealand (Central Sweden)

This region encompasses six provinces in central Sweden and includes the city of Stockholm and the historic university town of Uppsala. Svealand is the most populous district in Sweden, yet still offers large tracts of forest and lakeland in which to roam. It contains no less than 12 long-distance footpaths and four national parks.

The landscape is extremely varied, including open farmlands, wooded plains, gentle hills covered by forests of birch and pine, broad river valleys, mountains rising above tree limit and a coastline fringed by thousands of islands. Stockholm itself is situated on 20 islands. On the south, Svealand borders enormous Lake Vänern, the largest in Sweden, and Vättern, the second largest. Nearby are myriads of other, smaller lakes.

The region is also rich in archeological and historical monuments. It was the ancient seat of the *Svea Rike,* the old Swedish kingdom whose name survives in the modern name for the country, *Sverige.* As you wander through the district, you come across ancient burial mounds, rune stones, old castles, Viking remains and, from more recent times, quaint wooden villages and the characteristic red farm cottages of the countryside. The provinces of Dalarna and Värmland are part of Sweden's folklore district, where native customs and costumes still survive.

Lodgings are readily available throughout Svealand, where you are seldom more than a day's walk from the nearest village or town. There are some 50 youth hostels in the region, along with countless hotels, guesthouses, summer cottages and campgrounds.

Dalarna. This is the largest and northernmost province in Svealand. It forms a transition between the wilder, more rugged lands of northern

Sweden and the gentler, more populated districts to the south. Southern Dalarna is a land of wooded, gently rolling hills and broad valleys. Northward, the land becomes higher and more rugged, the towns and villages more widely scattered. Northwestern Dalarna is mountain country, with numerous peaks rising above tree limit to elevations exceeding 1,000 meters. Here, the great ranges of Lappland and Jämtland-Härjedalen reach their southernmost limits, offering the most accessible mountain walking in Sweden. Four mountain districts, comprising a third of the province, offer excellent cross-country skiing and endless roaming. These four districts are 1) Transtrandsfjällen, near the resort town of Salen, Sweden's southernmost mountain ski center, 2) Fulufjäll, west of Särna, 3) Nipfjällen, northeast of Indre, and 4) Långfjället, northwest of Indre, which culminates in Dalarna's highest peak, 1,204-meter Storrvätteshogna. Dalarna also includes two national parks: Töfsingdalenin in the Långfjället Range, and Hamra in the forest wilderness north of Orsa. The forest reserves of Njupeskär, at the eastern base of Fulufjället, and Idrefjällen, near the Långfjället Range, have marked footpaths and offer easy access to the nearby mountains, with their numerous lakes and meadows, commanding peaks and vast stretches of dwarf heath. Because the mountains of Dalarna are the southernmost in Sweden, they offer the longest walking season and best weather of any of the country's ranges. There are also many excellent walking routes in the gentler country of central and southern Dalarna, including three long-distance footpaths, the 340-kilometer Siljansleden, which circles through the countryside around Lake Siljan; the 70-kilometer Ljusbodarnas fäbodstigar, outside Djursjön; and the 45-kilometer Malingsbo-Kloten rundan, in the Malingsbo-Kloten Forest. Numerous other marked walking routes are found throughout Dalarna. The province also contains hundreds of kilometers of marked and illuminated ski tracks, which are found both in the mountain regions and near virtually all of the towns and villages. The Vasaloppet—or Vasa Ski Race—follows an 86-kilometer course from Sälen to Mora, commemorating the flight of 16th century King Gustav Vasa from the Danish conquerers. Held the first Sunday in March, the Vasaloppet attracts up to 10,000 participants.

Närke. Nestled between three of the four great lakes of central Sweden, the province of Närke embraces both rugged hill country and gentle plains devoted to agriculture. Vättern, the second largest lake in Sweden, is on the south; Vänern, the largest, lies to the west; and Hjälmaren stretches eastward from the town of Örebro, largest in the province. Great forests of birch and pine cover the hills and ring the thousand smaller lakes in the district. The forests have many short footpaths passing through meadows and woodlands, and by rushing streams, quiet lakes and rustic mountain huts. The forest of Tiveden in the south is famed among botanists for Lake Fagertärn, home of extremely rare red water lilies. The 50-kilometer Munkastigen passes through the Tiveden Forest, and the 274-kilometer Bergslagsleden connects Tiveden with the Malingsbo-Kloten Forest in Dalarna. This footpath also passes through Garphyttan National Park, which was established to preserve a cultivated area of historic interest. There are several short footpaths in this 108-hectare park. Närke also has a large number of nature reserves with footpaths of various lengths. Cross-country skiing is possible in the hill country of the northwest.

Södermanland & Uppland. These two provinces border the Baltic Sea in easternmost Svealand. The coastline is highly irregular, with thousands of islands and a labyrinth of waterways. Stockholm sits on 20 islands at the eastern end of Lake Mälaren, where it meets the sea. The entire lake, which straddles the boundary of Uppland to the north and Södermanland to the south, is strewn with hundreds of islands large and small. Uppland offers pleasant walking on footpaths and country lanes through gentle farmlands brightened by red cottages. Of particular interest are the 56-kilometer Roslagsleden and 31-kilometer Blå leden. The island national park of Ängsjö also offers splendid walking. The university town of Uppsala is an ancient seat of learning and culture in Sweden. Outside the town are burial mounds that legend says date back to the 6th century. Södermanland is a region of gentle hills scattered over forested plains, where birch and pine fringe the rocky shores of a thousand lakes. More than 400 rune stones are scattered through this historic province. The primary attraction for walkers, however, is the 500-kilometer Sörmlandsleden, Sweden's longest footpath, which winds through the lovely forest and lake country from Stockholm to the coastal town of Nyköping. Nearby, the nature reserve at Nynäs offers good short walks on marked footpaths.

Värmland. Lying in westernmost Svealand along the Norwegian border, Värmland is a land of blue, forested hills, broad river valleys, great forests, and more than 2,500 lakes, including Lake Vänern, the largest in Sweden. Värmland is rich in myth and folklore and provided the setting for Nobel laureate Selma Lagerlöf's *Saga of Gösta Berling*. Each summer there are traditional festivals, where native costumes, dances, and handicrafts are on display. Of particular interest to walkers is the nature reserve of Glaskogen, in the hills of western Värmland, which has a 250-kilometer network of paths winding through a forest region with two large lakes—Övre Gla and Stora Gla—and numerous small ones. One of Värmland's long-distance footpaths—the 30-kilometer Glaskogen—circles through the nature reserve. Another fine walk is on the 51-kilometer Fryksdalen-Klarälvdalen, which climbs westward from Segenäs, in the valley of the Klarälven River, one of the longest in Scandinavia, and crosses the forested ridge to the lakes near Rattsjöberg, at the head of Fryksdalen. The Klarälven Valley is known as the *Pilgrimsleden*—Pilgrim's Way—because it lay along the route taken by 11th century Christian pilgrims to the shrine of St. Olov at Trondheim, Norway. Fryksdalen, Värmland's other major valley, is filled with two long, finger-like lakes, which are connected by waterways to enormous Vänern in the south. At the northern end of the Klarälven Valley, near the Dalarna border, rises 700-meter Granberget, which lies along a marked footpath between Sysslebäck and N. Finnskoga. It is possible to combine walks with canoe trips on Värmland's network of lakes, streams and canals. The province is one of the major canoe centers in Europe and offers the finest canoeing in Sweden.

Västmanland. This province lies in the geographical center of Svealand. Its western portion consists of wooded hills, which give way on the east to a gently undulating plain. With its woods, lakes, country cottages, picturebook farms and quaint villages, Västmanland is said to represent the typical Swedish countryside. And though the region is one of the country's industrial centers, great areas of unspoiled forest and farmland still remain. Of particular interest to walkers is the 274-kilometer Berglagsleden and the 70-kilometer Bruksleden, a circular footpath in the countryside north and west of the town of Västerås, on the shores of Mälaren, the great island-studded lake that stretches eastward to Stockholm. Numerous other short footpaths are found throughout the region. Cross-country skiing is possible in the hills of western Västmanland.

Useful Addresses

See *Address Directory:*

Dalarna

Dala Turistservice. Provides general tourist information and information on walking and cross-country skiing in Dalarna. Staff speaks Swedish and English. Useful publications available from the office include:

- *Dalarna Holiday Guide* (in English). A tabloid brochure giving detailed tourist information about the region. Includes a sketch map showing the location of 79 footpaths, with a key listing each one, along with its location from the nearest town, its length and whether it can be used for cross-country skiing in the winter. Another sketch map shows the locations of ski centers, most of which have marked and illuminated ski tracks. Also includes sketch maps showing the locations of other tourist facilities, such as main roads, fishing spots and places with boats and canoes for hire. Includes lists of tourist offices, available tourist brochures (and the languages in which they are written), local festivals and points of interest. Also includes a 1:100,000 map of Dalarna in the centerfold.

- *Dalarna* (in English). Gives general tourist information on Dalarna and its several districts. Suggests places to walk and ski, but without specific directions. Includes a map of the province. Lists tourist offices and points of interest.

- *Skidspår och Vandringsleder markerade i terrängen runt om Mora* (in Swedish). Sketch map showing ski tracks near Mora.

- *Vinter i Dalarna* (in Swedish). Lists the winter activities available at the major sports centers in Dalarna. Indicates which have marked and illuminated ski tracks, as well as other facilities. Provides a calendar of events and lists the addresses and telephone numbers of local tourist offices. Most of the information can be understood even if you do not speak Swedish. A map shows the location of the ski centers.

Närke

Örebro läns Turistnämnd. Provides general tourist information on Örebro County in Närke. Can also provide some useful walking information. Staff speaks Swedish and English. Useful publications available from the office include:

- *Bergslagsleden: Allmän Beskrivning* (in Swedish). A leaflet providing an overview of the entire path, with a sketch map showing trailside lodgings and Topografiska Kartan sheets. Also gives information on group tours, lodgings, the length of each path section and cross-country skiing.

- *Bergslagsleden: Etappbeskrivning* (in Swedish). A series of leaflets describing individual sections of the path, with black and white reproductions of the 1:50,000 Topografiska kartan covering each section.

- *Örebro Län: Bergslagslänet* (in German). A brochure providing general tourist information for the county. Includes a color sketch map showing main features of interest—but not footpaths.

- *Tourist Guide: Örebro County Sweden* (in English). A booklet packed with useful information for traveling in the county. Includes a list of marked footpaths (including the Bergslagsleden) and of nature reserves with marked footpaths. Also lists campgrounds, holiday villages, youth hostels, hotels and other facilities and attractions.

Södermanland & Uppland

Södermanlands läns landsting turist- och friluftsnämnden. Provides general tourist information on Södermanland. Staff speaks Swedish and English. Useful publications available from the office include:

- *Nynäs* (in Swedish). Describes the Nynäs Nature Reserve, near Nyköping. Color sketch map shows some footpaths.

- *Södermanland* (in Swedish, English and German). Provides general information on Södermanland. Includes a color sketch map showing the route of the Sörmlandsleden.

- *Sörmlandsleden* (in Swedish). A pamphlet briefly describing the path. Includes a sketch map and list of local tourist information offices. Gives distances between points along the path and information on transportation to and from each point. Also includes information on lodgings and other facilities along the path.

Uppsala läns Landsting, Fritidsbyrån. Provides general tourist information on Uppland. Staff speaks Swedish and English.

Värmland

Värmlands Turisttrafikförbund. Provides general tourist information on Värmland. Staff speaks Swedish and English. Useful publications available from the office include:

* *Stugor i vinter-Värmland* (in Swedish). A brochure showing various chalets for rent in winter; includes black and white photo and floor plan of each. Color sketch map shows location of ski centers in Värmland. Smaller sketch maps of each center show nearby ski tracks. Includes information on booking chalets.

* *Värmland karta turistfakta* (in Swedish, with English and German inserts). A sketch map showing points of interest in Värmland, including several marked footpaths. Includes a list of tourist offices, descriptions of points of interest and indexes of hotels, restaurants, campgrounds and youth hostels.

* *Värmland Sweden* (in English). A glossy brochure giving general tourist information on Värmland. Lists major winter sports centers, as well as places of interest and activities for each district in Värmland. Each district is shown on a separate map. Also includes a map of the entire region, with points of interest and types of lodgings shown by symbols. Lists telephone numbers of local tourist offices.

* *Vinter Värmland* (in Swedish). Leaflet listing major ski centers, with facilities of each. Gives lengths of cross-country ski tracks.

Västmanland

Västmanlands läns landsting Turistavdelningen. Provides general tourist information on Västmanland. Can also provide some information on walking and cross-country skiing. Staff speaks Swedish and English. Useful publications available from the office include:

* *Bruksleden: Vandringsled i Västmanlands län* (in Swedish). A leaflet with a brief description of the path and information on bus connections and other facilities enroute. Gives telephone numbers for obtaining bus schedules and tourist and lodging information.

* *Västmanlands län* (in Swedish with symbols translated into English, French, German and Finnish). A 1:300,000 map of Västmanland, with symbols showing the locations of tourist information offices, hotels and motels, youth hostels, tourist lodges, summer chalets, campgrounds, viewpoints, illuminated ski tracks, downhill ski centers, historical sites, botanical sites, geological sites and other facilities and points of interest. Forested areas are shown in green.

* *Västmanland—Sweden in miniature* (in English). A glossy brochure

describing points of interest in Västmanland. Color sketch map shows roads and towns.

Maps

The mountain districts of Dalarna are covered by the Nya Fjällkartan 1:100,000, sheets W 1 and W 2, and 1:50,000 special sheets Grövelsjön, Idrefjällen and Fulufjället. The remainder of Svealand is covered by the following 1:50,000 Topografiska kartan:

Dalarna: sheets 11F Lindesberg NV and NO; 12D Uddeholm NO; 12E Säfsnäs NV, NO, SV and SO; 12F Ludvika NV, NO, SV and SO; 12G Avesta NV, NO, SV and SO; 13D Malung NV, NO, SV and SO; 13E Vansbro NV, NO, SV and SO; 13F Falun NV, NO, SV and SO; 13G Hofors NV and SV; 14C N. Finnskoga SO; 14D Sälen NO, SV and SO; 14E Mora NV, NO, SV and SO; 14F Rättvik NV, NO, SV and SO; 14G Ockelbo SV; 15D Särna NV, NO, SV and SO; 15E Älvho NV, NO, SV and SO; and 15F Voxna NV and SV.

Närke: sheets 9E Askersund NV, NO, SV and SO; 9F Finspång NV, NO and SV; 10E Karlskoga NV, NO, SV and SO; 10F Örebro NV, NO, SV and SO; 11G Filipstad NV, NO, SV and SO; and 11F Lindesberg NV, NO, SV and SO.

Södermanland: sheets 9G Katrineholm NV, NO and SO; 9H Nyköping NV, NO, SV and SO; 9I Nyhäshamn NV and NO; 10G Eskilstuna NV, NO, SV and SO; 10H Strängnäs NV, NO, SV and SO; and 10I Stockholm NV, NO, SV and SO.

Uppland: sheets 10H Strängnäs NV and NO; 10I Stockholm NV and NO; 10J Värmdö NV and SV; 11H Enköping NV, NO, SV and SO; 11I Uppsala NV, NO, SV and SO; 11J Norrtälje NV, NO and SO; 12H Söderfors NO and SO; 12I Östhammar NV, NO, SV and SO; 12J Grisslehamn NV and SV; 13H Gävle SO; and 13I Österlövsta SV and SO.

Värmland: sheets 9C Mellerud NO; 10B Årjäng NO; 10C Åmål NV, NO, SV and SO; 10D Karlstad NV, NO and SO; 10E Karlskoga NV and SV; 11B Koppom NO, SV and SO; 11C Arvika NV, NO, SV and SO; 11D Munkfors NV, NO, SV and SO; 11E Filipstad NV and SV; 12C Torsby NV, NO, SV and SO; 12D Uddeholm NV, NO, SV and SO; 12E Säfsnäs SV; 13C Dalby NV, NO, SV and SO; 13D Malung NV and SV; and 14C N. Finnskoga SV and SO.

Västermanland: sheets 10F Örebro NO and SO; 10G Eskilstuna NV and NO; 11F Lindesberg NO and SO; 11G Västerås NV, NO, SV and SO; 11H Enköping NV and SV; 12F Ludvika SO; 12G Avesta SV and SO; and 12H Söderfors NV, NO, SV and SO.

Guidebooks

In addition to the publications listed under the tourist offices' addresses for each province above and the various leaflets describing each of Svealand's 12 long-distance footpaths, the following guidebooks cover various districts and footpaths in the region:

* *Fjäll '81* (in Swedish). Describes a marked ski track/footpath, plus an alternative route, in the mountains of Dalarna. Available from the STF.

* *Vandringsguiden över Siljansleden* (in Swedish). A provisional guidebook with topographical maps describing the 340-kilometer Siljansleden circling around Lake Siljan and Lake Orsasjön in Dalarna. Available from the tourist offices in Mora, Orsa, Rättvik and Leksand. A detailed guidebook is in preparation.

* *Sörmlandsleden* (in Swedish). Gives a full route description of the path, along with information on access, lodgings and points of interest. Available from Friluftsfrämjandet.

* *Vandra i Sverige: Låglandsleder* (in Swedish). Briefly describes each of the long-distance footpaths in Svealand. Available from the STF.

Suggested Walks

As elsewhere in Sweden, the walking possibilities are numerous. Recommended walks are on the Bergslagsleden through the forests of Närke and Västmanland; on the Sörmlandsleden through the lake country of Södermanland; on the Fryksdalen-Klarälsdalen and Glaskogen in Värmland; on the Roslagsleden in Uppland; on the Bruksleden in southern Västmanland; on the Siljansleden of northern Dalarna; and on the footpaths in the mountains of Dalarna, including those in Töfsingdalen National Park and the forest reserves of Njupeskär and Idrefjällen. Other walks are possible on the Malingsbo-Kloten rundan and Ljusbodarnas fäbodstigar in Dalarna; on the Munkastigan in Närke; on the Brattforsheden in Värmland; and on the Blå leden in Uppland. For further information on each footpath, see the section on *Sweden's Long-Distance Footpaths*.

Cross-Country Skiing

The principal areas for cross-country skiing in Svealand are in the mountains of Dalarna and in the hills of Värmland, Västmanland and Närke. The provincial tourist associations in Dalarna and Värmland publish winter guides showing the locations of ski centers, listing marked and illuminated ski tracks and in one case showing the location of tracks on sketch maps. Three of these guides are listed under *Useful Addresses* above.

The STF maintains a marked ski track in the mountains of southern Härjedalen and northern Dalarna, from Tänndalen to Grövelsjön mountain station in the Langfjället Range. The 68-kilometer route is marked by red crossed boards affixed to long posts and is described in *Fjäll '81* see *Guidebooks*, above). You can also ski on several of the long-distance footpaths in the region, including the Bergsladsleden and Bruksleden. If you are an experienced cross-country skier and member of a recognized ski club, you can participate in the 86 kilometer Vasa Ski Race in Dalarna. The locations of marked and illuminated ski tracks are also often shown on general tourist maps for the various provinces. And once you have decided where you want to cross-country ski, you can sometimes obtain maps of the cross-country ski tracks from local tourist information offices, the addresses of which are available on request from the provincial tourist associations.

Address Directory

A

- *Ale Fritidsnämnd,* Ale. Tel. (031) 98 20 00.
- *Arvika Turistbyrå,* Stadshuset, S-671 00 Arvika. Tel (0570) 135 60.

B

- *Blekinge turist-och fritidskansli,* Landbrogatan 19, Box 22, S-371 01 Karlskrona. Tel. (0455) 105 82.
- *Bollnäs Turistbyrå,* Våggatan 6, Box 40, S-821 01 Bollnäs. Tel. (0278) 170 00 or 170 04.
- *Borgholms Turistbyrå,* Box 115, S-380 70 Borgholm. Tel. (0485) 103 00.

D

- *Dala Turistservice,* Tullkammareg 1, S-791 00 Falun. Tel. (023) 106 00 or 187 40.
- *Dalslands Turisttrafikförening,* Kyrkogatan 15, Box 89, S-662 00 Åmål. Tel. (0532) 122 40 or 143 66.
- *Danderyds fritidskontor,* Box 17, S-182 51 Djursholm. Tel. (08) 755 25 20.
- *Dial Press,* One Dag Hammerskjold Plaza, New York, New York 10017, U.S.A., 1972.

- *Döderhults naturskyddsförening,* Styrbjörn Ejneby, S-572 01 Oskarshamn. Tel. (0491) 177 06.
- *Domänverket,* Nationalparkerna, S-960 40 Jokkmokk. Tel. (0971) 104 38.
- *Domänverket i Björsjö nyttjandeförvaltning,* Tel. (0240) 300 10.
- *Domänverkets naturvårdssektion* (Swedish Forest Service, Nature Conservation Section), S-791 00 Falun. Tel. (023) 840 00.

E

- *Emergency:* Tel. 90 000.

F

- *Filipstads Turistbyrå,* Esso Motorhotell, Lasarettsgatan 2, S-682 00 Filipstad. Tel. (0590) 115 60.
- *Friluftsfrämjandet, Gävle,* Tel. (026) 11 44 00.
- *Friluftsfrämjandet,* Wallingatan 24, Box 708, S-101 30 Stockholm. Tel. (08) 23 43 50.
- *Friluftsmagasinet, Stockholm.* Two locations: Sveavägen 73, Stockholm, Tel. (08) 34 20 00, and Birger Jarlsgatan 33, Stockholm, Tel. (08) 10 96 51.
- *Friluftsmagasinet, Stockholm* (for mail orders). Box 49005 S-100 28 Stockholm. Tel. (08) 51 39 00 or 51 35 00.
- *Friluftsmagasinet, Göteborg,* Drottninggatan 35, Göteborg. Tel. (031) 11 62 26.
- *Friluftsmagasinet, Malmo,* Drottinggatan 2, Malmo. Tel. (040) 93 70 05.

G

- *GEO CENTER,* Honigwiesenstrasse 25, Postfach 80 08 30, D-7000 Stuttgart 80, Germany.
- *Gällivare Turistbyrå,* Lasarettsgatan 8, S-972 00 Gällivare. Tel. (0970) 136 30 or 110 00.
- *Gävle Turistbyrå,* Norra Kungsgatan 1, Box 125, S-801 03 Gävle. Tel. (026) 11 49 55.
- *Göteborgs Fritidsförvaltning,* Tel. (031) 61 10 00.
- *Gotlands Turistforening,* Skeppsbron 20, Box 81, S-621 Ol Visby. Tel. (0498) 190 10.
- *Gränna Turistbyrå,* Torget, Box 76, S-560 30 Gränna. Tel. (0390) 103 15.

H

- *Hässleholms Turistbyrå,* Stadshuset, Box 41, S-281 01 Hässleholm. Tel. (0451) 136 00.
- *Hemavans Högfjällshotel,* S-920 66 Hemavan. Tel. (0954) 431 20.
- *Hudiksvalls Fritidskonfor,* Trädgårdsgatan 19, Fack, S-824 01 Hudiksvall. Tel. (0650) 190 00.
- *Hudiksvalls Turistbyrå,* Storgatan 24, S-824 00 Hudiksvall. Tel. (0650) 139 20.

J

- *Jämtland-Härjedalens Turistförening,* Storgatan 16, Box 478, S-831 01 Östersund. Tel. (063) 12 70 55 or 12 45 90.
- *Jokkmokks Turistbyrå,* Jokkmokks Museum, Box 57, S-960 40 Jokkmokk. Tel. (0971) 113 30.

K

- *Kalmar länd Turisttrafikförbund,* Stortorget 36, Box 86, S-391 21 Kalmar. Tel. (0480) 282 70.
- *Karlshamns Turistbyrå,* Torget, Box 175, S-292 00 Karlshamn. Tel. (0454) 166 25.
- *Kartcentrum,* Götgatan 11, S-411 10 Göteborg. Tel. (031) 15 44 48.
- *Kisa Turistbyrå,* Tingshustorget 3, Box 71, S-590 41 Kisa. Tel. (0494) 122 60.
- *Kommungruppen för fritid i Gävleborgs län,* Brunnsgatan 63 A, S-802 22 Gävle. Tel (026) 12 95 40.
- *Kramfors Turistbyrå,* Torggatan 4, Box 57, S-872 00 Kramfors. Tel. (0612) 142 00.
- *Kristianstadts Turistbyrå,* Västra Storgatan 14, S-291 32 Kristianstad. Tel. (044) 12 1988 or 11 55 00.

L

- *Lapplandia Sporthotel,* S-980 28 Riksgränsen. Tel. (0980) 431 20.
- *Laxå Kommuns fritidskontor,* Box 66, S-695 01 Laxå. Tel. (0584) 108 30.
- *Leksands Turistbyrå,* Norsgatan, Box 52, S-793 01 Leksand. Tel. (0247) 104 11 or 104 16.
- *LiberKartor,* S-162 89 Vällingby. Tel. (08) 89 02 00.
- *Ljusdals Turistbyrå,* Fack 7, S-820 40 Järvsö. Tel. (0651) 120 77 or 403 26.

M

• *Malingsbo-Klotens Turistbyrå*, Malingsbo 8100, S-770 20 Söderbärke. Tel. (0240) 350 80 or 350 98.

• *Mora Turistbyrå*, Ångbåtskajen, S-792 00 Mora. Tel. (0250) 151 00.

N

• *Nässjö Turistbyrå*, Stortorget 4, Box 230, S-571 00 Nässjö. Tel. (0380) 188 75 or 132 70.

• *Nordkalottresor AB*, Box 242, S-951 23 Luleå. Tel. (0920) 690 80.

• *Norrbottens Turisttrafikförbund*, Box 72, S-951 01 Luleå. Tel. (0920) 6 98 85.

O

• *Örebro läns Turistnämnd*, Box 1816, S-701 18 Örebro. Tel. (019) 14 00 70.

• *Orsa Turistbyrå*, Centralgatan 3, S-794 00 Orsa. Tel. (0250) 400 60.

• *Oskarshamns Turistbyrå*, Hantverksgatan 18-20, Box 6, S-572 01 Oskarshamn. Tel. (0491) 105 49.

• *Ostergötlands Länturistnämnd*, Platensgatan 11 B, Box 325, S-581 03 Linköping. Tel. (013) 13 02 30.

P

• *Poststyrelsen*, Diligenssektionen, S-105 00 Stockholm. Tel. (08) 781.

• *Postverkets Diligenstrafik*, Fack, S-921 00 Lycksele. Tel. (0950) 129.

R

• *Rättviks Turistbyrå*, Torget, S-795 00 Rättvik. Tel. (0248) 110 50.

• *Ronneby Turistbyrå*, Snäckebacksplan, Box 114, S-372 00 Ronneby. Tel. (0457) 150 70.

S

• *STF*, see *Svenska turistföreningen*.

• *Skånes Turisttrafikförbund*, Östergatan 8, Box 4277, S-203 14 Malmö. Tel. (040) 11 08 04 or 11 08 05.

• *Skogsvårdsstyrelsen i Värmlands län*, S-651 05 Karlstad. Tel. (054) 15 01 50.

- *Söderhamns Turistbyrå,* Kungsgatan 11, Box 114, S-826 00 Söderhamn. Tel. (0270) 118 62 or 160 60.
- *Södermanlands läns Landsting Turist- och Friluftsnämnden,* Repslageregatan 19, Box 333, S-611 01 Nyköping. Tel. (0155) 171 60 or 165 50.
- *Statens Naturvårdsverk* (National Environmental Protection Board), S-171 20 Solna 1. Tel. (08) 98 18 00.
- *Storliens Högfjällshotell,* S-830 19 Storlien. Tel. (0647) 701 70.
- *Svenska Fjällklubben,* Villagatan 24, S-114 32 Stockholm. Tel. (08) 20 14 56.
- *Svenska Klätterförbundet,* Box 14037, S-700 14 Örebro. Tel. (0586) 52 959.
- *Svenska turistföreningen (STF),* Box 7615, S-103 94 Stockholm. Tel. (08) 22 72 00.
- *Sverek,* Sverige Rekreation AB, Domänverket, S-171 93 Solna. Tel. (08) 85 03 30.
- *Sveriges Meteorologiska och Hydrologiska Institut* (Swedish Meteorological and Hydrological Institute), Tel. (011) 17 01 03.
- *Sveriges Turistråd,* Hamngatan 27, Box 7306, S-103 85 Stockholm. Tel. (08) 22 32 80.
- *Swedish National Tourist Office,* London, 3 Cork Street, London W1X 1HA. Tel. (01) 437 5816.
- *Swedish National Tourist Office,* New York, 75 Rockefeller Plaza, New York, New York 10019. Tel. (212) 582-2802.

T

- *Til Fjälls Resor AB,* Box 478, S-831 01 Östersund. Tel. (063) 12 45 90.
- *Turism och Fritid i Jönköpings län,* Västra Storgatan 18 A, Fack, S-551 01 Jönköping. Tel. (036) 16 95 90.
- *Turism och Fritid i Kronoberg,* Linnégatan 1, Box 36 S-351 03 Växjö. Tel. (0470) 475 75.

U

- *Upplysningar lämnas även av Fritid Centrum,* Tel. (031) 80 16 40.
- *Uposala läns Landsting, Fritidsbyrån,* Nedre Slottsgatan 10A, S-751 25 Uppsala. Tel. (018) 10 22 00.

V

- *Vägsjöfors friluftscenter,* Vägsjöfors herrgård, S-685 00 Torsby. Tel. (0560) 311 77.

- *Värmlands Turisttrafikförbund,* Box 323, S-651 05 Karlstad. Tel. (054) 10 21 60.
- *Västerbottens Länsturistnämnd,* Box 337, S-901, 07 Umeå. Tel. (090) 13 90 20.
- *Västergötlands Turisttrafikförening,* Billingehus, Box 77, S-541 01 Skövde. Tel. (0500) 825 00.
- *Västernorrlands läns Landsting,* Turist- och näringslivssektionen, Fack, S-871 01 Härnösand. Tel. (0611) 156 70.
- *Västerviks Turistbyrå,* Fiskartorget, S-593 00 Västervik. Tel. (040) 136 95 or 169 20.
- *Västkustens Turisttrafikförbund,* Kungsportsplatsen 2, S-411 10 Göteborg. Tel. (031) 13 77 92 or 13 61 08.
- *Västmanlands läns landsting Turistavdeiningen,* Hållgatan 2, S-722 11 Västerås. Tel. (021) 18 53 00.
- *Västmanlands länsstyrelse,* S-721 86 Västerås. Tel. (021) 11 02 00.
- *Vaxholms fritidskontor,* Norrgårdsvägen 101, S-184 00 Vaxholm. Tel. (0764) 601 00.
- *Vaxholms Turistbyrå,* Hamngatan 4, S-185 00 Vaxholm. Tel. (0764) 314 80.

A Quick Reference

In a hurry? Turn to the pages listed below. They will give you the most important information on walking in Sweden.

Search & Rescue, page 317.

Weather Forecasts, page 289.

Associations to Contact for Information:
On Walking, page 290.
On the Principal Footpaths in Sweden, page 319.
Tourist Information, page 315.

Maps, page 293.

Guidebooks, page 294.

Equipment, page 305.

Address Directory, page 388.

About the Author

CRAIG EVANS is an avid walker, winter mountaineer, writer, editor and photographer. He worked his way through college as a reporter for the *San Jose Mercury-News* in San Jose, California, and wrote an award-winning student travel publication, *Tripping,* which was distributed through West Coast student travel offices from 1973 to 1975. Mr. Evans then spent a year as editor of BACKPACKER Magazine and was project editor for the revised edition of BACKPACKER's *Backpacking Equipment Buyer's Guide* (a comprehensive, 285-page book that includes articles on how virtually every type of hiking equipment is made, as well as individual product reports on more than 1,000 pieces of gear). He has written articles on walking and traveling in Europe, and compiled reports on lightweight stoves, binoculars, winter tents and winter footwear for the equipment sections in BACKPACKER Magazine.

Mr. Evans visited Europe for the first time in 1971, and during the next two years traveled and walked in virtually every one of the Western European countries. He has since returned to Europe six times.

In 1973, he spent six months in the Alps, walking more than 2,000 kilometers (1,300 miles) from Menton, France, to Trieste, Italy. He has also led walking tours in the Alps.

For the *On Foot Through Europe* series, Mr. Evans worked for three years compiling information, checking facts and writing. He visited virtually every one of Europe's major walking organizations and alpine clubs, taking time to accompany members on the trails they know best. In the end, he had collected more than 450 kilos (half a ton) of information in 12 languages—the information from which this book was distilled.

To this, he added the experience gained backpacking in the East and West coast mountains of the United States, the Arizona desert and the Canadian Rockies.

Born in Klamath Falls, Oregon, in 1949, he holds a Bachelor of Arts degree in English from the California State University, San Jose. He now lives in Washington, D.C.